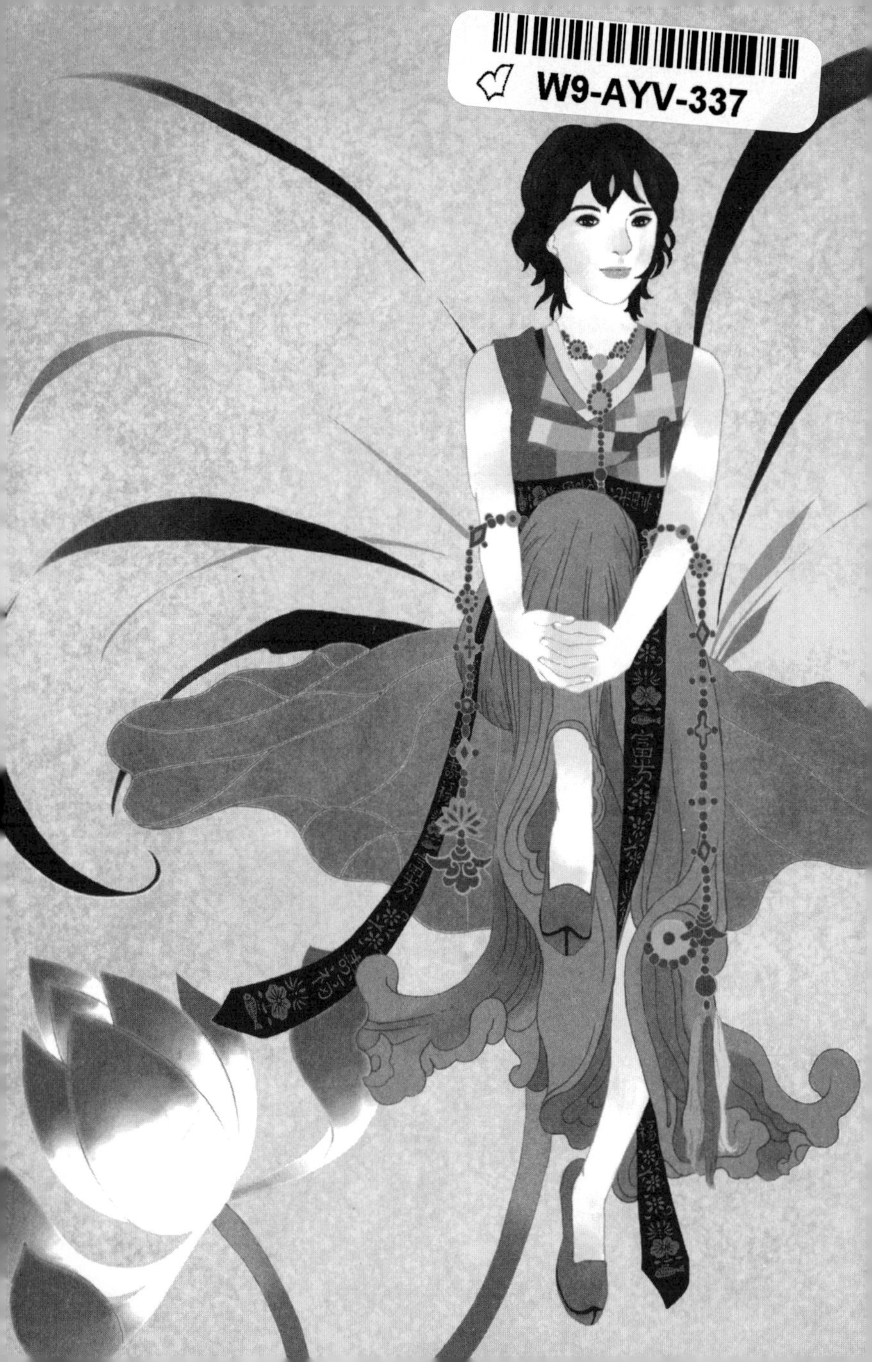

From the Author

It's raining now, in these dry winter days, for the first time in a long while.

At the end of last year, I moved back to my hometown of Busan.
It's a homecoming after 14 years.
I'm also taking some small trips.

As I began this book, I felt strongly that many of the tales that I wish to tell originate from my most private imagination and complete empathy. I saw precisely the means that would serve as both my wings and my boundary. And so this story (even though it tells of another life, and other persons) makes me feel as if I was opening, page by page, my own diary.

Each time the story changes, I experience many personal changes as well. No—as I reach some point of change in my life, the story changes, too. The finale that I had first planned in the beginning is so different from the finale that's possible right now that I'm enjoying it myself.

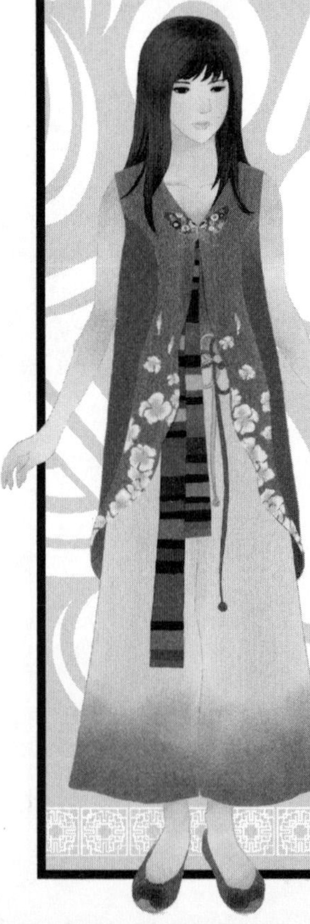

Right now, I am approaching the time when I meet many things with all five senses. More substantive and real encounters are happening. I walk much more and touch much more, take in much more and meet much more.

I would like to be a person who can collect the multitude of stories linked to the world—like spores that float around without yet having taken shape—water them, and cultivate them so that they may flourish into healthy greens.

Though I tell people all the time, like a bad habit, that I want to run away and that drawing these manuscripts is difficult, in truth I enjoy this work so very much. Taking a deep breath now, I want to put down each and every word carefully, and well enough so that I can proudly say there is no more of this story for me to leave behind—and that the future, already opened, can be left to Sunbi.

To the readers and fans walking with me, and the hard-working lone soldiers of the editing staff, I wish you all good fortune in the new year of 2007, and hope you all can have just a little more happiness in your lives.

March 2007
MARLEY

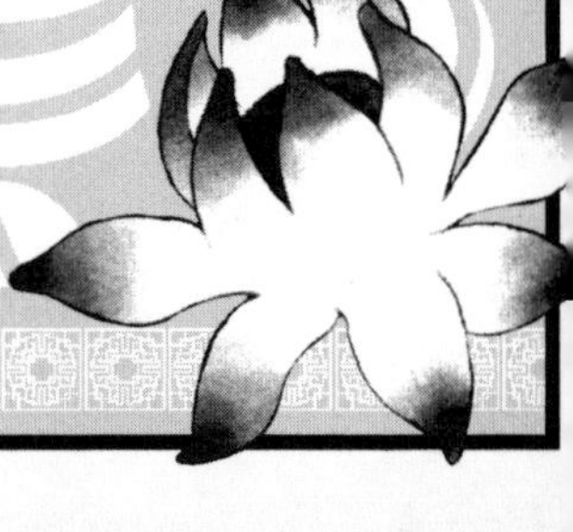

Dokebi Bride

Vol. 5

MARLEY

YA
Marley

NETCOMICS

Dokebi Bride Vol. 5

Story and Art by Marley

English translation rights in USA,
Canada, UK, NZ, Australia arranged by
Ecomix Media Company
395-21 Seogyo-dong, Mapo-gu, Seoul, Korea 121-840
info@ecomixmedia.com

- Produced by **Ecomix Media Company**
- Translator Ernest Woo
- Editor Jeffrey Tompkins
- Managing Editor Soyoung Jung
- Cover Designer purj
- Graphic Designers Eunsook Lee, Hyekyoung Choi
- President & Publisher Heewoon Chung

P.O. Box 3036, Jersey City, NJ 07303-3036
info@netcomics.com
www.NETCOMICS.com

ISBN: 978-1-60009-079-0

First printing: March 2007
10 9 8 7 6 5 4 3 2 1
Printed in Korea

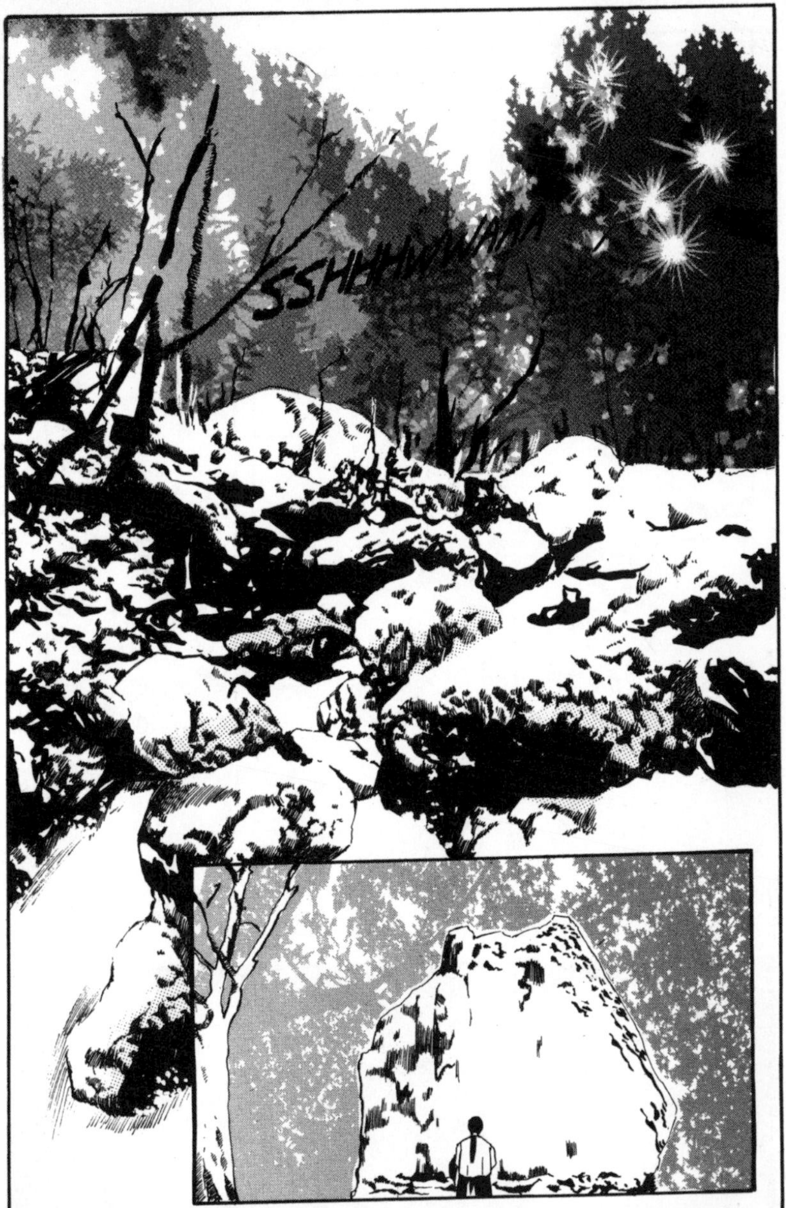
SSHHHWWAAA

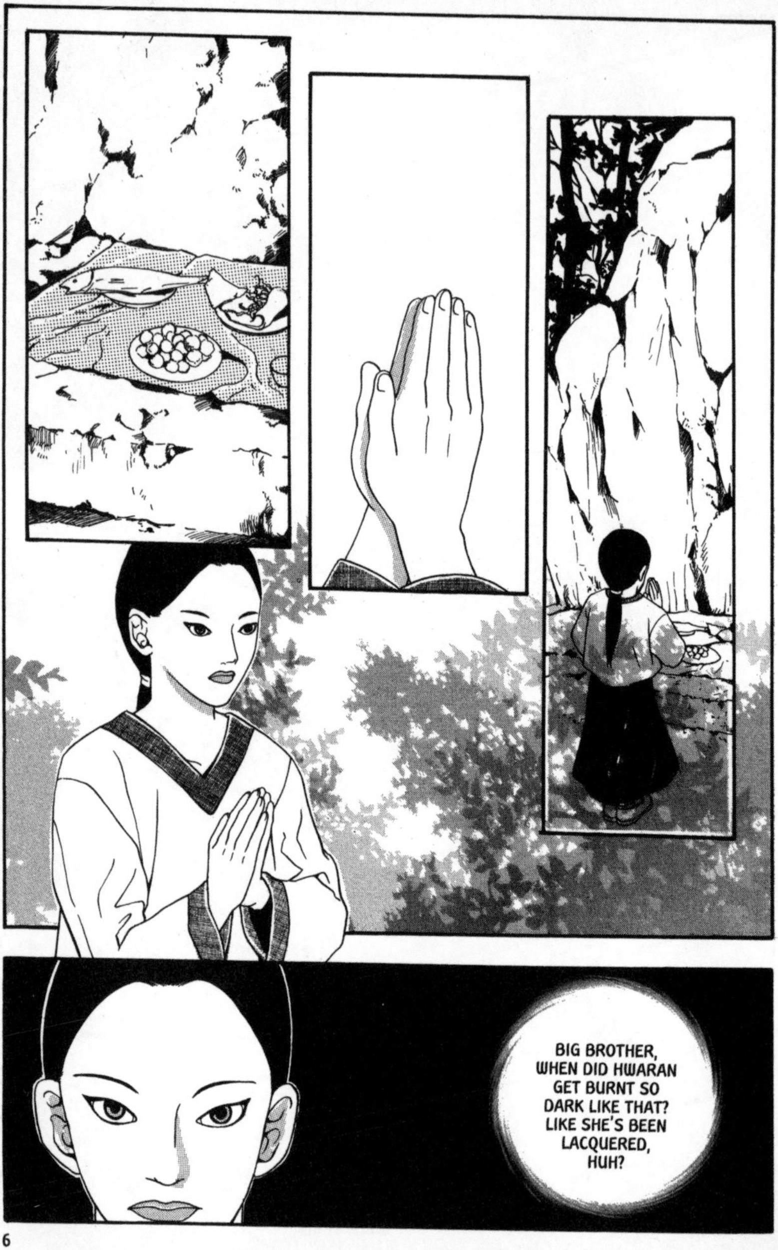
BIG BROTHER, WHEN DID HWARAN GET BURNT SO DARK LIKE THAT? LIKE SHE'S BEEN LACQUERED, HUH?

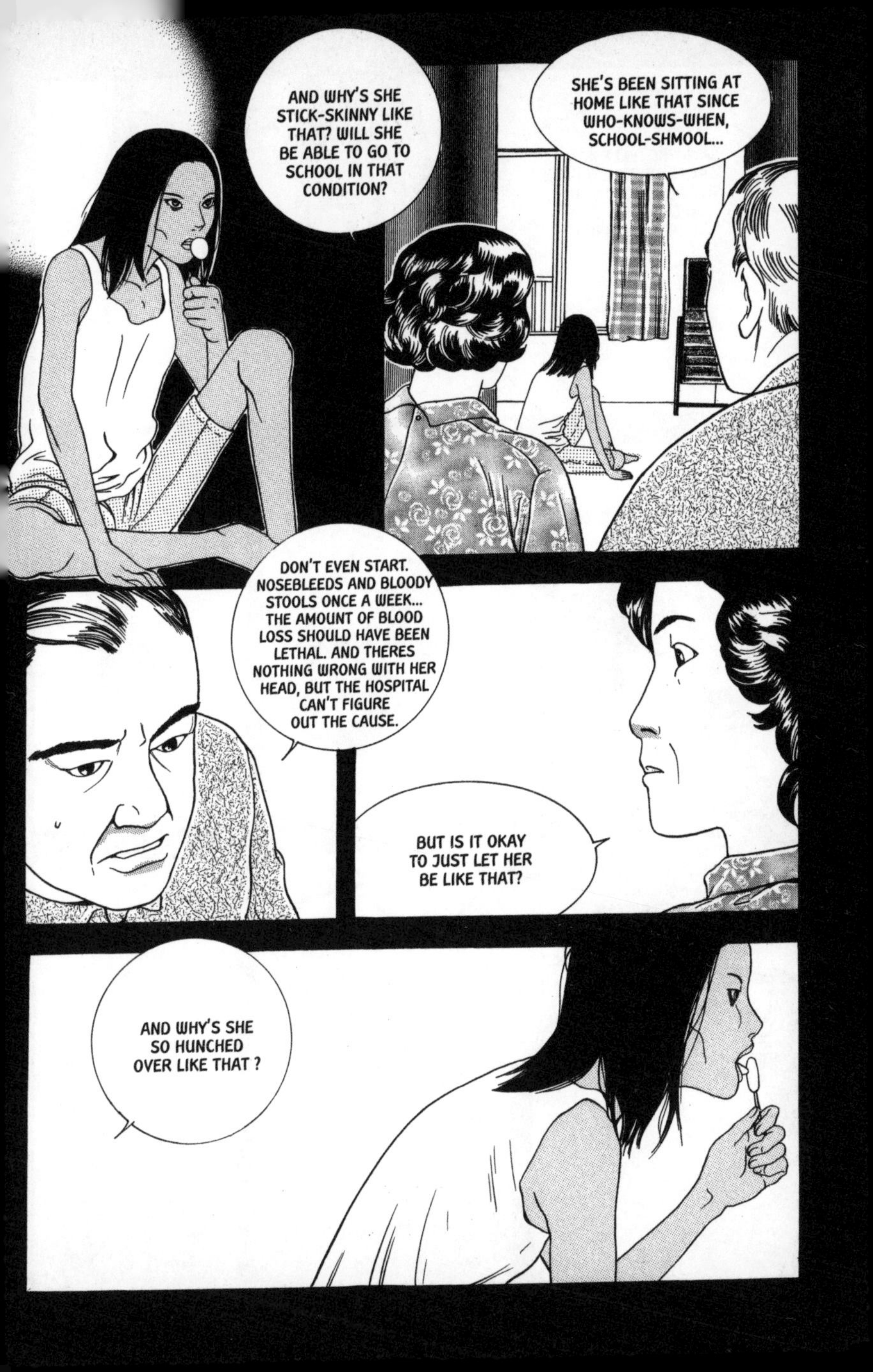
AND WHY'S SHE STICK-SKINNY LIKE THAT? WILL SHE BE ABLE TO GO TO SCHOOL IN THAT CONDITION?
SHE'S BEEN SITTING AT HOME LIKE THAT SINCE WHO-KNOWS-WHEN, SCHOOL-SHMOOL...
DON'T EVEN START. NOSEBLEEDS AND BLOODY STOOLS ONCE A WEEK... THE AMOUNT OF BLOOD LOSS SHOULD HAVE BEEN LETHAL. AND THERES NOTHING WRONG WITH HER HEAD, BUT THE HOSPITAL CAN'T FIGURE OUT THE CAUSE.
BUT IS IT OKAY TO JUST LET HER BE LIKE THAT?
AND WHY'S SHE SO HUNCHED OVER LIKE THAT ?

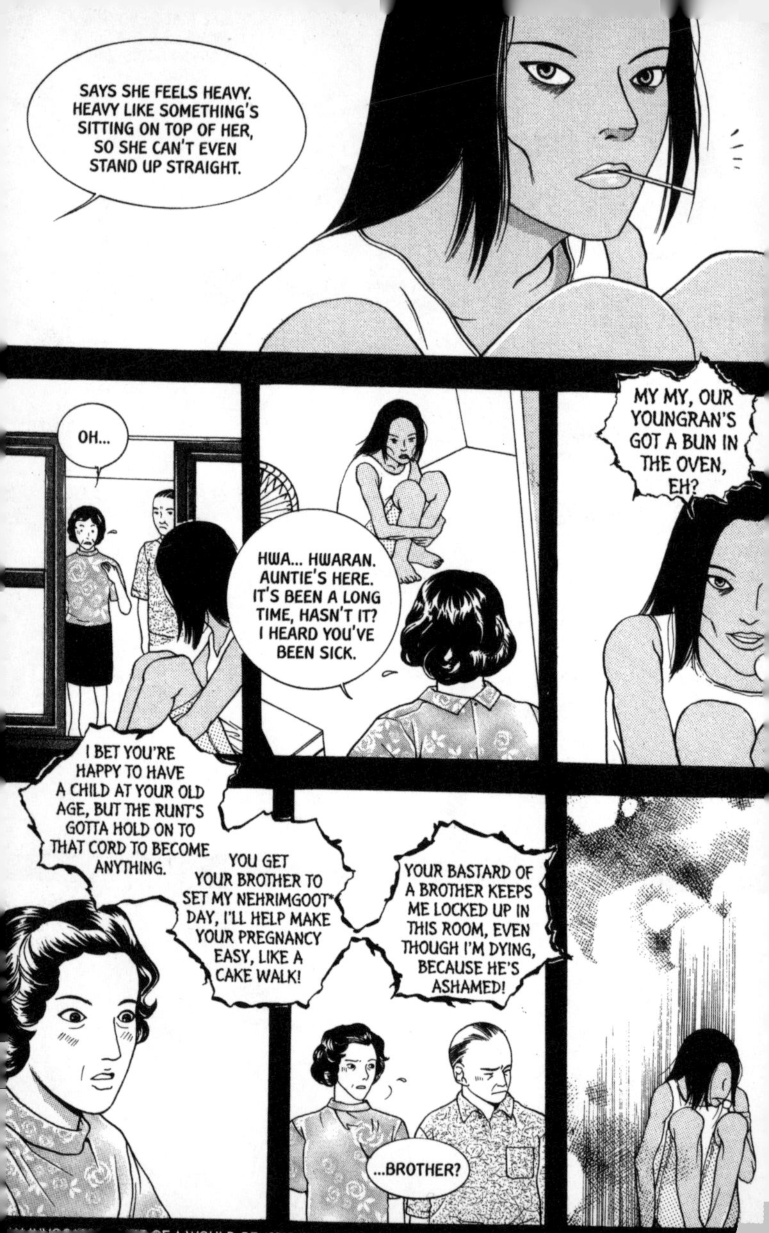
SAYS SHE FEELS HEAVY. HEAVY LIKE SOMETHING'S SITTING ON TOP OF HER, SO SHE CAN'T EVEN STAND UP STRAIGHT.
OH...
HWA... HWARAN. AUNTIE'S HERE. IT'S BEEN A LONG TIME, HASN'T IT? I HEARD YOU'VE BEEN SICK.
MY MY, OUR YOUNGRAN'S GOT A BUN IN THE OVEN, EH?
I BET YOU'RE HAPPY TO HAVE A CHILD AT YOUR OLD AGE, BUT THE RUNT'S GOTTA HOLD ON TO THAT CORD TO BECOME ANYTHING.
YOU GET YOUR BROTHER TO SET MY NEHRIMGOOT* DAY, I'LL HELP MAKE YOUR PREGNANCY EASY, LIKE A CAKE WALK!
YOUR BASTARD OF A BROTHER KEEPS ME LOCKED UP IN THIS ROOM, EVEN THOUGH I'M DYING, BECAUSE HE'S ASHAMED!
...BROTHER?

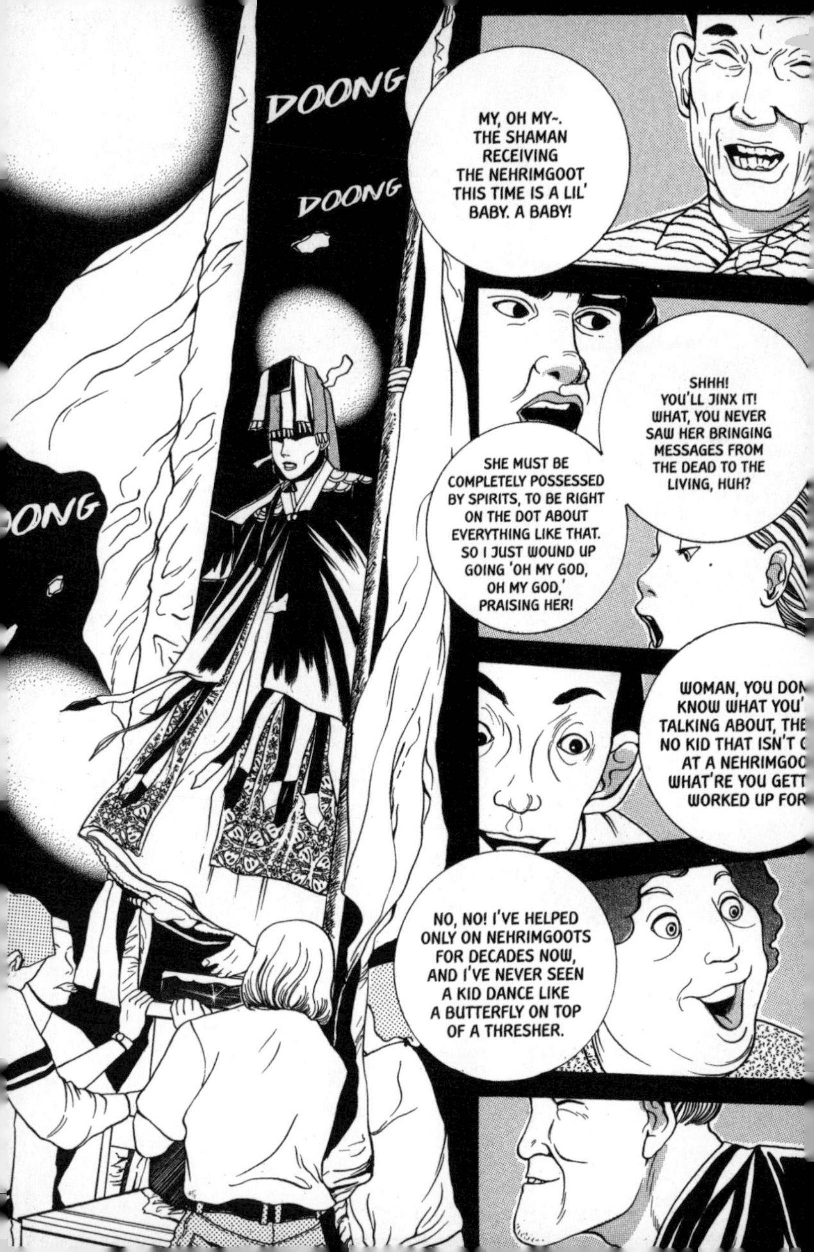

DOONG
DOONG
ONG
MY, OH MY~. THE SHAMAN RECEIVING THE NEHRIMGOOT THIS TIME IS A LIL' BABY. A BABY!
SHE MUST BE COMPLETELY POSSESSED BY SPIRITS, TO BE RIGHT ON THE DOT ABOUT EVERYTHING LIKE THAT. SO I JUST WOUND UP GOING 'OH MY GOD, OH MY GOD,' PRAISING HER!
SHHH! YOU'LL JINX IT! WHAT, YOU NEVER SAW HER BRINGING MESSAGES FROM THE DEAD TO THE LIVING, HUH?
WOMAN, YOU DON KNOW WHAT YOU' TALKING ABOUT, THE NO KID THAT ISN'T AT A NEHRIMGOO WHAT'RE YOU GETT WORKED UP FOR
NO, NO! I'VE HELPED ONLY ON NEHRIMGOOTS FOR DECADES NOW, AND I'VE NEVER SEEN A KID DANCE LIKE A BUTTERFLY ON TOP OF A THRESHER.

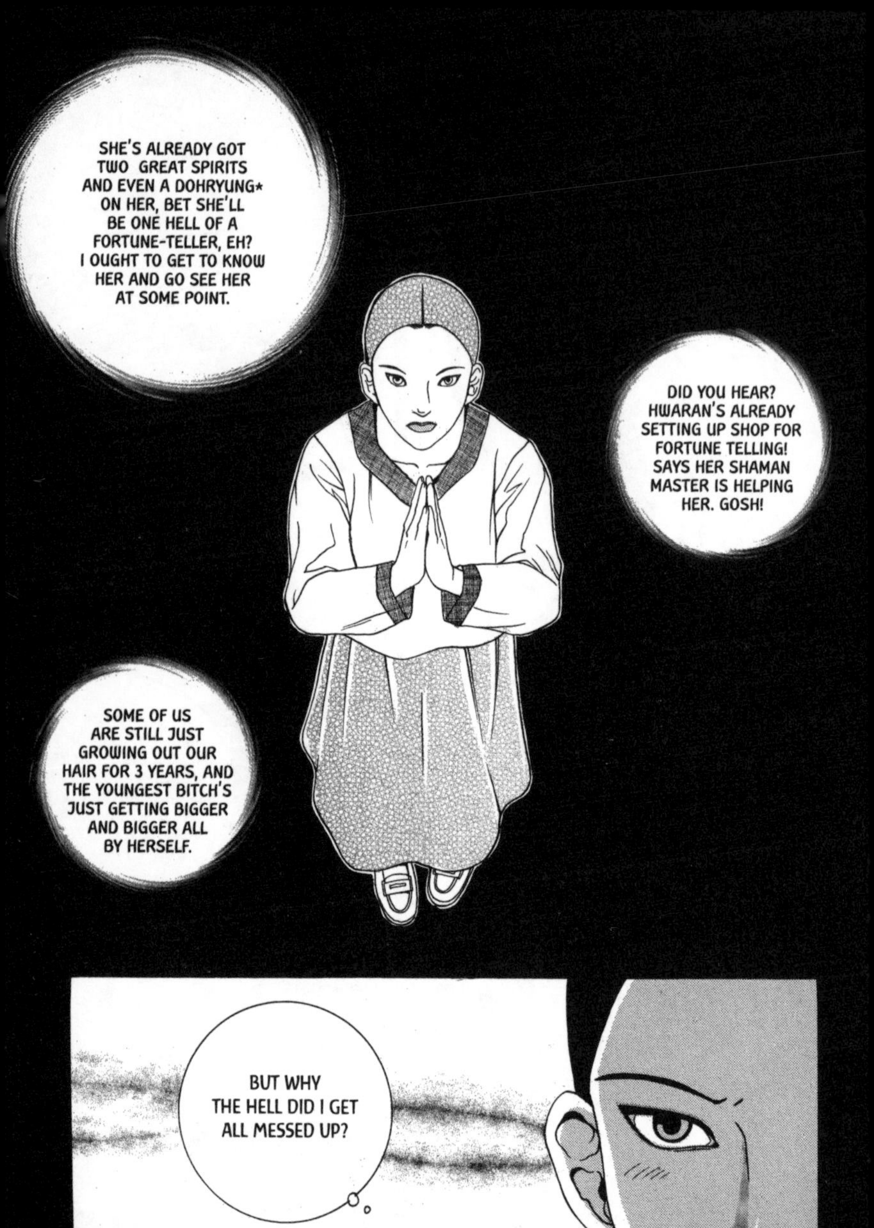
SHE'S ALREADY GOT TWO GREAT SPIRITS AND EVEN A DOHRYUNG* ON HER, BET SHE'LL BE ONE HELL OF A FORTUNE-TELLER, EH? I OUGHT TO GET TO KNOW HER AND GO SEE HER AT SOME POINT.
DID YOU HEAR? HWARAN'S ALREADY SETTING UP SHOP FOR FORTUNE TELLING! SAYS HER SHAMAN MASTER IS HELPING HER. GOSH!
SOME OF US ARE STILL JUST GROWING OUT OUR HAIR FOR 3 YEARS, AND THE YOUNGEST BITCH'S JUST GETTING BIGGER AND BIGGER ALL BY HERSELF.
BUT WHY THE HELL DID I GET ALL MESSED UP?

* DOHRYUNG: THE SPIRIT OF A BOY THAT DIED AT A YOUNG AGE, WHO FORETELLS ONE'S FATE. ALSO CALLED BABY DONGJA, DONGJA, YOUNGDU, TAEJU

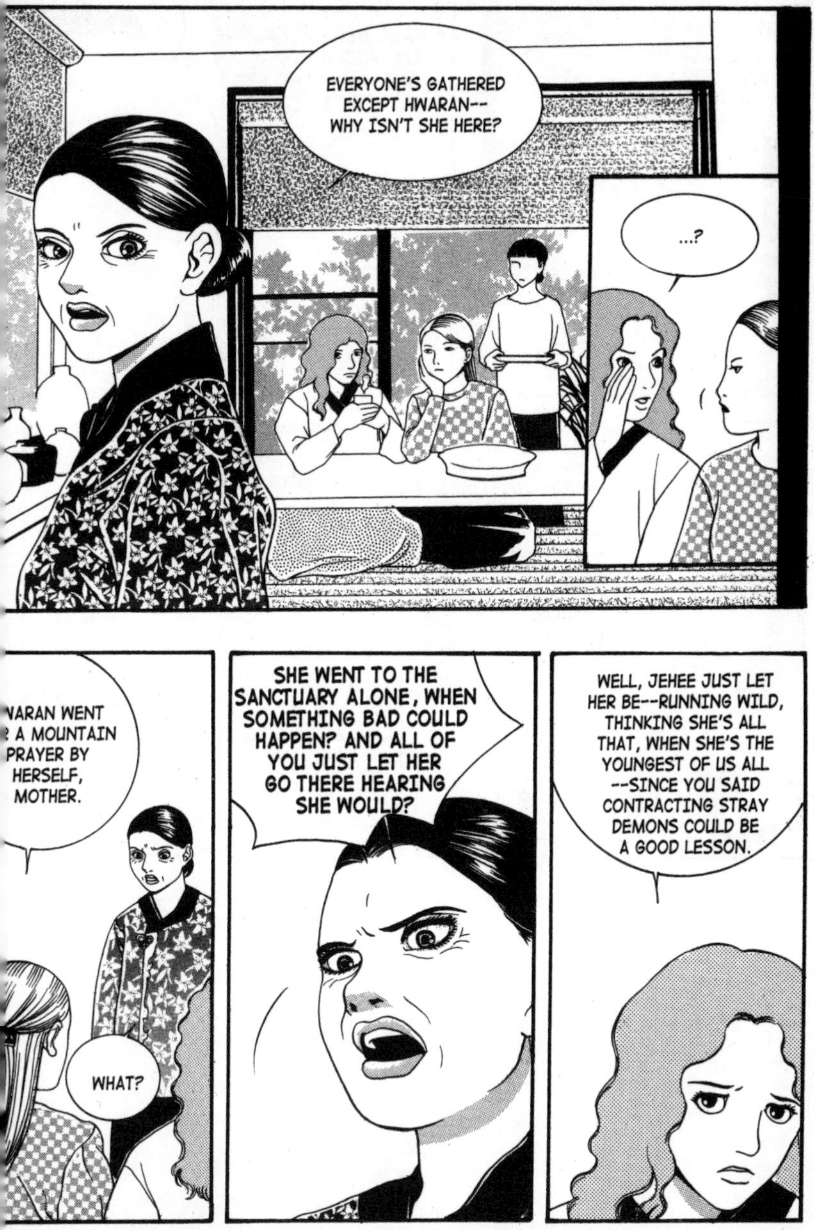

EVERYONE'S GATHERED EXCEPT HWARAN-- WHY ISN'T SHE HERE?
...?
VARAN WENT ? A MOUNTAIN PRAYER BY HERSELF, MOTHER.
WHAT?
SHE WENT TO THE SANCTUARY ALONE, WHEN SOMETHING BAD COULD HAPPEN? AND ALL OF YOU JUST LET HER GO THERE HEARING SHE WOULD?
WELL, JEHEE JUST LET HER BE--RUNNING WILD, THINKING SHE'S ALL THAT, WHEN SHE'S THE YOUNGEST OF US ALL --SINCE YOU SAID CONTRACTING STRAY DEMONS COULD BE A GOOD LESSON.

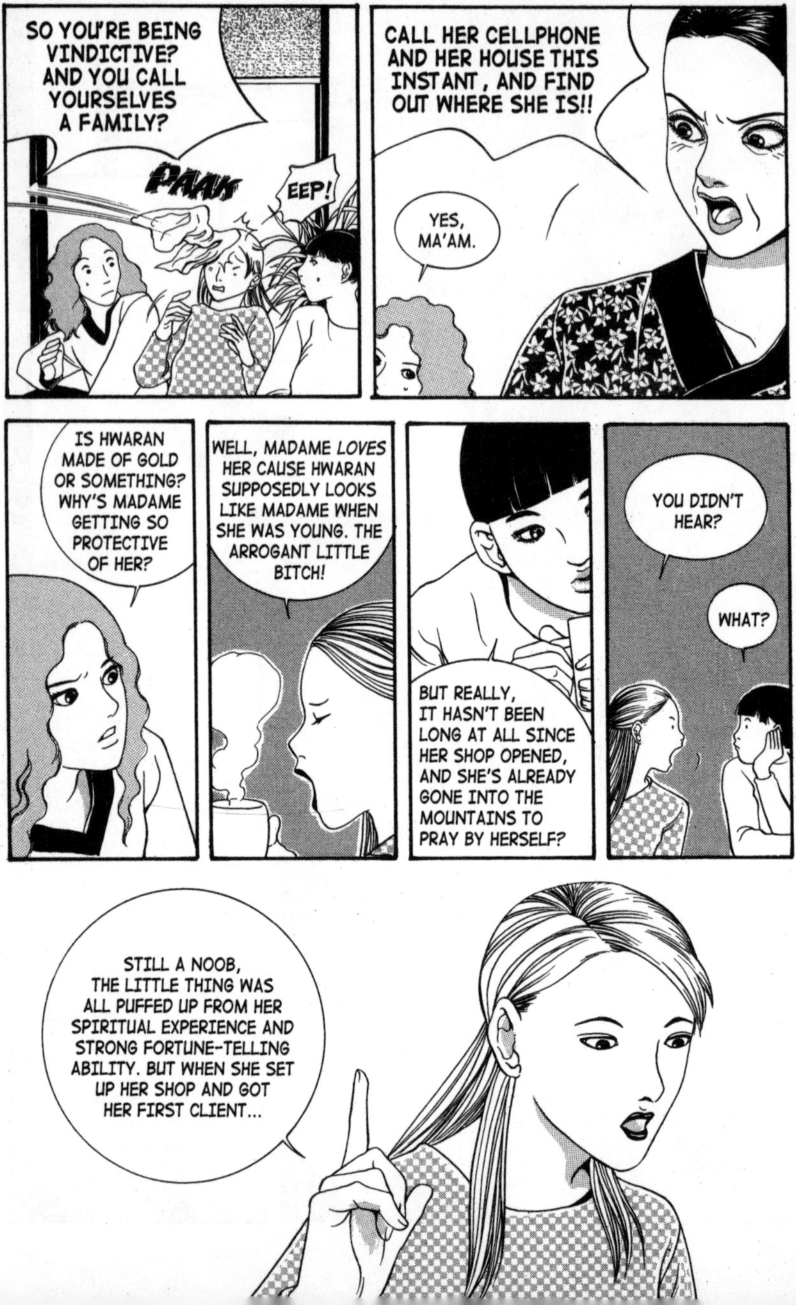
SO YOU'RE BEING VINDICTIVE? AND YOU CALL YOURSELVES A FAMILY?
PAAK
EEP!
CALL HER CELLPHONE AND HER HOUSE THIS INSTANT, AND FIND OUT WHERE SHE IS!!
YES, MA'AM.
IS HWARAN MADE OF GOLD OR SOMETHING? WHY'S MADAME GETTING SO PROTECTIVE OF HER?
WELL, MADAME *LOVES* HER CAUSE HWARAN SUPPOSEDLY LOOKS LIKE MADAME WHEN SHE WAS YOUNG. THE ARROGANT LITTLE BITCH!
BUT REALLY, IT HASN'T BEEN LONG AT ALL SINCE HER SHOP OPENED, AND SHE'S ALREADY GONE INTO THE MOUNTAINS TO PRAY BY HERSELF?
YOU DIDN'T HEAR?
WHAT?
STILL A NOOB, THE LITTLE THING WAS ALL PUFFED UP FROM HER SPIRITUAL EXPERIENCE AND STRONG FORTUNE-TELLING ABILITY. BUT WHEN SHE SET UP HER SHOP AND GOT HER FIRST CLIENT...

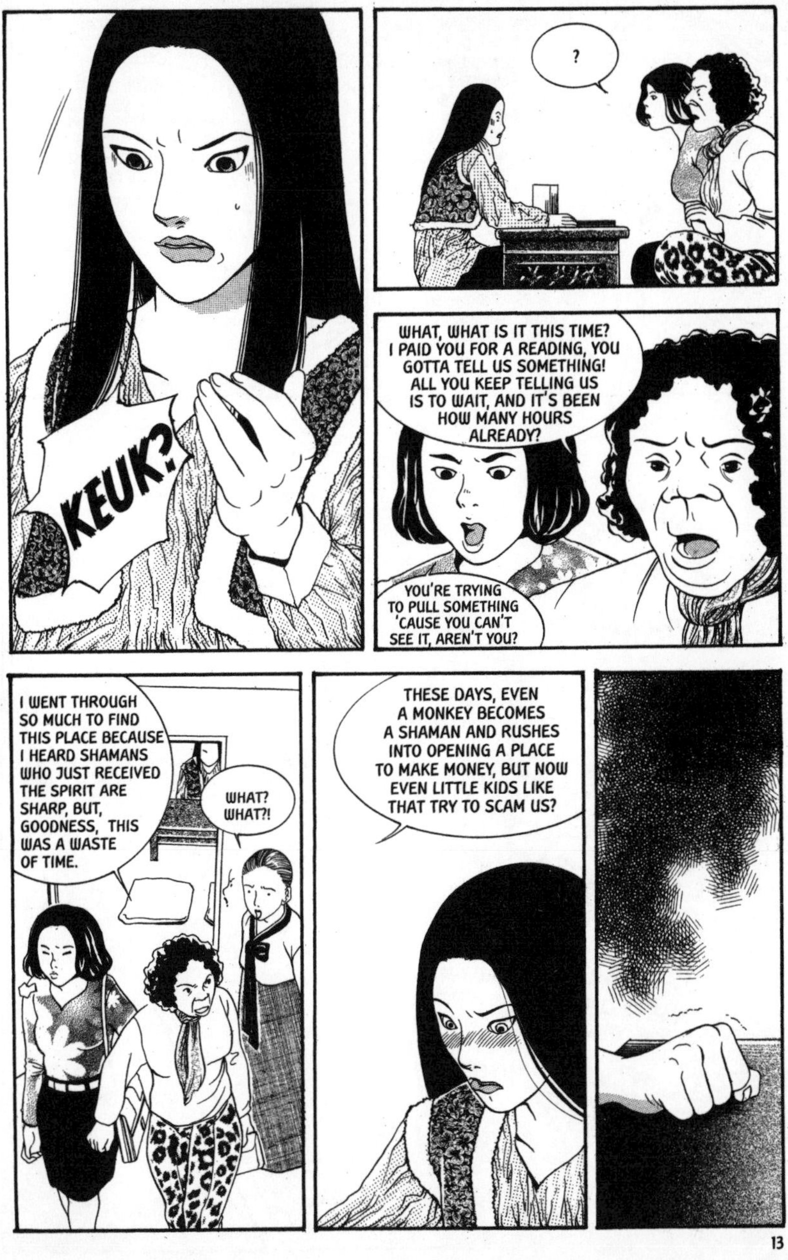
KEUK?
?
WHAT, WHAT IS IT THIS TIME? I PAID YOU FOR A READING, YOU GOTTA TELL US SOMETHING! ALL YOU KEEP TELLING US IS TO WAIT, AND IT'S BEEN HOW MANY HOURS ALREADY?
YOU'RE TRYING TO PULL SOMETHING 'CAUSE YOU CAN'T SEE IT, AREN'T YOU?
I WENT THROUGH SO MUCH TO FIND THIS PLACE BECAUSE I HEARD SHAMANS WHO JUST RECEIVED THE SPIRIT ARE SHARP, BUT, GOODNESS, THIS WAS A WASTE OF TIME.
WHAT? WHAT?!
THESE DAYS, EVEN A MONKEY BECOMES A SHAMAN AND RUSHES INTO OPENING A PLACE TO MAKE MONEY, BUT NOW EVEN LITTLE KIDS LIKE THAT TRY TO SCAM US?

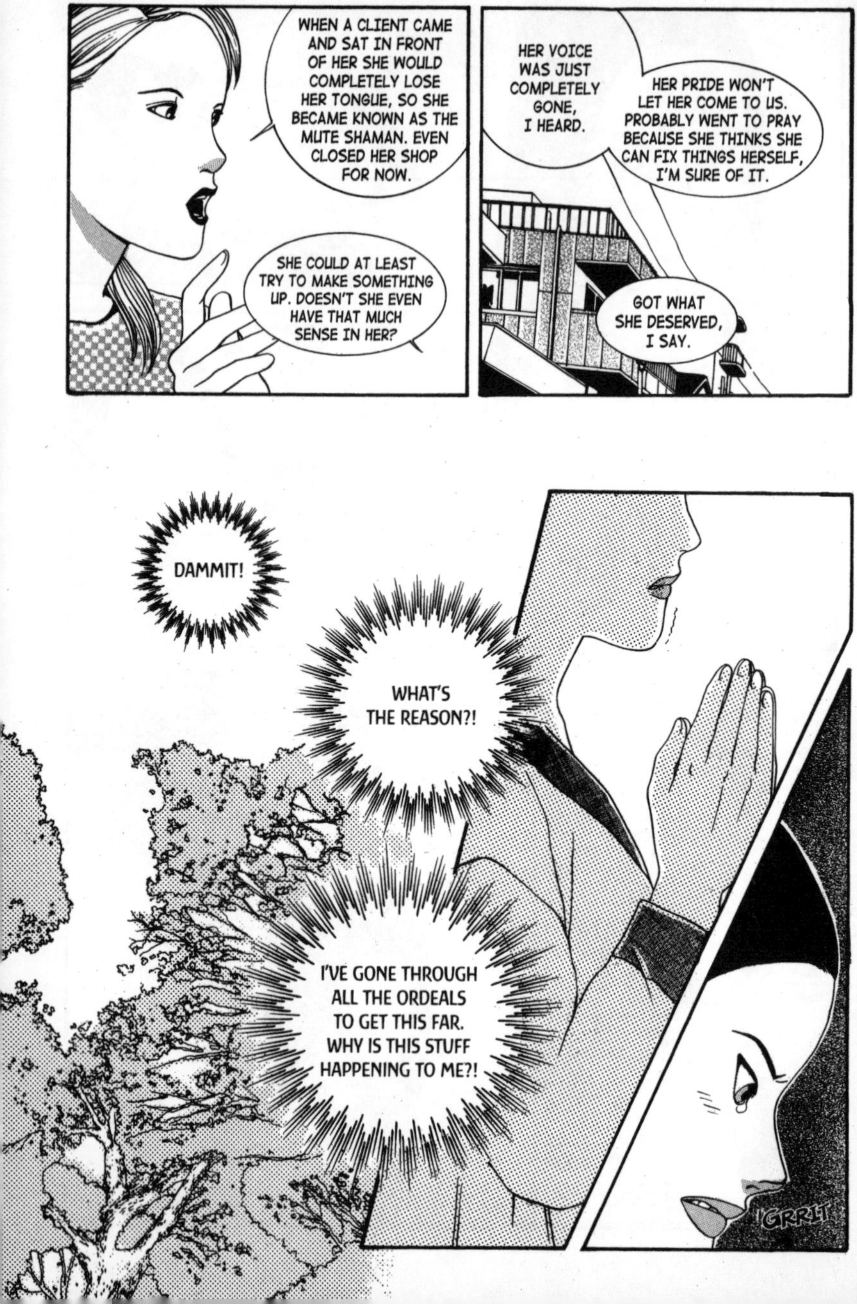
WHEN A CLIENT CAME AND SAT IN FRONT OF HER SHE WOULD COMPLETELY LOSE HER TONGUE, SO SHE BECAME KNOWN AS THE MUTE SHAMAN. EVEN CLOSED HER SHOP FOR NOW.
SHE COULD AT LEAST TRY TO MAKE SOMETHING UP. DOESN'T SHE EVEN HAVE THAT MUCH SENSE IN HER?
HER VOICE WAS JUST COMPLETELY GONE, I HEARD.
HER PRIDE WON'T LET HER COME TO US. PROBABLY WENT TO PRAY BECAUSE SHE THINKS SHE CAN FIX THINGS HERSELF, I'M SURE OF IT.
GOT WHAT SHE DESERVED, I SAY.
DAMMIT!
WHAT'S THE REASON?!
I'VE GONE THROUGH ALL THE ORDEALS TO GET THIS FAR. WHY IS THIS STUFF HAPPENING TO ME?!
GRRIT

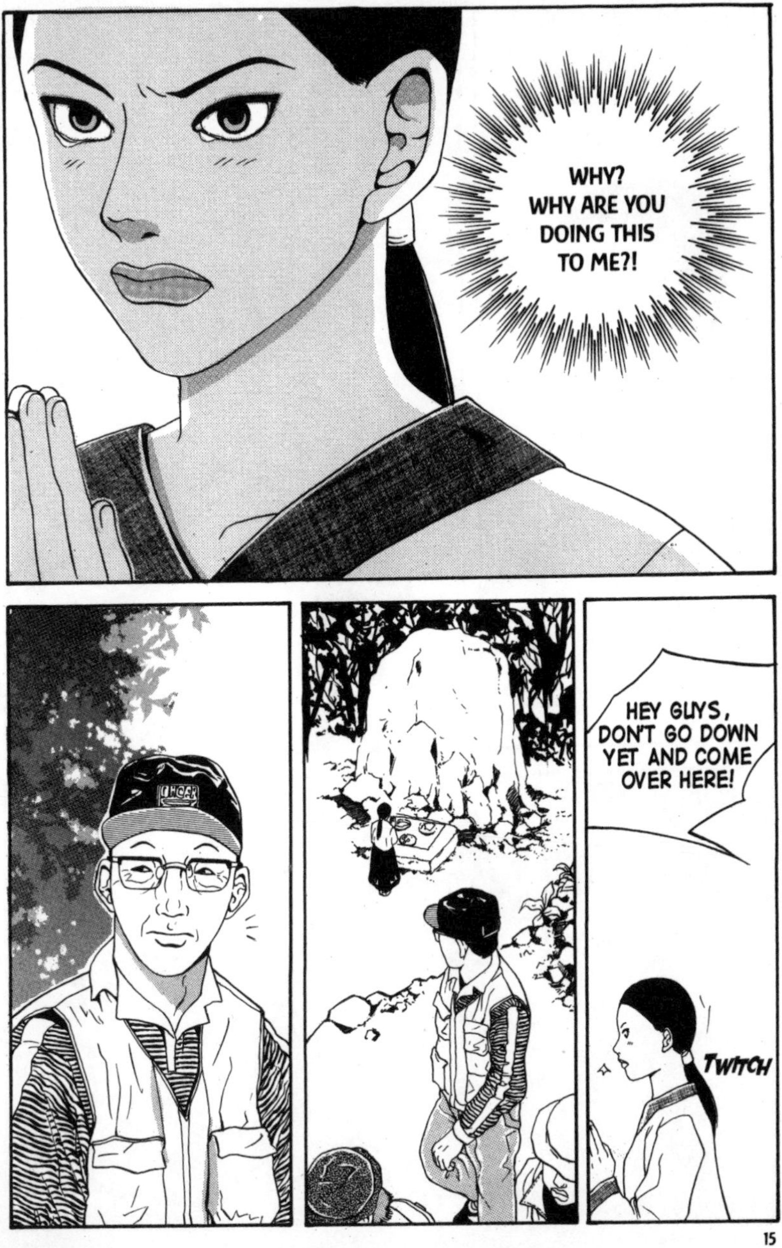
WHY?
WHY ARE YOU
DOING THIS
TO ME?!
HEY GUYS,
DON'T GO DOWN
YET AND COME
OVER HERE!
TWITCH

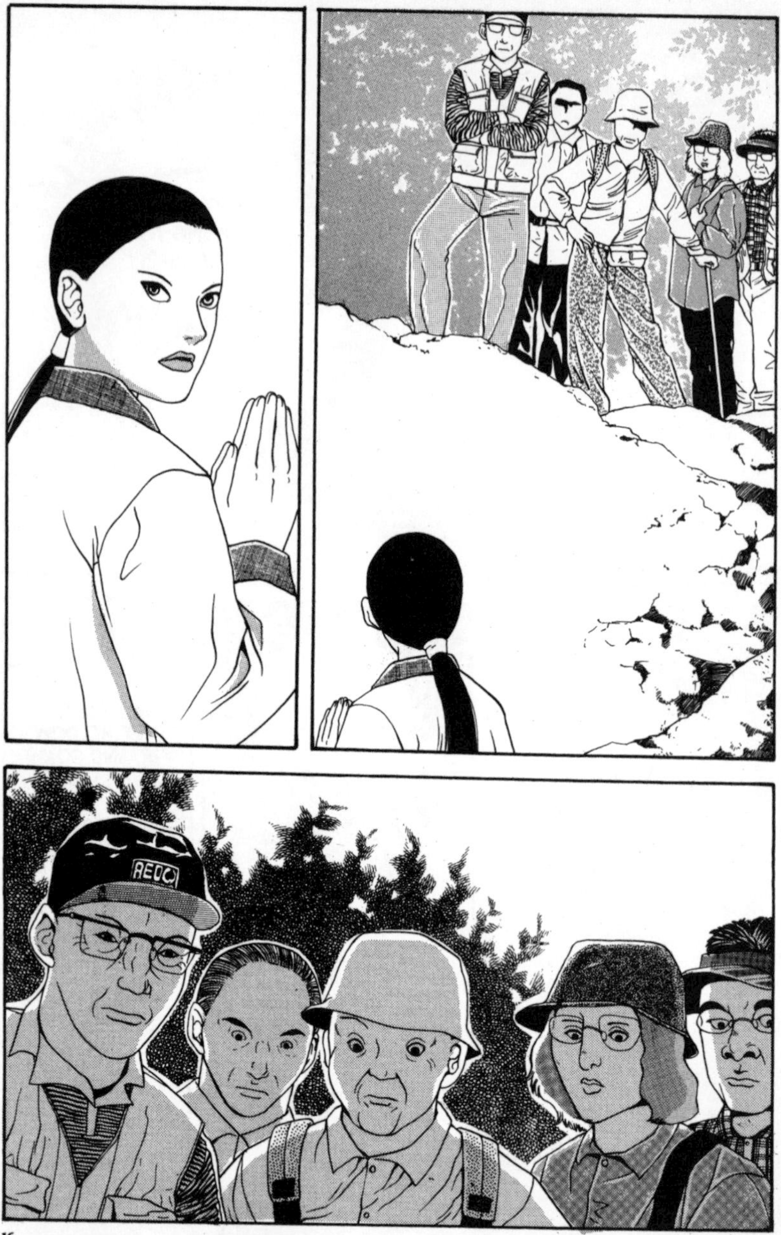

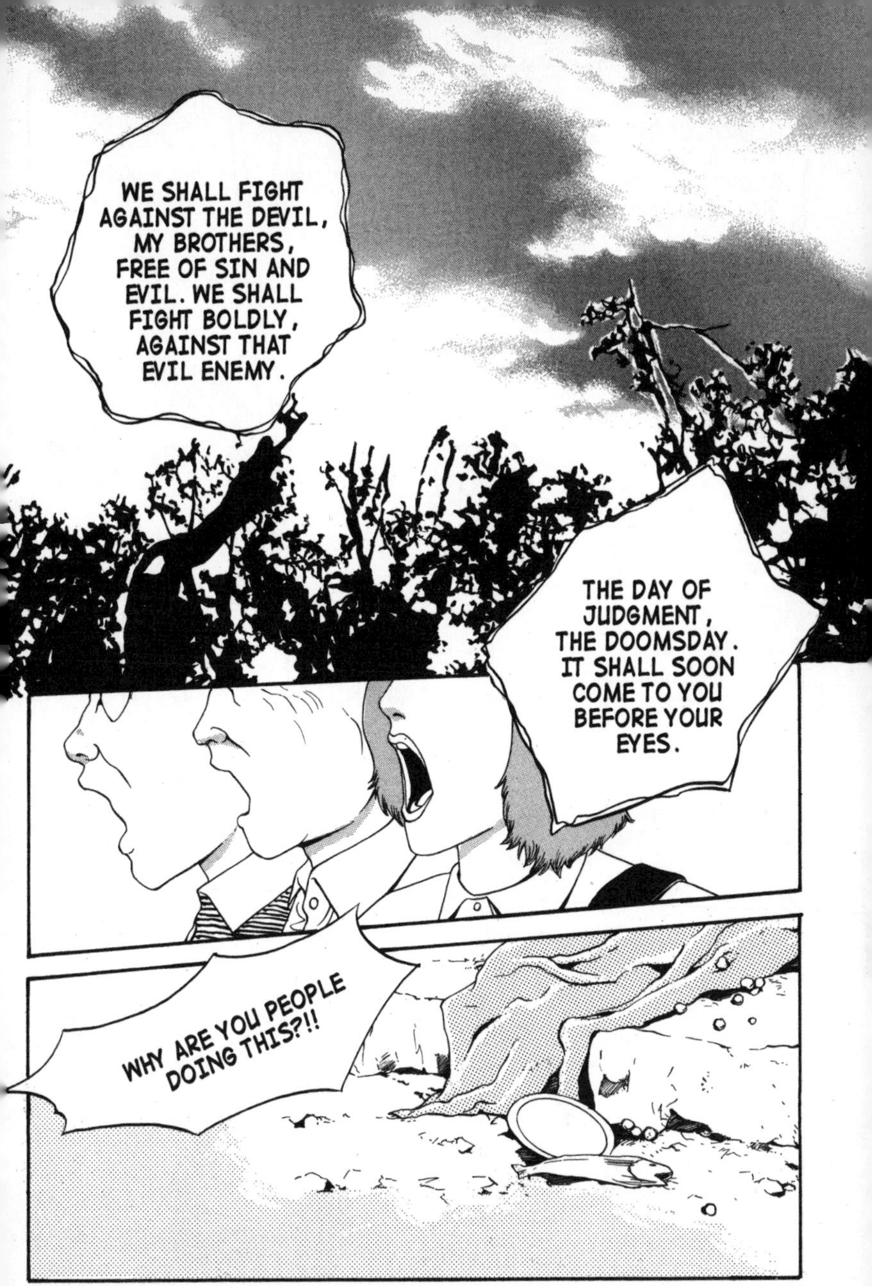
WE SHALL FIGHT AGAINST THE DEVIL, MY BROTHERS, FREE OF SIN AND EVIL. WE SHALL FIGHT BOLDLY, AGAINST THAT EVIL ENEMY.
THE DAY OF JUDGMENT, THE DOOMSDAY. IT SHALL SOON COME TO YOU BEFORE YOUR EYES.
WHY ARE YOU PEOPLE DOING THIS?!!

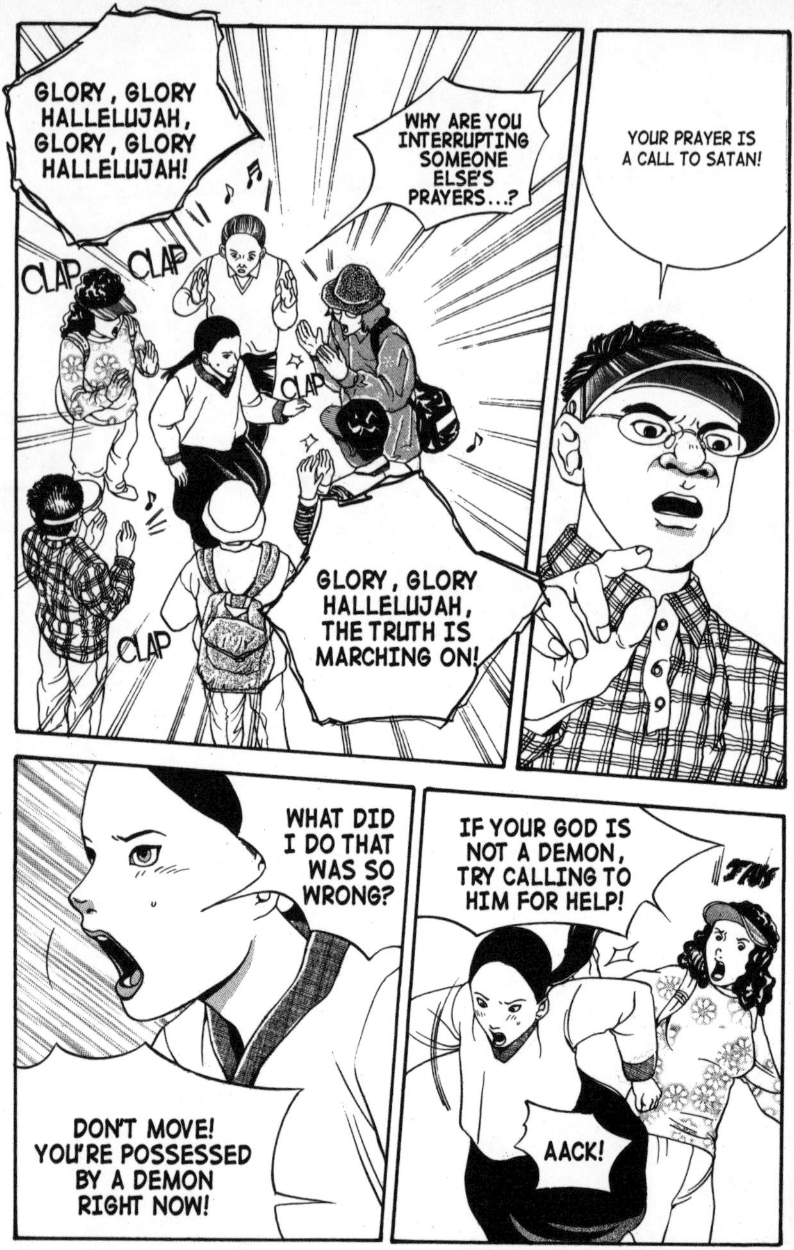
GLORY, GLORY HALLELUJAH, GLORY, GLORY HALLELUJAH!
WHY ARE YOU INTERRUPTING SOMEONE ELSE'S PRAYERS...?
CLAP
CLAP
CLAP
CLAP
GLORY, GLORY HALLELUJAH, THE TRUTH IS MARCHING ON!
YOUR PRAYER IS A CALL TO SATAN!
WHAT DID I DO THAT WAS SO WRONG?
DON'T MOVE! YOU'RE POSSESSED BY A DEMON RIGHT NOW!
IF YOUR GOD IS NOT A DEMON, TRY CALLING TO HIM FOR HELP!
AACK!

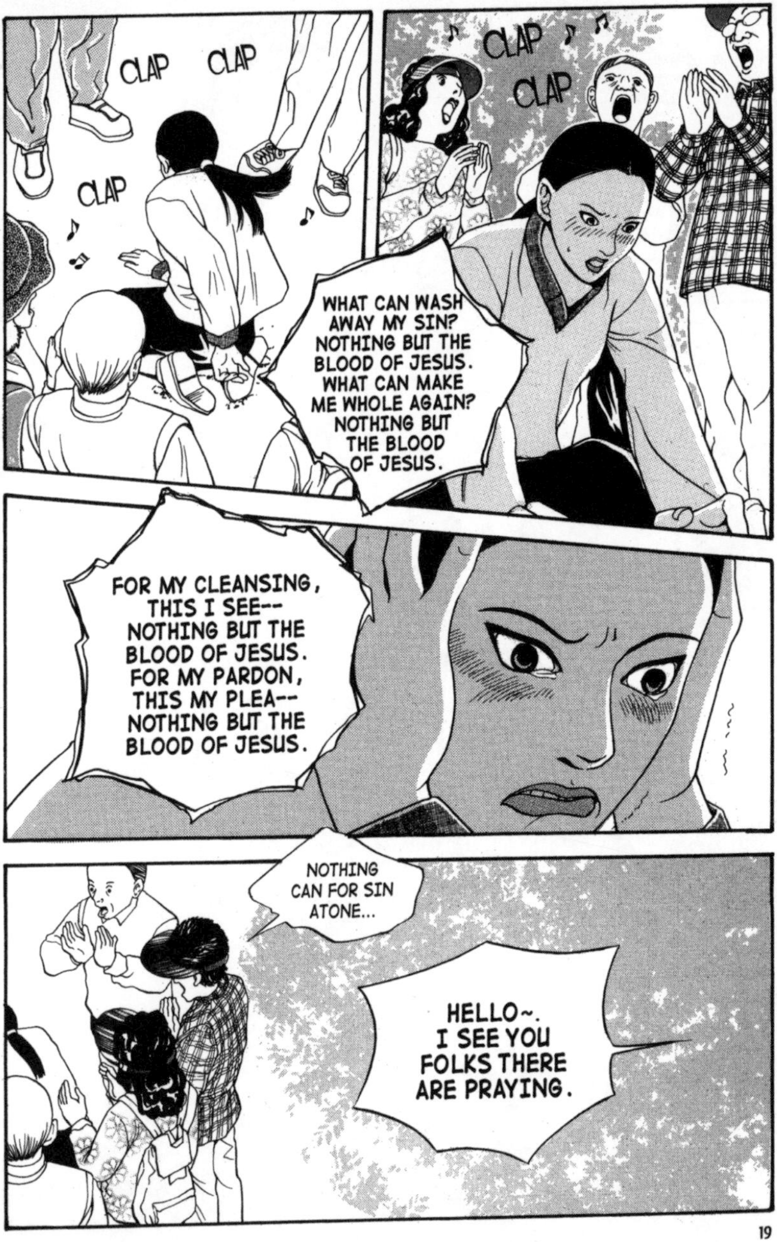
CLAP CLAP
CLAP
CLAP
CLAP
WHAT CAN WASH AWAY MY SIN? NOTHING BUT THE BLOOD OF JESUS. WHAT CAN MAKE ME WHOLE AGAIN? NOTHING BUT THE BLOOD OF JESUS.
FOR MY CLEANSING, THIS I SEE-- NOTHING BUT THE BLOOD OF JESUS. FOR MY PARDON, THIS MY PLEA-- NOTHING BUT THE BLOOD OF JESUS.
NOTHING CAN FOR SIN ATONE...
HELLO~. I SEE YOU FOLKS THERE ARE PRAYING.

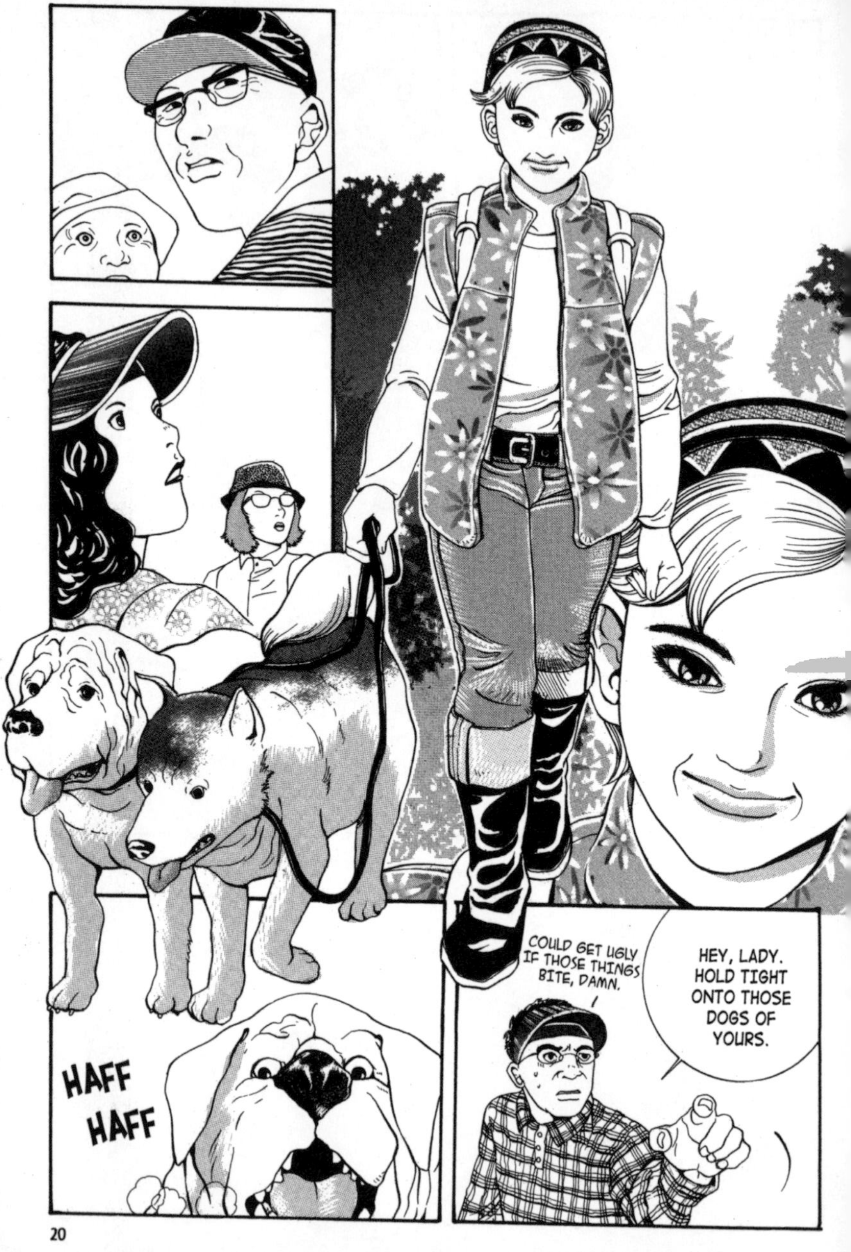
HAFF
HAFF
COULD GET UGLY IF THOSE THINGS BITE, DAMN.
HEY, LADY. HOLD TIGHT ONTO THOSE DOGS OF YOURS.

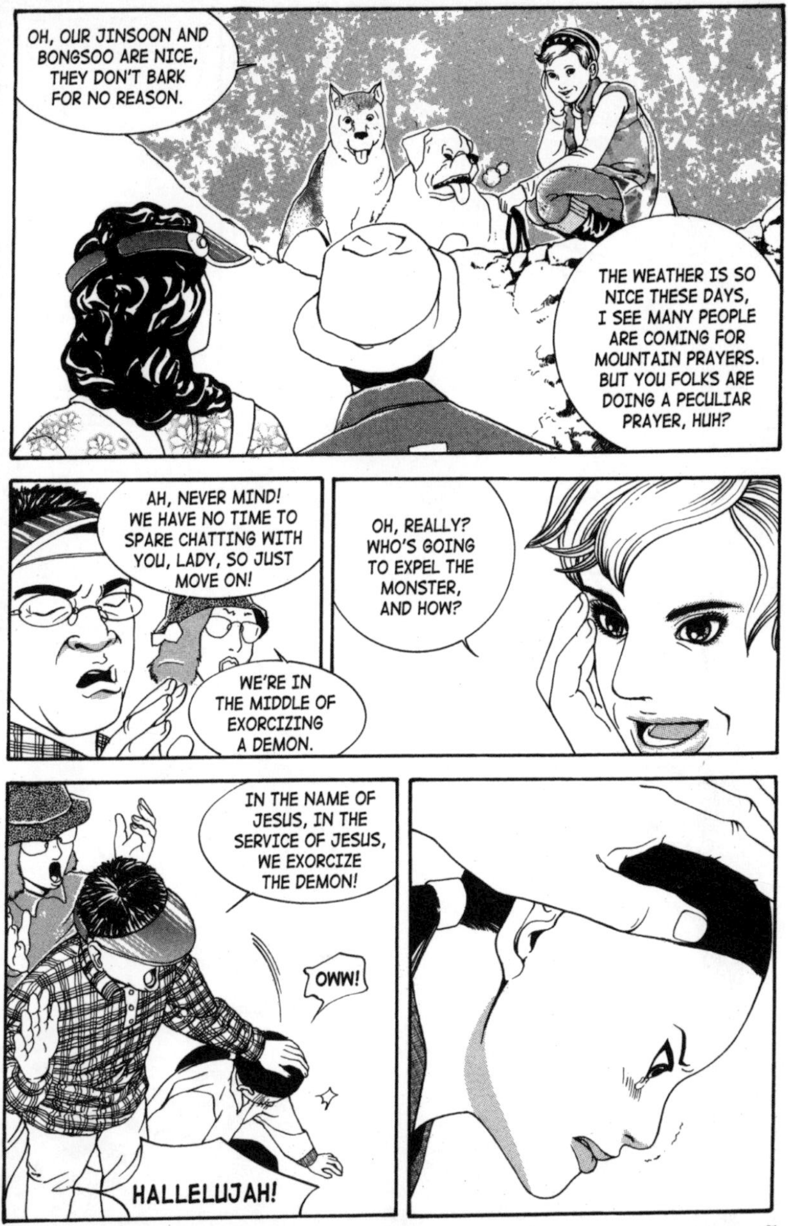
OH, OUR JINSOON AND BONGSOO ARE NICE, THEY DON'T BARK FOR NO REASON.
THE WEATHER IS SO NICE THESE DAYS, I SEE MANY PEOPLE ARE COMING FOR MOUNTAIN PRAYERS. BUT YOU FOLKS ARE DOING A PECULIAR PRAYER, HUH?
AH, NEVER MIND! WE HAVE NO TIME TO SPARE CHATTING WITH YOU, LADY, SO JUST MOVE ON!
WE'RE IN THE MIDDLE OF EXORCIZING A DEMON.
OH, REALLY? WHO'S GOING TO EXPEL THE MONSTER, AND HOW?
IN THE NAME OF JESUS, IN THE SERVICE OF JESUS, WE EXORCIZE THE DEMON!
OWW!
HALLELUJAH!

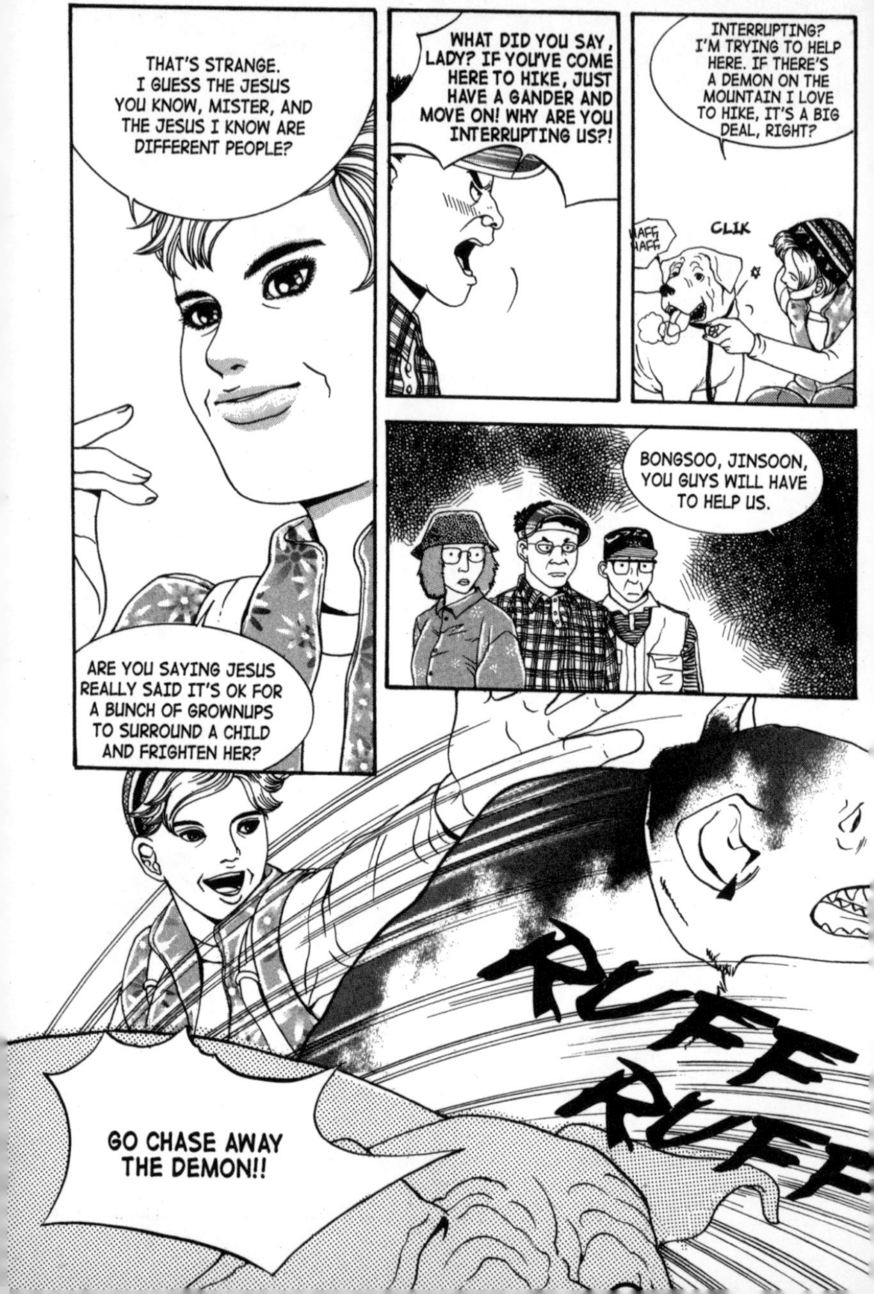
THAT'S STRANGE. I GUESS THE JESUS YOU KNOW, MISTER, AND THE JESUS I KNOW ARE DIFFERENT PEOPLE?
ARE YOU SAYING JESUS REALLY SAID IT'S OK FOR A BUNCH OF GROWNUPS TO SURROUND A CHILD AND FRIGHTEN HER?
WHAT DID YOU SAY, LADY? IF YOU'VE COME HERE TO HIKE, JUST HAVE A GANDER AND MOVE ON! WHY ARE YOU INTERRUPTING US?!
INTERRUPTING? I'M TRYING TO HELP HERE. IF THERE'S A DEMON ON THE MOUNTAIN I LOVE TO HIKE, IT'S A BIG DEAL, RIGHT?
HAFF HAFF
CLIK
BONGSOO, JINSOON, YOU GUYS WILL HAVE TO HELP US.
GO CHASE AWAY THE DEMON!!
RUFF RUFF

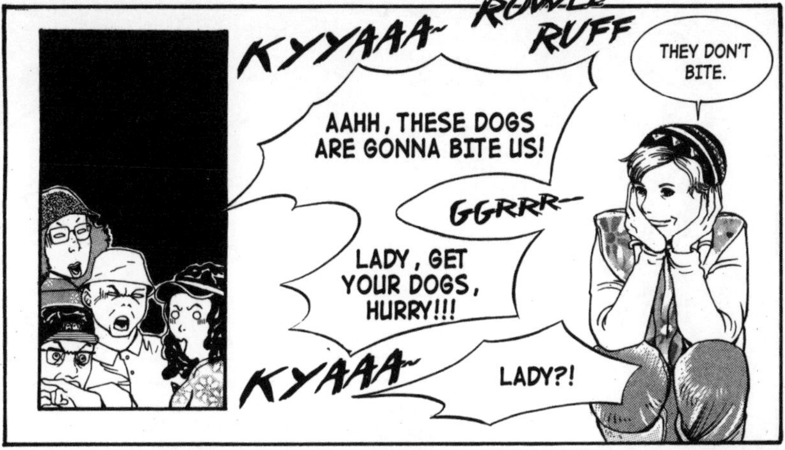
KYYAAA~
ROWLL
RUFF
THEY DON'T BITE.
AAHH, THESE DOGS ARE GONNA BITE US!
GGRRR-
LADY, GET YOUR DOGS, HURRY!!!
KYAAA~
LADY?!

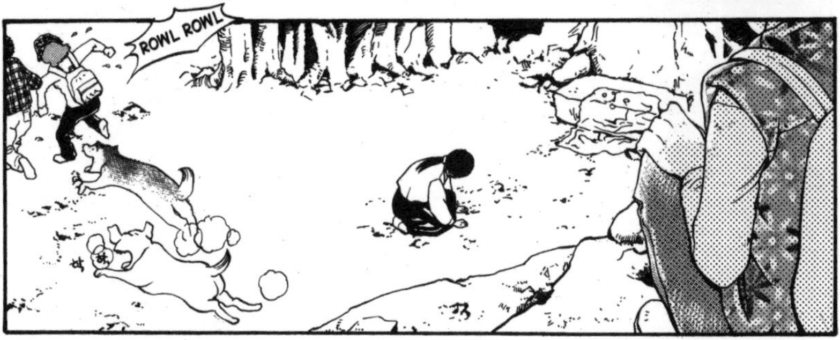
ROWL ROWL

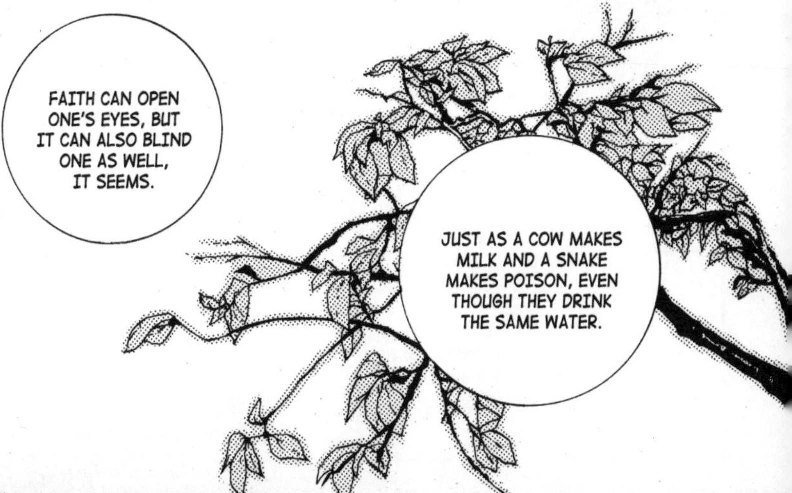
FAITH CAN OPEN ONE'S EYES, BUT IT CAN ALSO BLIND ONE AS WELL, IT SEEMS.
JUST AS A COW MAKES MILK AND A SNAKE MAKES POISON, EVEN THOUGH THEY DRINK THE SAME WATER.

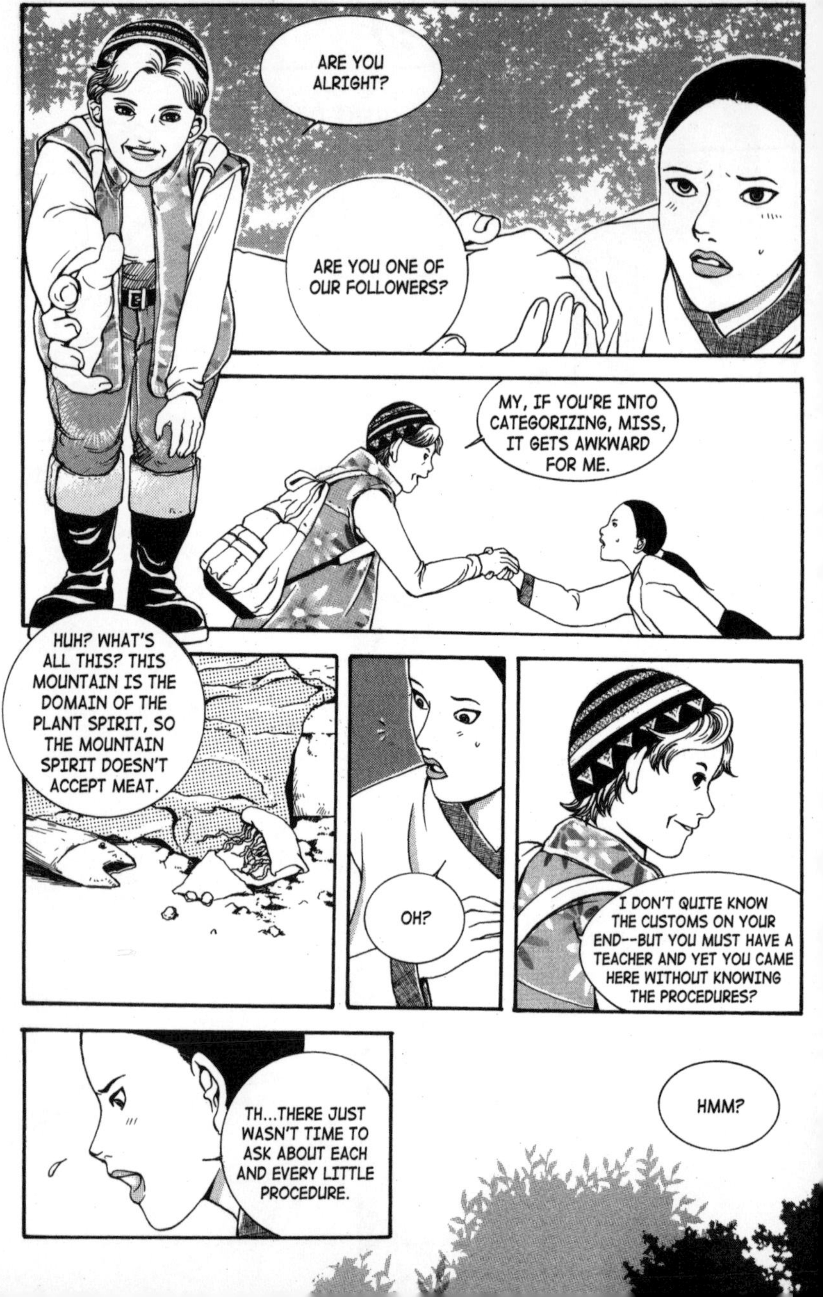

ARE YOU ALRIGHT?
ARE YOU ONE OF OUR FOLLOWERS?
MY, IF YOU'RE INTO CATEGORIZING, MISS, IT GETS AWKWARD FOR ME.
HUH? WHAT'S ALL THIS? THIS MOUNTAIN IS THE DOMAIN OF THE PLANT SPIRIT, SO THE MOUNTAIN SPIRIT DOESN'T ACCEPT MEAT.
OH?
I DON'T QUITE KNOW THE CUSTOMS ON YOUR END--BUT YOU MUST HAVE A TEACHER AND YET YOU CAME HERE WITHOUT KNOWING THE PROCEDURES?
TH...THERE JUST WASN'T TIME TO ASK ABOUT EACH AND EVERY LITTLE PROCEDURE.
HMM?

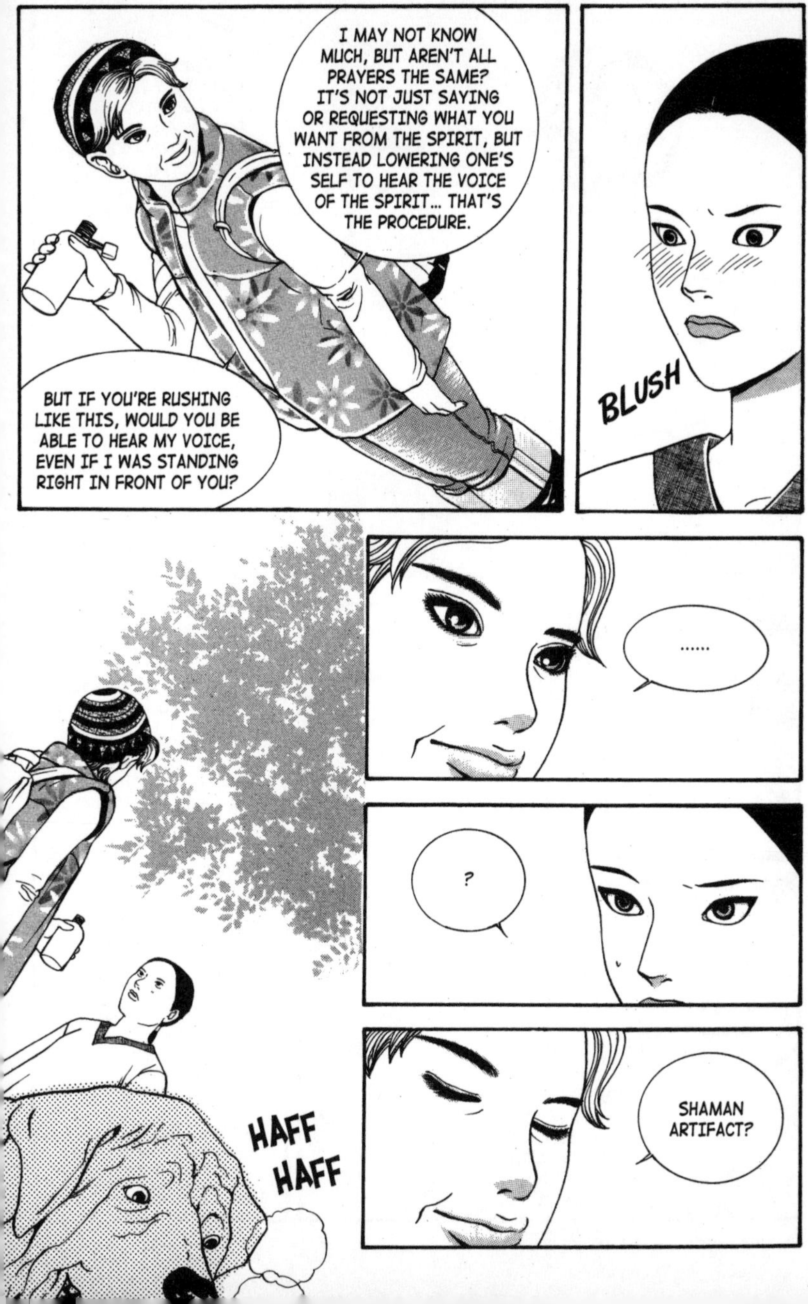
I MAY NOT KNOW MUCH, BUT AREN'T ALL PRAYERS THE SAME? IT'S NOT JUST SAYING OR REQUESTING WHAT YOU WANT FROM THE SPIRIT, BUT INSTEAD LOWERING ONE'S SELF TO HEAR THE VOICE OF THE SPIRIT... THAT'S THE PROCEDURE.
BUT IF YOU'RE RUSHING LIKE THIS, WOULD YOU BE ABLE TO HEAR MY VOICE, EVEN IF I WAS STANDING RIGHT IN FRONT OF YOU?
BLUSH
HAFF HAFF
......
?
SHAMAN ARTIFACT?

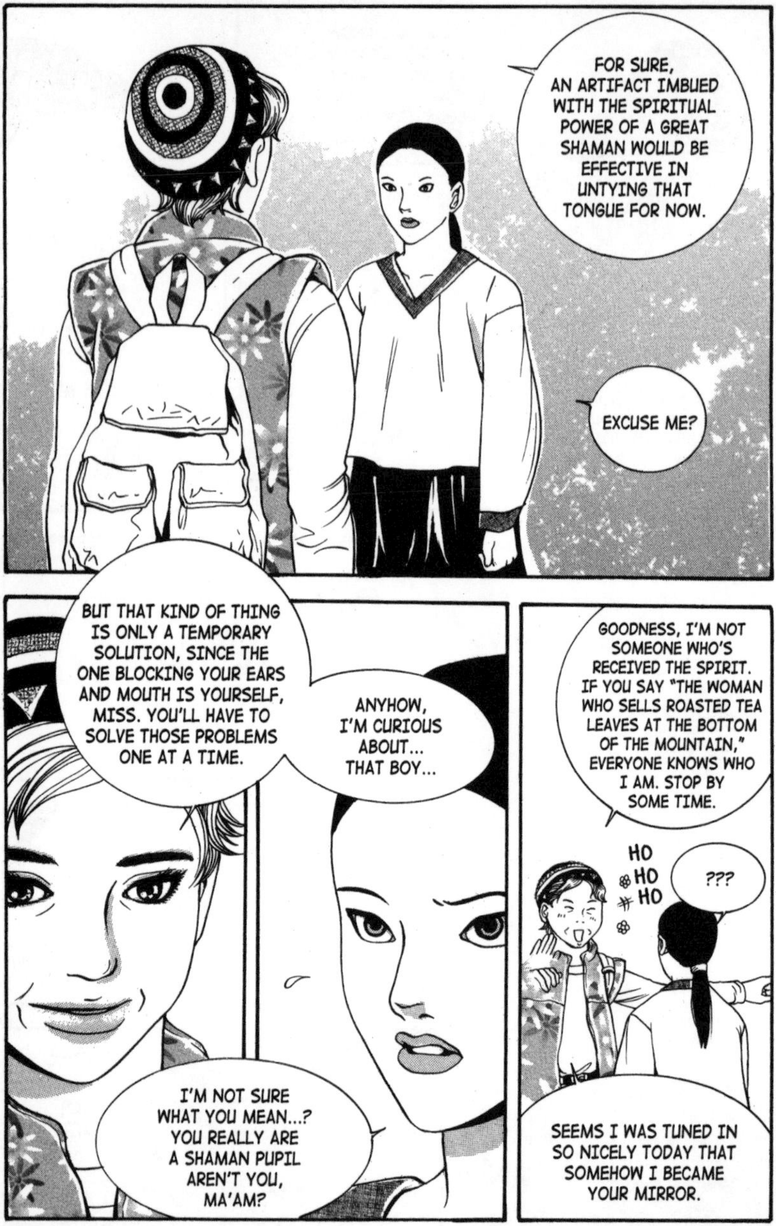
FOR SURE, AN ARTIFACT IMBUED WITH THE SPIRITUAL POWER OF A GREAT SHAMAN WOULD BE EFFECTIVE IN UNTYING THAT TONGUE FOR NOW.
EXCUSE ME?
BUT THAT KIND OF THING IS ONLY A TEMPORARY SOLUTION, SINCE THE ONE BLOCKING YOUR EARS AND MOUTH IS YOURSELF, MISS. YOU'LL HAVE TO SOLVE THOSE PROBLEMS ONE AT A TIME.
ANYHOW, I'M CURIOUS ABOUT... THAT BOY...
I'M NOT SURE WHAT YOU MEAN...? YOU REALLY ARE A SHAMAN PUPIL AREN'T YOU, MA'AM?
GOODNESS, I'M NOT SOMEONE WHO'S RECEIVED THE SPIRIT. IF YOU SAY "THE WOMAN WHO SELLS ROASTED TEA LEAVES AT THE BOTTOM OF THE MOUNTAIN," EVERYONE KNOWS WHO I AM. STOP BY SOME TIME.
HO HO HO
???
SEEMS I WAS TUNED IN SO NICELY TODAY THAT SOMEHOW I BECAME YOUR MIRROR.

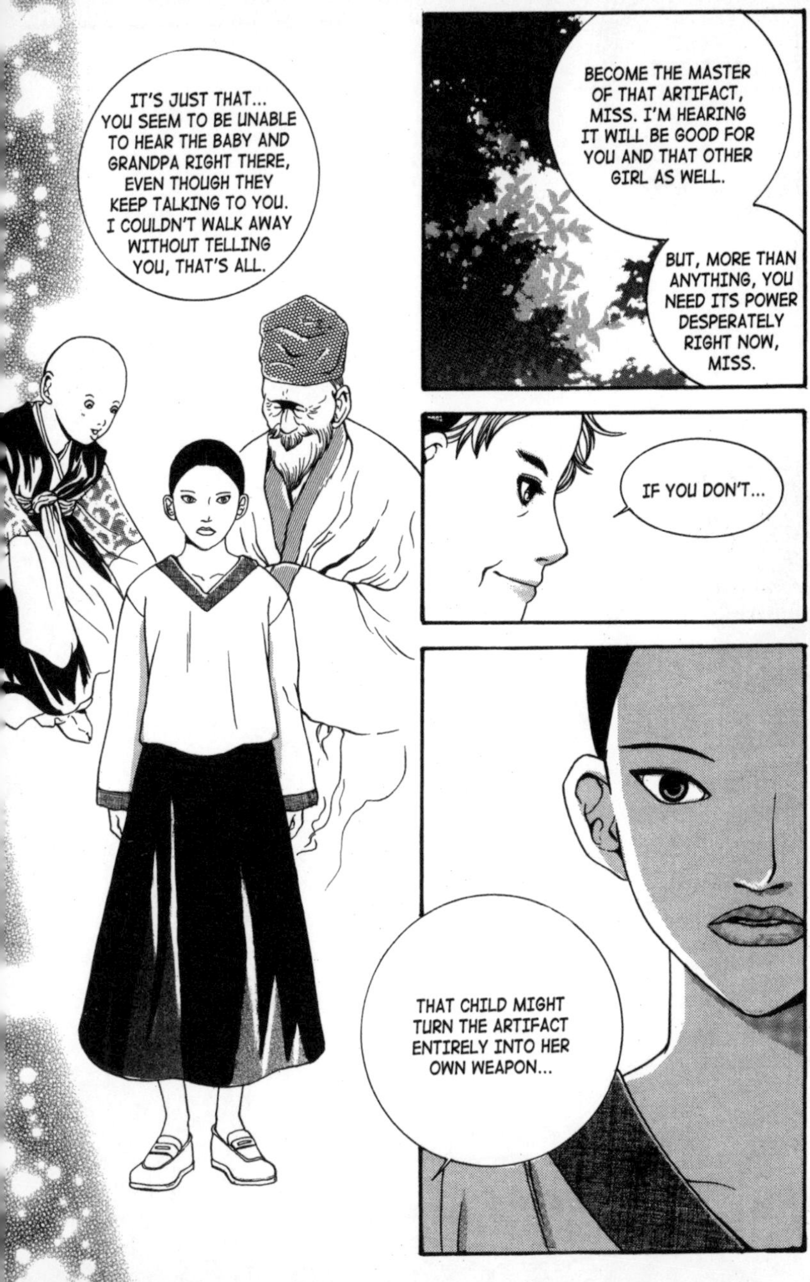
IT'S JUST THAT... YOU SEEM TO BE UNABLE TO HEAR THE BABY AND GRANDPA RIGHT THERE, EVEN THOUGH THEY KEEP TALKING TO YOU. I COULDN'T WALK AWAY WITHOUT TELLING YOU, THAT'S ALL.
BECOME THE MASTER OF THAT ARTIFACT, MISS. I'M HEARING IT WILL BE GOOD FOR YOU AND THAT OTHER GIRL AS WELL.
BUT, MORE THAN ANYTHING, YOU NEED ITS POWER DESPERATELY RIGHT NOW, MISS.
IF YOU DON'T...
THAT CHILD MIGHT TURN THE ARTIFACT ENTIRELY INTO HER OWN WEAPON...

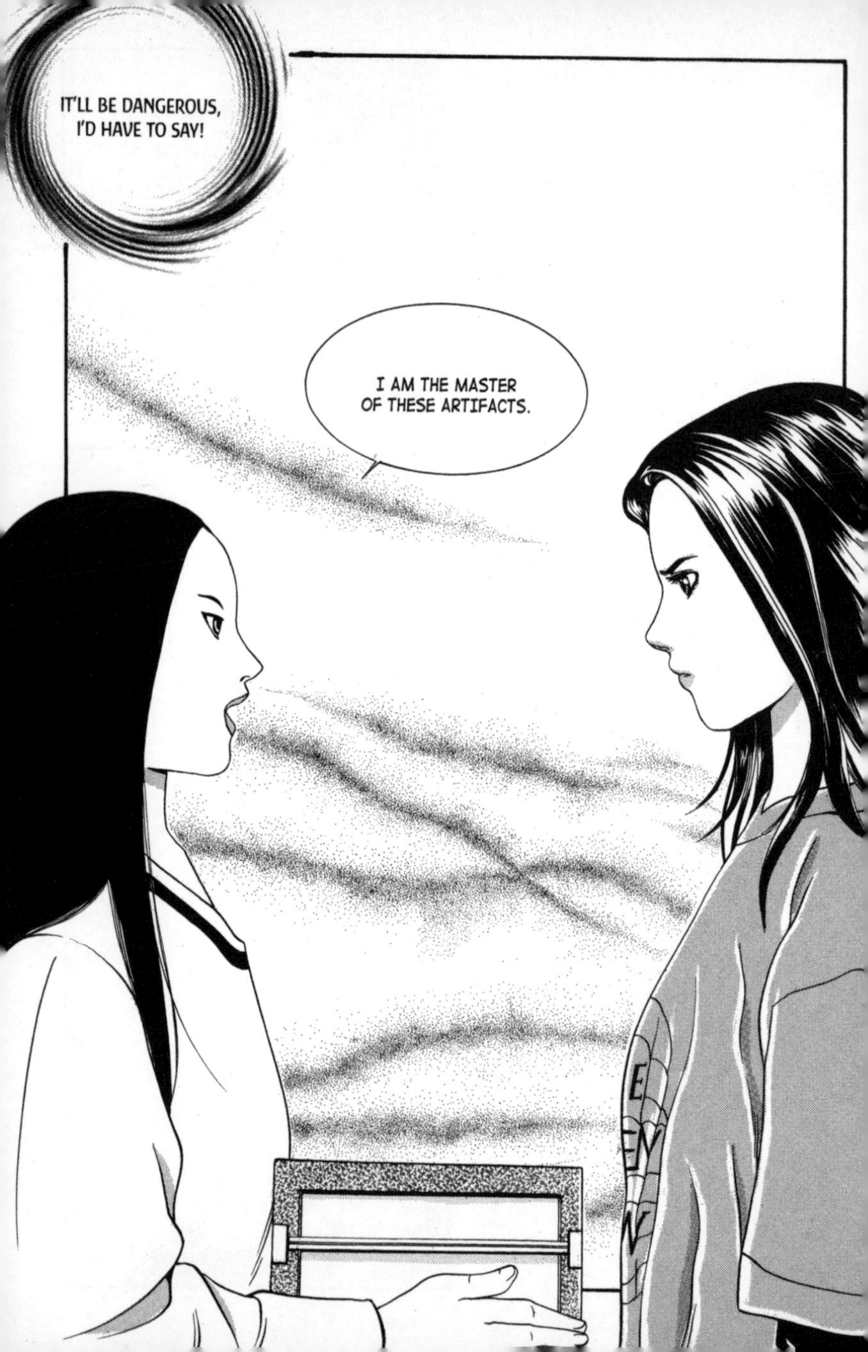
IT'LL BE DANGEROUS, I'D HAVE TO SAY!
I AM THE MASTER OF THESE ARTIFACTS.

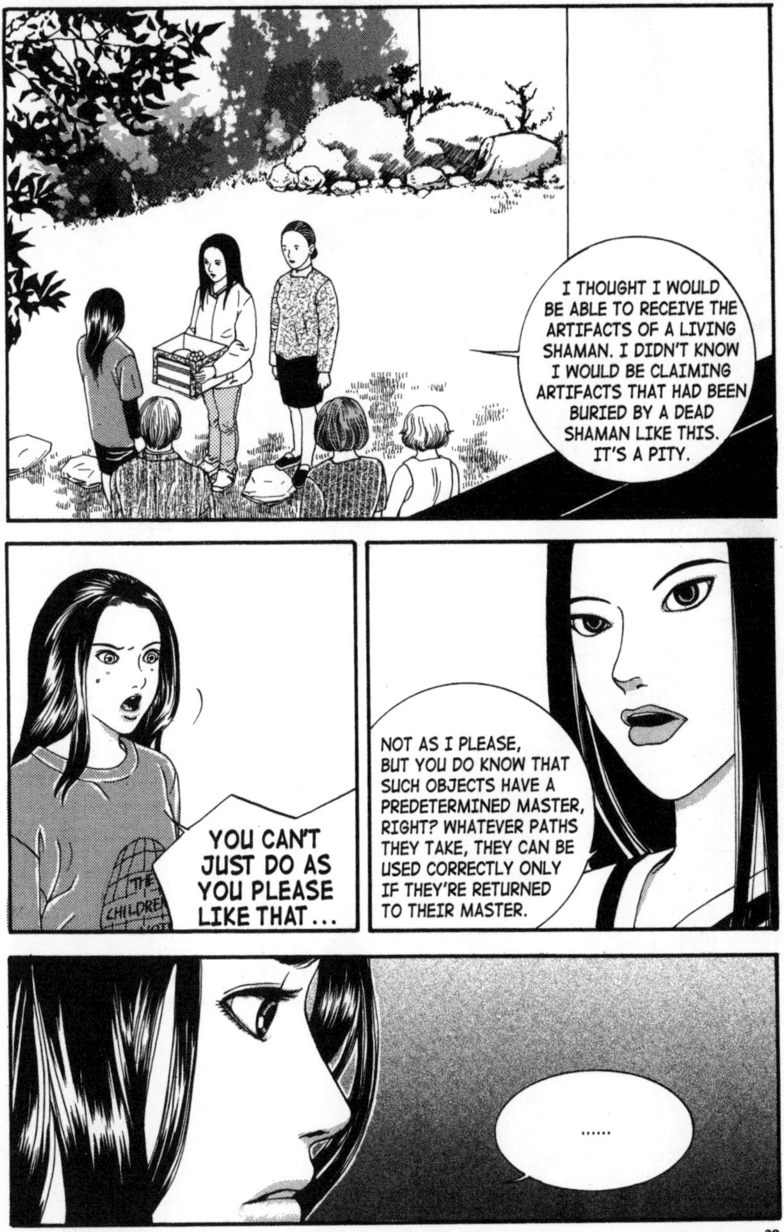
I THOUGHT I WOULD BE ABLE TO RECEIVE THE ARTIFACTS OF A LIVING SHAMAN. I DIDN'T KNOW I WOULD BE CLAIMING ARTIFACTS THAT HAD BEEN BURIED BY A DEAD SHAMAN LIKE THIS. IT'S A PITY.
YOU CAN'T JUST DO AS YOU PLEASE LIKE THAT...
NOT AS I PLEASE, BUT YOU DO KNOW THAT SUCH OBJECTS HAVE A PREDETERMINED MASTER, RIGHT? WHATEVER PATHS THEY TAKE, THEY CAN BE USED CORRECTLY ONLY IF THEY'RE RETURNED TO THEIR MASTER.
......

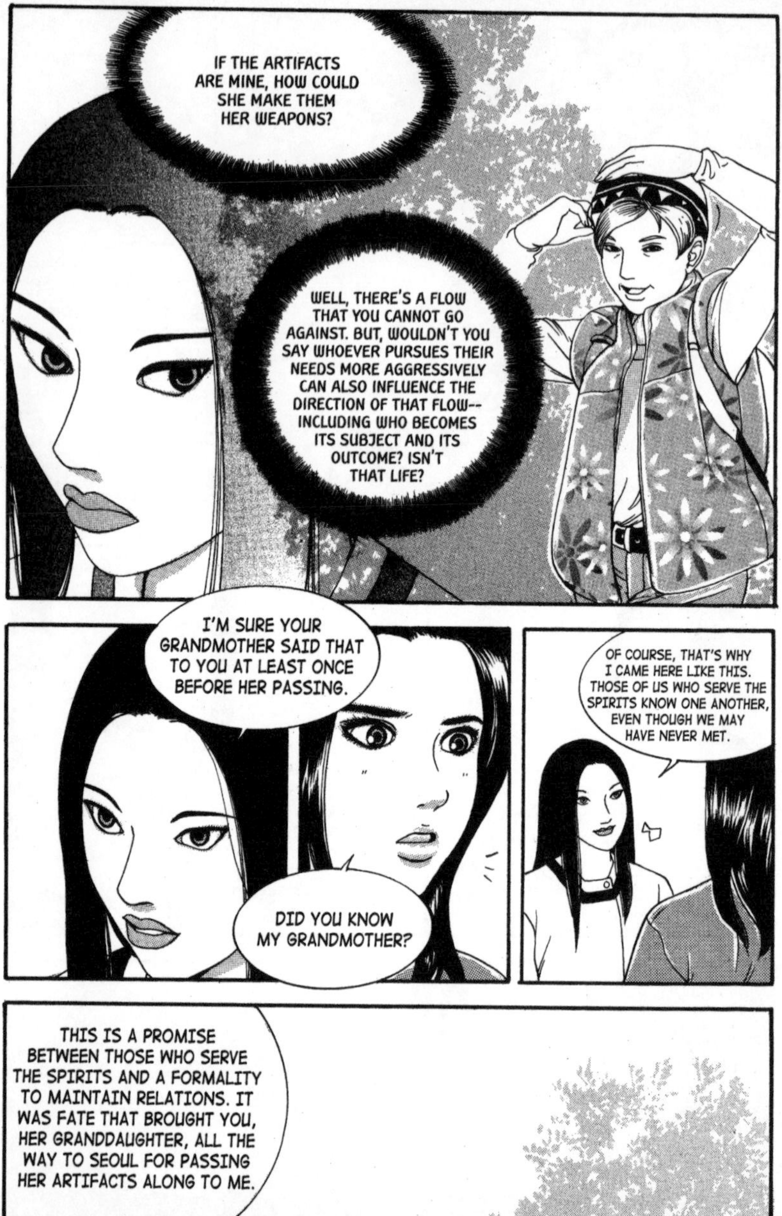
IF THE ARTIFACTS ARE MINE, HOW COULD SHE MAKE THEM HER WEAPONS?
WELL, THERE'S A FLOW THAT YOU CANNOT GO AGAINST. BUT, WOULDN'T YOU SAY WHOEVER PURSUES THEIR NEEDS MORE AGGRESSIVELY CAN ALSO INFLUENCE THE DIRECTION OF THAT FLOW-- INCLUDING WHO BECOMES ITS SUBJECT AND ITS OUTCOME? ISN'T THAT LIFE?
I'M SURE YOUR GRANDMOTHER SAID THAT TO YOU AT LEAST ONCE BEFORE HER PASSING.
DID YOU KNOW MY GRANDMOTHER?
OF COURSE, THAT'S WHY I CAME HERE LIKE THIS. THOSE OF US WHO SERVE THE SPIRITS KNOW ONE ANOTHER, EVEN THOUGH WE MAY HAVE NEVER MET.
THIS IS A PROMISE BETWEEN THOSE WHO SERVE THE SPIRITS AND A FORMALITY TO MAINTAIN RELATIONS. IT WAS FATE THAT BROUGHT YOU, HER GRANDDAUGHTER, ALL THE WAY TO SEOUL FOR PASSING HER ARTIFACTS ALONG TO ME.

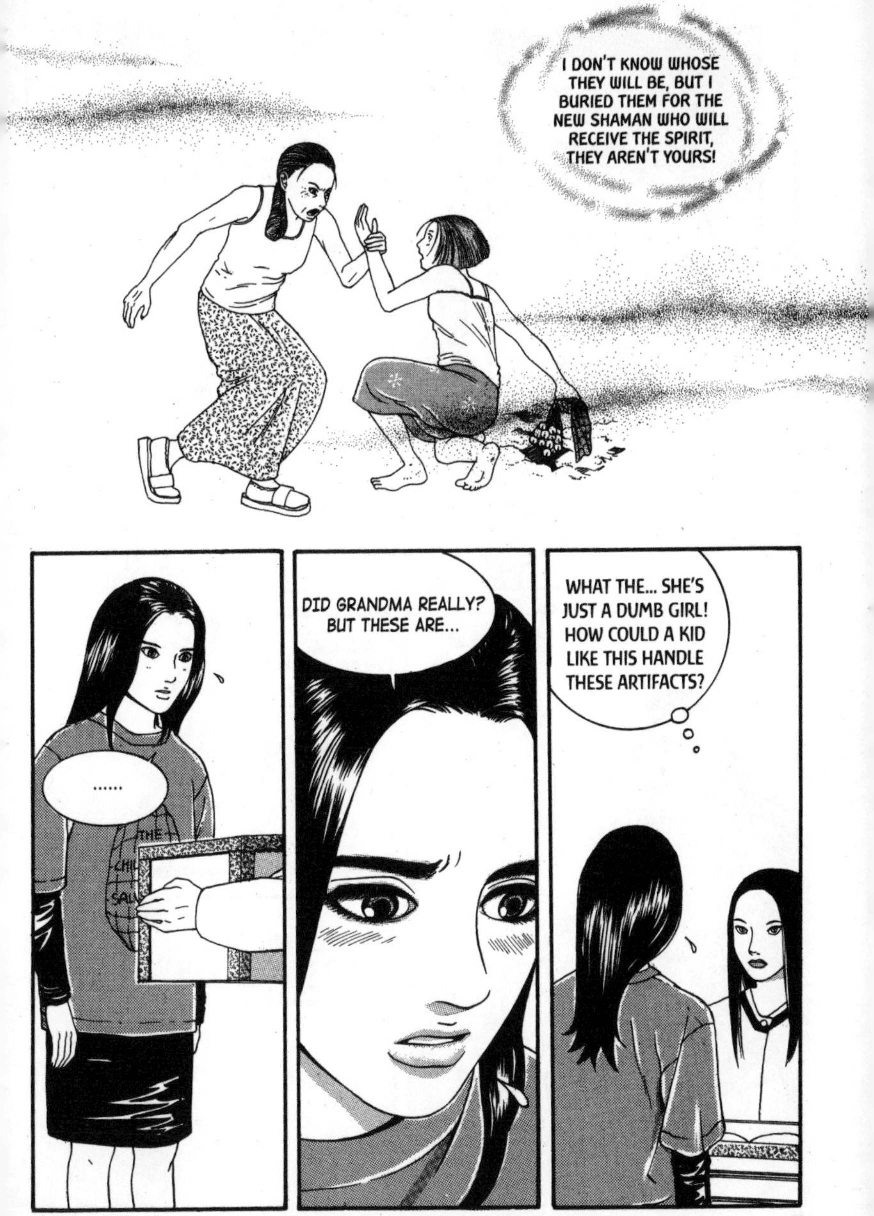
I DON'T KNOW WHOSE THEY WILL BE, BUT I BURIED THEM FOR THE NEW SHAMAN WHO WILL RECEIVE THE SPIRIT, THEY AREN'T YOURS!
......
DID GRANDMA REALLY? BUT THESE ARE...
WHAT THE... SHE'S JUST A DUMB GIRL! HOW COULD A KID LIKE THIS HANDLE THESE ARTIFACTS?

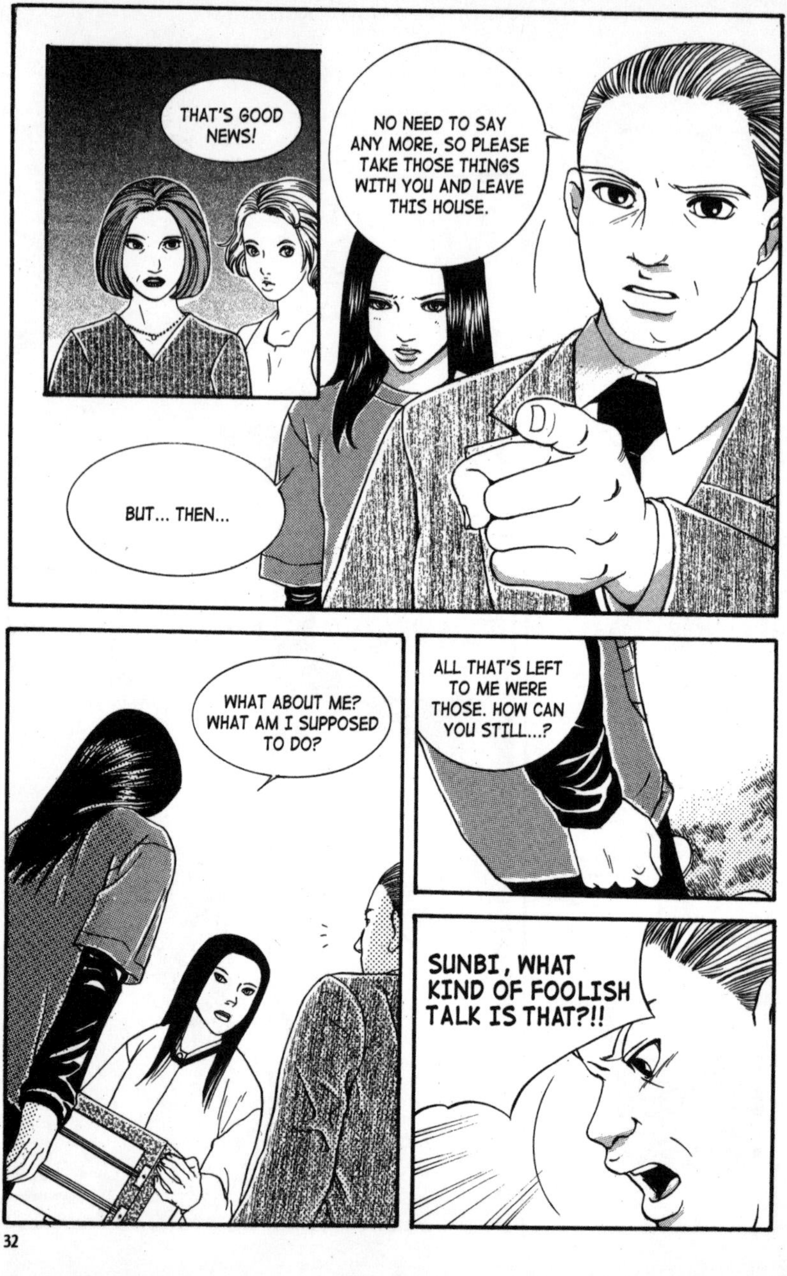
THAT'S GOOD NEWS!
NO NEED TO SAY ANY MORE, SO PLEASE TAKE THOSE THINGS WITH YOU AND LEAVE THIS HOUSE.
BUT... THEN...
WHAT ABOUT ME? WHAT AM I SUPPOSED TO DO?
ALL THAT'S LEFT TO ME WERE THOSE. HOW CAN YOU STILL...?
SUNBI, WHAT KIND OF FOOLISH TALK IS THAT?!!

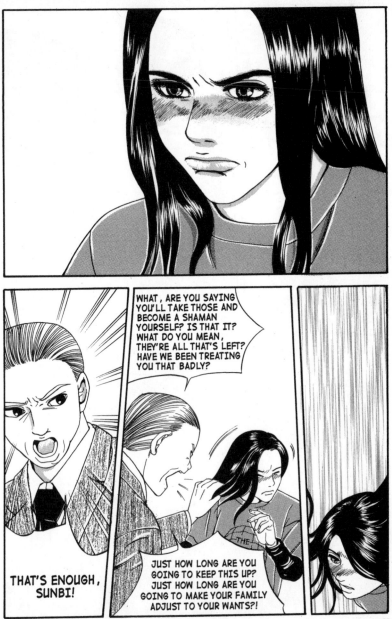

THAT'S ENOUGH, SUNBI!
WHAT, ARE YOU SAYING YOU'LL TAKE THOSE AND BECOME A SHAMAN YOURSELF? IS THAT IT? WHAT DO YOU MEAN, THEY'RE ALL THAT'S LEFT? HAVE WE BEEN TREATING YOU THAT BADLY?
THE
JUST HOW LONG ARE YOU GOING TO KEEP THIS UP? JUST HOW LONG ARE YOU GOING TO MAKE YOUR FAMILY ADJUST TO YOUR WANTS?!

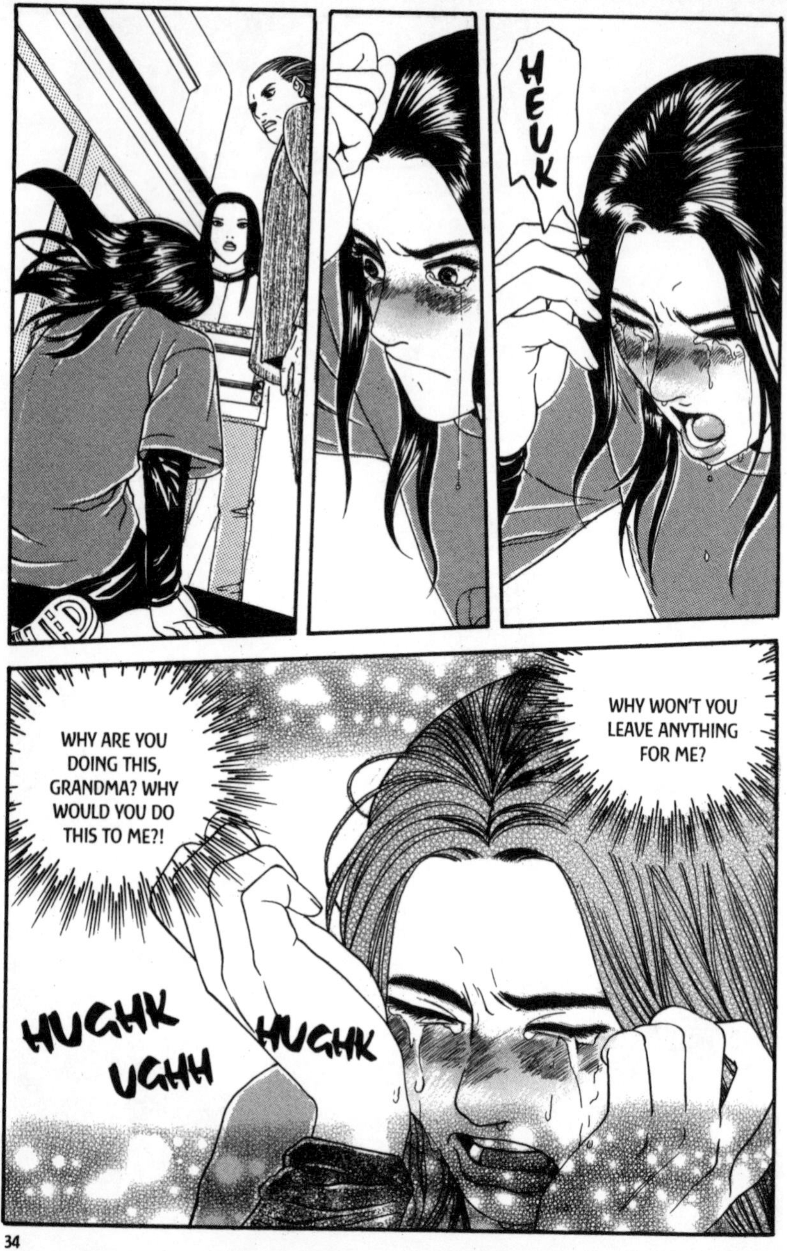
HEUK
WHY ARE YOU DOING THIS, GRANDMA? WHY WOULD YOU DO THIS TO ME?!
WHY WON'T YOU LEAVE ANYTHING FOR ME?
HUGHK
UGHH
HUGHK

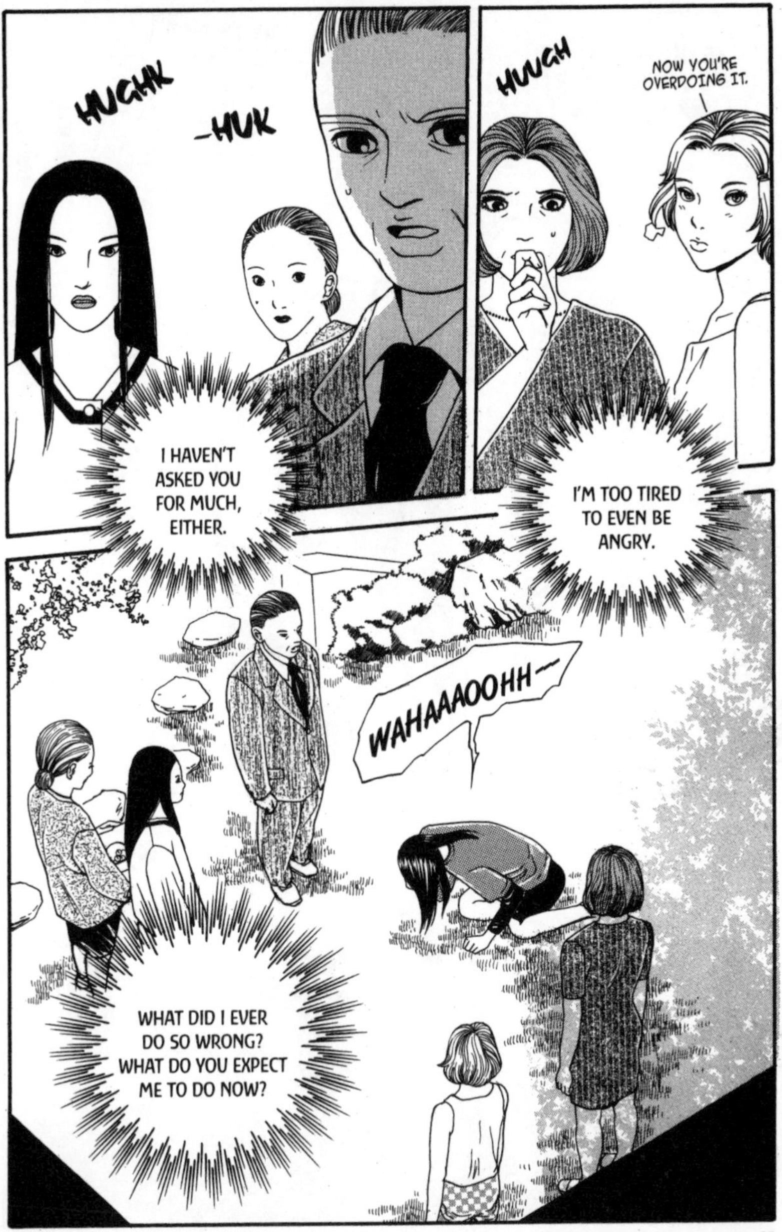
HUGHK
-HUK
I HAVEN'T ASKED YOU FOR MUCH, EITHER.
HUUGH
NOW YOU'RE OVERDOING IT.
I'M TOO TIRED TO EVEN BE ANGRY.
WAHAAAOOHH—
WHAT DID I EVER DO SO WRONG? WHAT DO YOU EXPECT ME TO DO NOW?

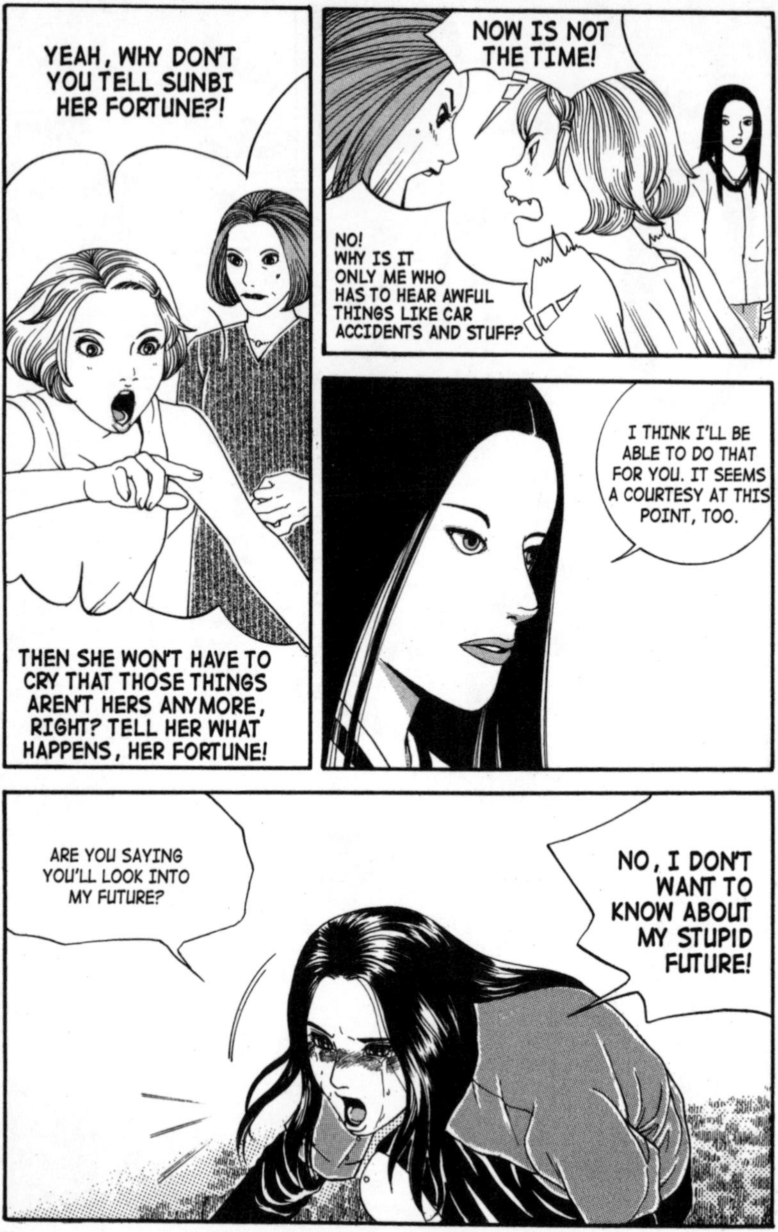

YEAH, WHY DON'T YOU TELL SUNBI HER FORTUNE?!
THEN SHE WON'T HAVE TO CRY THAT THOSE THINGS AREN'T HERS ANYMORE, RIGHT? TELL HER WHAT HAPPENS, HER FORTUNE!
NOW IS NOT THE TIME!
NO! WHY IS IT ONLY ME WHO HAS TO HEAR AWFUL THINGS LIKE CAR ACCIDENTS AND STUFF?
I THINK I'LL BE ABLE TO DO THAT FOR YOU. IT SEEMS A COURTESY AT THIS POINT, TOO.
ARE YOU SAYING YOU'LL LOOK INTO MY FUTURE?
NO, I DON'T WANT TO KNOW ABOUT MY STUPID FUTURE!

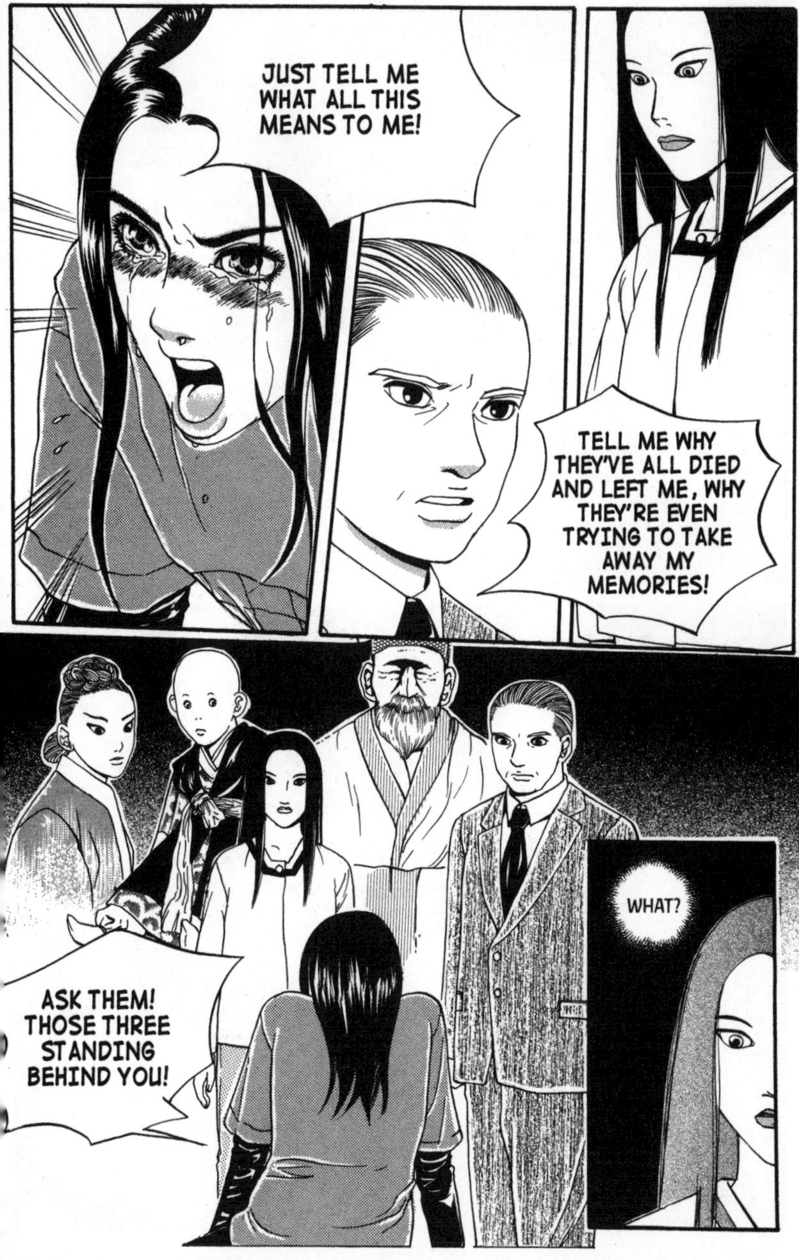
JUST TELL ME WHAT ALL THIS MEANS TO ME!
TELL ME WHY THEY'VE ALL DIED AND LEFT ME, WHY THEY'RE EVEN TRYING TO TAKE AWAY MY MEMORIES!
ASK THEM! THOSE THREE STANDING BEHIND YOU!
WHAT?

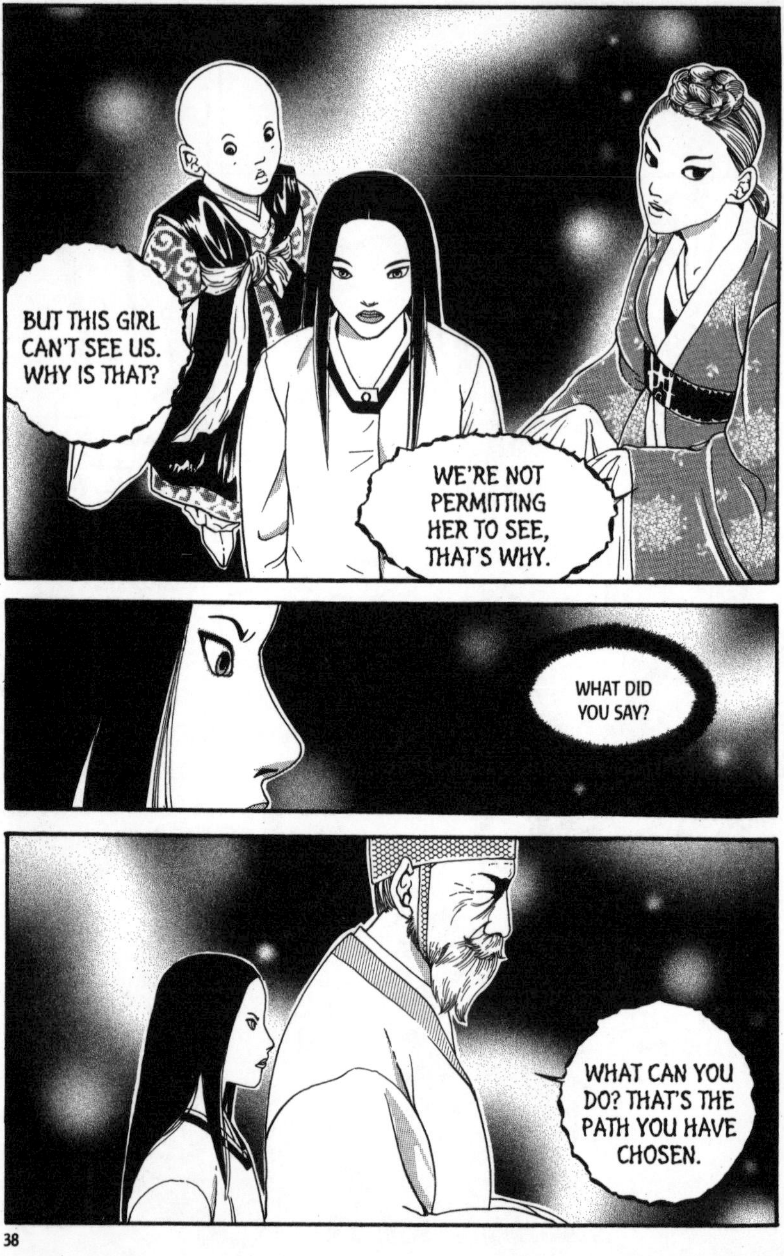

BUT THIS GIRL CAN'T SEE US. WHY IS THAT?
WE'RE NOT PERMITTING HER TO SEE, THAT'S WHY.
WHAT DID YOU SAY?
WHAT CAN YOU DO? THAT'S THE PATH YOU HAVE CHOSEN.

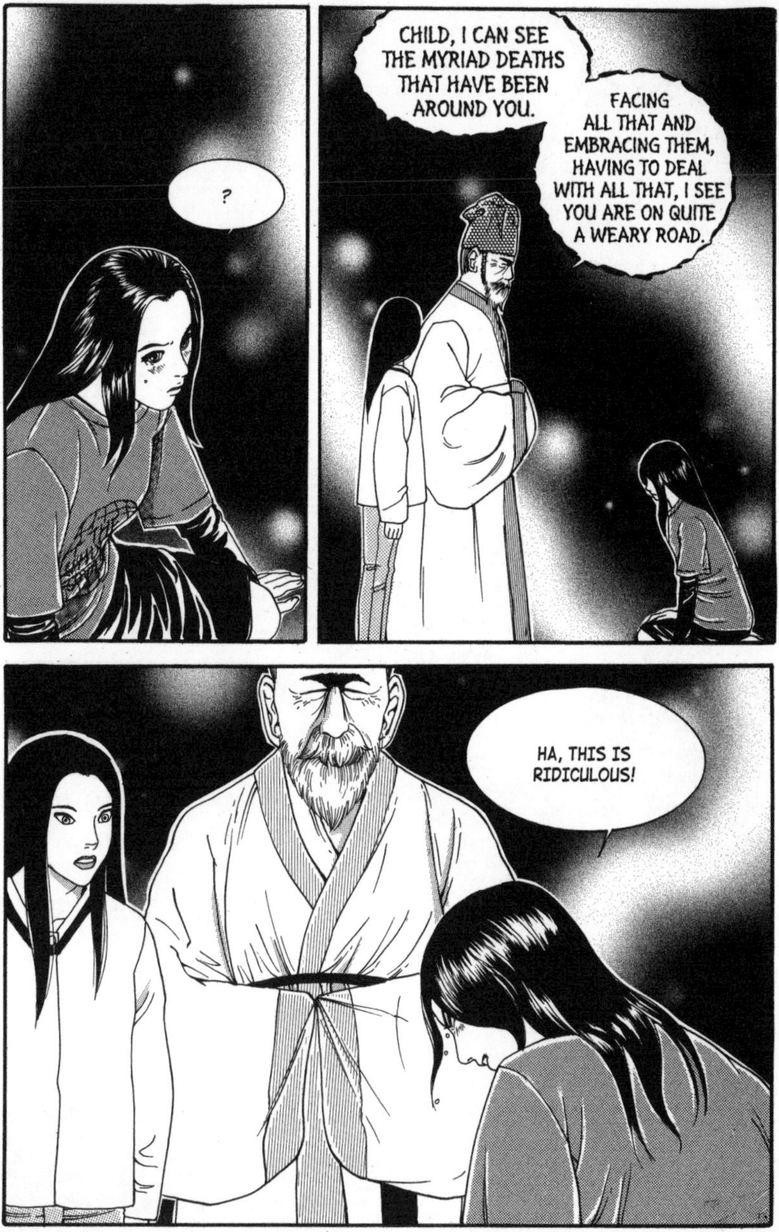
?
CHILD, I CAN SEE THE MYRIAD DEATHS THAT HAVE BEEN AROUND YOU.
FACING ALL THAT AND EMBRACING THEM, HAVING TO DEAL WITH ALL THAT, I SEE YOU ARE ON QUITE A WEARY ROAD.
HA, THIS IS RIDICULOUS!

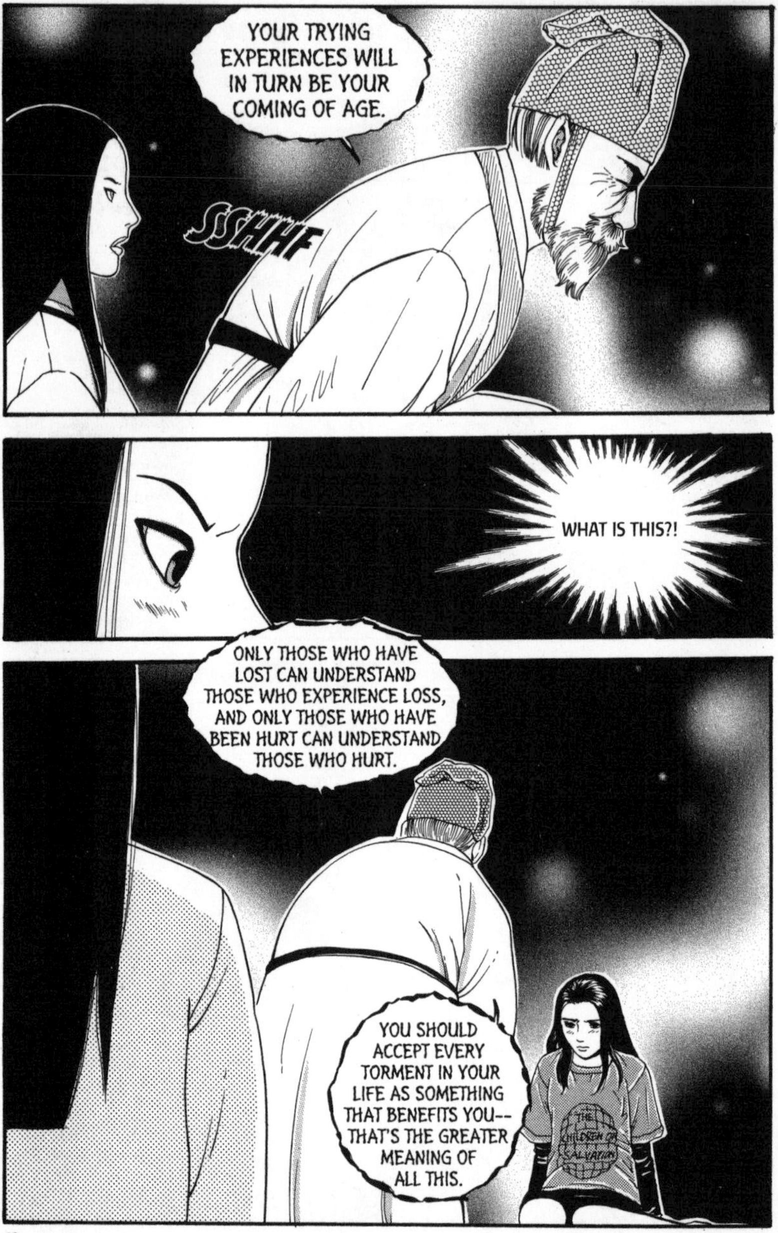
YOUR TRYING EXPERIENCES WILL IN TURN BE YOUR COMING OF AGE.
SSHHF
WHAT IS THIS?!
ONLY THOSE WHO HAVE LOST CAN UNDERSTAND THOSE WHO EXPERIENCE LOSS, AND ONLY THOSE WHO HAVE BEEN HURT CAN UNDERSTAND THOSE WHO HURT.
YOU SHOULD ACCEPT EVERY TORMENT IN YOUR LIFE AS SOMETHING THAT BENEFITS YOU-- THAT'S THE GREATER MEANING OF ALL THIS.

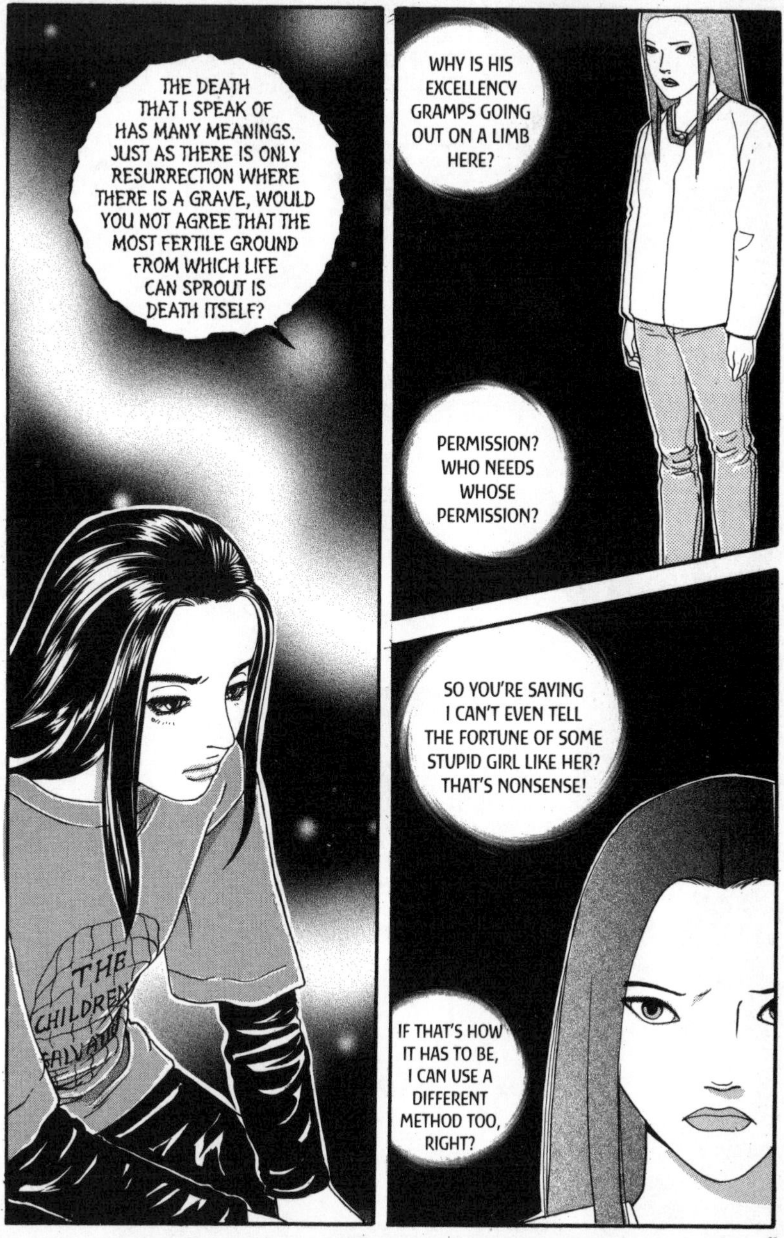
THE DEATH THAT I SPEAK OF HAS MANY MEANINGS. JUST AS THERE IS ONLY RESURRECTION WHERE THERE IS A GRAVE, WOULD YOU NOT AGREE THAT THE MOST FERTILE GROUND FROM WHICH LIFE CAN SPROUT IS DEATH ITSELF?
THE CHILDREN
WHY IS HIS EXCELLENCY GRAMPS GOING OUT ON A LIMB HERE?
PERMISSION? WHO NEEDS WHOSE PERMISSION?
SO YOU'RE SAYING I CAN'T EVEN TELL THE FORTUNE OF SOME STUPID GIRL LIKE HER? THAT'S NONSENSE!
IF THAT'S HOW IT HAS TO BE, I CAN USE A DIFFERENT METHOD TOO, RIGHT?

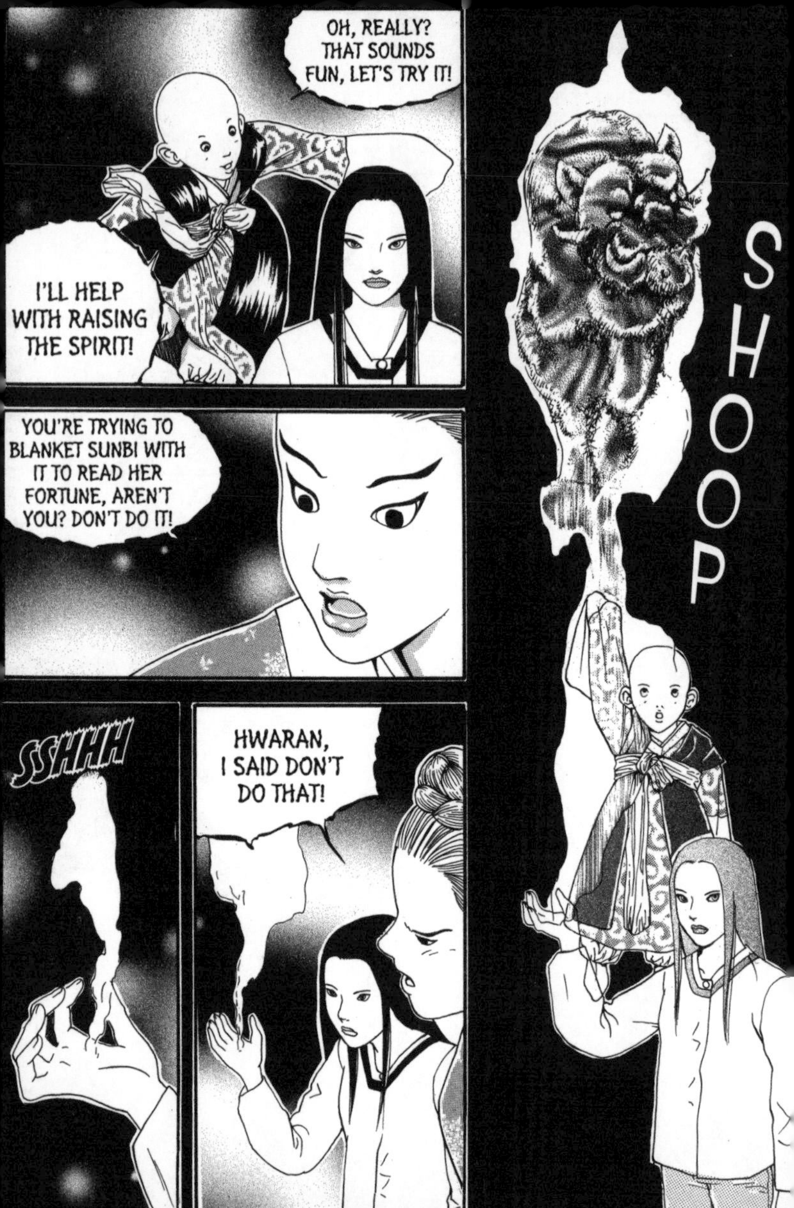
OH, REALLY? THAT SOUNDS FUN, LET'S TRY IT!
I'LL HELP WITH RAISING THE SPIRIT!
YOU'RE TRYING TO BLANKET SUNBI WITH IT TO READ HER FORTUNE, AREN'T YOU? DON'T DO IT!
SSHHH
HWARAN, I SAID DON'T DO THAT!
SHOOP

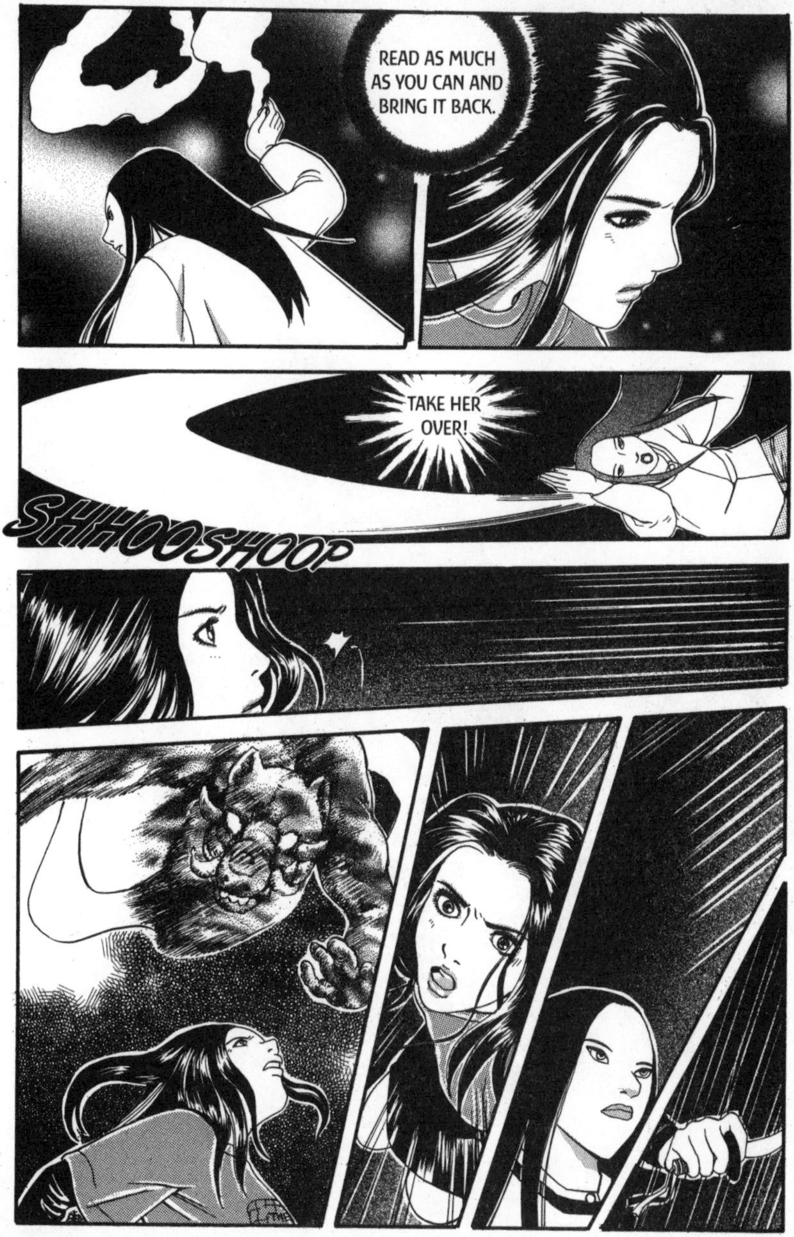
READ AS MUCH AS YOU CAN AND BRING IT BACK.
TAKE HER OVER!
SHHOOSHOOP

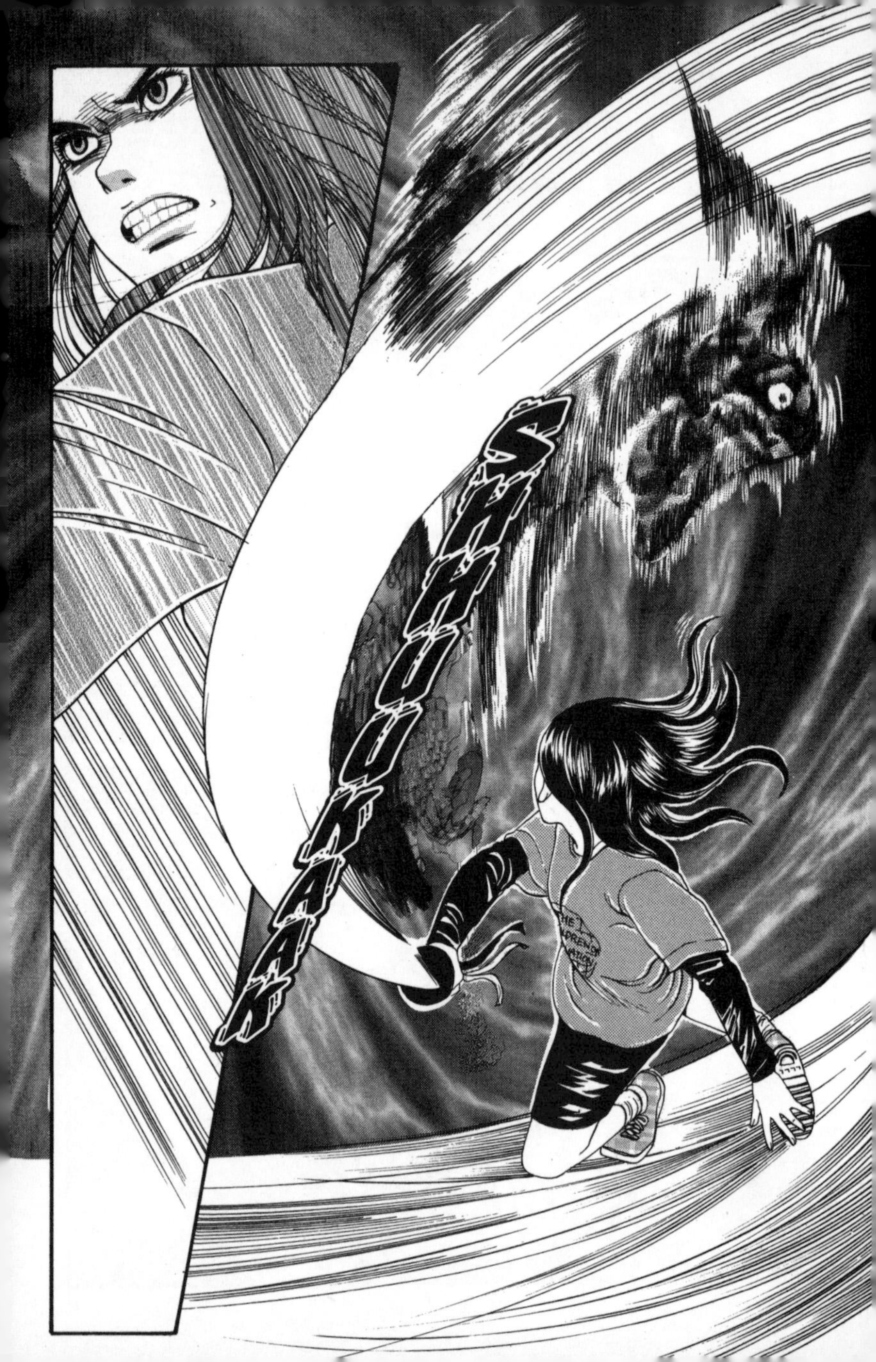
SHHUUKAAA

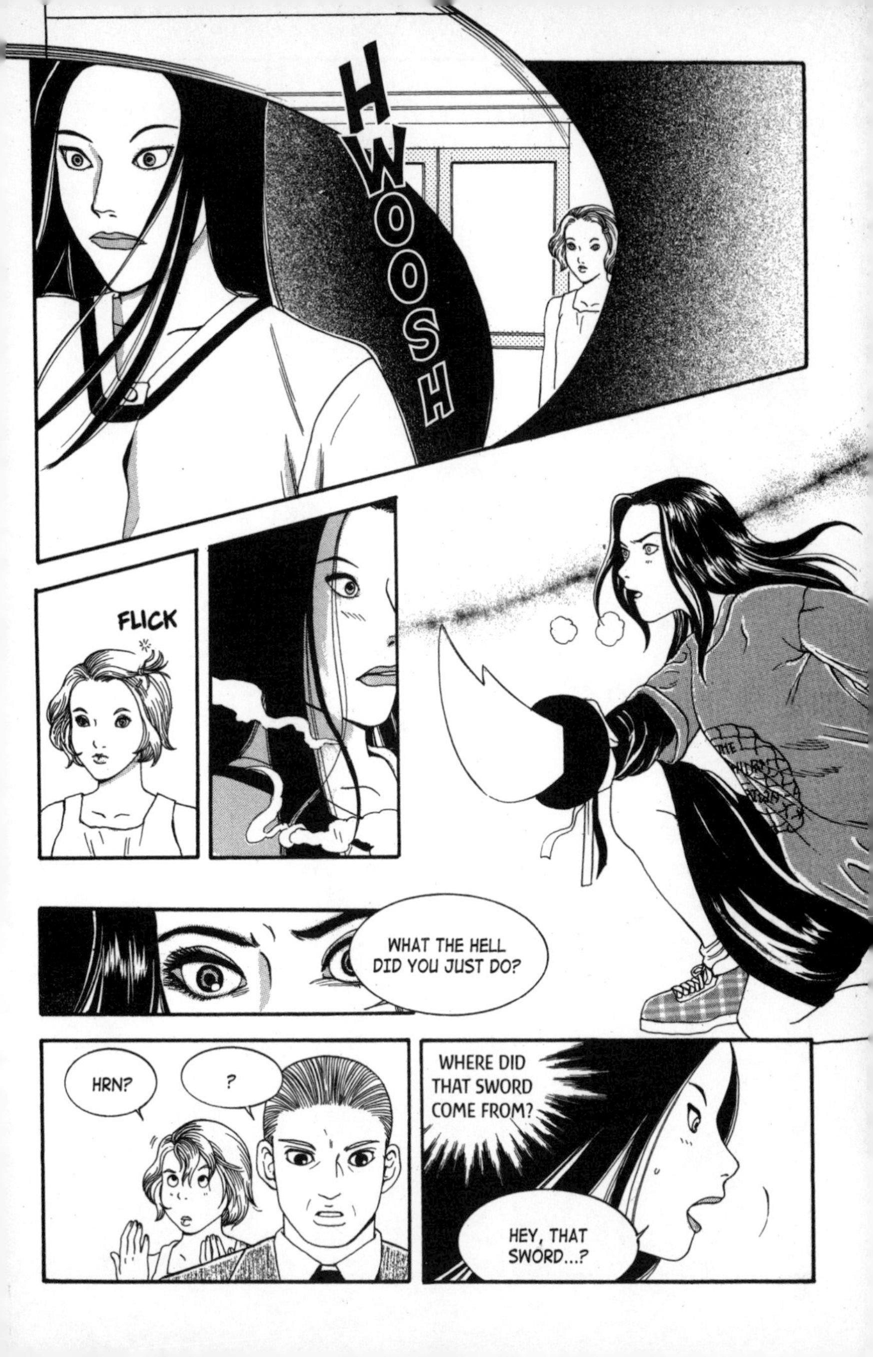
HWOOSH
FLICK
WHAT THE HELL DID YOU JUST DO?
HRN?
?
WHERE DID THAT SWORD COME FROM?
HEY, THAT SWORD...?

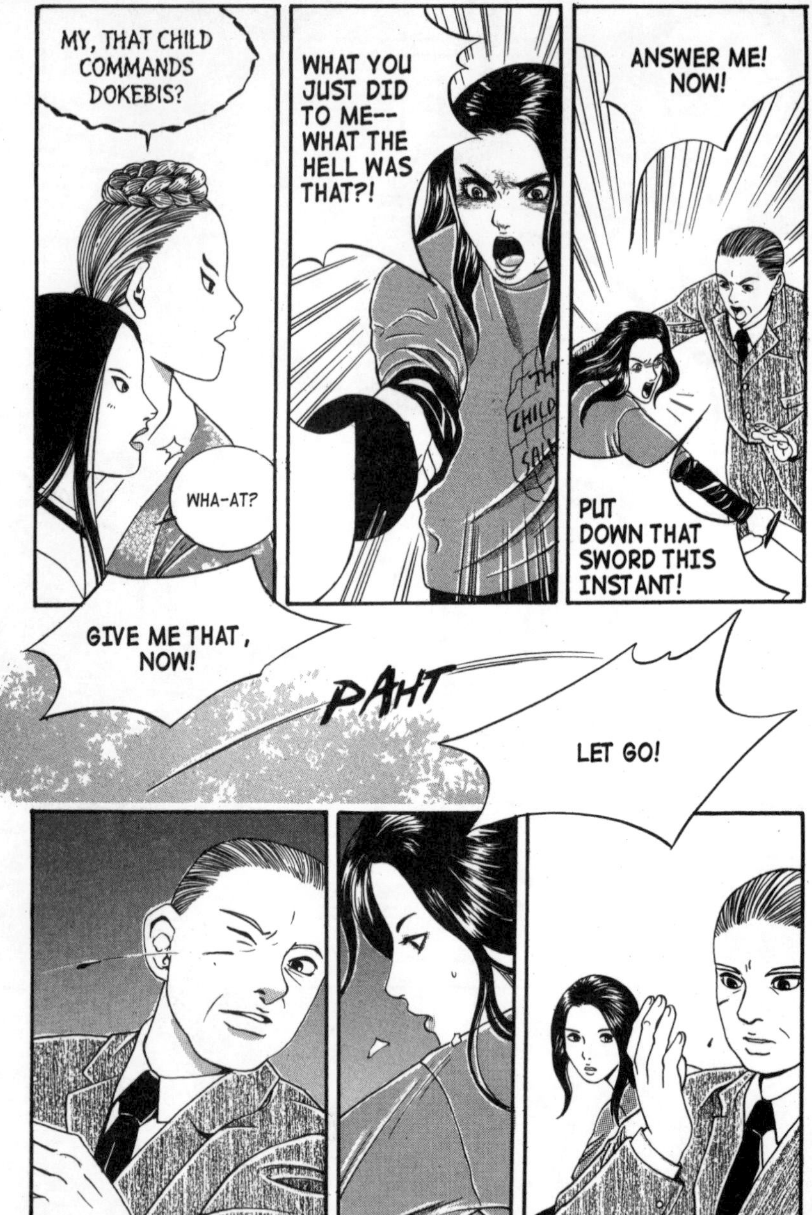
MY, THAT CHILD COMMANDS DOKEBIS?
WHA-AT?
WHAT YOU JUST DID TO ME-- WHAT THE HELL WAS THAT?!
ANSWER ME! NOW!
PUT DOWN THAT SWORD THIS INSTANT!
GIVE ME THAT, NOW!
PAHT
LET GO!

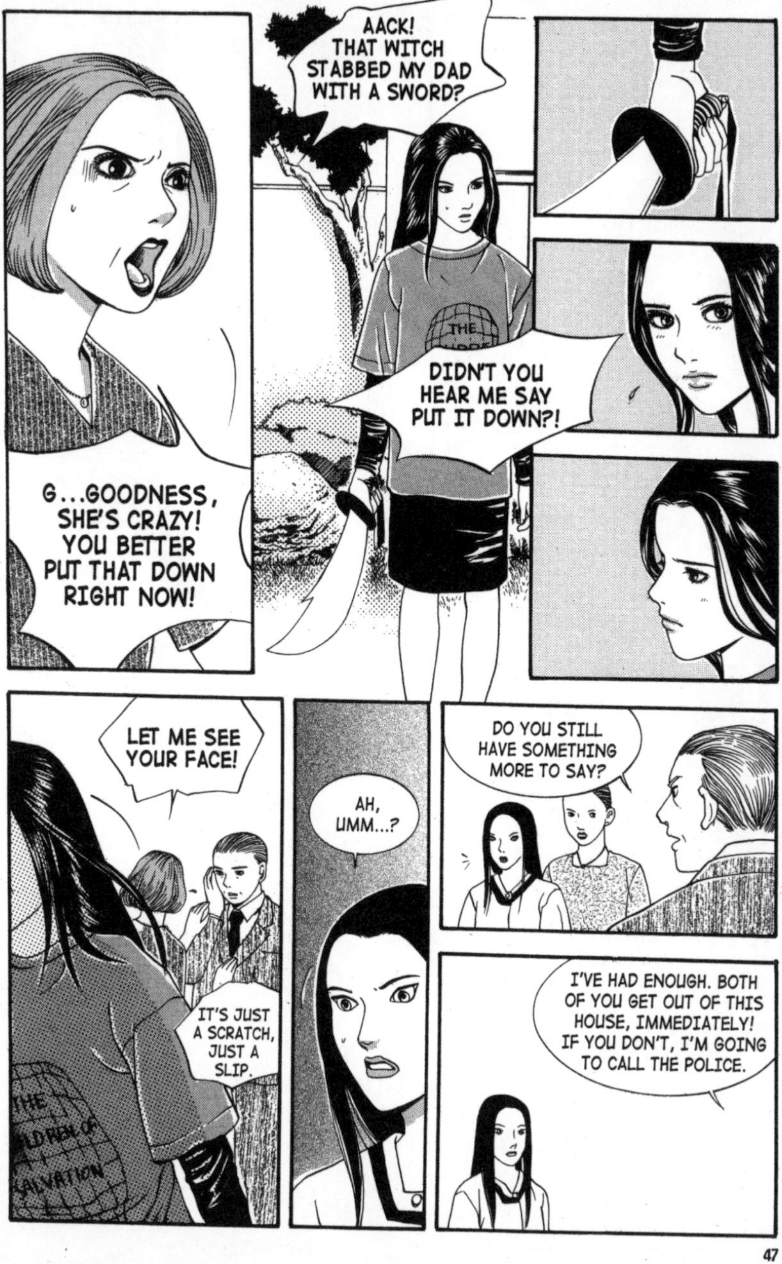
G...GOODNESS, SHE'S CRAZY! YOU BETTER PUT THAT DOWN RIGHT NOW!
AACK! THAT WITCH STABBED MY DAD WITH A SWORD?
DIDN'T YOU HEAR ME SAY PUT IT DOWN?!
LET ME SEE YOUR FACE!
IT'S JUST A SCRATCH, JUST A SLIP.
AH, UMM...?
DO YOU STILL HAVE SOMETHING MORE TO SAY?
I'VE HAD ENOUGH. BOTH OF YOU GET OUT OF THIS HOUSE, IMMEDIATELY! IF YOU DON'T, I'M GOING TO CALL THE POLICE.

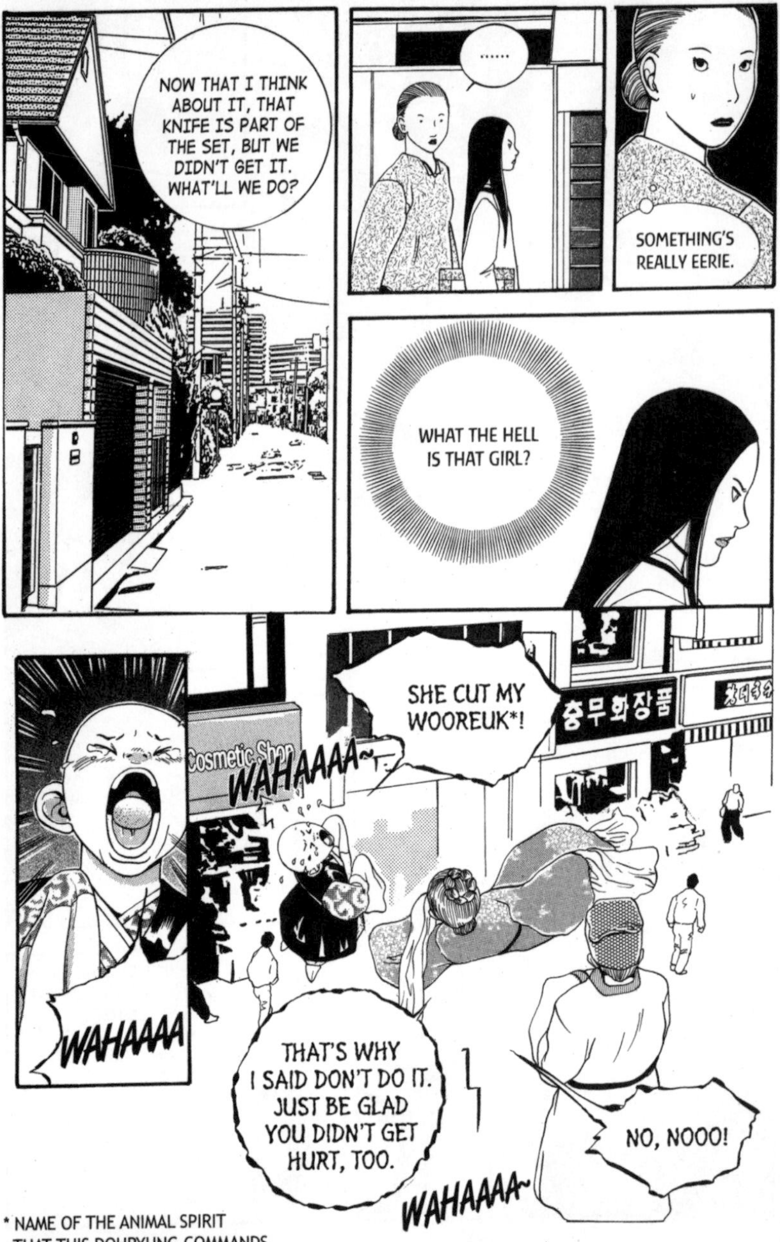
NOW THAT I THINK ABOUT IT, THAT KNIFE IS PART OF THE SET, BUT WE DIDN'T GET IT. WHAT'LL WE DO?
......
SOMETHING'S REALLY EERIE.
WHAT THE HELL IS THAT GIRL?
WAHAAAA
SHE CUT MY WOOREUK*!
충무화장품
Cosmetic Shop
WAHAAAA~
THAT'S WHY I SAID DON'T DO IT. JUST BE GLAD YOU DIDN'T GET HURT, TOO.
NO, NOOO!
WAHAAAA~

* NAME OF THE ANIMAL SPIRIT THAT THIS DOHRYUNG COMMANDS

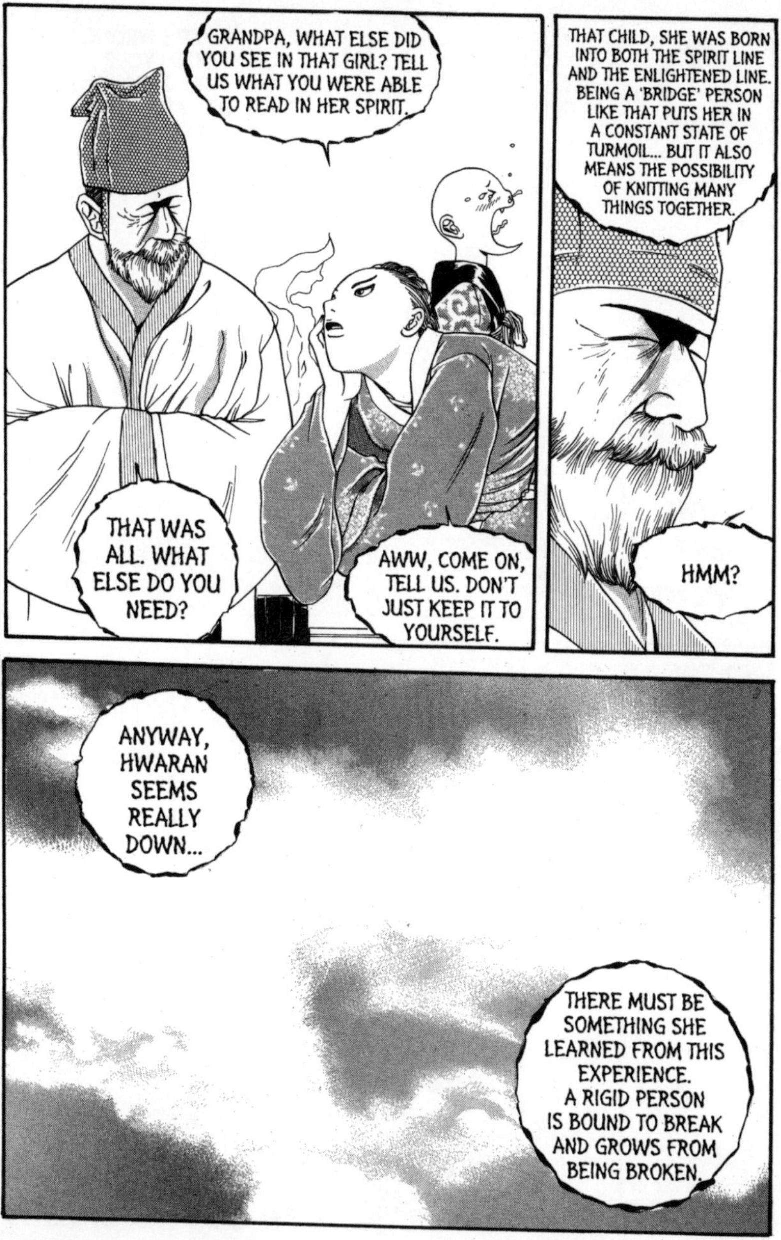
GRANDPA, WHAT ELSE DID YOU SEE IN THAT GIRL? TELL US WHAT YOU WERE ABLE TO READ IN HER SPIRIT.
THAT WAS ALL. WHAT ELSE DO YOU NEED?
AWW, COME ON, TELL US. DON'T JUST KEEP IT TO YOURSELF.
THAT CHILD, SHE WAS BORN INTO BOTH THE SPIRIT LINE AND THE ENLIGHTENED LINE. BEING A 'BRIDGE' PERSON LIKE THAT PUTS HER IN A CONSTANT STATE OF TURMOIL... BUT IT ALSO MEANS THE POSSIBILITY OF KNITTING MANY THINGS TOGETHER.
HMM?
ANYWAY, HWARAN SEEMS REALLY DOWN...
THERE MUST BE SOMETHING SHE LEARNED FROM THIS EXPERIENCE. A RIGID PERSON IS BOUND TO BREAK AND GROWS FROM BEING BROKEN.

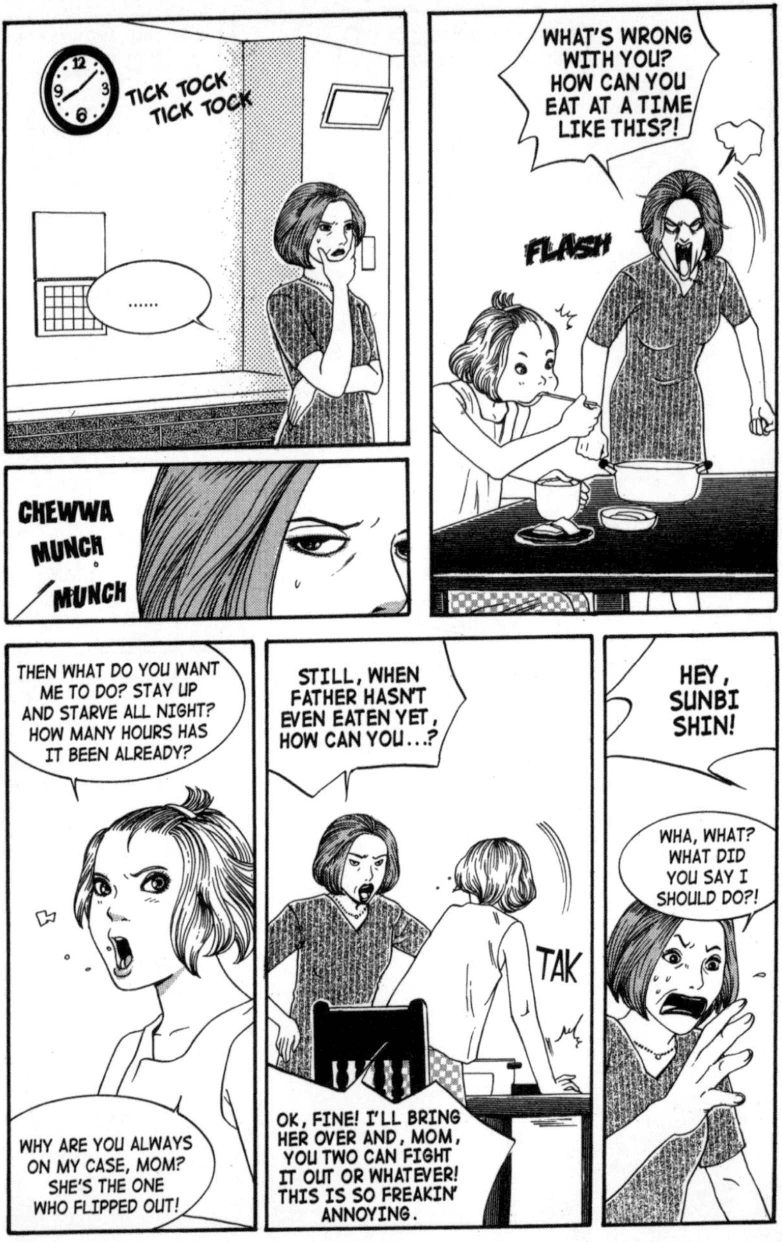
TICK TOCK
TICK TOCK
......
CHEWWA
MUNCH
MUNCH
WHAT'S WRONG WITH YOU? HOW CAN YOU EAT AT A TIME LIKE THIS?!
FLASH
THEN WHAT DO YOU WANT ME TO DO? STAY UP AND STARVE ALL NIGHT? HOW MANY HOURS HAS IT BEEN ALREADY?
WHY ARE YOU ALWAYS ON MY CASE, MOM? SHE'S THE ONE WHO FLIPPED OUT!
STILL, WHEN FATHER HASN'T EVEN EATEN YET, HOW CAN YOU...?
TAK
OK, FINE! I'LL BRING HER OVER AND, MOM, YOU TWO CAN FIGHT IT OUT OR WHATEVER! THIS IS SO FREAKIN' ANNOYING.
HEY, SUNBI SHIN!
WHA, WHAT? WHAT DID YOU SAY I SHOULD DO?!

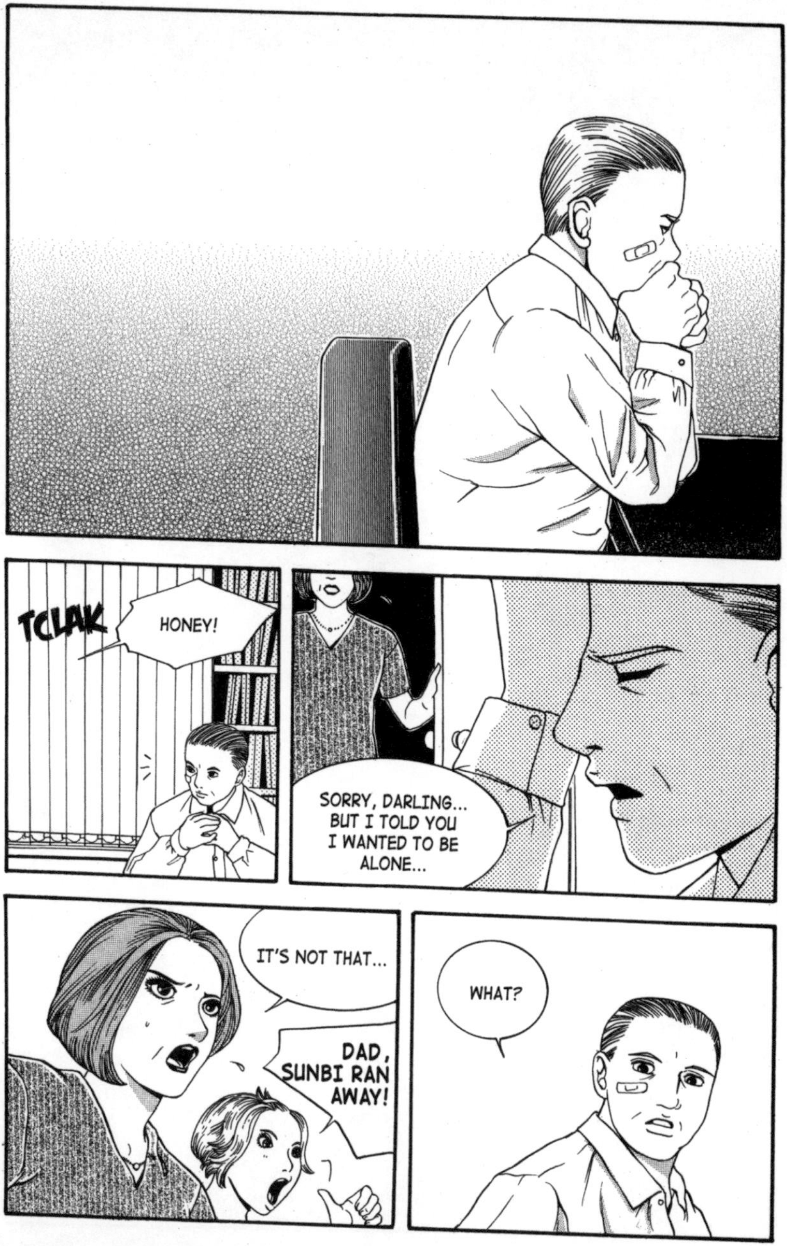
TCLAK
HONEY!
SORRY, DARLING... BUT I TOLD YOU I WANTED TO BE ALONE...
IT'S NOT THAT...
DAD, SUNBI RAN AWAY!
WHAT?

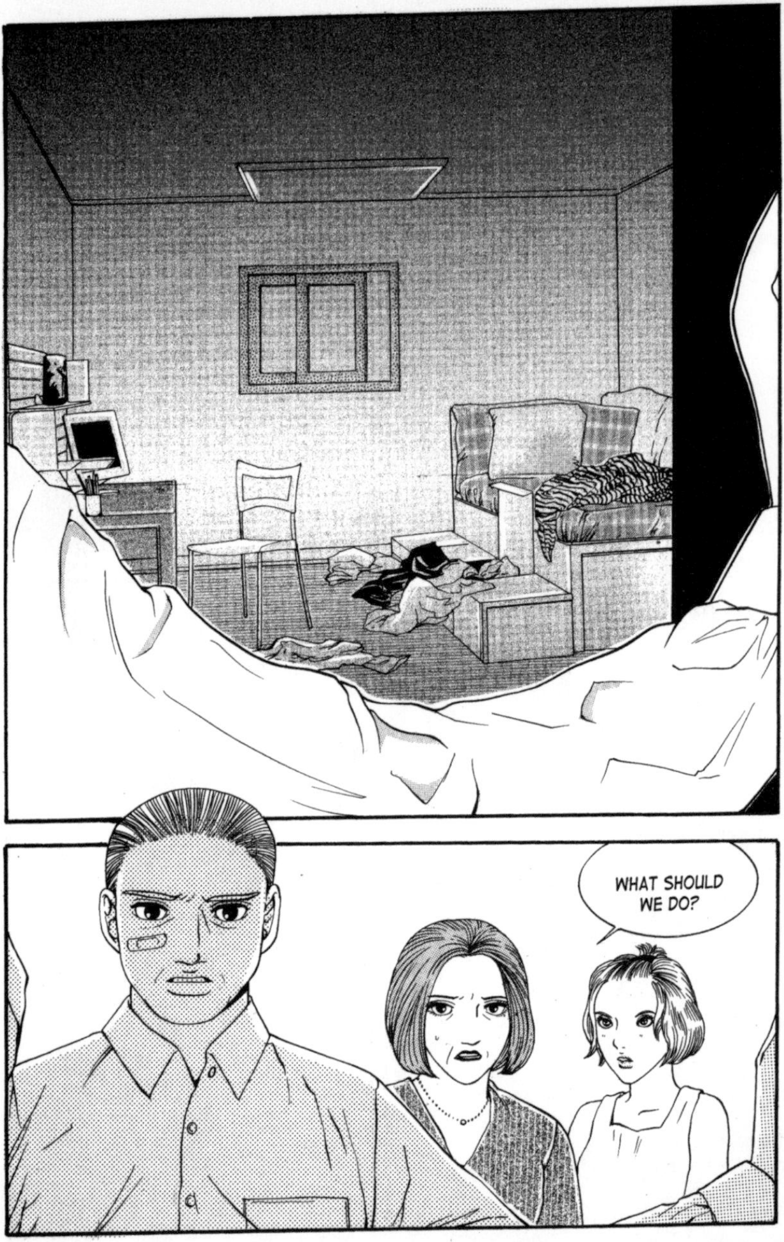
WHAT SHOULD WE DO?

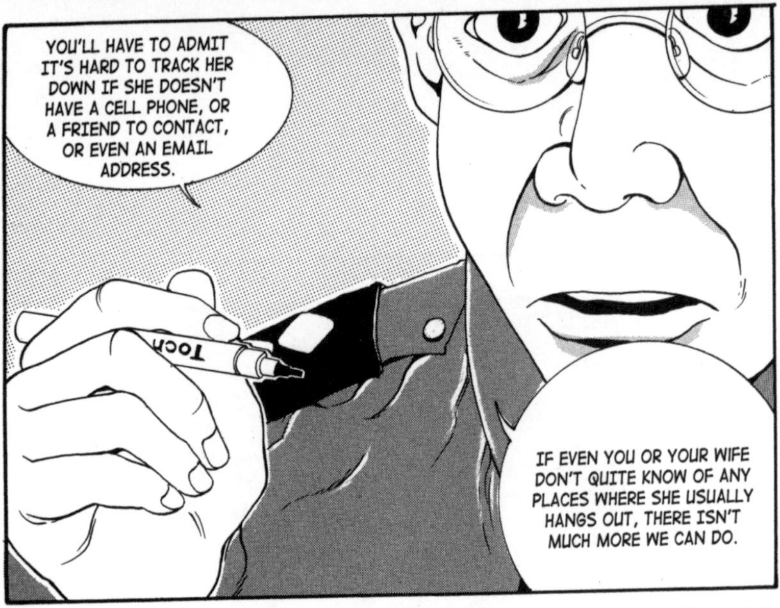
YOU'LL HAVE TO ADMIT IT'S HARD TO TRACK HER DOWN IF SHE DOESN'T HAVE A CELL PHONE, OR A FRIEND TO CONTACT, OR EVEN AN EMAIL ADDRESS.
IF EVEN YOU OR YOUR WIFE DON'T QUITE KNOW OF ANY PLACES WHERE SHE USUALLY HANGS OUT, THERE ISN'T MUCH MORE WE CAN DO.

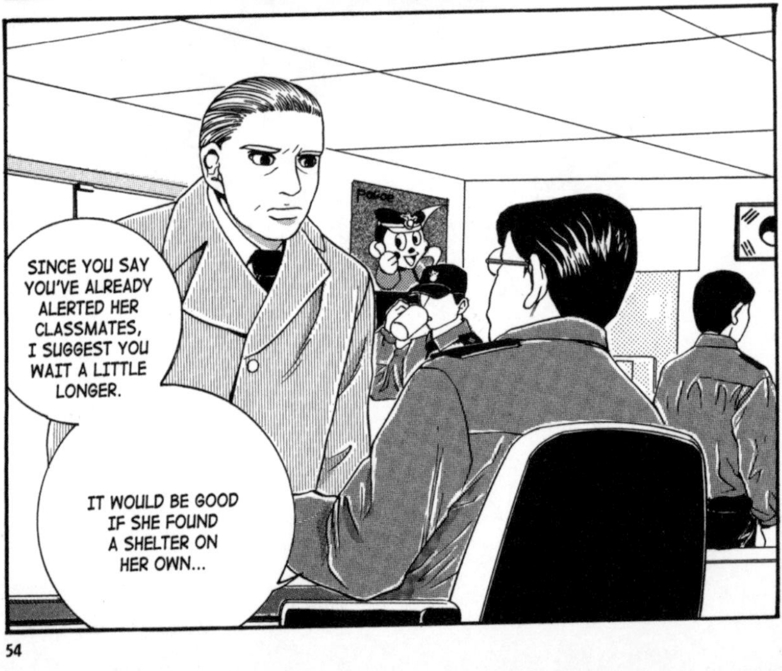
SINCE YOU SAY YOU'VE ALREADY ALERTED HER CLASSMATES, I SUGGEST YOU WAIT A LITTLE LONGER.
IT WOULD BE GOOD IF SHE FOUND A SHELTER ON HER OWN...

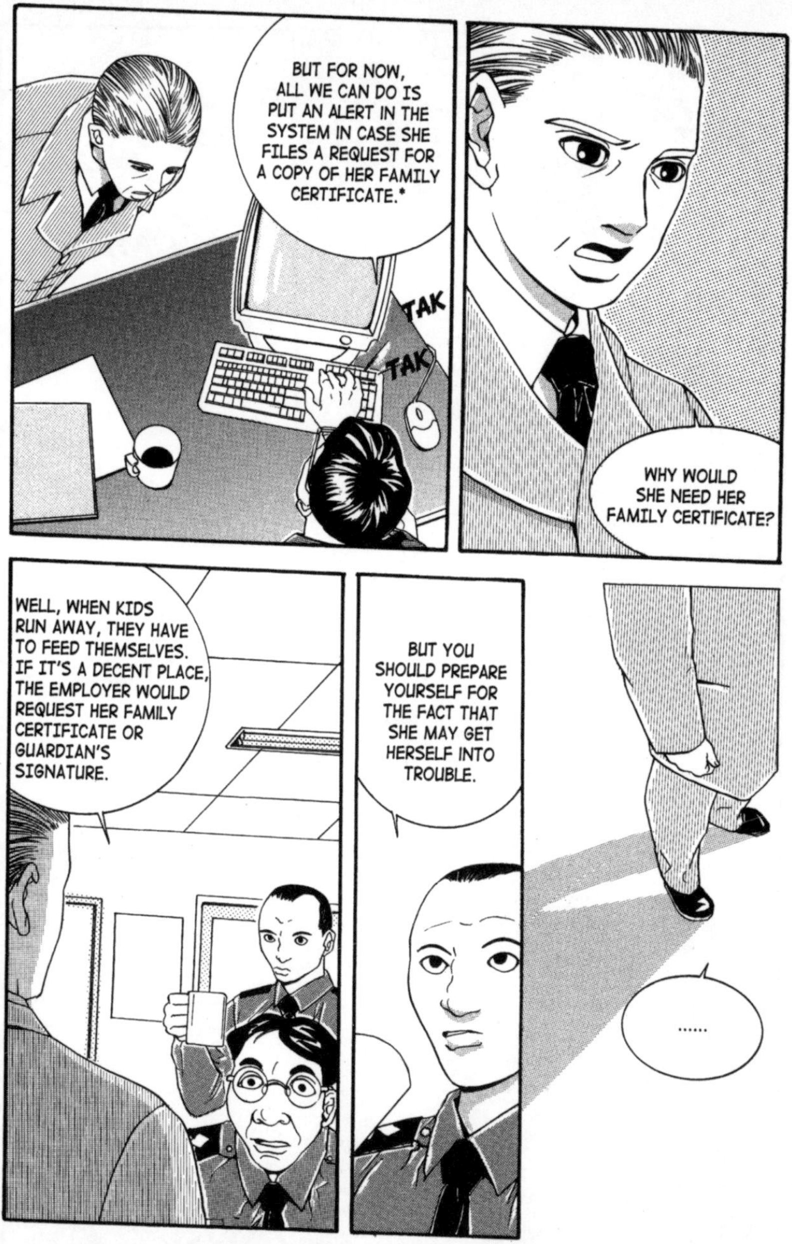
BUT FOR NOW, ALL WE CAN DO IS PUT AN ALERT IN THE SYSTEM IN CASE SHE FILES A REQUEST FOR A COPY OF HER FAMILY CERTIFICATE.*
TAK
TAK
WHY WOULD SHE NEED HER FAMILY CERTIFICATE?
WELL, WHEN KIDS RUN AWAY, THEY HAVE TO FEED THEMSELVES. IF IT'S A DECENT PLACE, THE EMPLOYER WOULD REQUEST HER FAMILY CERTIFICATE OR GUARDIAN'S SIGNATURE.
BUT YOU SHOULD PREPARE YOURSELF FOR THE FACT THAT SHE MAY GET HERSELF INTO TROUBLE.
......

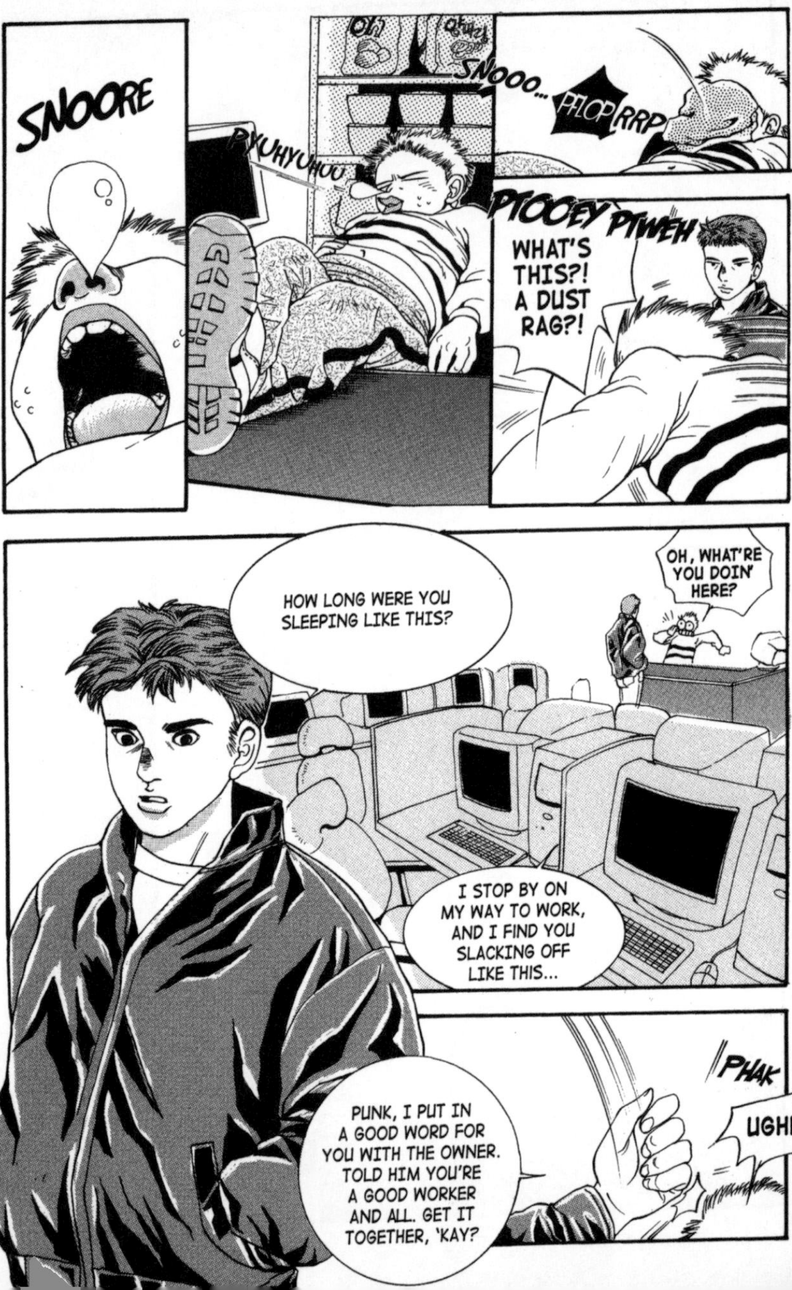
SNOORE
PYUHYUHOO
SNOOO...
PFLOP
RRP
PTOOEY
PIWEH
WHAT'S THIS?! A DUST RAG?!
HOW LONG WERE YOU SLEEPING LIKE THIS?
OH, WHAT'RE YOU DOIN' HERE?
I STOP BY ON MY WAY TO WORK, AND I FIND YOU SLACKING OFF LIKE THIS...
PUNK, I PUT IN A GOOD WORD FOR YOU WITH THE OWNER. TOLD HIM YOU'RE A GOOD WORKER AND ALL. GET IT TOGETHER, 'KAY?
PHAK
UGHK

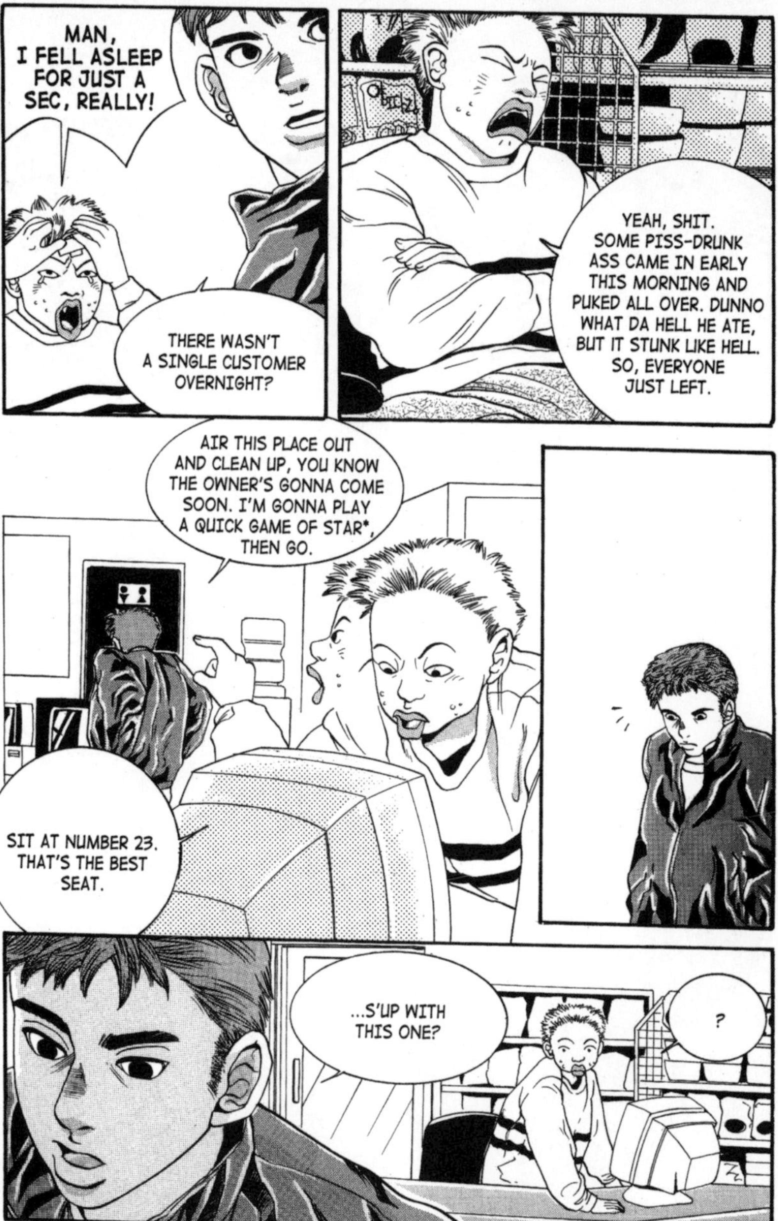
MAN, I FELL ASLEEP FOR JUST A SEC, REALLY!
THERE WASN'T A SINGLE CUSTOMER OVERNIGHT?
YEAH, SHIT. SOME PISS-DRUNK ASS CAME IN EARLY THIS MORNING AND PUKED ALL OVER. DUNNO WHAT DA HELL HE ATE, BUT IT STUNK LIKE HELL. SO, EVERYONE JUST LEFT.
AIR THIS PLACE OUT AND CLEAN UP, YOU KNOW THE OWNER'S GONNA COME SOON. I'M GONNA PLAY A QUICK GAME OF STAR*, THEN GO.
SIT AT NUMBER 23. THAT'S THE BEST SEAT.
...S'UP WITH THIS ONE?
?

* STAR: SLANG FOR ONLINE GAME "STARCRAFT"

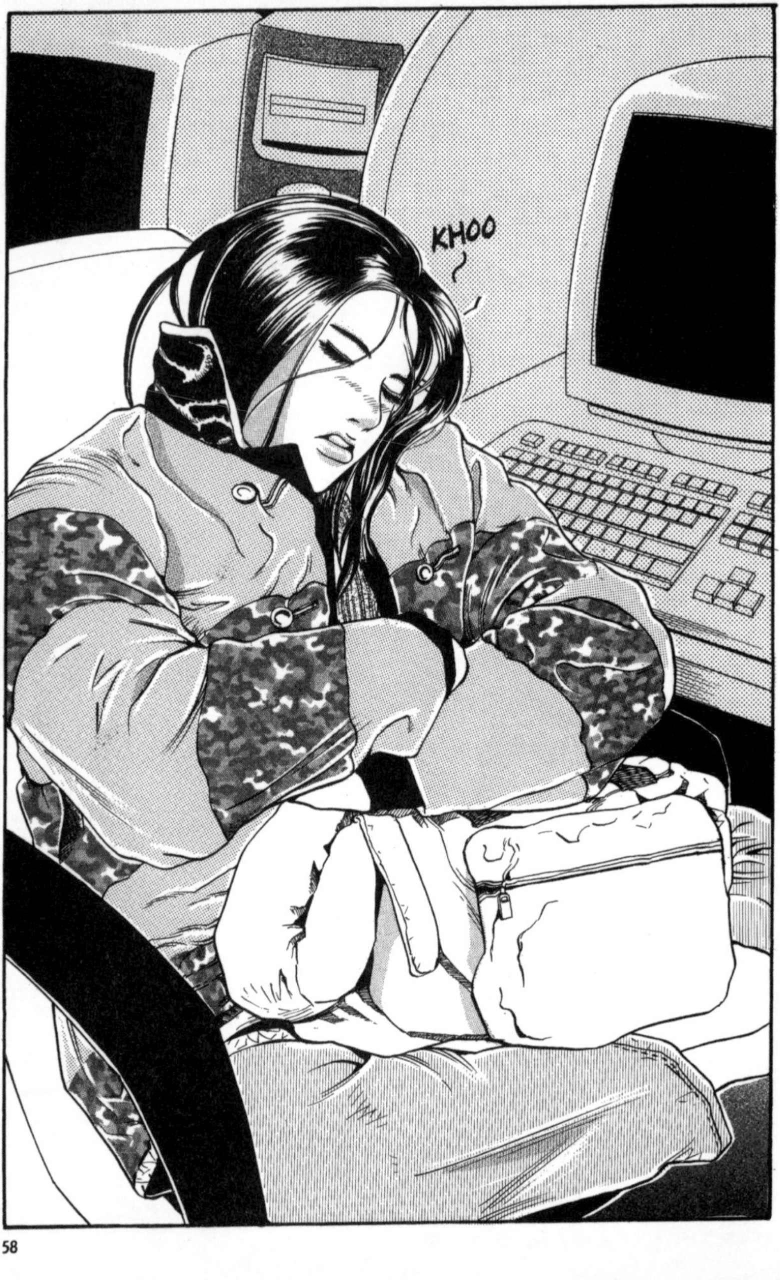
KHOO

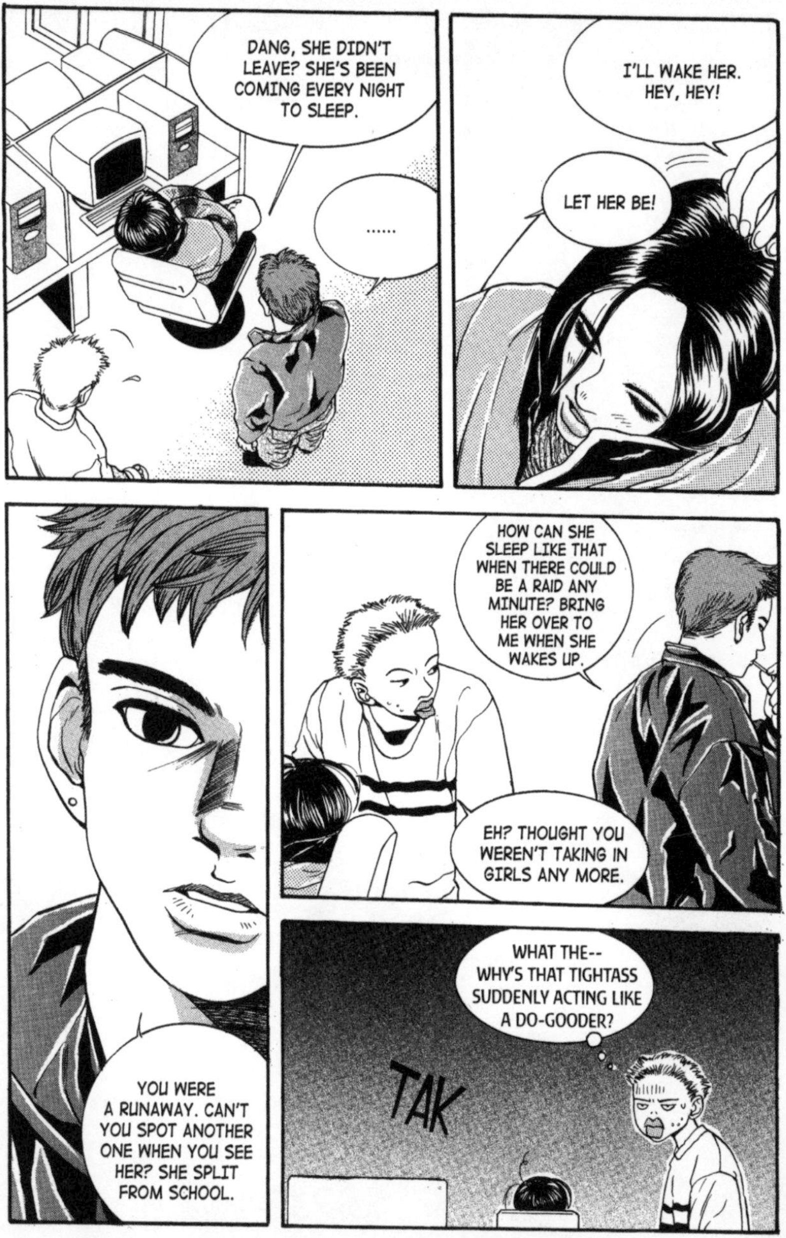
DANG, SHE DIDN'T LEAVE? SHE'S BEEN COMING EVERY NIGHT TO SLEEP.
......
I'LL WAKE HER. HEY, HEY!
LET HER BE!
YOU WERE A RUNAWAY. CAN'T YOU SPOT ANOTHER ONE WHEN YOU SEE HER? SHE SPLIT FROM SCHOOL.
HOW CAN SHE SLEEP LIKE THAT WHEN THERE COULD BE A RAID ANY MINUTE? BRING HER OVER TO ME WHEN SHE WAKES UP.
EH? THOUGHT YOU WEREN'T TAKING IN GIRLS ANY MORE.
WHAT THE-- WHY'S THAT TIGHTASS SUDDENLY ACTING LIKE A DO-GOODER?
TAK

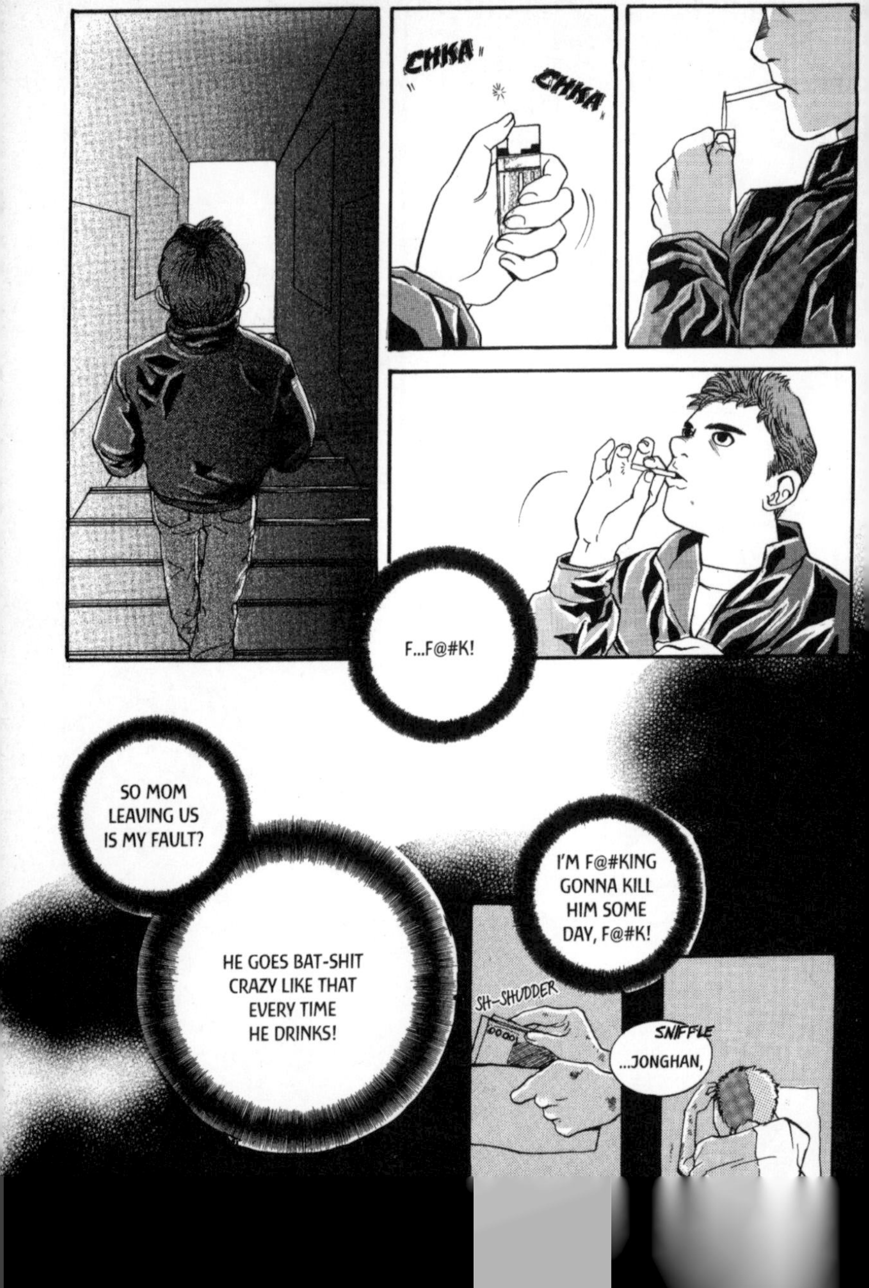

CHKA
CHKA
F...F@#K!
SO MOM LEAVING US IS MY FAULT?
HE GOES BAT-SHIT CRAZY LIKE THAT EVERY TIME HE DRINKS!
I'M F@#KING GONNA KILL HIM SOME DAY, F@#K!
SH-SHUDDER
SNIFFLE
...JONGHAN,

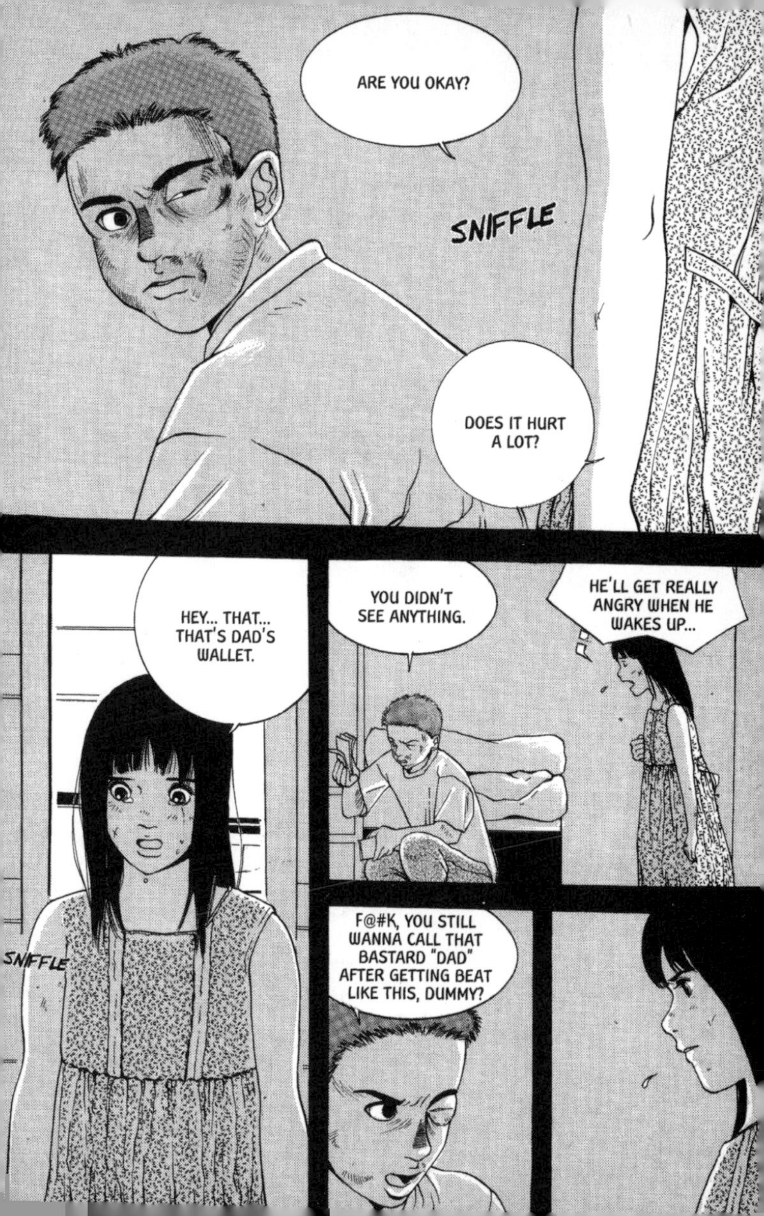
ARE YOU OKAY?
SNIFFLE
DOES IT HURT A LOT?
HEY... THAT... THAT'S DAD'S WALLET.
SNIFFLE
YOU DIDN'T SEE ANYTHING.
HE'LL GET REALLY ANGRY WHEN HE WAKES UP...
F@#K, YOU STILL WANNA CALL THAT BASTARD "DAD" AFTER GETTING BEAT LIKE THIS, DUMMY?

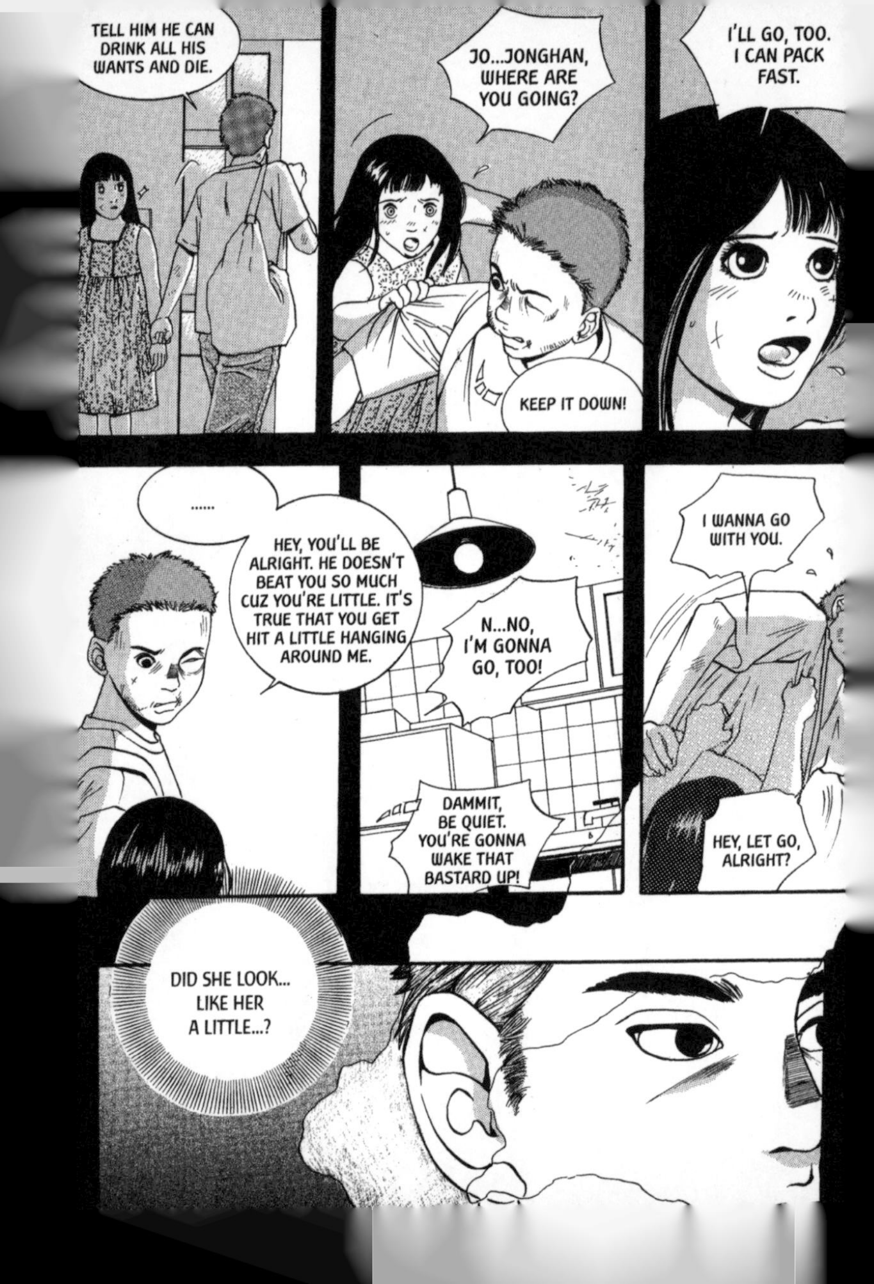
TELL HIM HE CAN DRINK ALL HIS WANTS AND DIE.
JO...JONGHAN, WHERE ARE YOU GOING?
KEEP IT DOWN!
I'LL GO, TOO. I CAN PACK FAST.
......
HEY, YOU'LL BE ALRIGHT. HE DOESN'T BEAT YOU SO MUCH CUZ YOU'RE LITTLE. IT'S TRUE THAT YOU GET HIT A LITTLE HANGING AROUND ME.
N...NO, I'M GONNA GO, TOO!
DAMMIT, BE QUIET. YOU'RE GONNA WAKE THAT BASTARD UP!
I WANNA GO WITH YOU.
HEY, LET GO, ALRIGHT?
DID SHE LOOK... LIKE HER A LITTLE...?

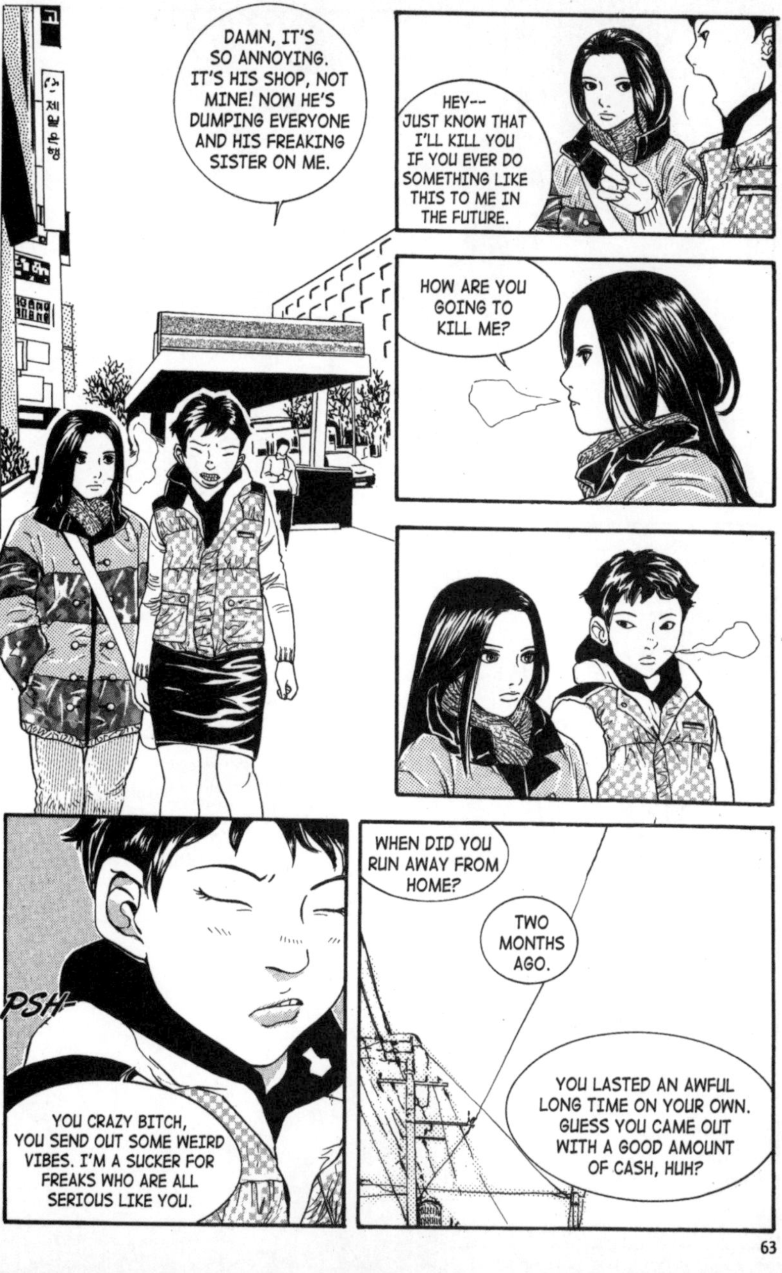

제일은행
DAMN, IT'S SO ANNOYING. IT'S HIS SHOP, NOT MINE! NOW HE'S DUMPING EVERYONE AND HIS FREAKING SISTER ON ME.
HEY-- JUST KNOW THAT I'LL KILL YOU IF YOU EVER DO SOMETHING LIKE THIS TO ME IN THE FUTURE.
HOW ARE YOU GOING TO KILL ME?
PSH-
YOU CRAZY BITCH, YOU SEND OUT SOME WEIRD VIBES. I'M A SUCKER FOR FREAKS WHO ARE ALL SERIOUS LIKE YOU.
WHEN DID YOU RUN AWAY FROM HOME?
TWO MONTHS AGO.
YOU LASTED AN AWFUL LONG TIME ON YOUR OWN. GUESS YOU CAME OUT WITH A GOOD AMOUNT OF CASH, HUH?

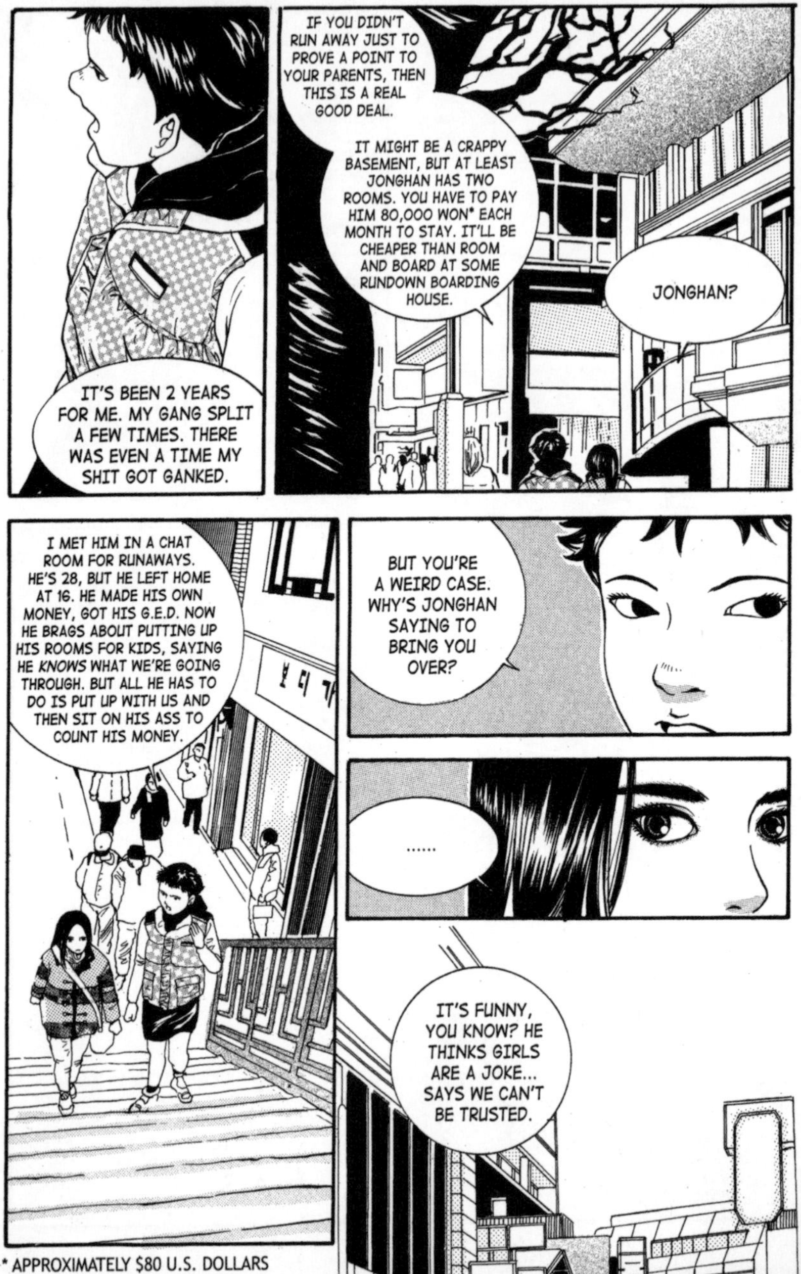
IT'S BEEN 2 YEARS FOR ME. MY GANG SPLIT A FEW TIMES. THERE WAS EVEN A TIME MY SHIT GOT GANKED.
IF YOU DIDN'T RUN AWAY JUST TO PROVE A POINT TO YOUR PARENTS, THEN THIS IS A REAL GOOD DEAL.
IT MIGHT BE A CRAPPY BASEMENT, BUT AT LEAST JONGHAN HAS TWO ROOMS. YOU HAVE TO PAY HIM 80,000 WON* EACH MONTH TO STAY. IT'LL BE CHEAPER THAN ROOM AND BOARD AT SOME RUNDOWN BOARDING HOUSE.
JONGHAN?
I MET HIM IN A CHAT ROOM FOR RUNAWAYS. HE'S 28, BUT HE LEFT HOME AT 16. HE MADE HIS OWN MONEY, GOT HIS G.E.D. NOW HE BRAGS ABOUT PUTTING UP HIS ROOMS FOR KIDS, SAYING HE *KNOWS* WHAT WE'RE GOING THROUGH. BUT ALL HE HAS TO DO IS PUT UP WITH US AND THEN SIT ON HIS ASS TO COUNT HIS MONEY.
BUT YOU'RE A WEIRD CASE. WHY'S JONGHAN SAYING TO BRING YOU OVER?
......
IT'S FUNNY, YOU KNOW? HE THINKS GIRLS ARE A JOKE... SAYS WE CAN'T BE TRUSTED.

* APPROXIMATELY $80 U.S. DOLLARS

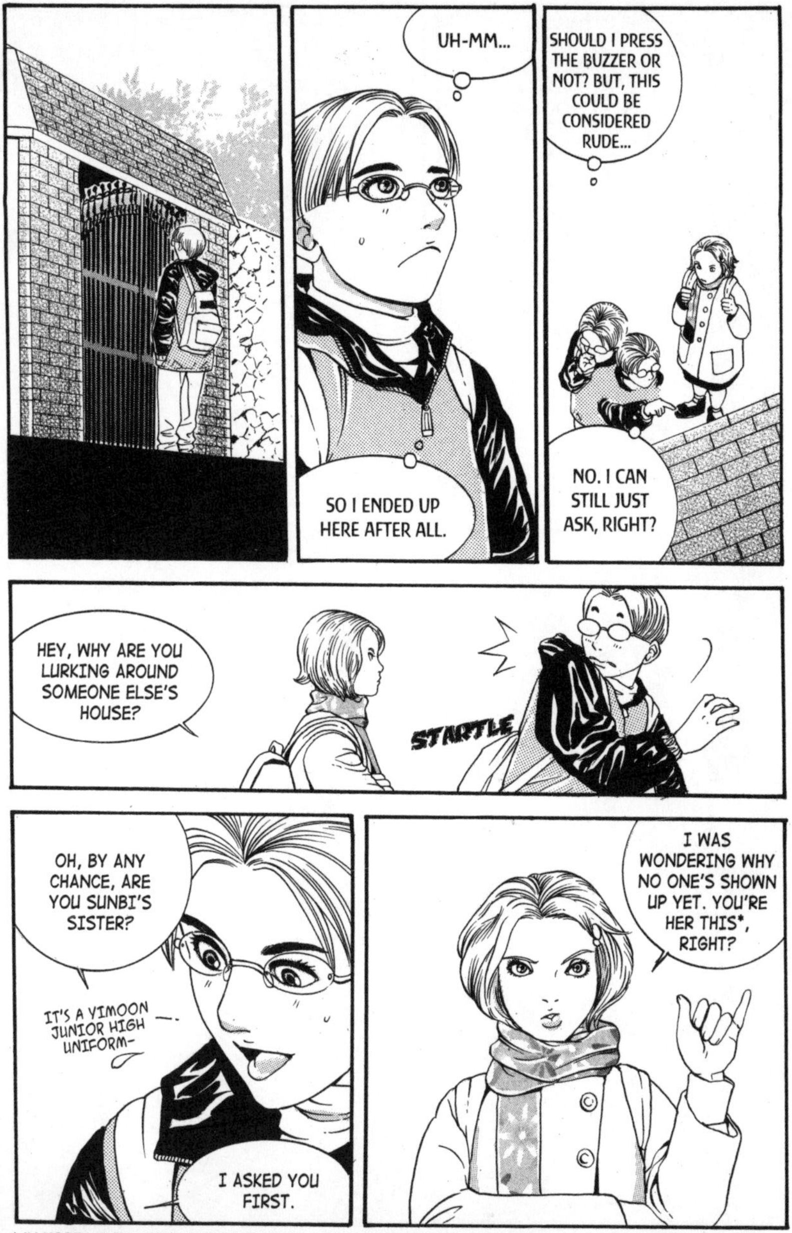
UH-MM...
SO I ENDED UP HERE AFTER ALL.
SHOULD I PRESS THE BUZZER OR NOT? BUT, THIS COULD BE CONSIDERED RUDE...
NO. I CAN STILL JUST ASK, RIGHT?
HEY, WHY ARE YOU LURKING AROUND SOMEONE ELSE'S HOUSE?
STARTLE
OH, BY ANY CHANCE, ARE YOU SUNBI'S SISTER?
IT'S A YIMOON JUNIOR HIGH UNIFORM-
I ASKED YOU FIRST.
I WAS WONDERING WHY NO ONE'S SHOWN UP YET. YOU'RE HER THIS*, RIGHT?

* IN KOREA AND JAPAN, HOLDING UP THE PINKY WHEN SPEAKING OF TWO PEOPLE MEANS THEY ARE IN A RELATIONSHIP--THOUGH NOT IN CHINA, WHERE IT IS CONSIDERED VULGAR AND/OR OFFENSIVE.

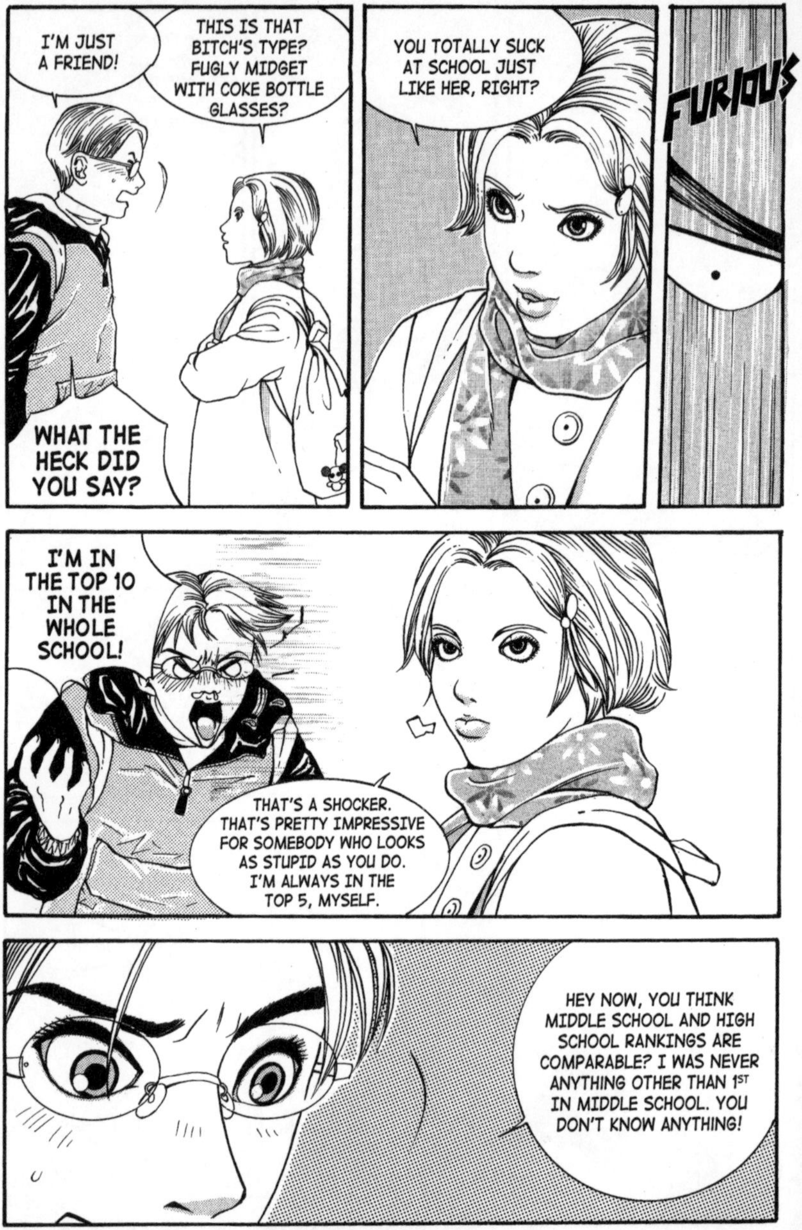
I'M JUST A FRIEND!
THIS IS THAT BITCH'S TYPE? FUGLY MIDGET WITH COKE BOTTLE GLASSES?
WHAT THE HECK DID YOU SAY?
YOU TOTALLY SUCK AT SCHOOL JUST LIKE HER, RIGHT?
FURIOUS
I'M IN THE TOP 10 IN THE WHOLE SCHOOL!
THAT'S A SHOCKER. THAT'S PRETTY IMPRESSIVE FOR SOMEBODY WHO LOOKS AS STUPID AS YOU DO. I'M ALWAYS IN THE TOP 5, MYSELF.
HEY NOW, YOU THINK MIDDLE SCHOOL AND HIGH SCHOOL RANKINGS ARE COMPARABLE? I WAS NEVER ANYTHING OTHER THAN 1ST IN MIDDLE SCHOOL. YOU DON'T KNOW ANYTHING!

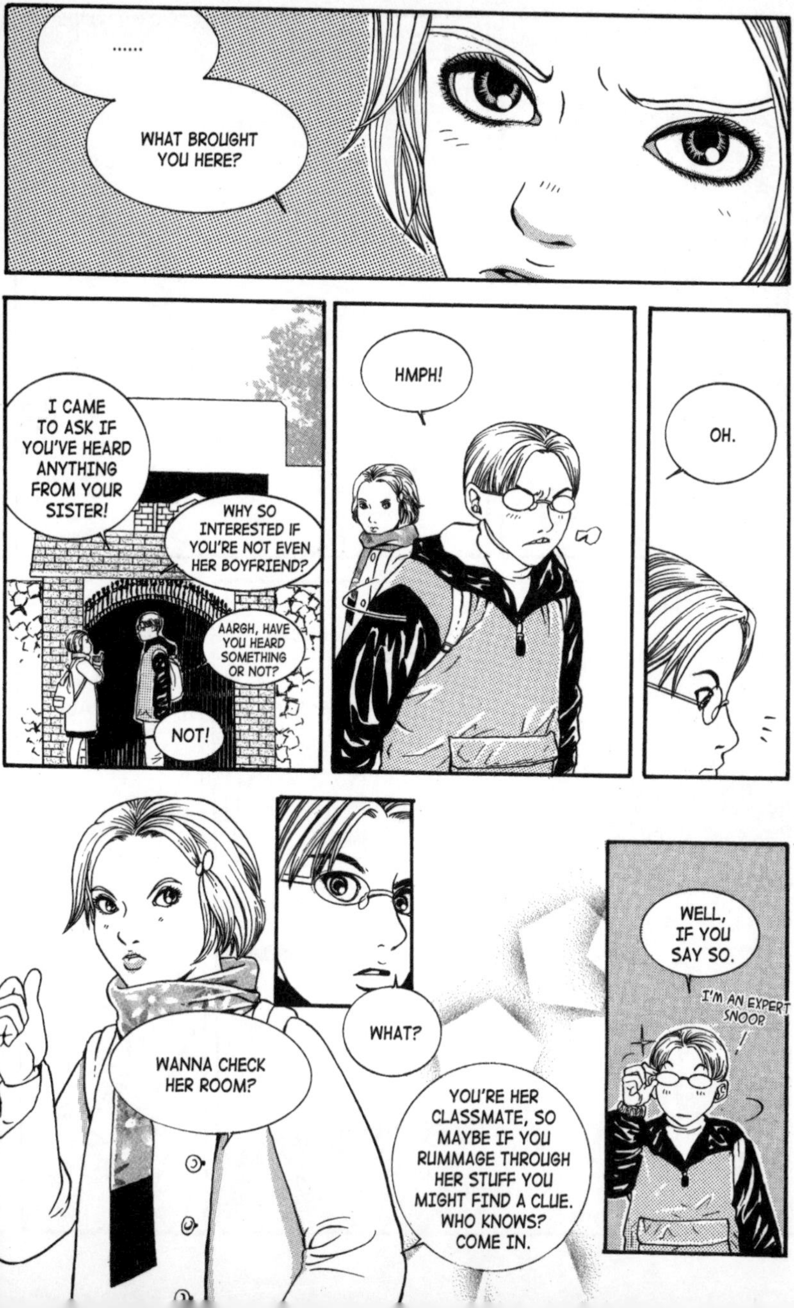
......
WHAT BROUGHT YOU HERE?
I CAME TO ASK IF YOU'VE HEARD ANYTHING FROM YOUR SISTER!
WHY SO INTERESTED IF YOU'RE NOT EVEN HER BOYFRIEND?
AARGH, HAVE YOU HEARD SOMETHING OR NOT?
NOT!
HMPH!
OH.
WANNA CHECK HER ROOM?
WHAT?
YOU'RE HER CLASSMATE, SO MAYBE IF YOU RUMMAGE THROUGH HER STUFF YOU MIGHT FIND A CLUE. WHO KNOWS? COME IN.
WELL, IF YOU SAY SO.
I'M AN EXPERT SNOOP!

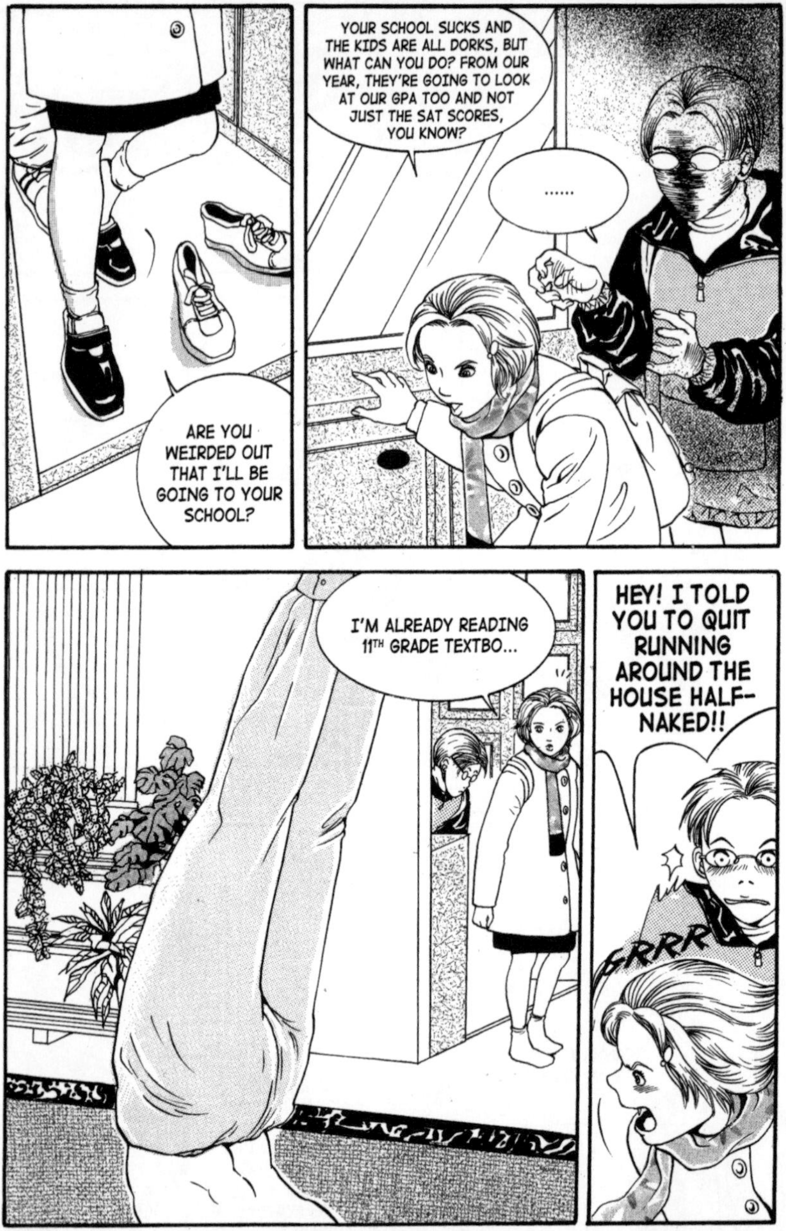
ARE YOU WEIRDED OUT THAT I'LL BE GOING TO YOUR SCHOOL?
YOUR SCHOOL SUCKS AND THE KIDS ARE ALL DORKS, BUT WHAT CAN YOU DO? FROM OUR YEAR, THEY'RE GOING TO LOOK AT OUR GPA TOO AND NOT JUST THE SAT SCORES, YOU KNOW?
......
I'M ALREADY READING 11TH GRADE TEXTBO...
HEY! I TOLD YOU TO QUIT RUNNING AROUND THE HOUSE HALF-NAKED!!
GRRR

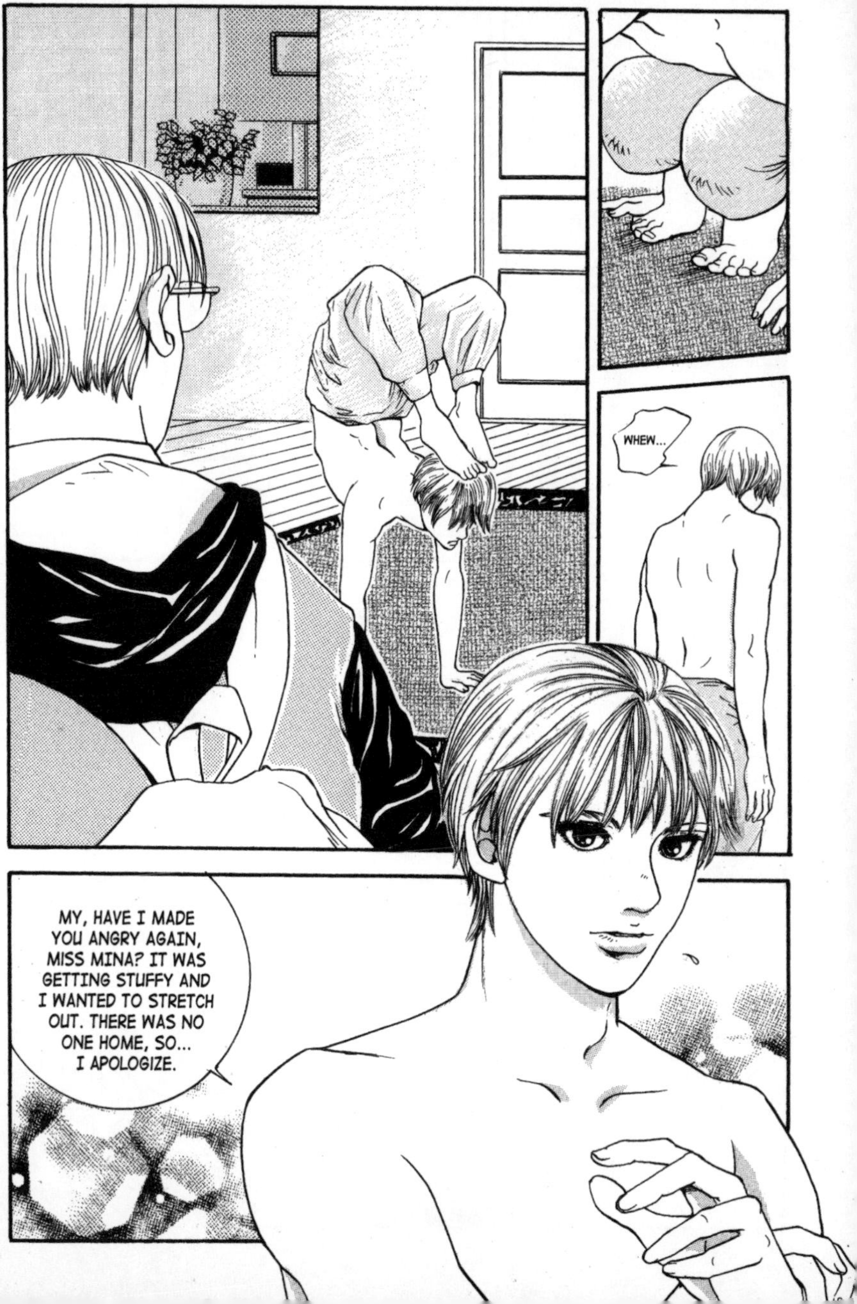
WHEW...
MY, HAVE I MADE YOU ANGRY AGAIN, MISS MINA? IT WAS GETTING STUFFY AND I WANTED TO STRETCH OUT. THERE WAS NO ONE HOME, SO... I APOLOGIZE.

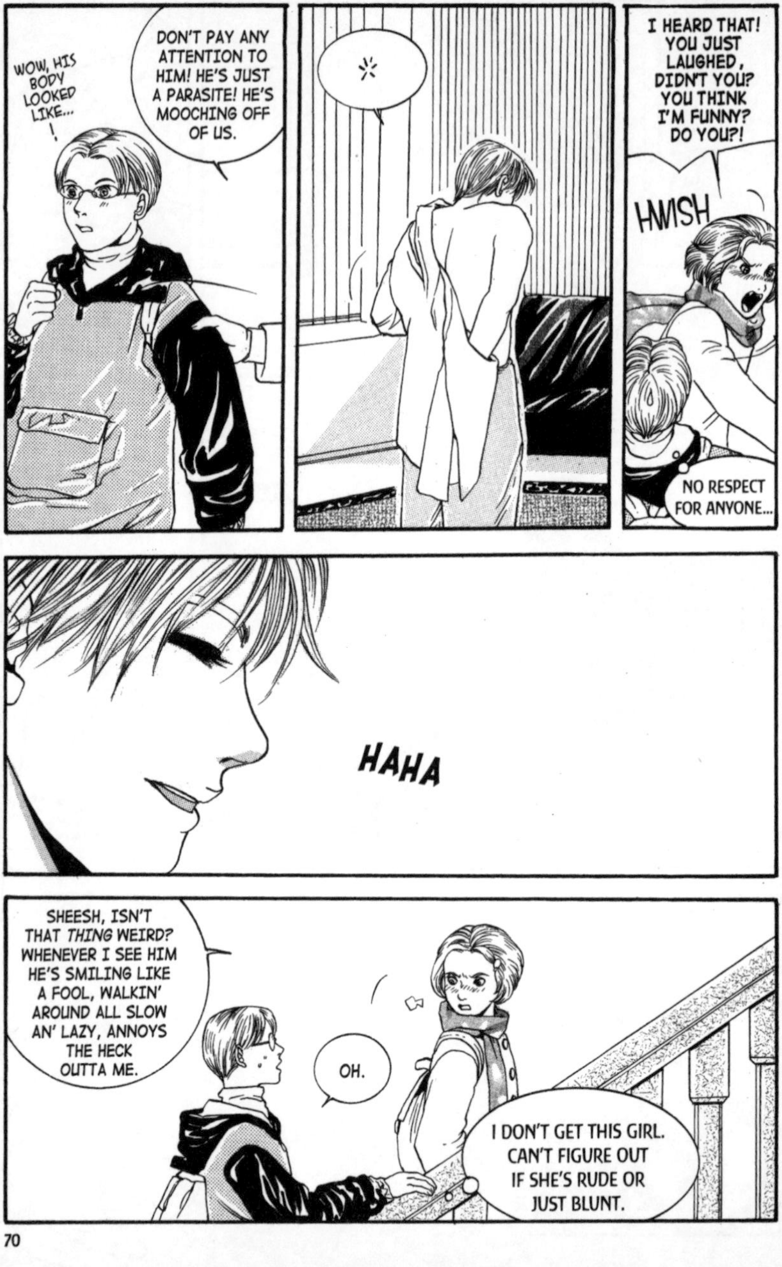
WOW, HIS BODY LOOKED LIKE... !
DON'T PAY ANY ATTENTION TO HIM! HE'S JUST A PARASITE! HE'S MOOCHING OFF OF US.
I HEARD THAT! YOU JUST LAUGHED, DIDN'T YOU? YOU THINK I'M FUNNY? DO YOU?!
HWISH
NO RESPECT FOR ANYONE...
HAHA
SHEESH, ISN'T THAT THING WEIRD? WHENEVER I SEE HIM HE'S SMILING LIKE A FOOL, WALKIN' AROUND ALL SLOW AN' LAZY, ANNOYS THE HECK OUTTA ME.
OH.
I DON'T GET THIS GIRL. CAN'T FIGURE OUT IF SHE'S RUDE OR JUST BLUNT.

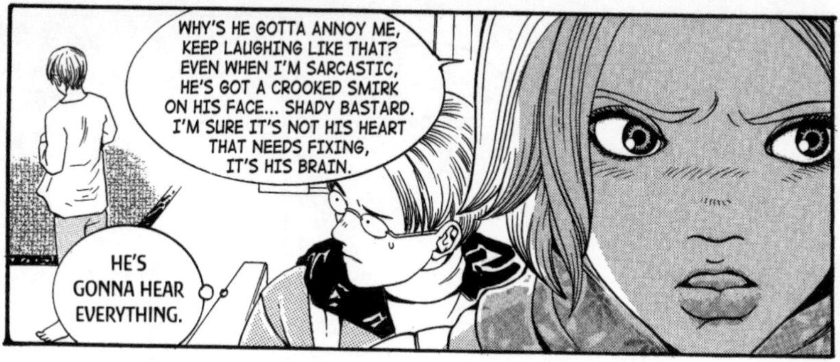
WHY'S HE GOTTA ANNOY ME, KEEP LAUGHING LIKE THAT? EVEN WHEN I'M SARCASTIC, HE'S GOT A CROOKED SMIRK ON HIS FACE... SHADY BASTARD. I'M SURE IT'S NOT HIS HEART THAT NEEDS FIXING, IT'S HIS BRAIN.
HE'S GONNA HEAR EVERYTHING.

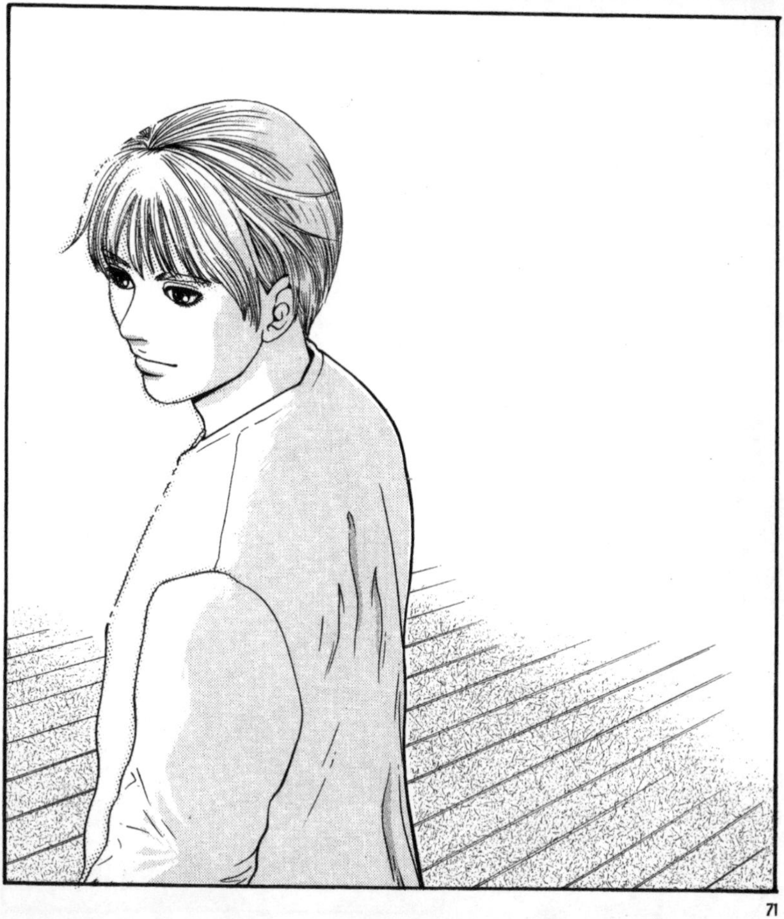

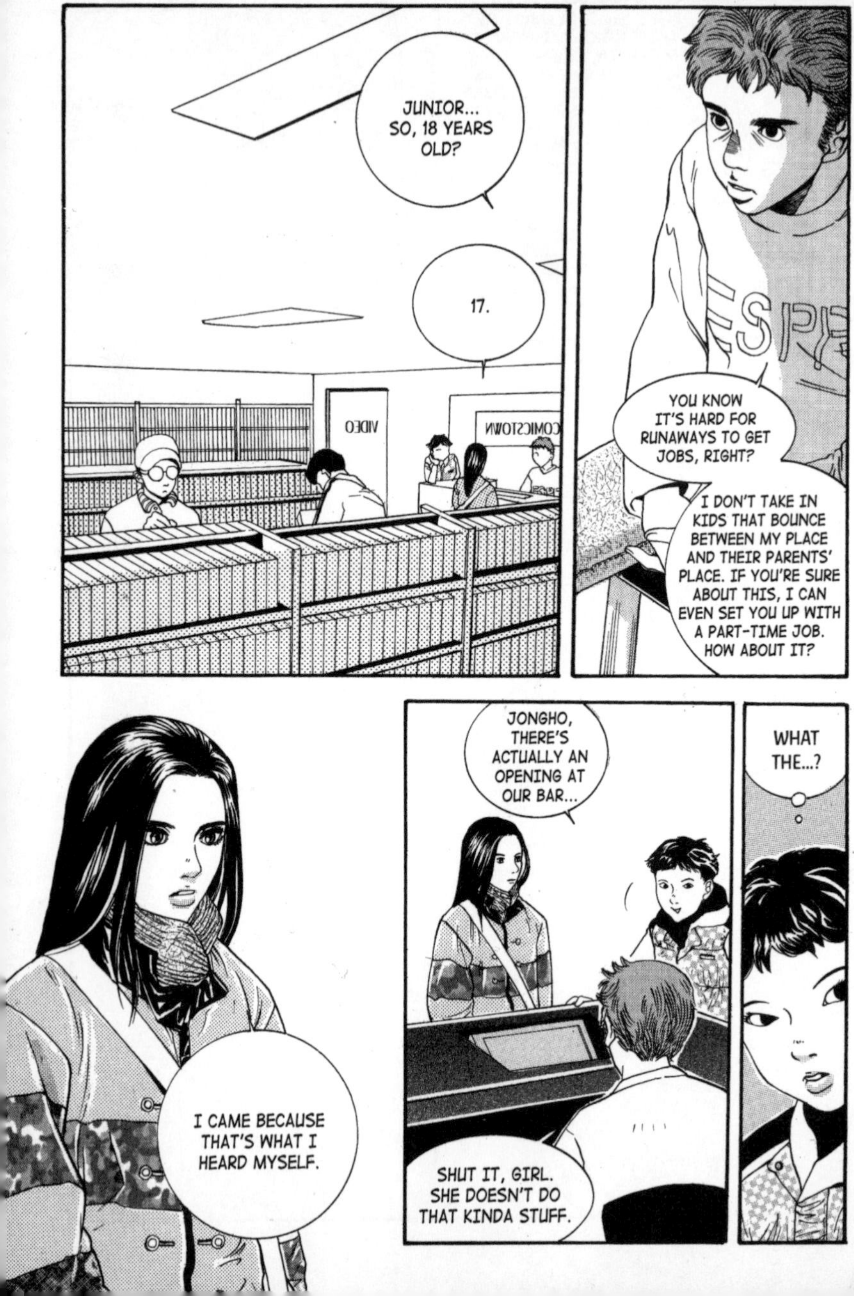
JUNIOR... SO, 18 YEARS OLD?
17.
YOU KNOW IT'S HARD FOR RUNAWAYS TO GET JOBS, RIGHT?
I DON'T TAKE IN KIDS THAT BOUNCE BETWEEN MY PLACE AND THEIR PARENTS' PLACE. IF YOU'RE SURE ABOUT THIS, I CAN EVEN SET YOU UP WITH A PART-TIME JOB. HOW ABOUT IT?
I CAME BECAUSE THAT'S WHAT I HEARD MYSELF.
JONGHO, THERE'S ACTUALLY AN OPENING AT OUR BAR...
SHUT IT, GIRL. SHE DOESN'T DO THAT KINDA STUFF.
WHAT THE...?

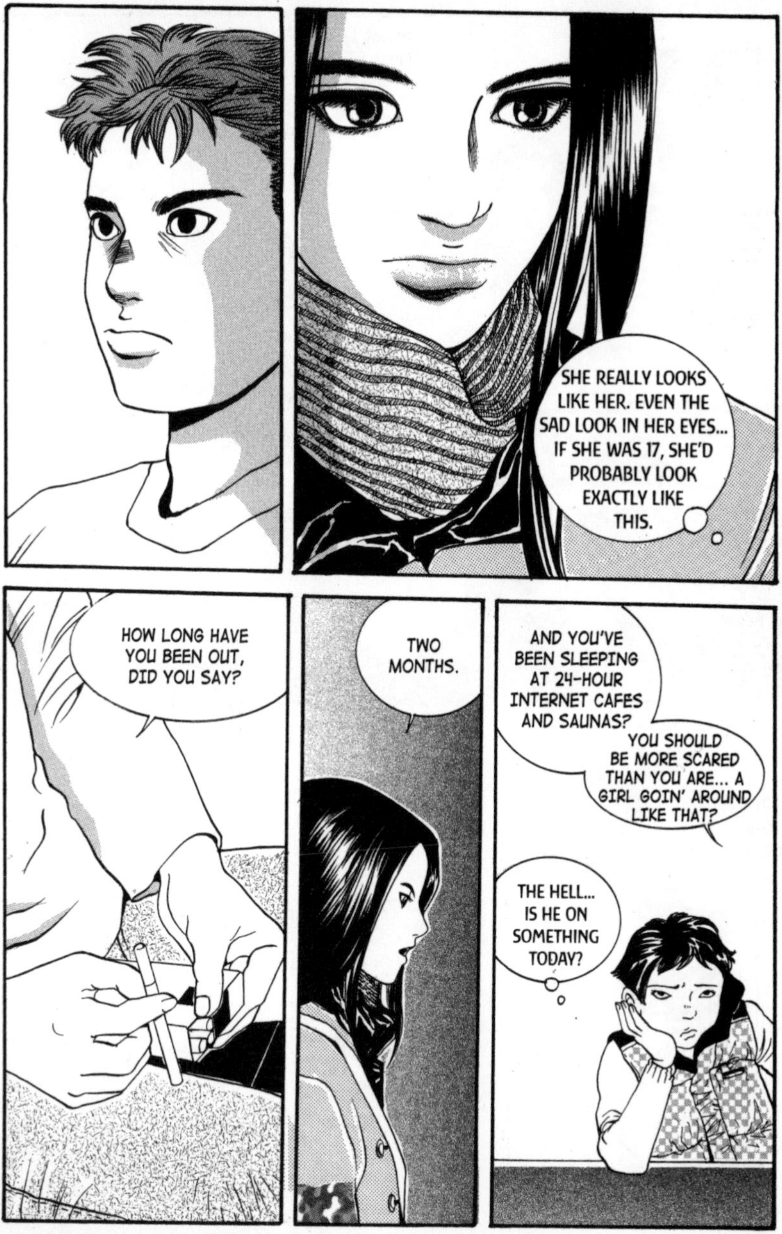
SHE REALLY LOOKS LIKE HER. EVEN THE SAD LOOK IN HER EYES... IF SHE WAS 17, SHE'D PROBABLY LOOK EXACTLY LIKE THIS.
HOW LONG HAVE YOU BEEN OUT, DID YOU SAY?
TWO MONTHS.
AND YOU'VE BEEN SLEEPING AT 24-HOUR INTERNET CAFES AND SAUNAS?
YOU SHOULD BE MORE SCARED THAN YOU ARE... A GIRL GOIN' AROUND LIKE THAT?
THE HELL... IS HE ON SOMETHING TODAY?

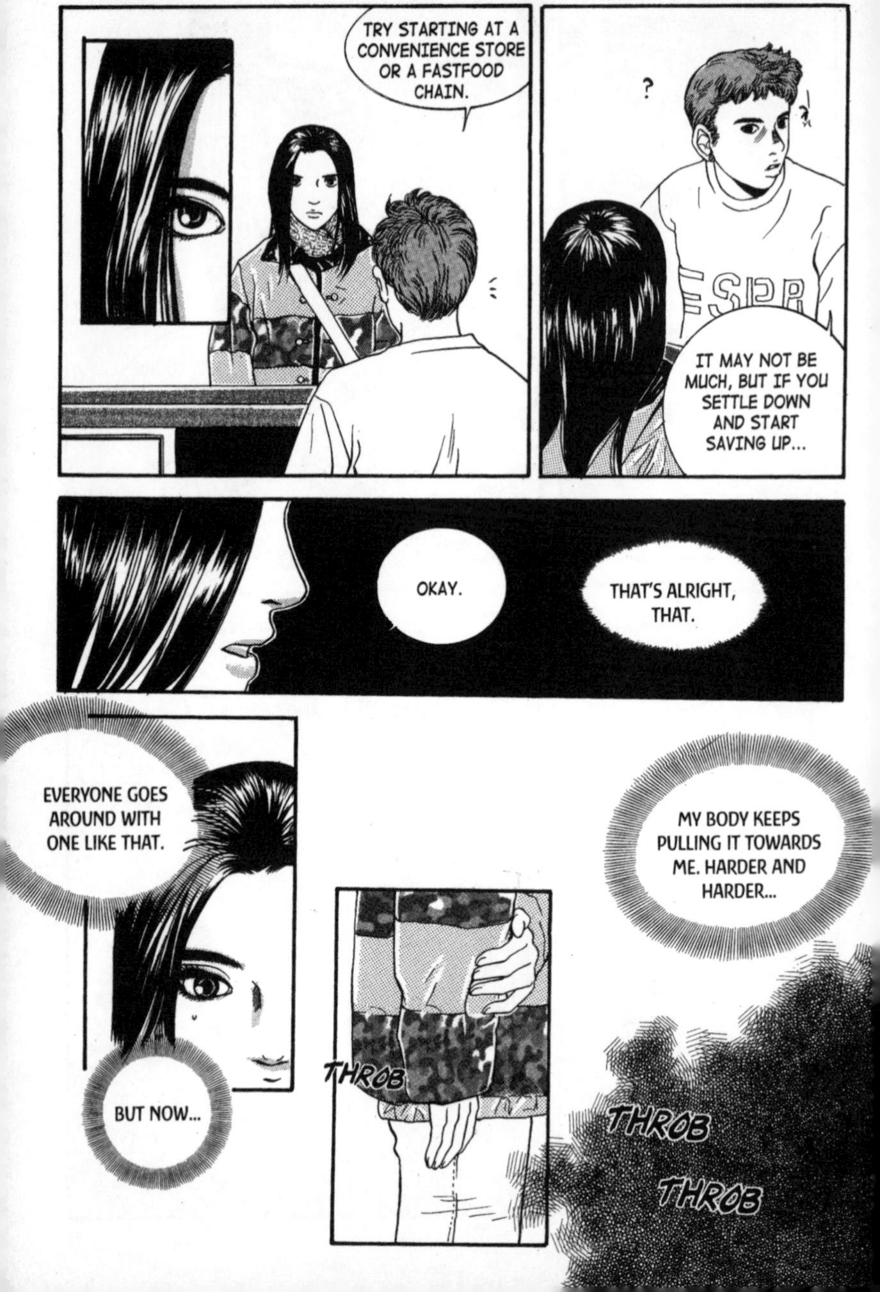
TRY STARTING AT A CONVENIENCE STORE OR A FASTFOOD CHAIN.
?
IT MAY NOT BE MUCH, BUT IF YOU SETTLE DOWN AND START SAVING UP...
OKAY.
THAT'S ALRIGHT, THAT.
EVERYONE GOES AROUND WITH ONE LIKE THAT.
BUT NOW...
THROB
MY BODY KEEPS PULLING IT TOWARDS ME. HARDER AND HARDER...
THROB
THROB

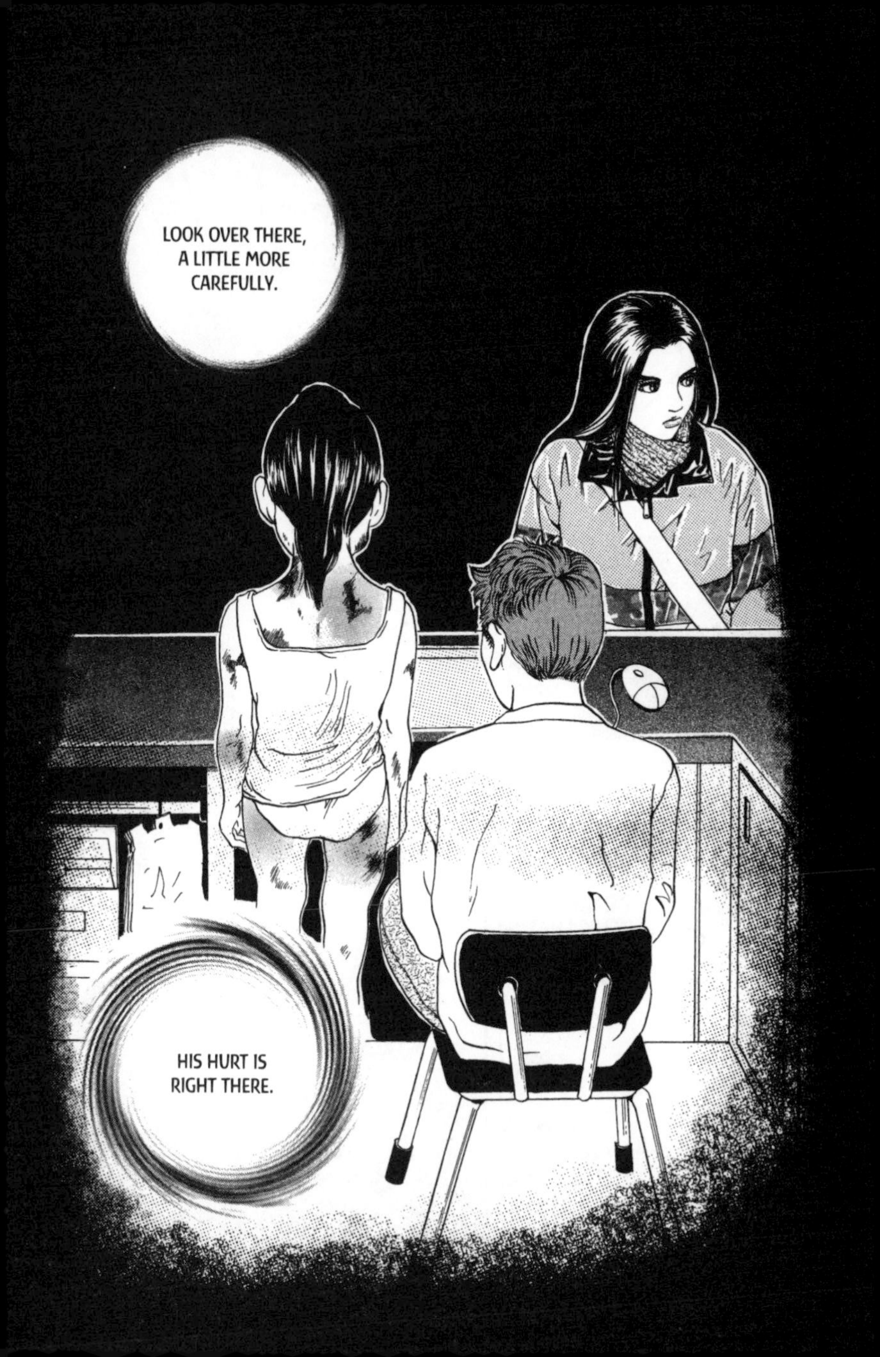
LOOK OVER THERE, A LITTLE MORE CAREFULLY.
HIS HURT IS RIGHT THERE.

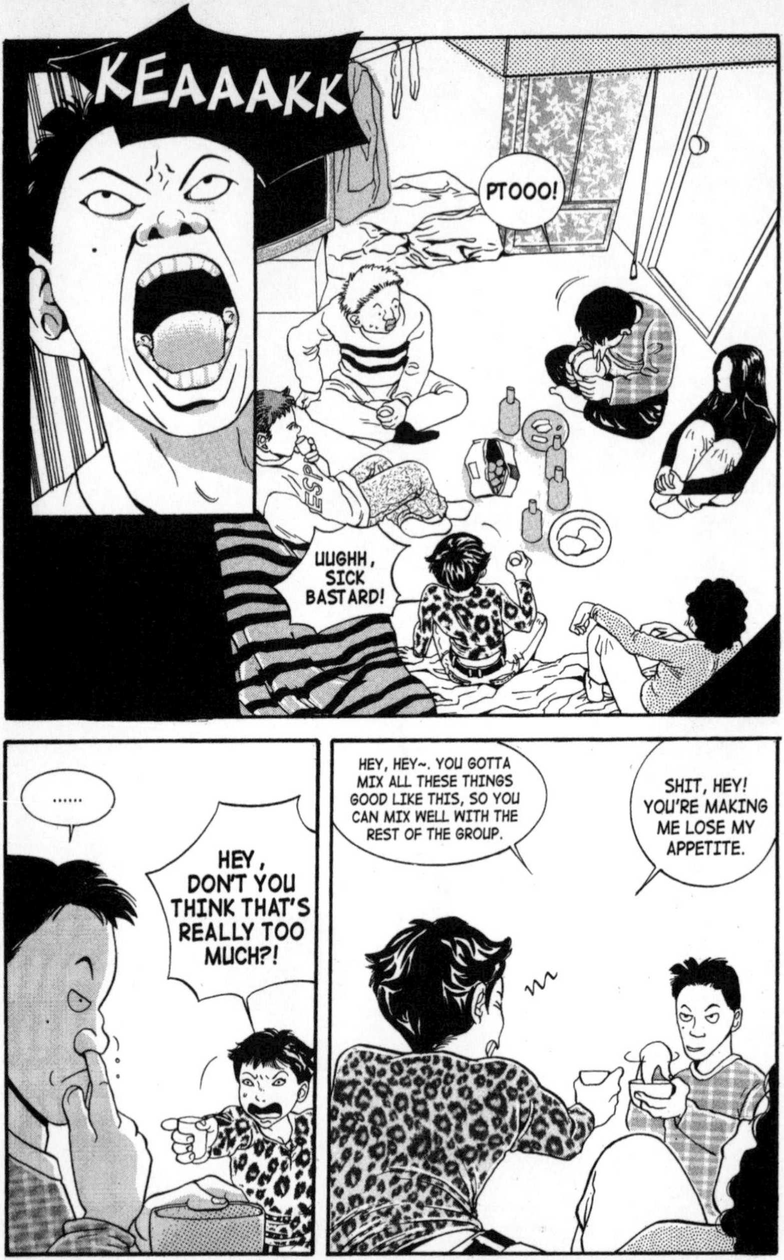
KEAAAKK
PTOOO!
UUGHH, SICK BASTARD!
......
HEY, DON'T YOU THINK THAT'S REALLY TOO MUCH?!
HEY, HEY~. YOU GOTTA MIX ALL THESE THINGS GOOD LIKE THIS, SO YOU CAN MIX WELL WITH THE REST OF THE GROUP.
SHIT, HEY! YOU'RE MAKING ME LOSE MY APPETITE.

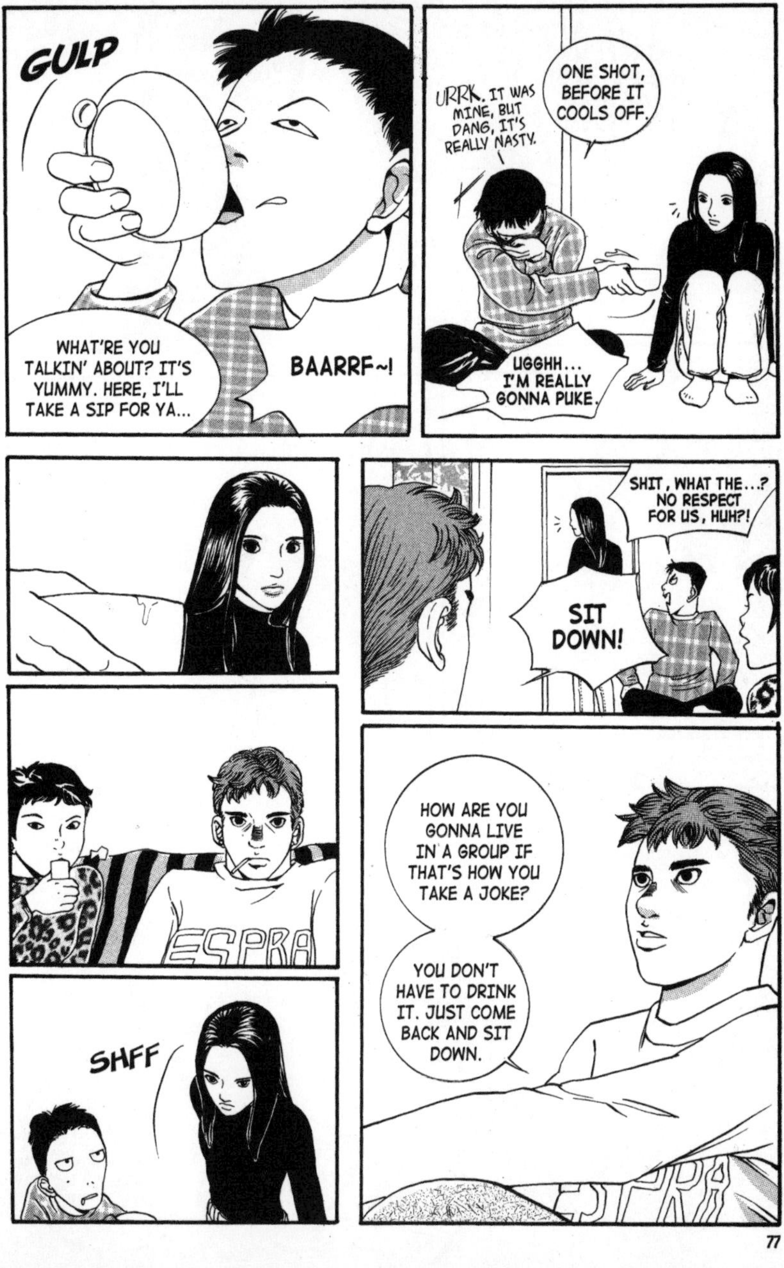

GULP
WHAT'RE YOU TALKIN' ABOUT? IT'S YUMMY. HERE, I'LL TAKE A SIP FOR YA...
BAARRF~!
URRK. IT WAS MINE, BUT DANG, IT'S REALLY NASTY.
ONE SHOT, BEFORE IT COOLS OFF.
UGGHH... I'M REALLY GONNA PUKE.
ESPRA
SHFF
SHIT, WHAT THE...? NO RESPECT FOR US, HUH?!
SIT DOWN!
HOW ARE YOU GONNA LIVE IN A GROUP IF THAT'S HOW YOU TAKE A JOKE?
YOU DON'T HAVE TO DRINK IT. JUST COME BACK AND SIT DOWN.

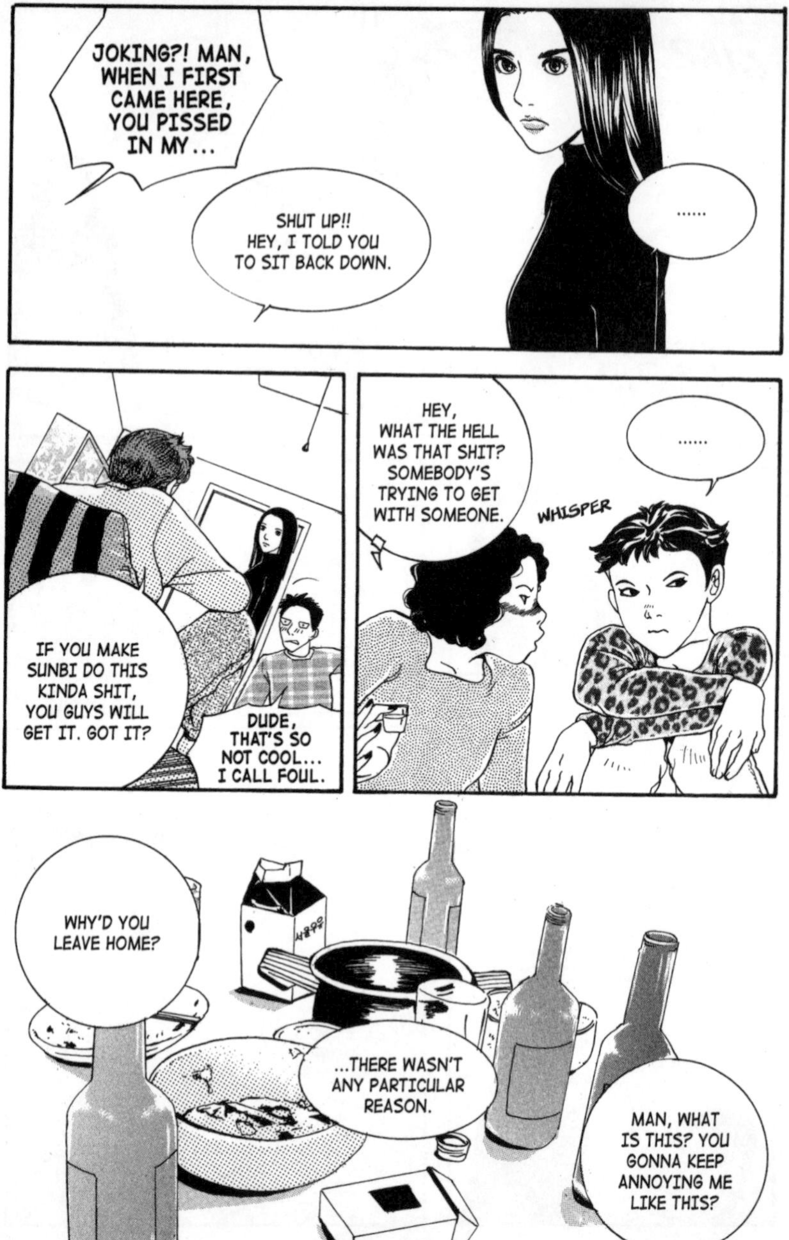
JOKING?! MAN, WHEN I FIRST CAME HERE, YOU PISSED IN MY...
SHUT UP!! HEY, I TOLD YOU TO SIT BACK DOWN.
......
IF YOU MAKE SUNBI DO THIS KINDA SHIT, YOU GUYS WILL GET IT. GOT IT?
DUDE, THAT'S SO NOT COOL... I CALL FOUL.
HEY, WHAT THE HELL WAS THAT SHIT? SOMEBODY'S TRYING TO GET WITH SOMEONE.
WHISPER
......
WHY'D YOU LEAVE HOME?
...THERE WASN'T ANY PARTICULAR REASON.
MAN, WHAT IS THIS? YOU GONNA KEEP ANNOYING ME LIKE THIS?

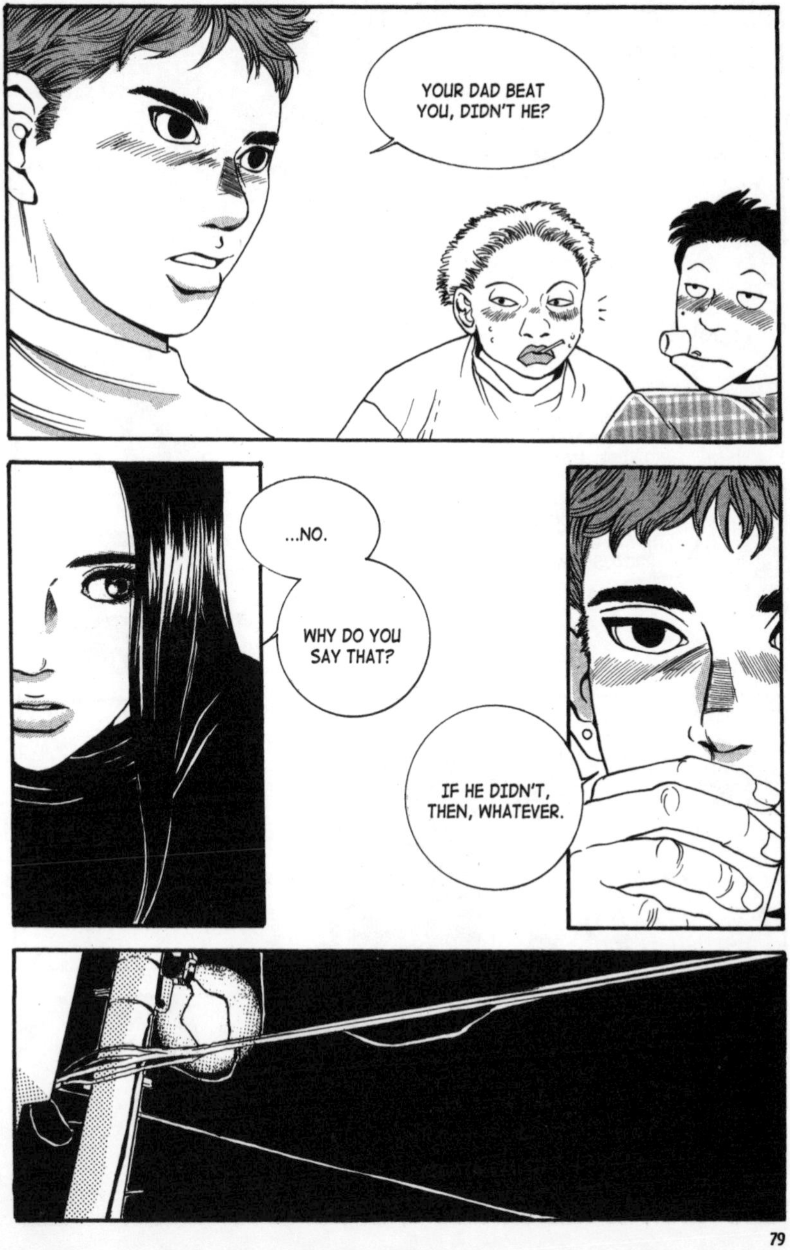
YOUR DAD BEAT YOU, DIDN'T HE?
...NO.
WHY DO YOU SAY THAT?
IF HE DIDN'T, THEN, WHATEVER.

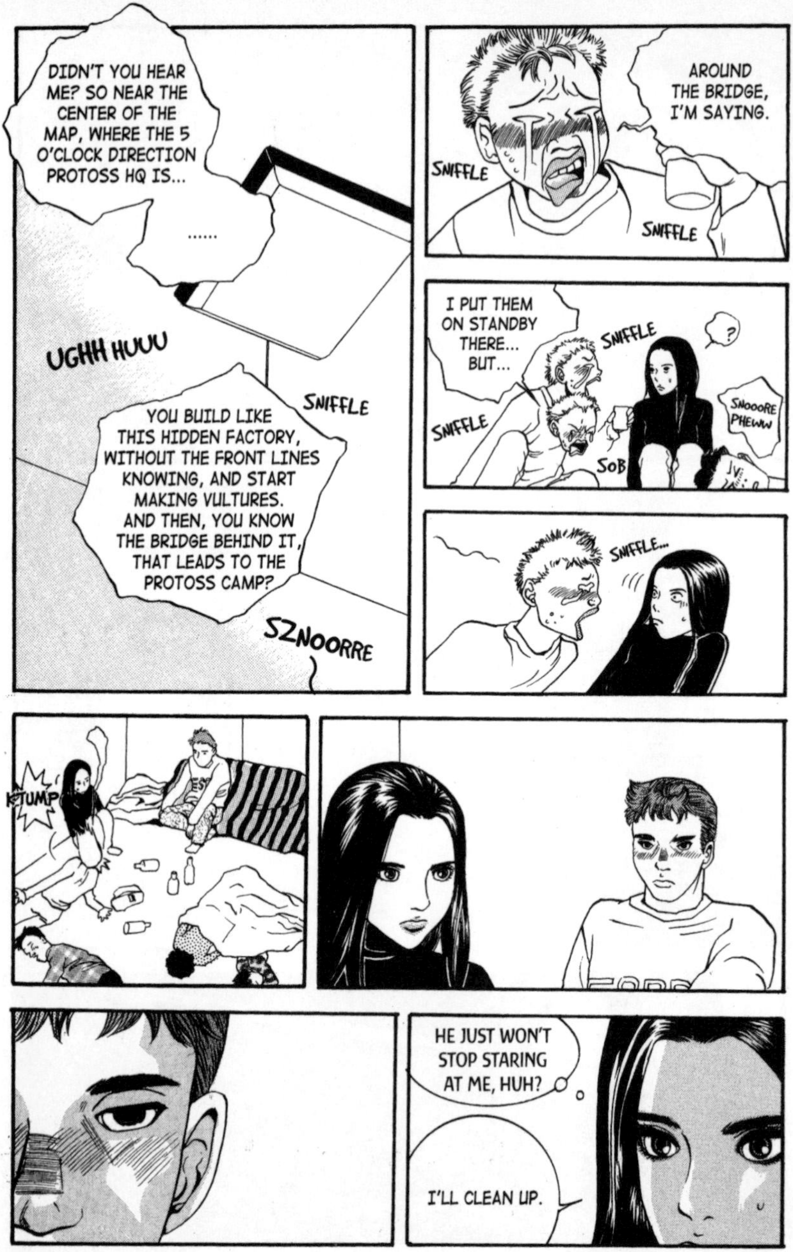

DIDN'T YOU HEAR ME? SO NEAR THE CENTER OF THE MAP, WHERE THE 5 O'CLOCK DIRECTION PROTOSS HQ IS...
......
UGHH HUUU
YOU BUILD LIKE THIS HIDDEN FACTORY, WITHOUT THE FRONT LINES KNOWING, AND START MAKING VULTURES. AND THEN, YOU KNOW THE BRIDGE BEHIND IT, THAT LEADS TO THE PROTOSS CAMP?
SNIFFLE
SZNOORRE
SNIFFLE
AROUND THE BRIDGE, I'M SAYING.
SNIFFLE
I PUT THEM ON STANDBY THERE... BUT...
SNIFFLE
?
SNIFFLE
SNOOORE PHEWW
SOB
SNIFFLE...
K-TUMP
HE JUST WON'T STOP STARING AT ME, HUH?
I'LL CLEAN UP.

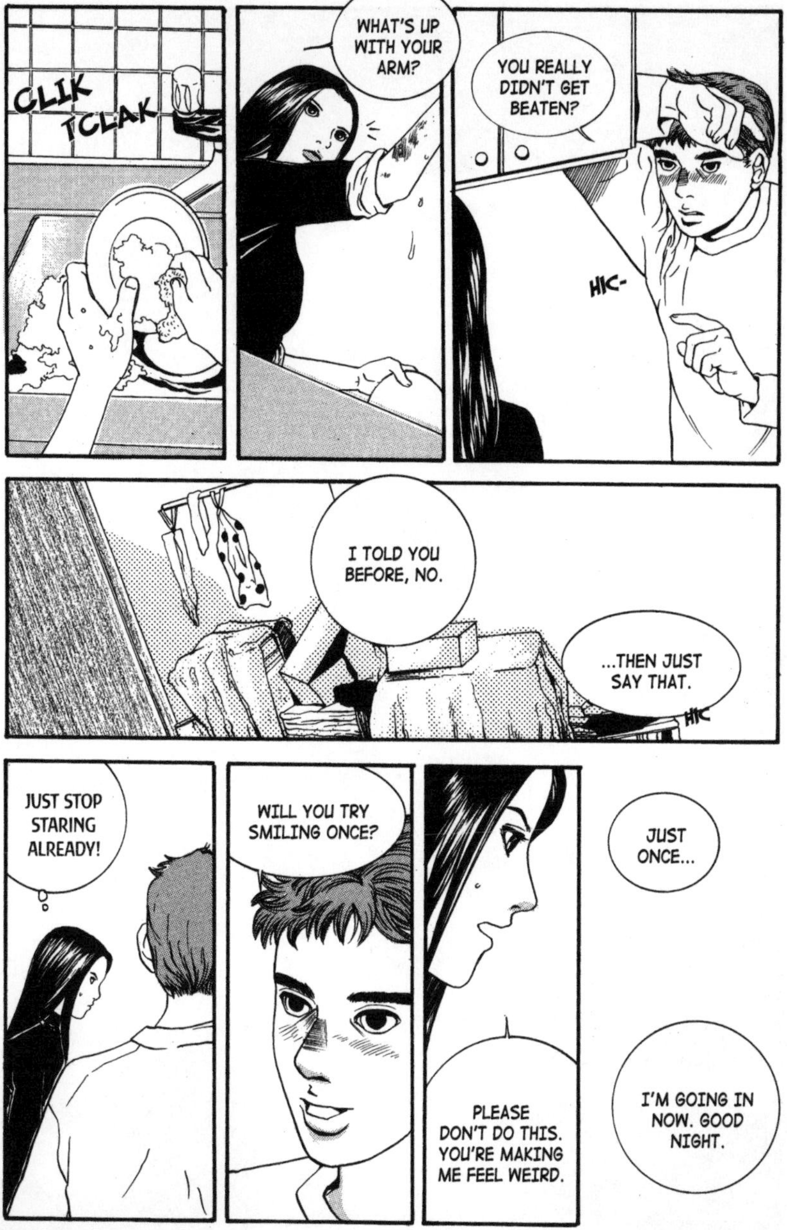
CLIK
TCLAK
WHAT'S UP WITH YOUR ARM?
YOU REALLY DIDN'T GET BEATEN?
HIC-
I TOLD YOU BEFORE, NO.
...THEN JUST SAY THAT.
HIC
JUST STOP STARING ALREADY!
WILL YOU TRY SMILING ONCE?
PLEASE DON'T DO THIS. YOU'RE MAKING ME FEEL WEIRD.
JUST ONCE...
I'M GOING IN NOW. GOOD NIGHT.

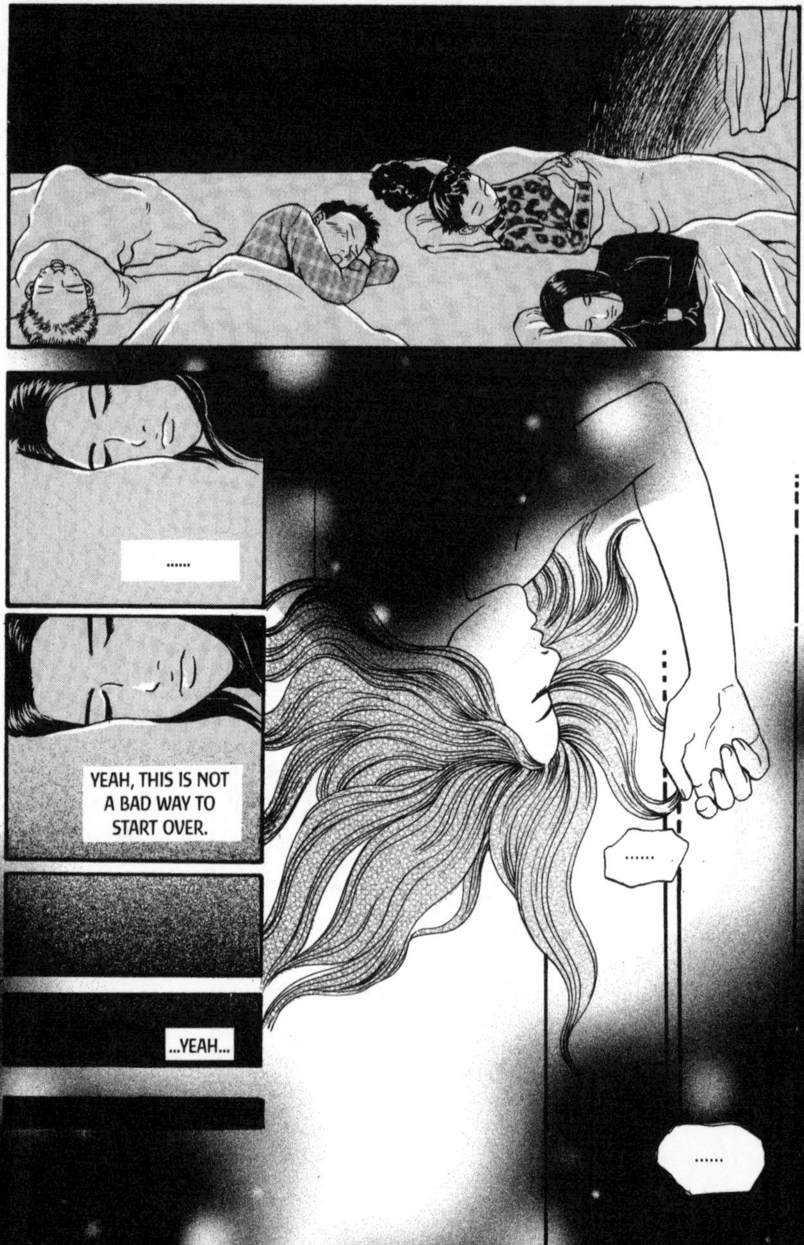
......
YEAH, THIS IS NOT A BAD WAY TO START OVER.
...YEAH...
......
......

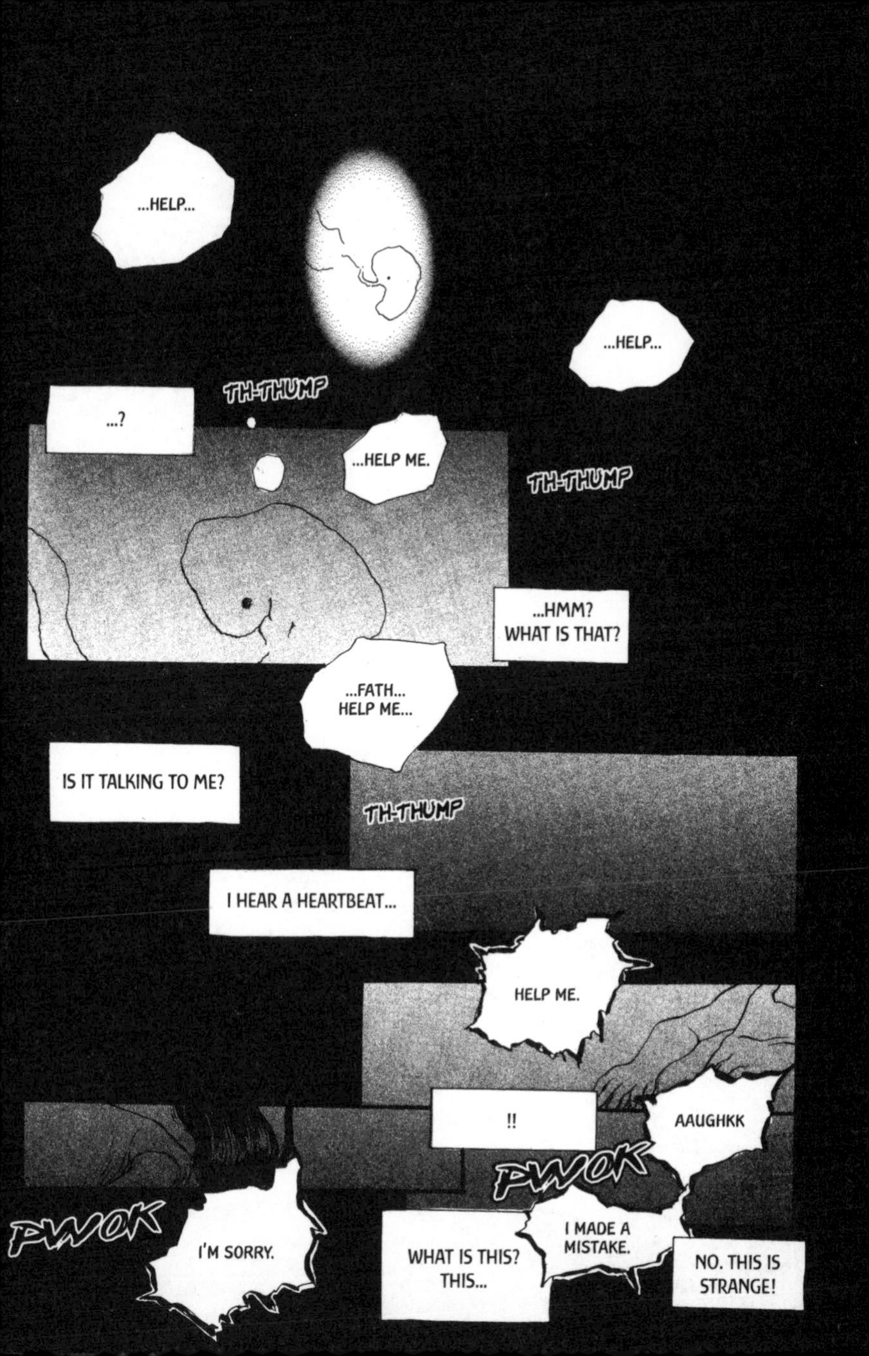
...HELP...
...HELP...
TH-THUMP
...?
...HELP ME.
TH-THUMP
...HMM? WHAT IS THAT?
...FATH... HELP ME...
IS IT TALKING TO ME?
TH-THUMP
I HEAR A HEARTBEAT...
HELP ME.
!!
AAUGHKK
PWOK
PWOK
I'M SORRY.
WHAT IS THIS? THIS...
I MADE A MISTAKE.
NO. THIS IS STRANGE!

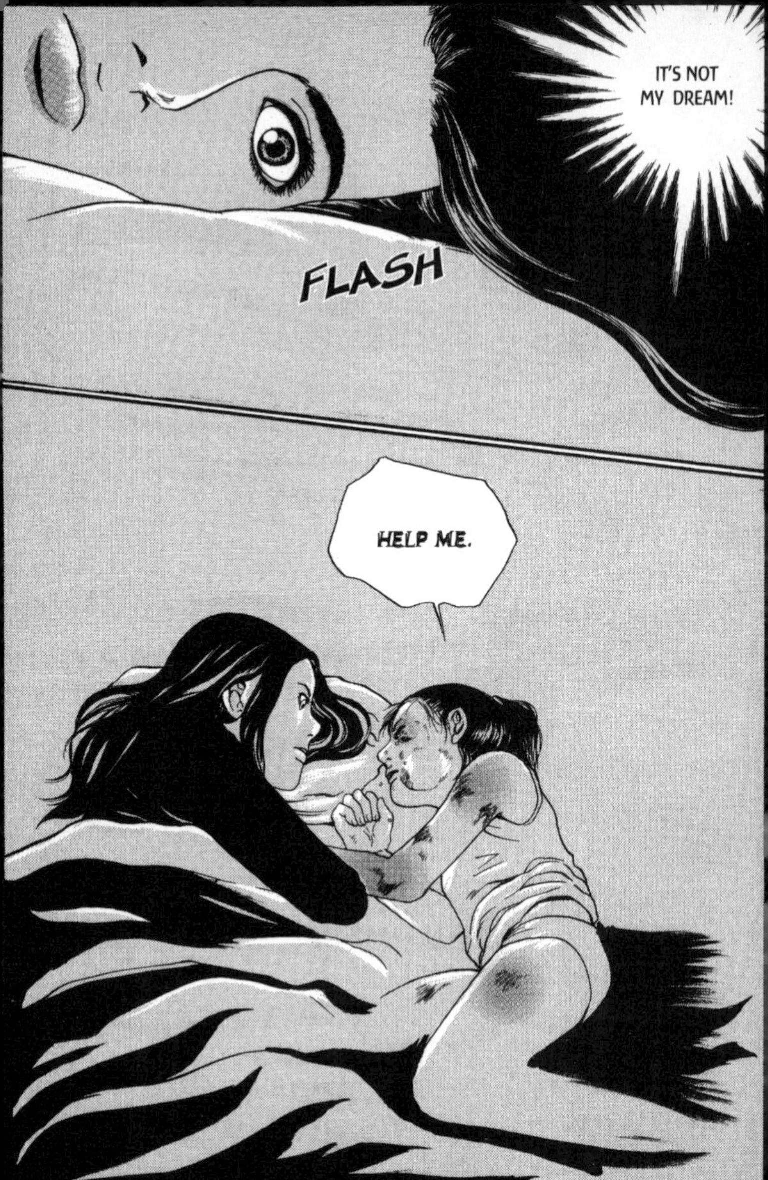
IT'S NOT MY DREAM!
FLASH
HELP ME.

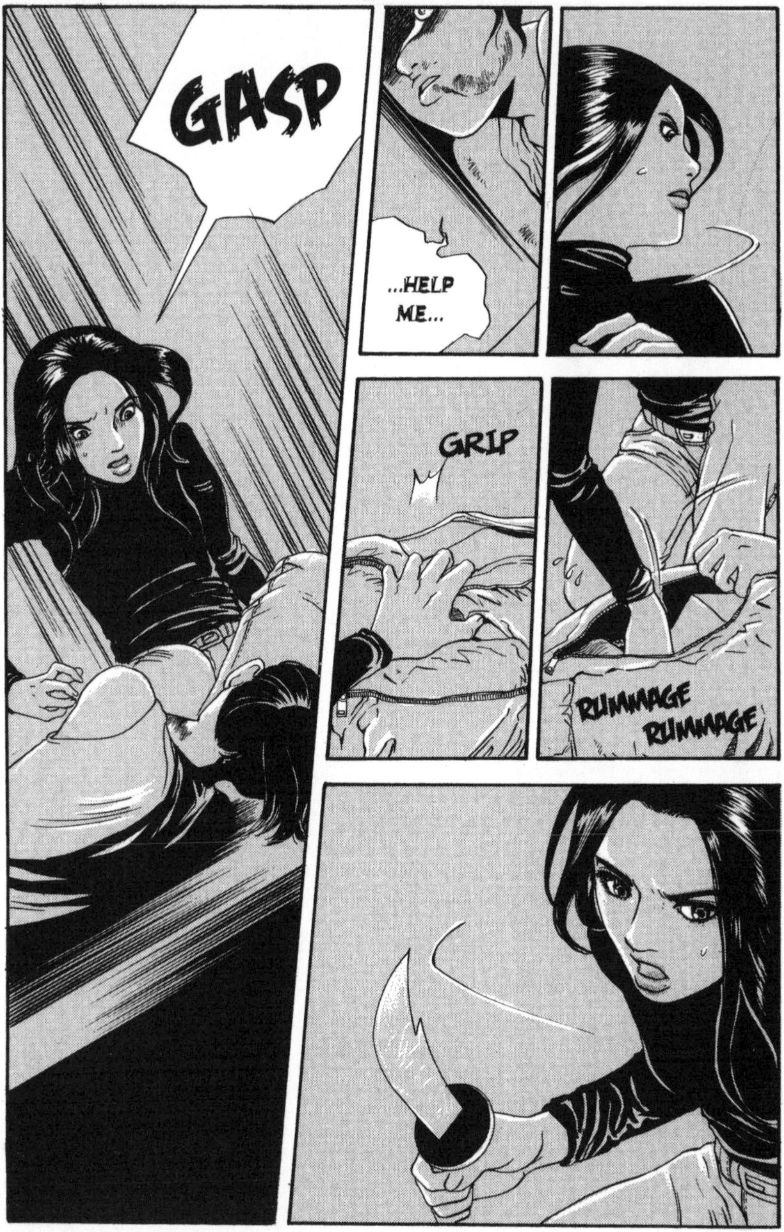
GASP
...HELP
ME...
GRIP
RUMMAGE
RUMMAGE

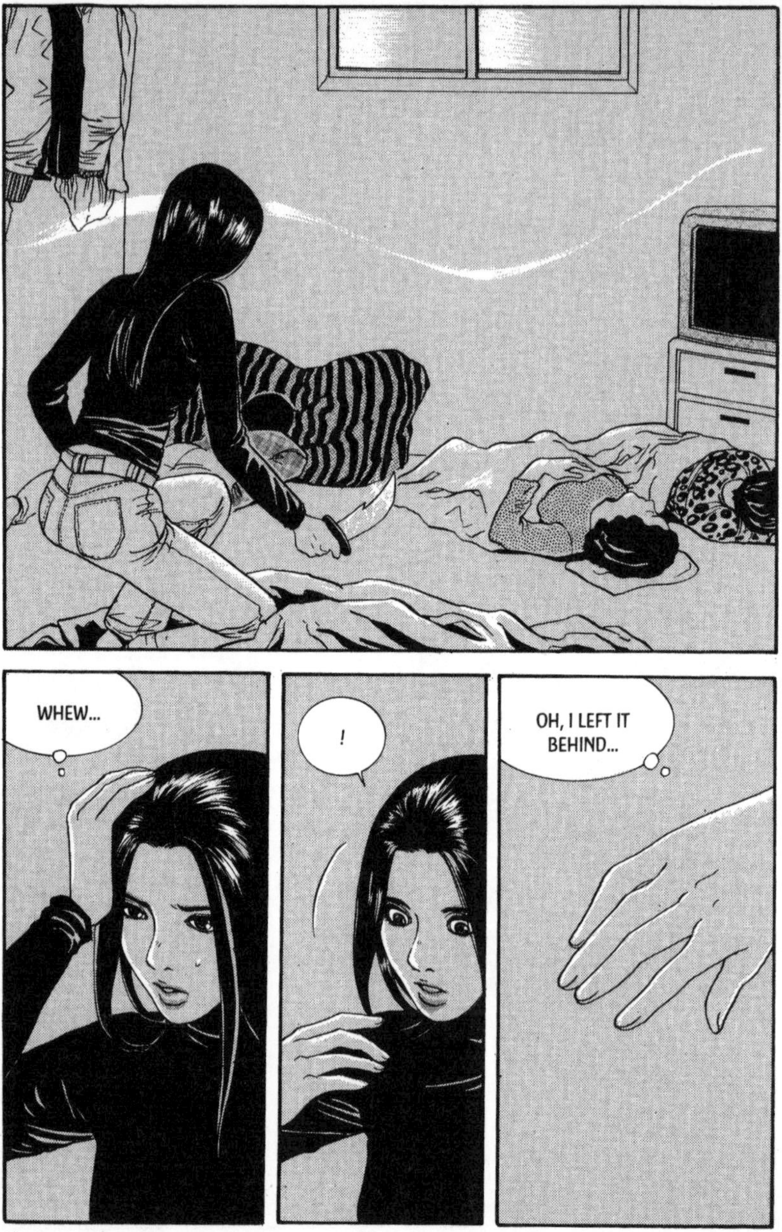
WHEW...
!
OH, I LEFT IT BEHIND...

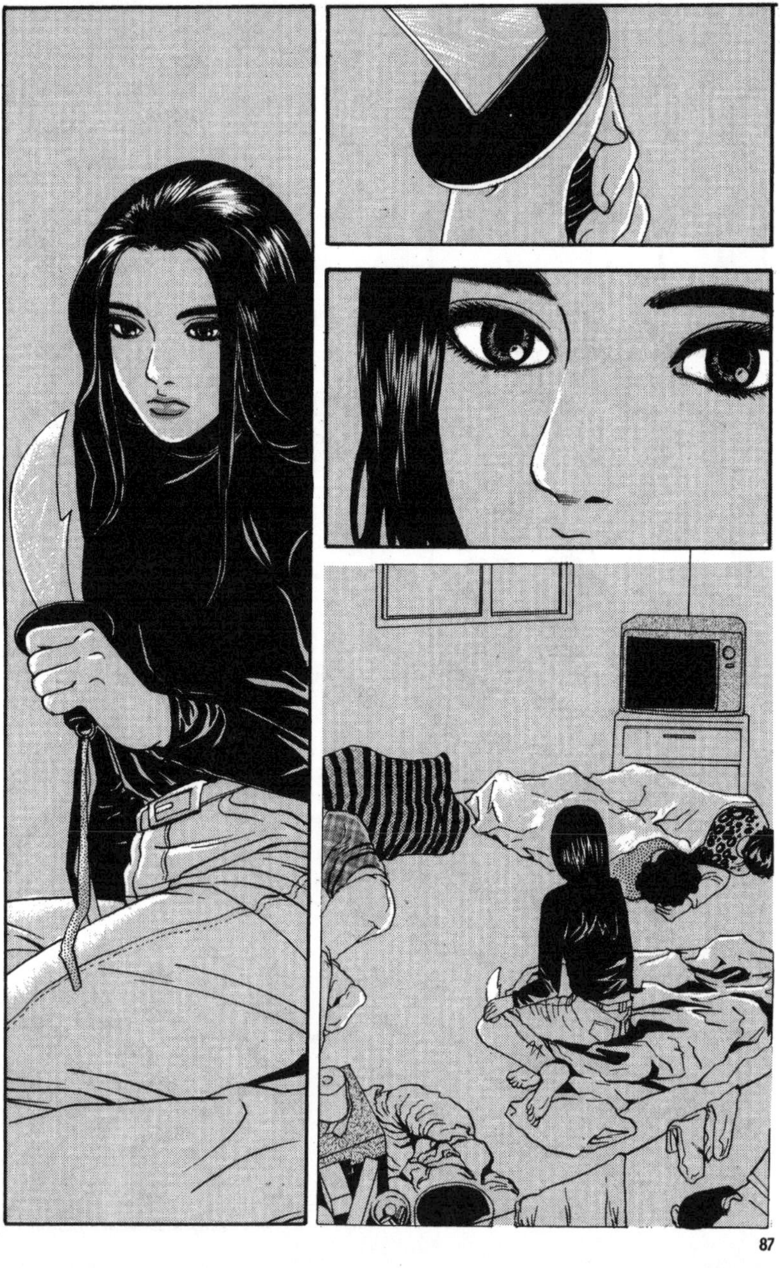

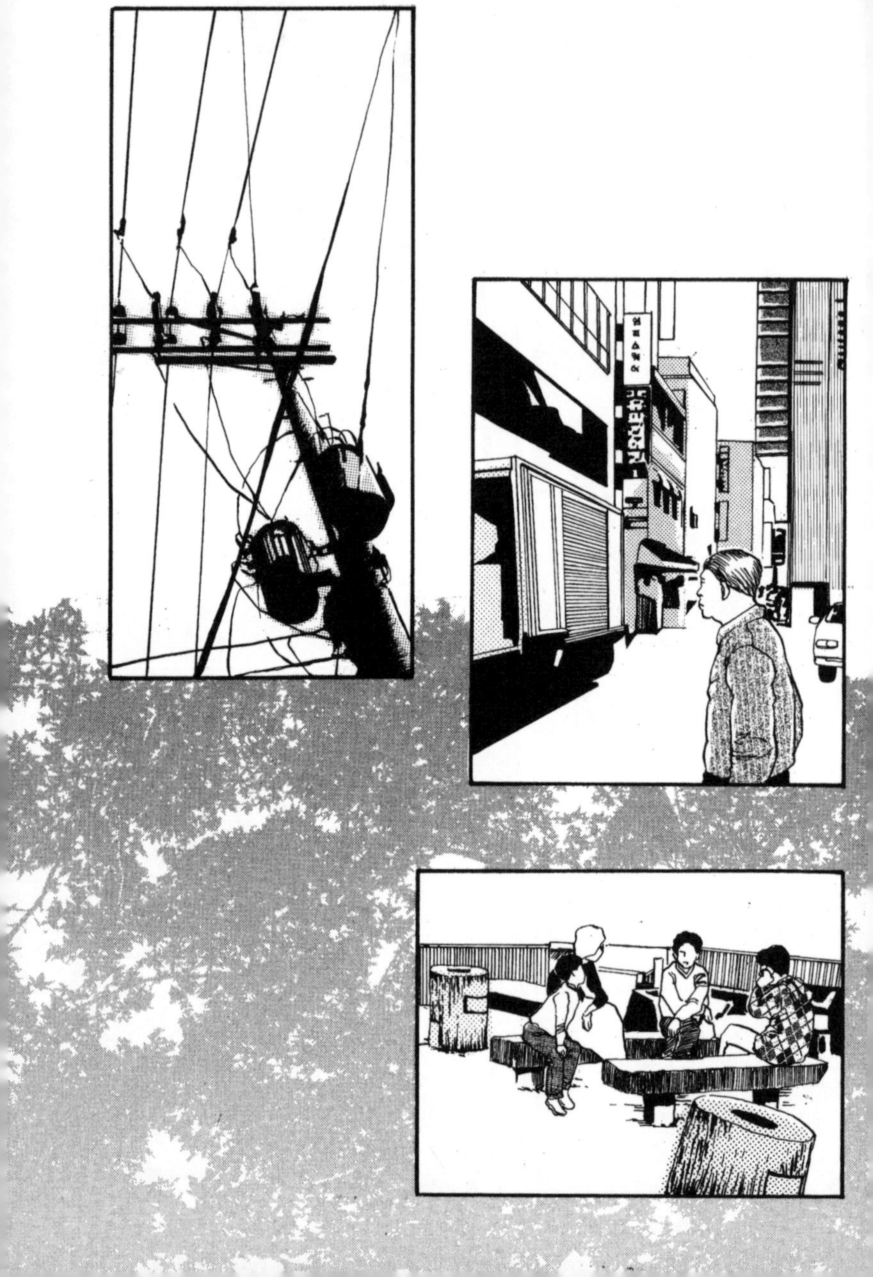

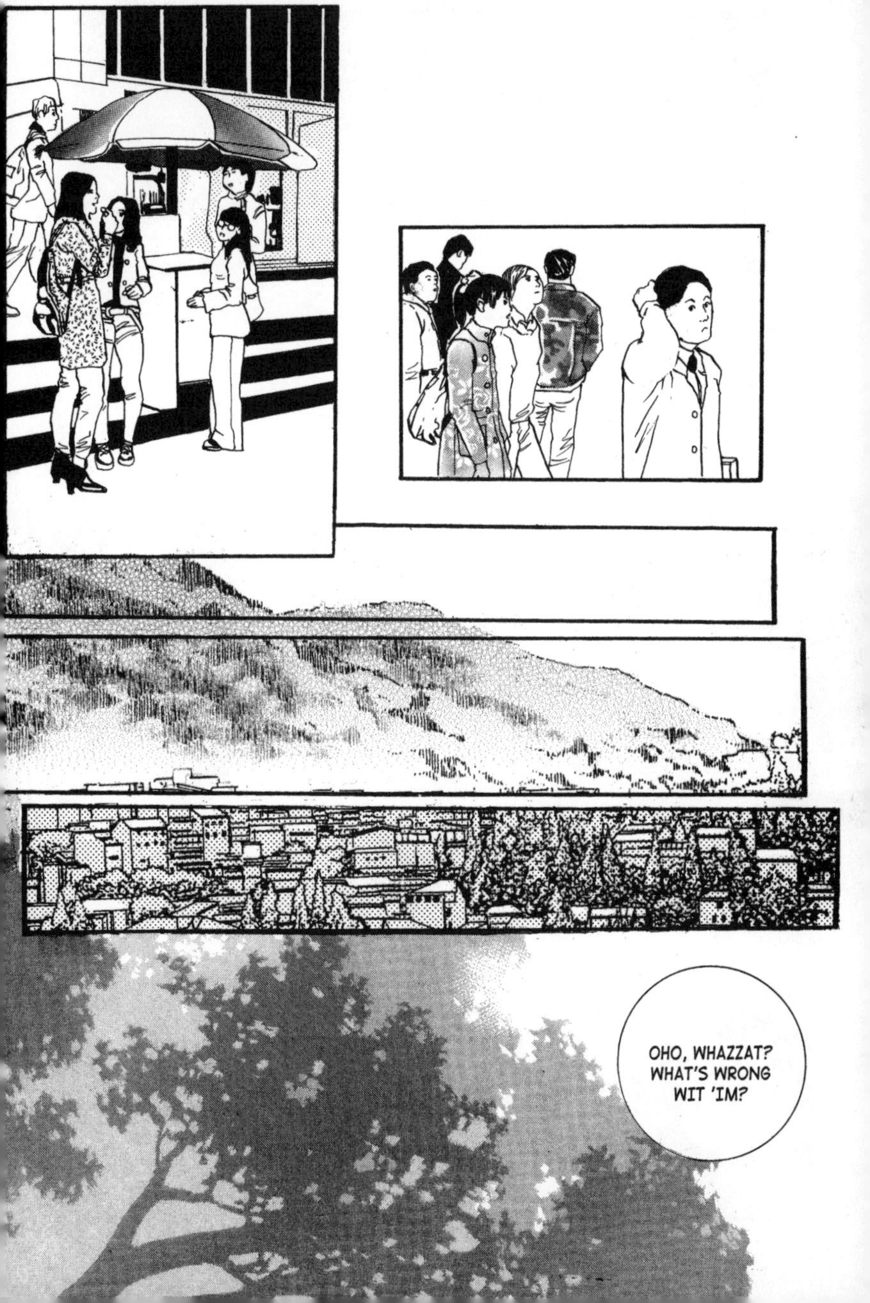
OHO, WHAZZAT? WHAT'S WRONG WIT 'IM?

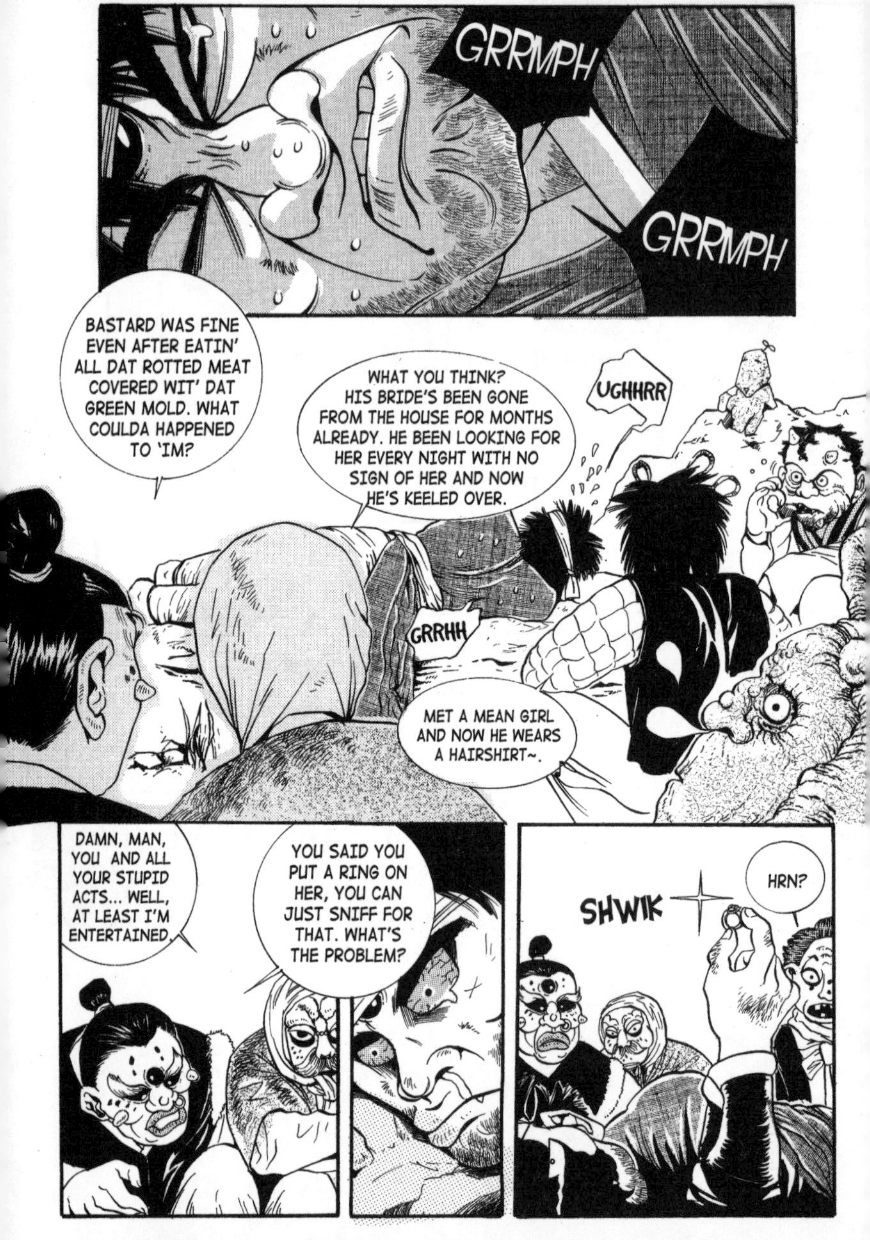
GRRMPH
GRRMPH
BASTARD WAS FINE EVEN AFTER EATIN' ALL DAT ROTTED MEAT COVERED WIT' DAT GREEN MOLD. WHAT COULDA HAPPENED TO 'IM?
WHAT YOU THINK? HIS BRIDE'S BEEN GONE FROM THE HOUSE FOR MONTHS ALREADY. HE BEEN LOOKING FOR HER EVERY NIGHT WITH NO SIGN OF HER AND NOW HE'S KEELED OVER.
UGHHRR
GRRHH
MET A MEAN GIRL AND NOW HE WEARS A HAIRSHIRT~.
DAMN, MAN, YOU AND ALL YOUR STUPID ACTS... WELL, AT LEAST I'M ENTERTAINED.
YOU SAID YOU PUT A RING ON HER, YOU CAN JUST SNIFF FOR THAT. WHAT'S THE PROBLEM?
SHWIK
HRN?

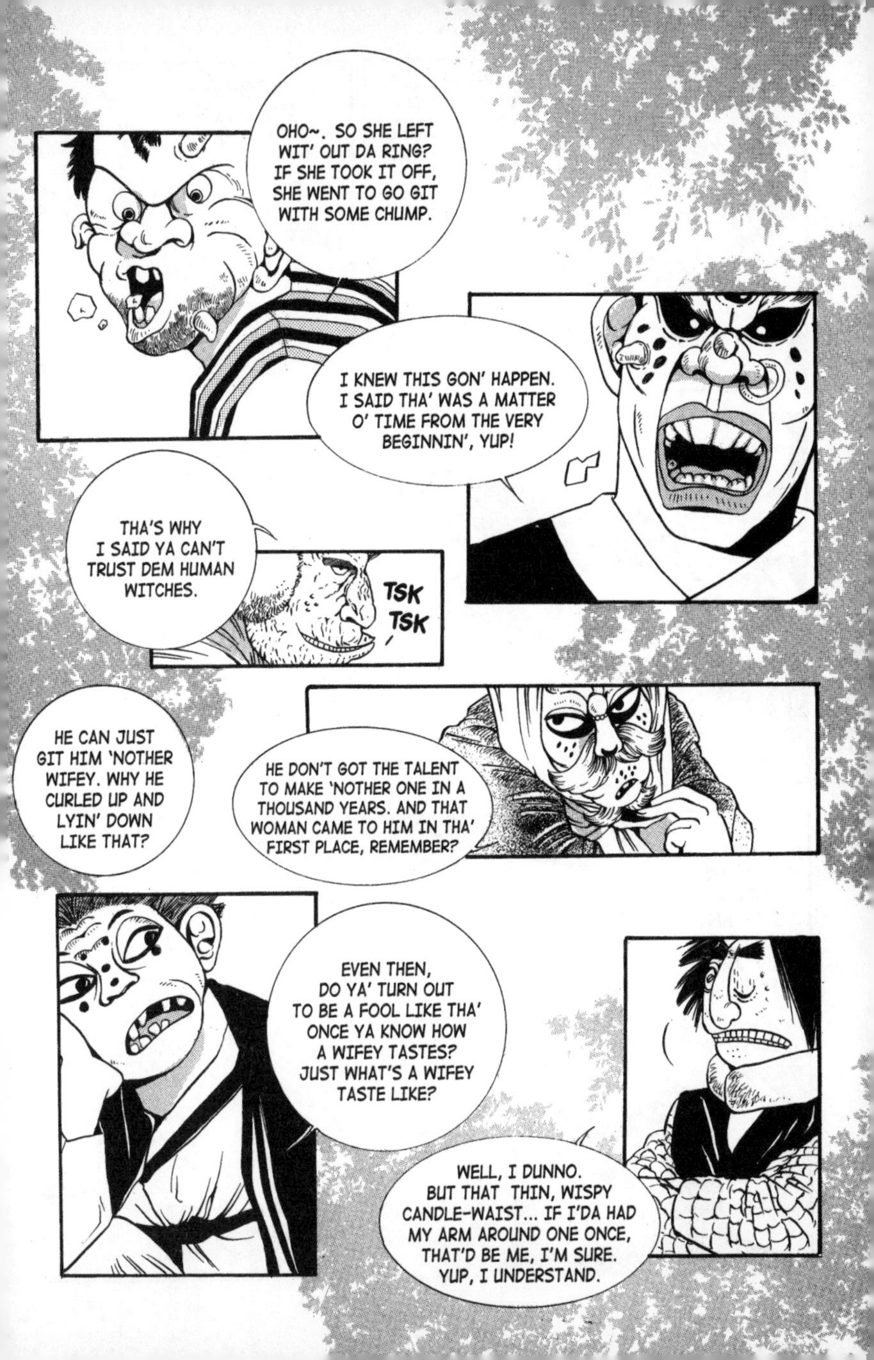
OHO~. SO SHE LEFT WIT' OUT DA RING? IF SHE TOOK IT OFF, SHE WENT TO GO GIT WITH SOME CHUMP.
I KNEW THIS GON' HAPPEN. I SAID THA' WAS A MATTER O' TIME FROM THE VERY BEGINNIN', YUP!
THA'S WHY I SAID YA CAN'T TRUST DEM HUMAN WITCHES.
TSK TSK
HE CAN JUST GIT HIM 'NOTHER WIFEY. WHY HE CURLED UP AND LYIN' DOWN LIKE THAT?
HE DON'T GOT THE TALENT TO MAKE 'NOTHER ONE IN A THOUSAND YEARS. AND THAT WOMAN CAME TO HIM IN THA' FIRST PLACE, REMEMBER?
EVEN THEN, DO YA' TURN OUT TO BE A FOOL LIKE THA' ONCE YA KNOW HOW A WIFEY TASTES? JUST WHAT'S A WIFEY TASTE LIKE?
WELL, I DUNNO. BUT THAT THIN, WISPY CANDLE-WAIST... IF I'DA HAD MY ARM AROUND ONE ONCE, THAT'D BE ME, I'M SURE. YUP, I UNDERSTAND.

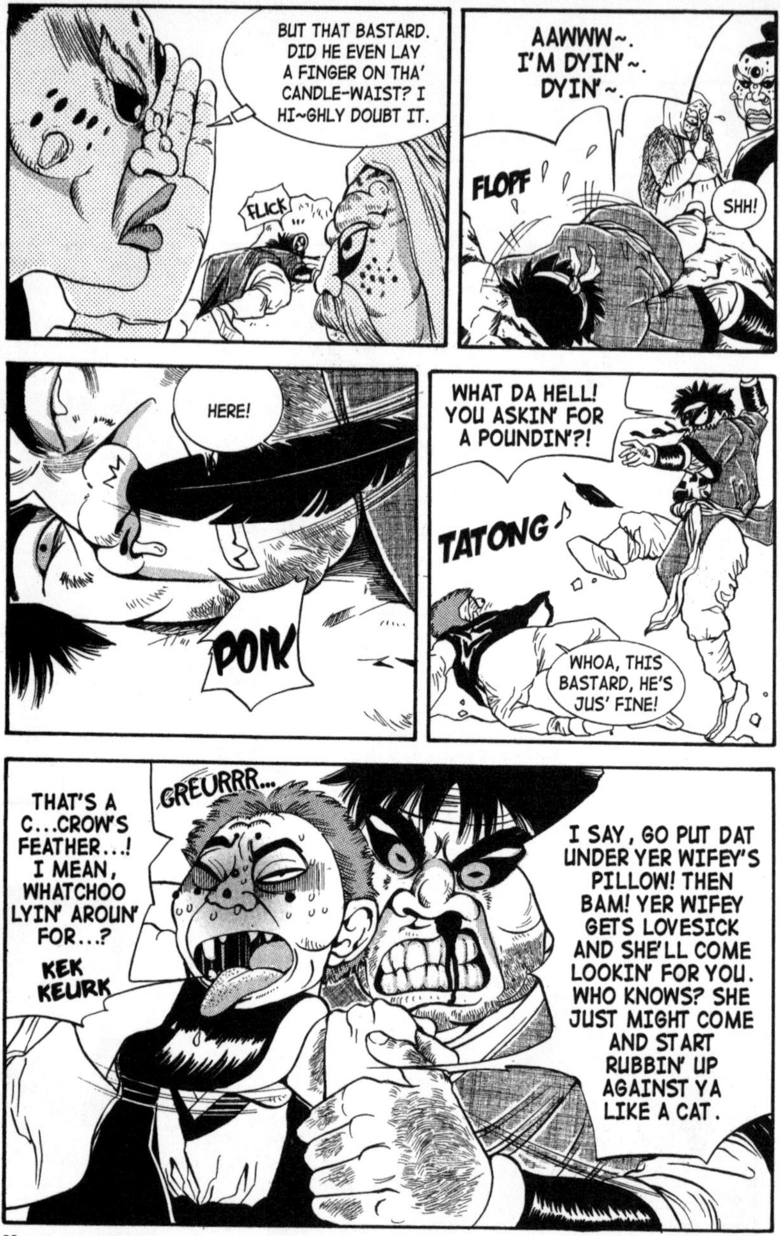
BUT THAT BASTARD. DID HE EVEN LAY A FINGER ON THA' CANDLE-WAIST? I HI~GHLY DOUBT IT.
FLICK
AAWWW~. I'M DYIN'~. DYIN'~.
FLOPF
SHH!
HERE!
POIK
WHAT DA HELL! YOU ASKIN' FOR A POUNDIN'?!
TATONG
WHOA, THIS BASTARD, HE'S JUS' FINE!
THAT'S A C...CROW'S FEATHER...! I MEAN, WHATCHOO LYIN' AROUN' FOR...?
GREURRR...
KEK KEURK
I SAY, GO PUT DAT UNDER YER WIFEY'S PILLOW! THEN BAM! YER WIFEY GETS LOVESICK AND SHE'LL COME LOOKIN' FOR YOU. WHO KNOWS? SHE JUST MIGHT COME AND START RUBBIN' UP AGAINST YA LIKE A CAT.

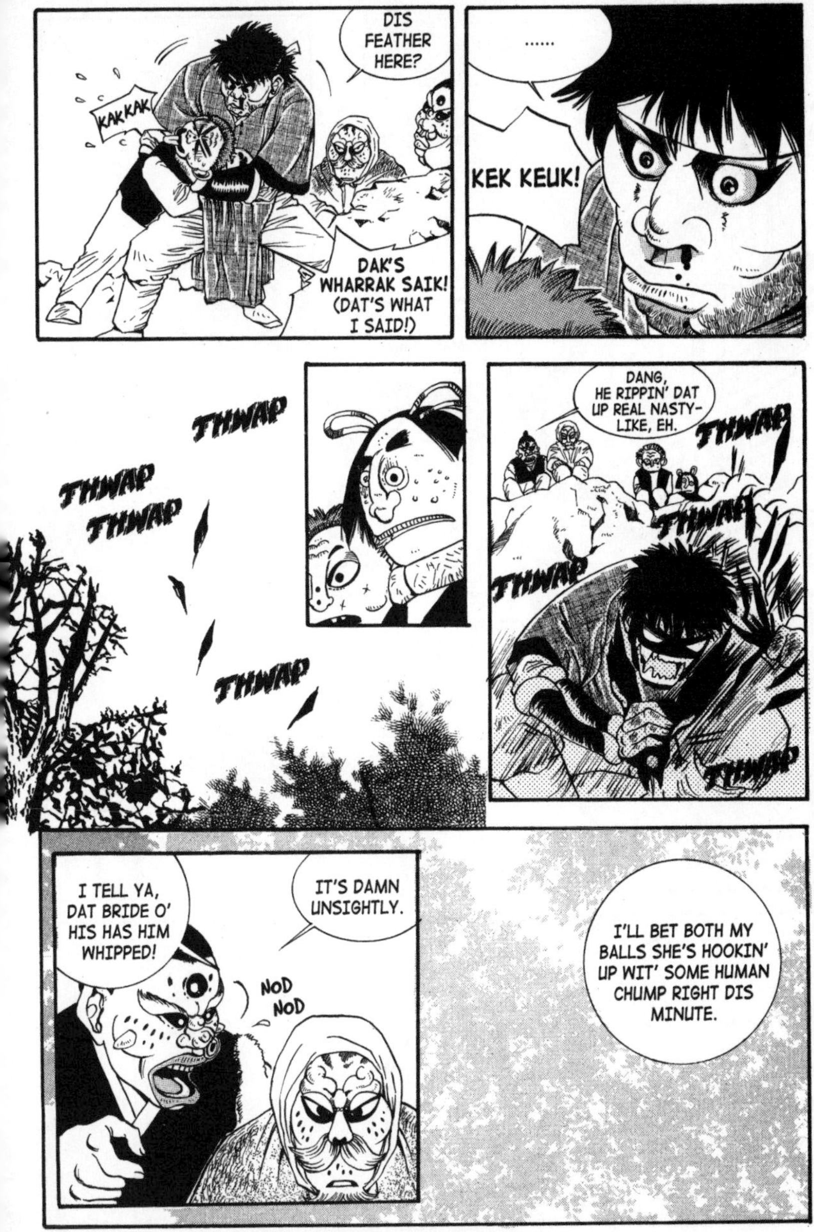
KAKKAK
DIS FEATHER HERE?
DAK'S WHARRAK SAIK! (DAT'S WHAT I SAID!)
......
KEK KEUK!
THWAP
THWAP
THWAP
THWAP
DANG, HE RIPPIN' DAT UP REAL NASTY-LIKE, EH.
THWAP
THWAP
THWAP
THWAP
I TELL YA, DAT BRIDE O' HIS HAS HIM WHIPPED!
NOD NOD
IT'S DAMN UNSIGHTLY.
I'LL BET BOTH MY BALLS SHE'S HOOKIN' UP WIT' SOME HUMAN CHUMP RIGHT DIS MINUTE.

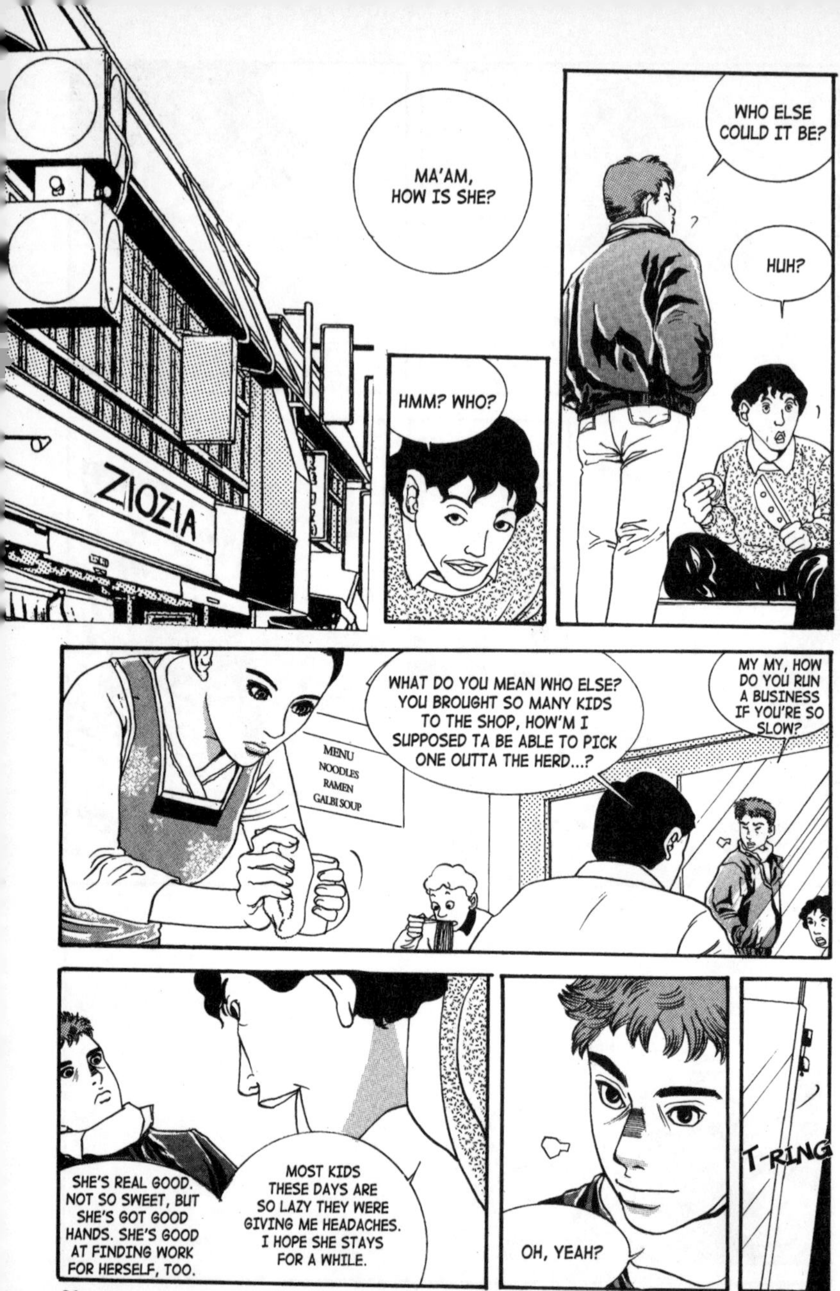
ZIOZIA
MA'AM, HOW IS SHE?
HMM? WHO?
WHO ELSE COULD IT BE?
HUH?
MENU
NOODLES
RAMEN
GALBI SOUP
WHAT DO YOU MEAN WHO ELSE? YOU BROUGHT SO MANY KIDS TO THE SHOP, HOW'M I SUPPOSED TA BE ABLE TO PICK ONE OUTTA THE HERD...?
MY MY, HOW DO YOU RUN A BUSINESS IF YOU'RE SO SLOW?
SHE'S REAL GOOD. NOT SO SWEET, BUT SHE'S GOT GOOD HANDS. SHE'S GOOD AT FINDING WORK FOR HERSELF, TOO.
MOST KIDS THESE DAYS ARE SO LAZY THEY WERE GIVING ME HEADACHES. I HOPE SHE STAYS FOR A WHILE.
OH, YEAH?
T-RING

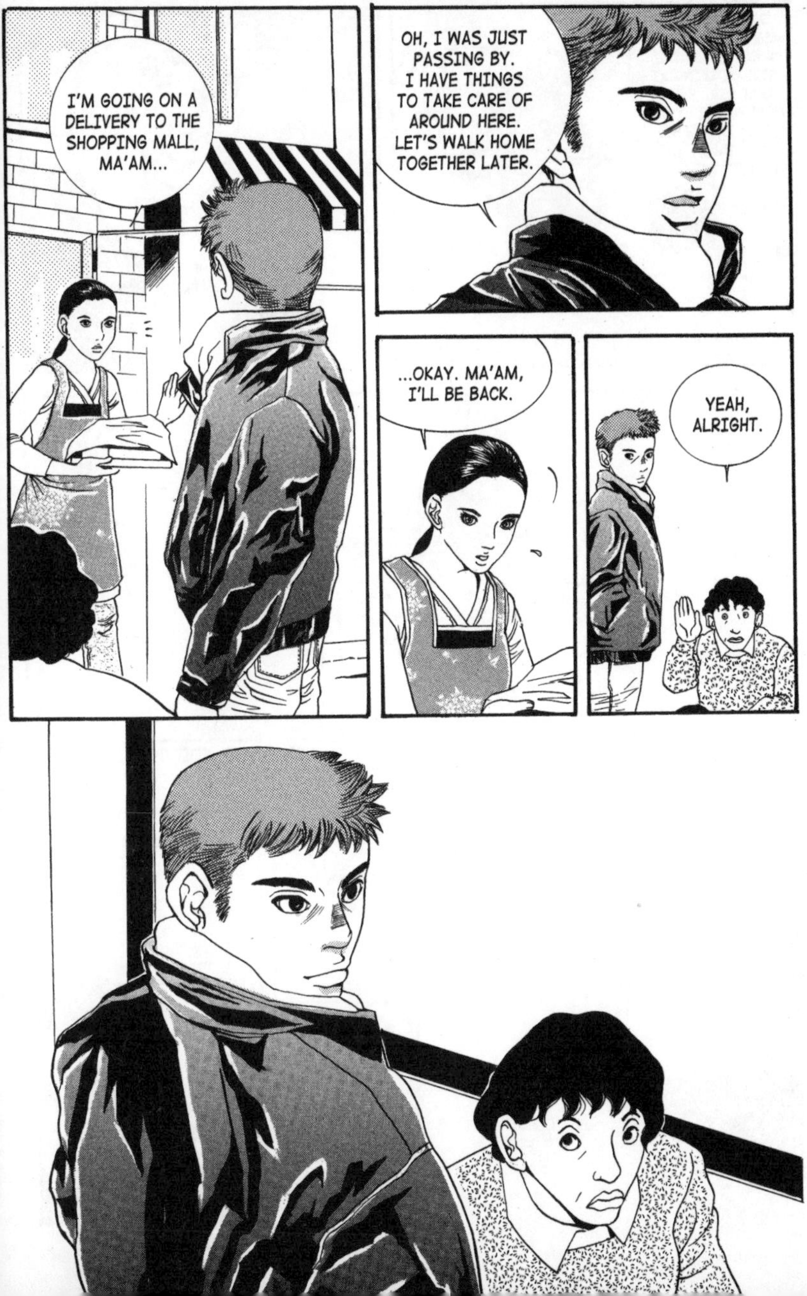
I'M GOING ON A DELIVERY TO THE SHOPPING MALL, MA'AM...
OH, I WAS JUST PASSING BY. I HAVE THINGS TO TAKE CARE OF AROUND HERE. LET'S WALK HOME TOGETHER LATER.
...OKAY. MA'AM, I'LL BE BACK.
YEAH, ALRIGHT.

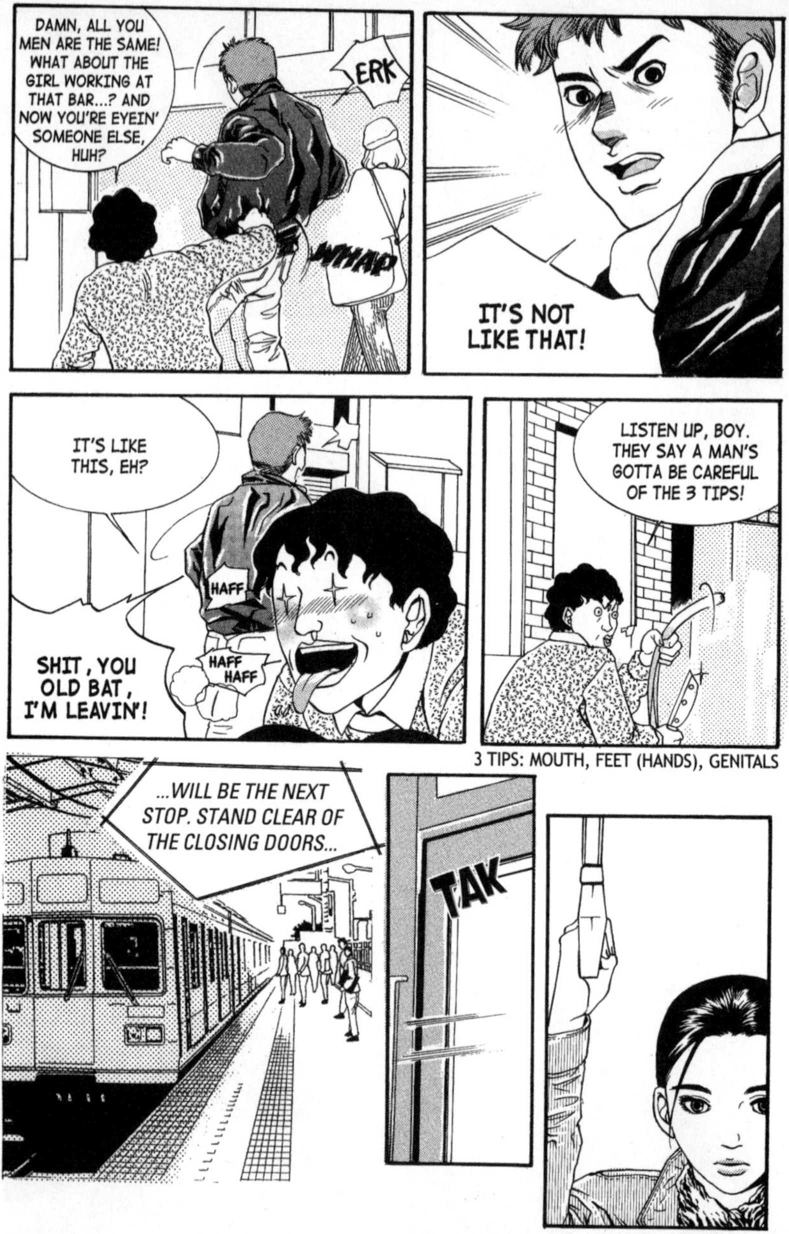
DAMN, ALL YOU MEN ARE THE SAME! WHAT ABOUT THE GIRL WORKING AT THAT BAR...? AND NOW YOU'RE EYEIN' SOMEONE ELSE, HUH?
ERK
WHAP
IT'S NOT LIKE THAT!
IT'S LIKE THIS, EH?
HAFF
HAFF HAFF
SHIT, YOU OLD BAT, I'M LEAVIN'!
LISTEN UP, BOY. THEY SAY A MAN'S GOTTA BE CAREFUL OF THE 3 TIPS!
3 TIPS: MOUTH, FEET (HANDS), GENITALS
...WILL BE THE NEXT STOP. STAND CLEAR OF THE CLOSING DOORS...
TAK

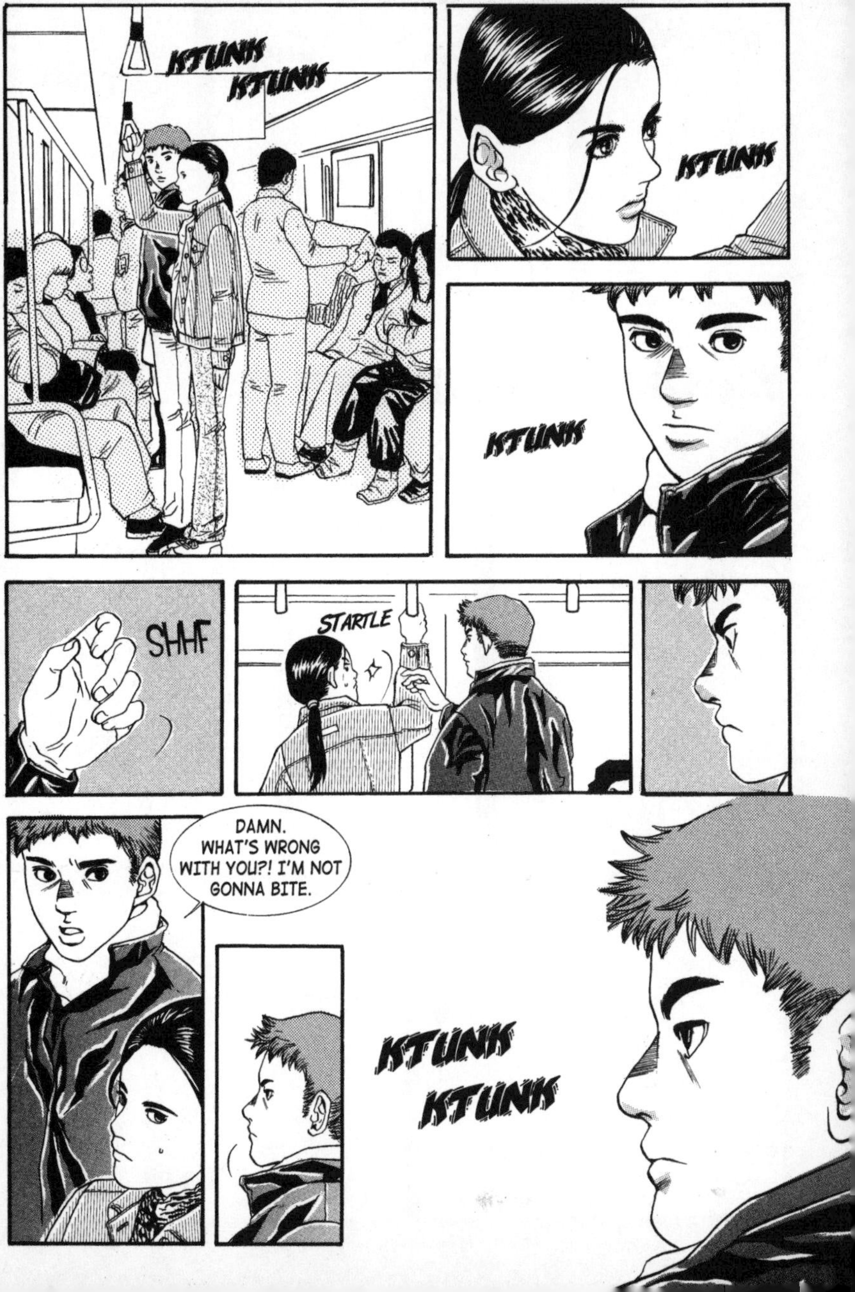
KTUNK
KTUNK
KTUNK
KTUNK
SHHF
STARTLE
DAMN. WHAT'S WRONG WITH YOU?! I'M NOT GONNA BITE.
KTUNK
KTUNK

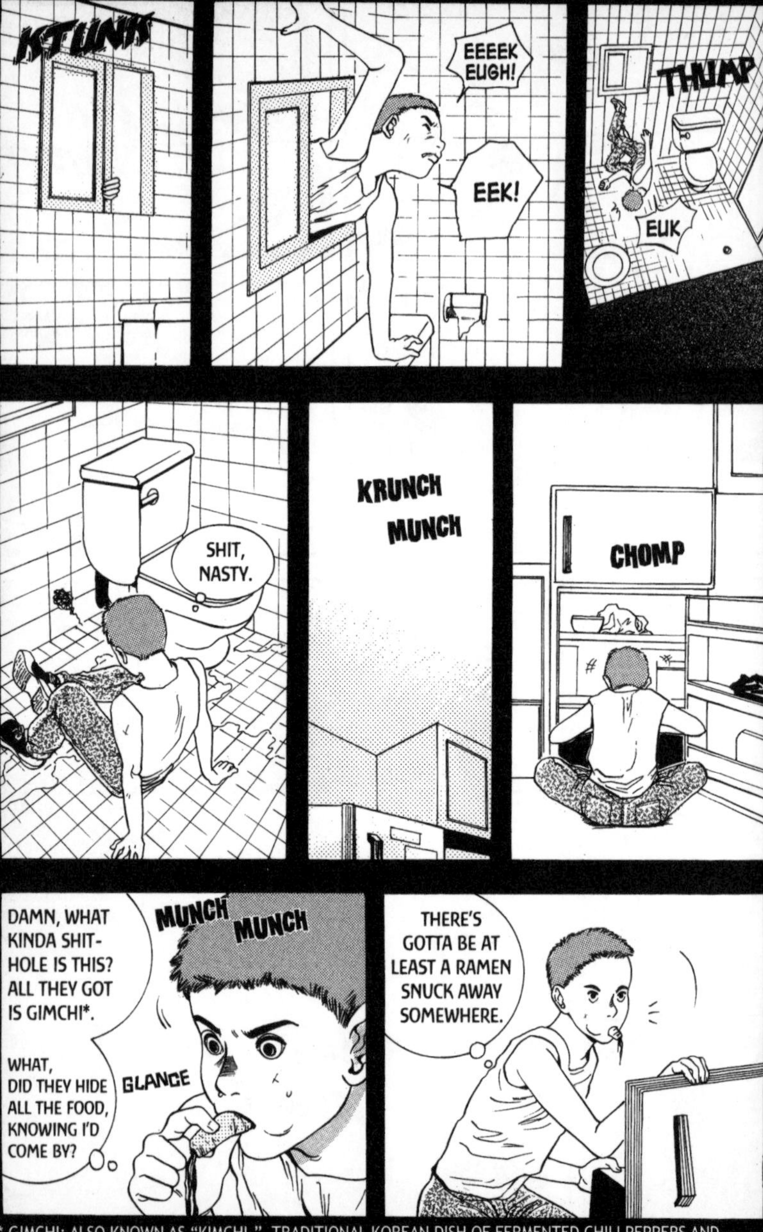
KTUNK
EEEEK EUGH!
EEK!
THUMP
EUK
SHIT, NASTY.
KRUNCH
MUNCH
CHOMP
DAMN, WHAT KINDA SHIT-HOLE IS THIS? ALL THEY GOT IS GIMCHI*.
WHAT, DID THEY HIDE ALL THE FOOD, KNOWING I'D COME BY?
MUNCH
MUNCH
GLANCE
THERE'S GOTTA BE AT LEAST A RAMEN SNUCK AWAY SOMEWHERE.

* GIMCHI: ALSO KNOWN AS "KIMCHI," TRADITIONAL KOREAN DISH OF FERMENTED CHILI PEPPERS AND VEGETABLES, USUALLY MADE FROM KOREAN CABBAGE.

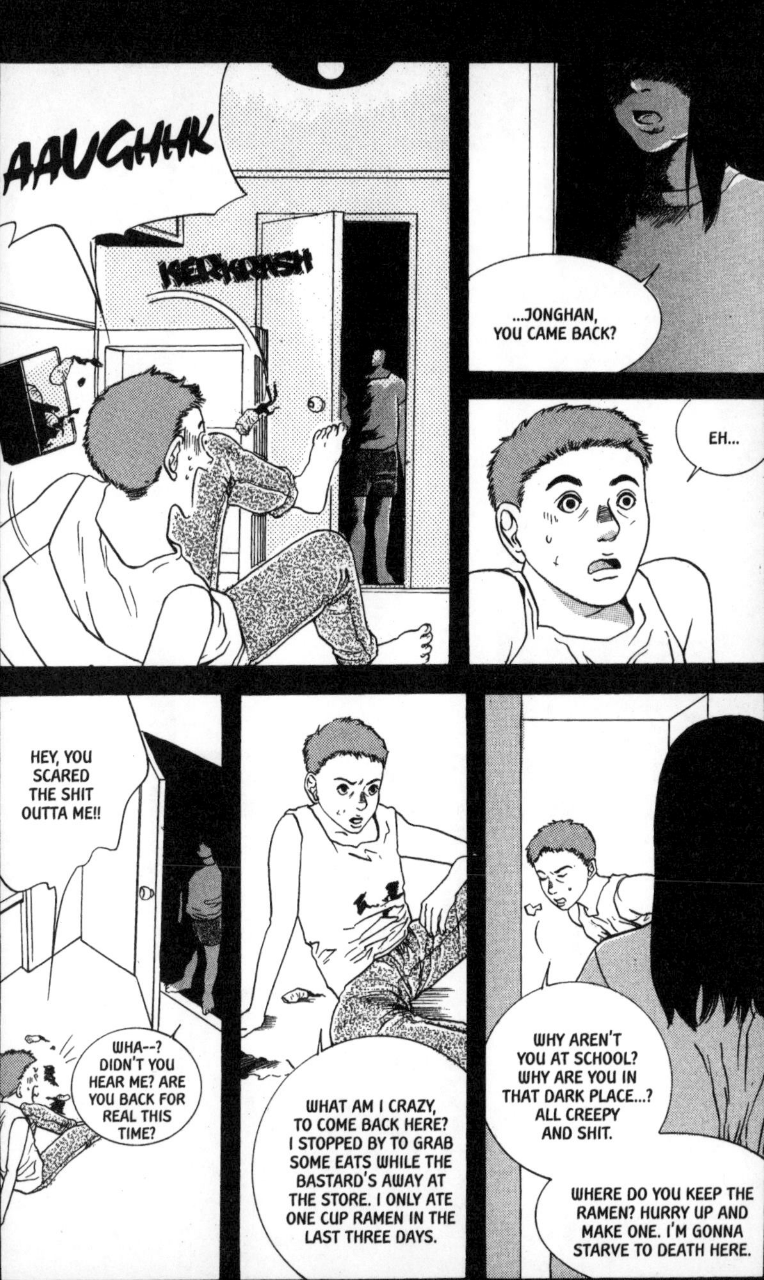
AAUGHHK
KERKRASH
...JONGHAN, YOU CAME BACK?
EH...
HEY, YOU SCARED THE SHIT OUTTA ME!!
WHA--? DIDN'T YOU HEAR ME? ARE YOU BACK FOR REAL THIS TIME?
WHAT AM I CRAZY, TO COME BACK HERE? I STOPPED BY TO GRAB SOME EATS WHILE THE BASTARD'S AWAY AT THE STORE. I ONLY ATE ONE CUP RAMEN IN THE LAST THREE DAYS.
WHY AREN'T YOU AT SCHOOL? WHY ARE YOU IN THAT DARK PLACE...? ALL CREEPY AND SHIT.
WHERE DO YOU KEEP THE RAMEN? HURRY UP AND MAKE ONE. I'M GONNA STARVE TO DEATH HERE.

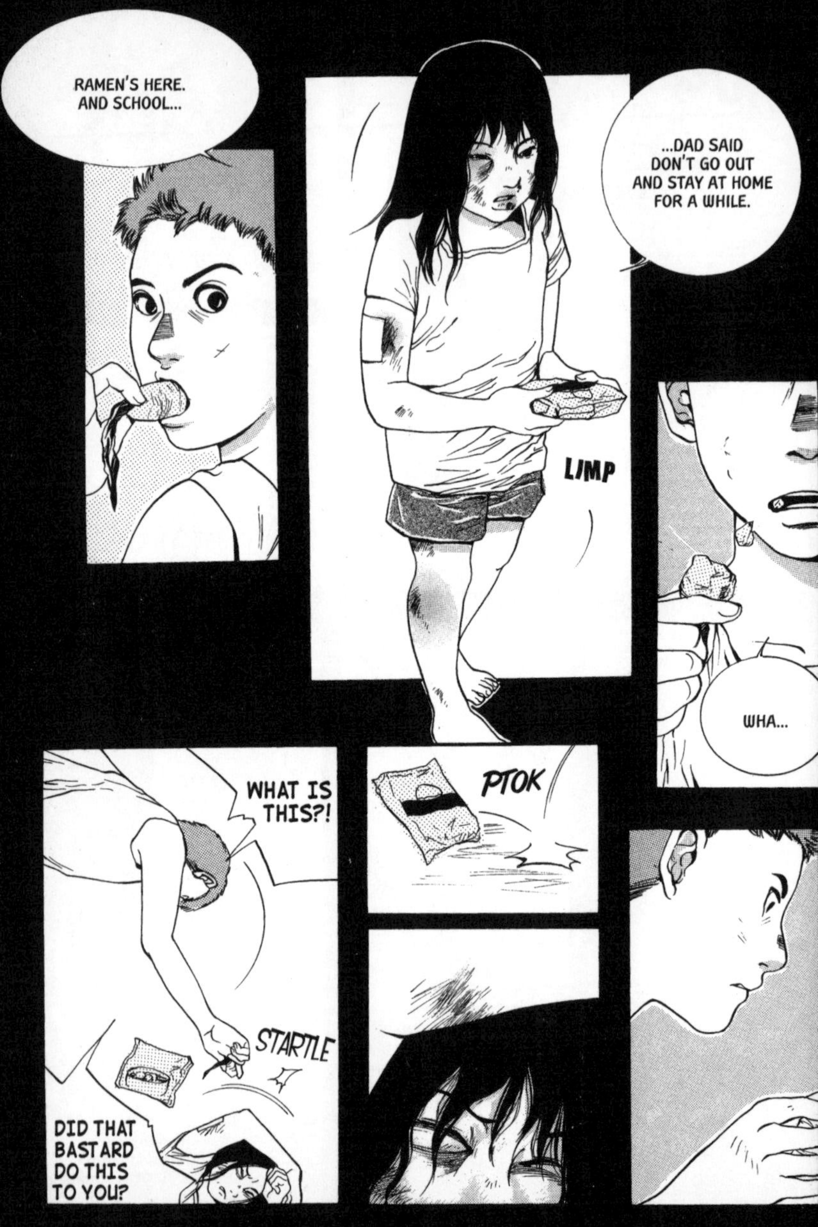

RAMEN'S HERE. AND SCHOOL...
...DAD SAID DON'T GO OUT AND STAY AT HOME FOR A WHILE.
LIMP
WHA...
WHAT IS THIS?!
STARTLE
DID THAT BASTARD DO THIS TO YOU?
PTOK

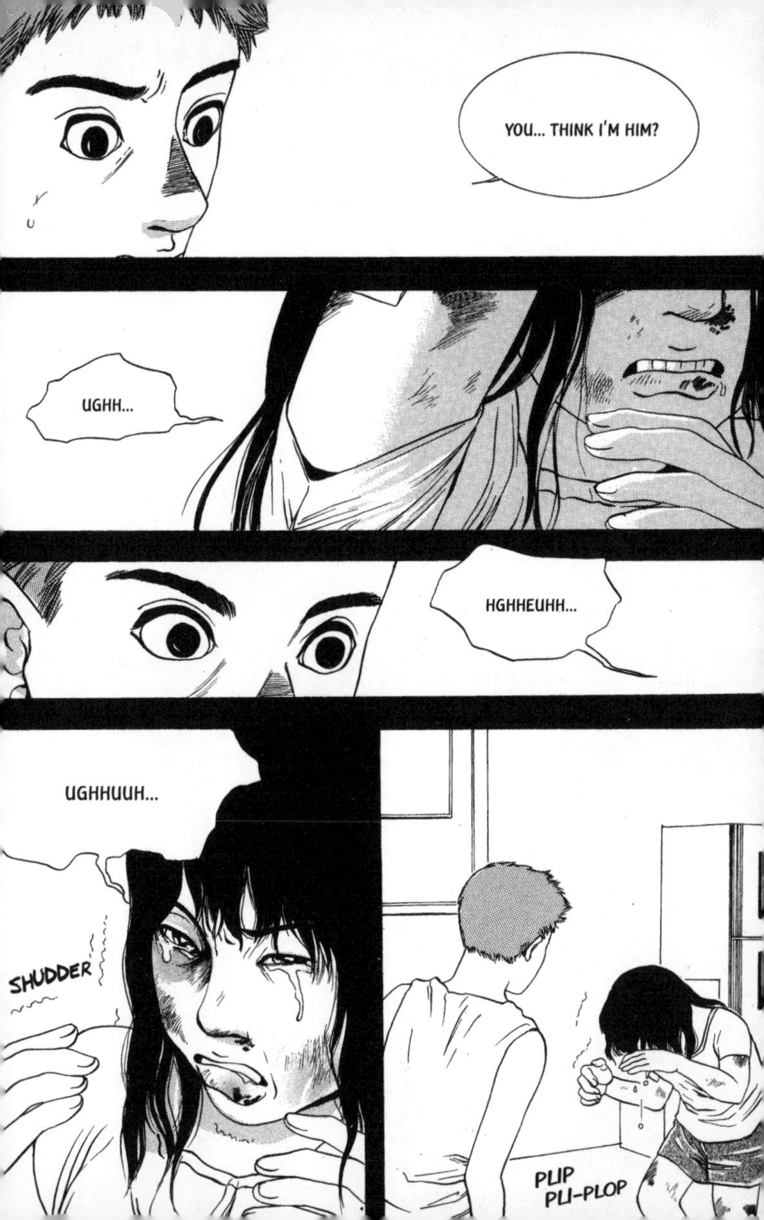
YOU... THINK I'M HIM?
UGHH...
HGHHEUHH...
UGHHUUH...
SHUDDER
PLIP
PLI-PLOP

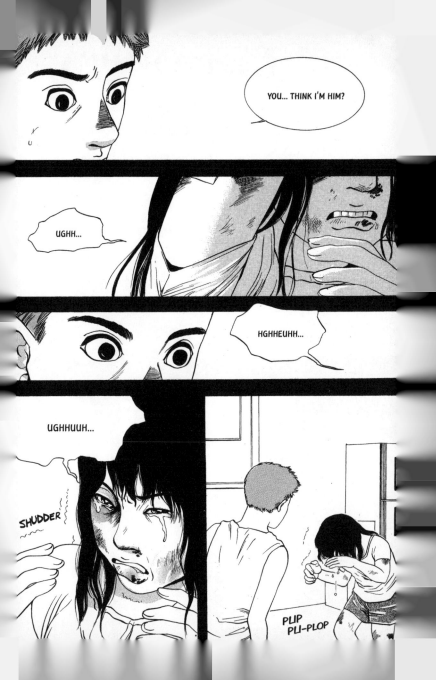

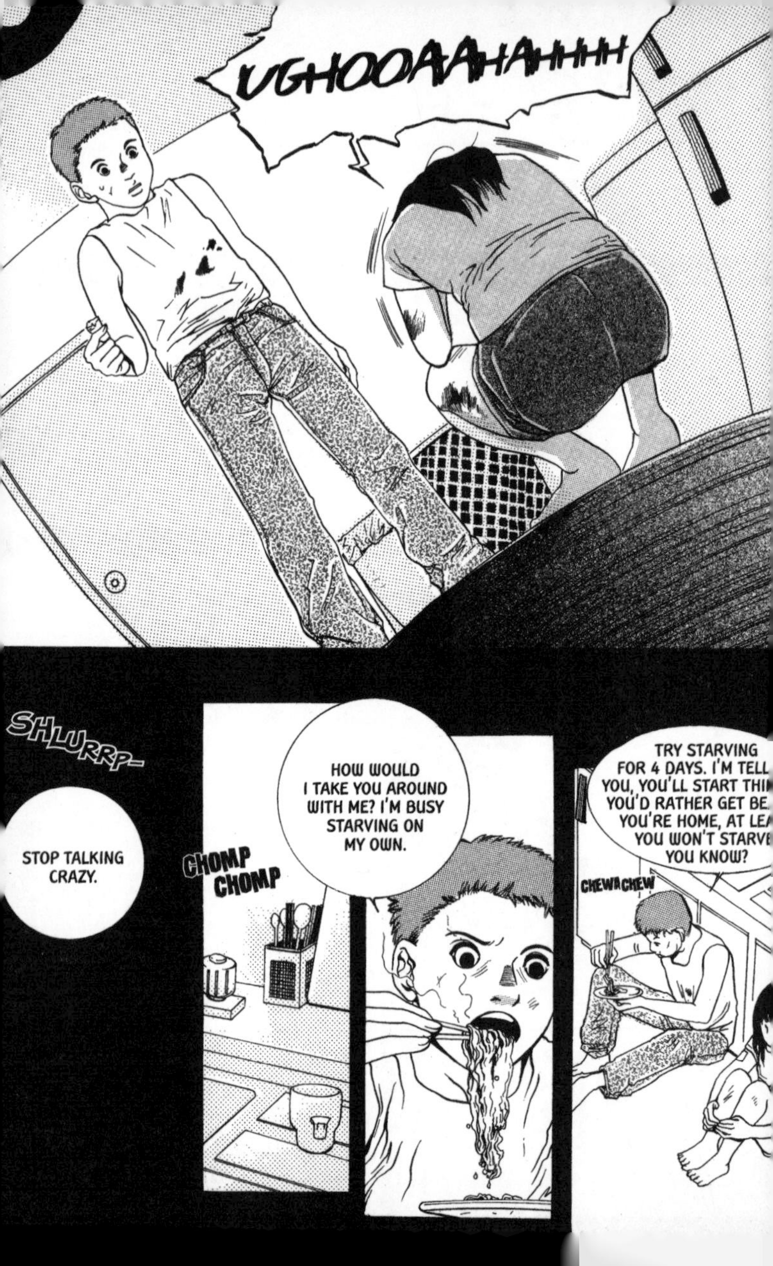
UGHOOAAHAHHHH
SHLURRP-
STOP TALKING CRAZY.
CHOMP CHOMP
HOW WOULD I TAKE YOU AROUND WITH ME? I'M BUSY STARVING ON MY OWN.
CHEWACHEW
TRY STARVING FOR 4 DAYS. I'M TELL YOU, YOU'LL START THI YOU'D RATHER GET BE YOU'RE HOME, AT LEA YOU WON'T STARVE YOU KNOW?

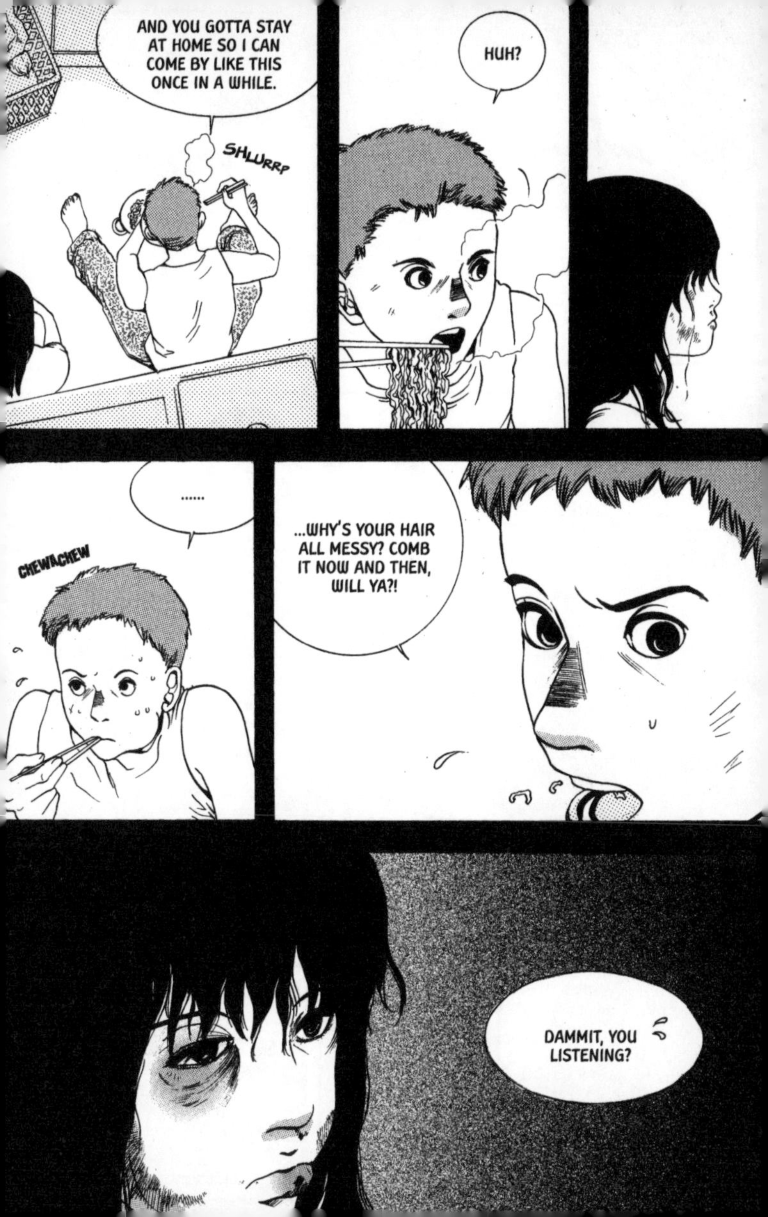
AND YOU GOTTA STAY AT HOME SO I CAN COME BY LIKE THIS ONCE IN A WHILE.
SHLURRP
HUH?
......
CHEWACHEW
...WHY'S YOUR HAIR ALL MESSY? COMB IT NOW AND THEN, WILL YA?!
DAMMIT, YOU LISTENING?

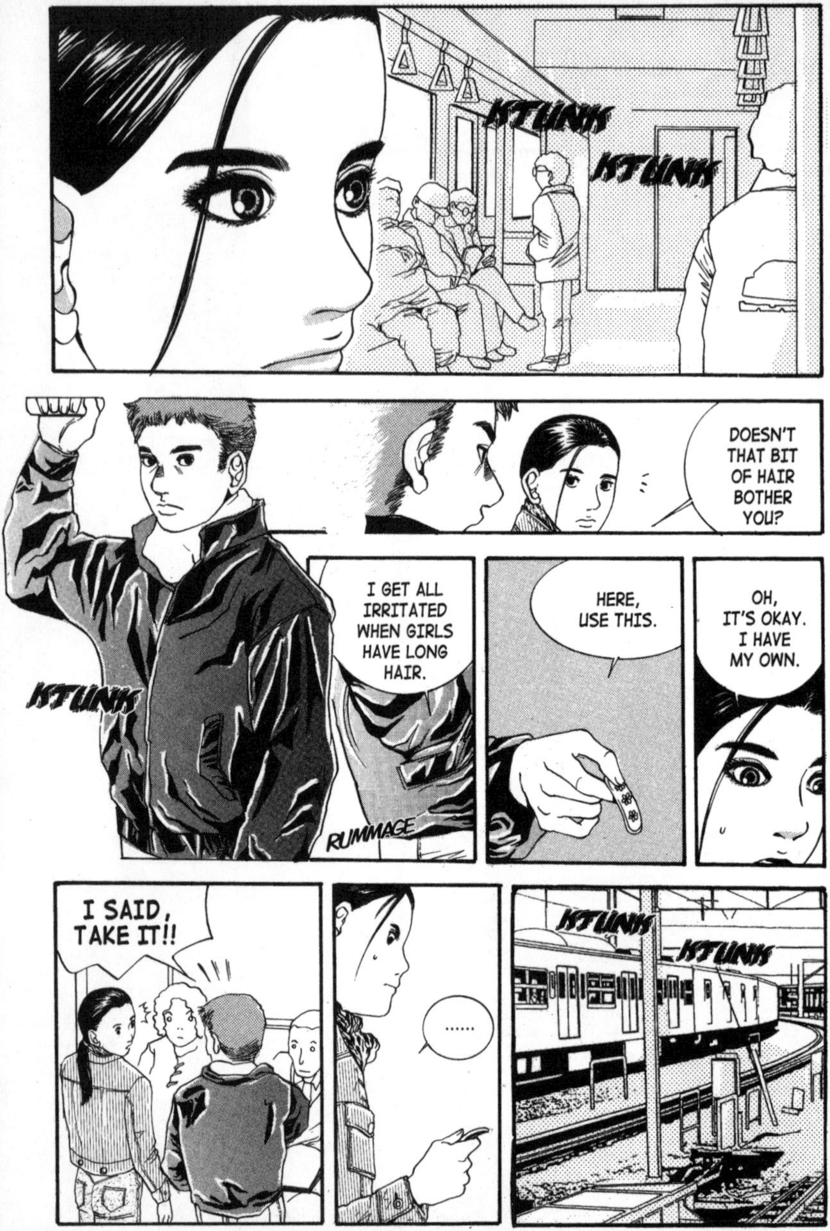
KTUNK
KTUNK
DOESN'T THAT BIT OF HAIR BOTHER YOU?
KTUNK
I GET ALL IRRITATED WHEN GIRLS HAVE LONG HAIR.
RUMMAGE
HERE, USE THIS.
OH, IT'S OKAY. I HAVE MY OWN.
I SAID, TAKE IT!!
......
KTUNK
KTUNK

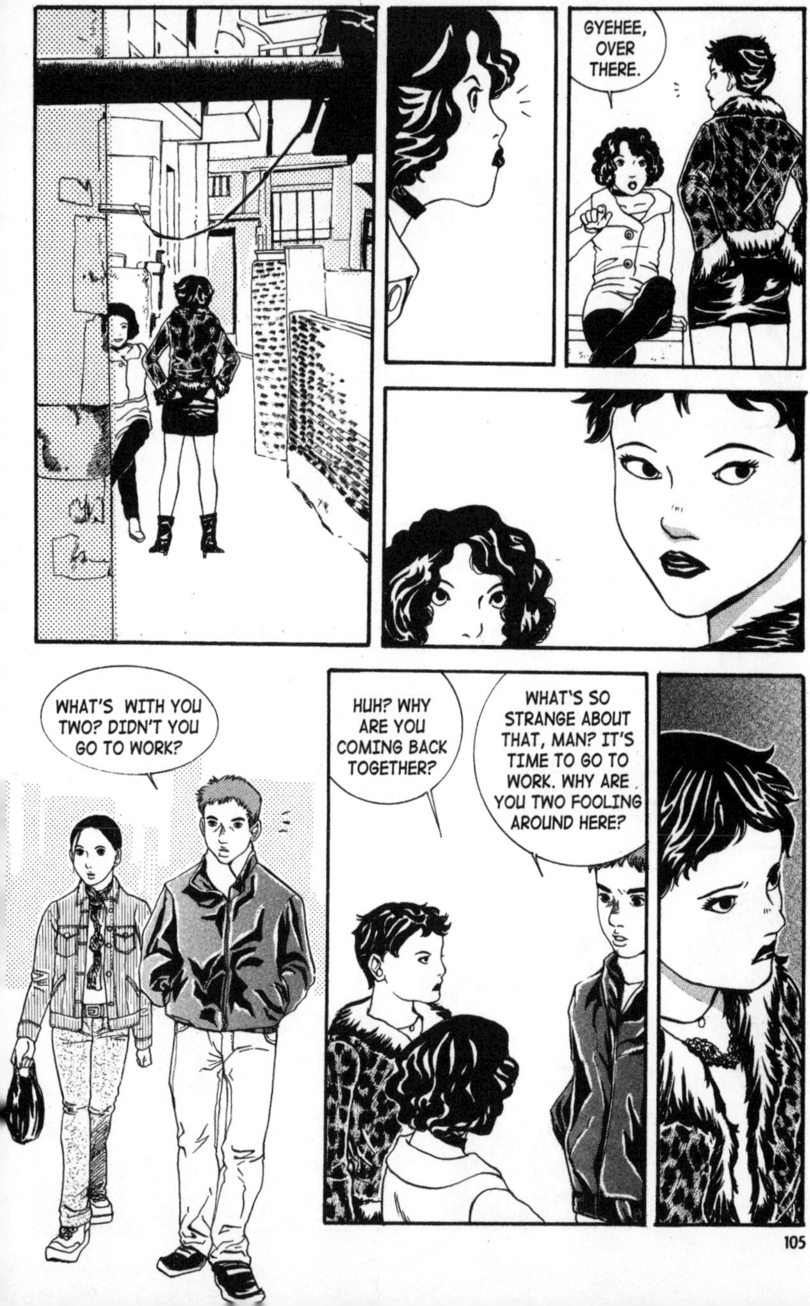
GYEHEE, OVER THERE.
WHAT'S WITH YOU TWO? DIDN'T YOU GO TO WORK?
HUH? WHY ARE YOU COMING BACK TOGETHER?
WHAT'S SO STRANGE ABOUT THAT, MAN? IT'S TIME TO GO TO WORK. WHY ARE YOU TWO FOOLING AROUND HERE?

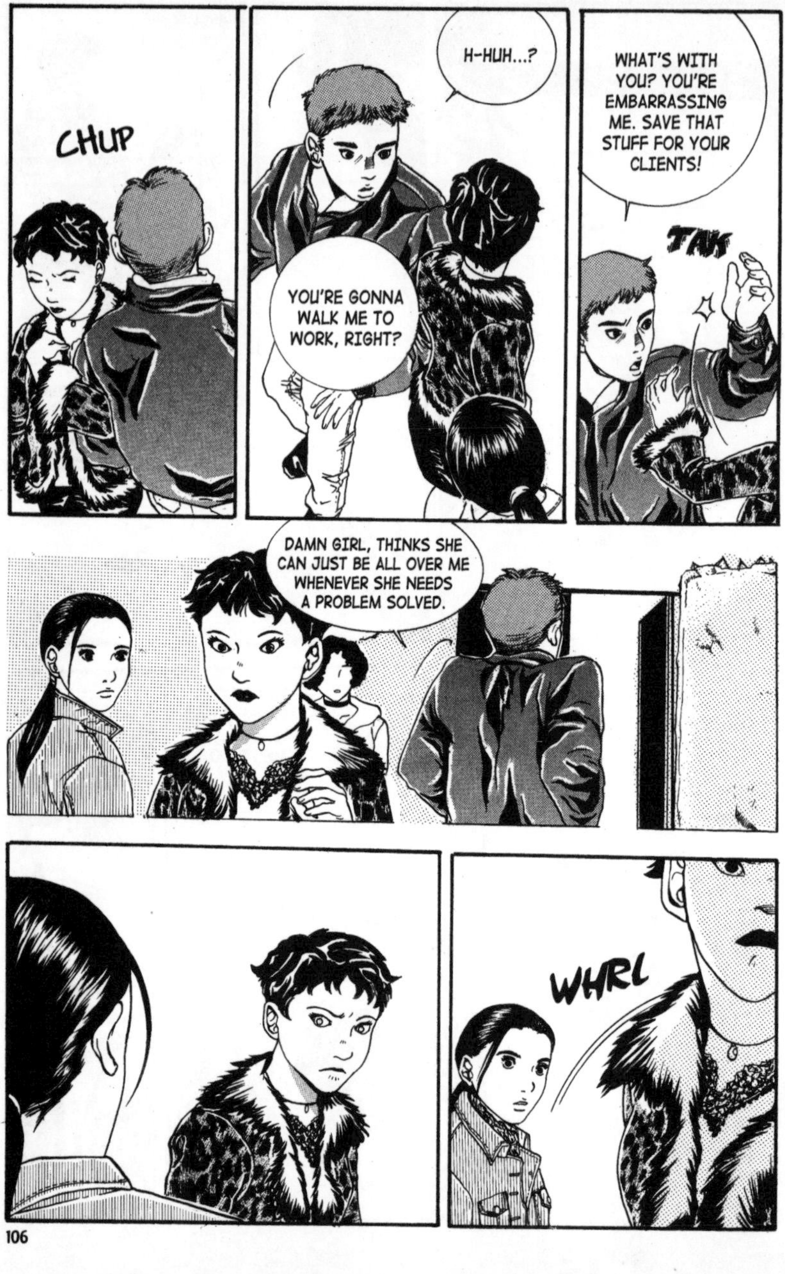
CHUP
H-HUH...?
YOU'RE GONNA WALK ME TO WORK, RIGHT?
WHAT'S WITH YOU? YOU'RE EMBARRASSING ME. SAVE THAT STUFF FOR YOUR CLIENTS!
TAK
DAMN GIRL, THINKS SHE CAN JUST BE ALL OVER ME WHENEVER SHE NEEDS A PROBLEM SOLVED.
WHRL

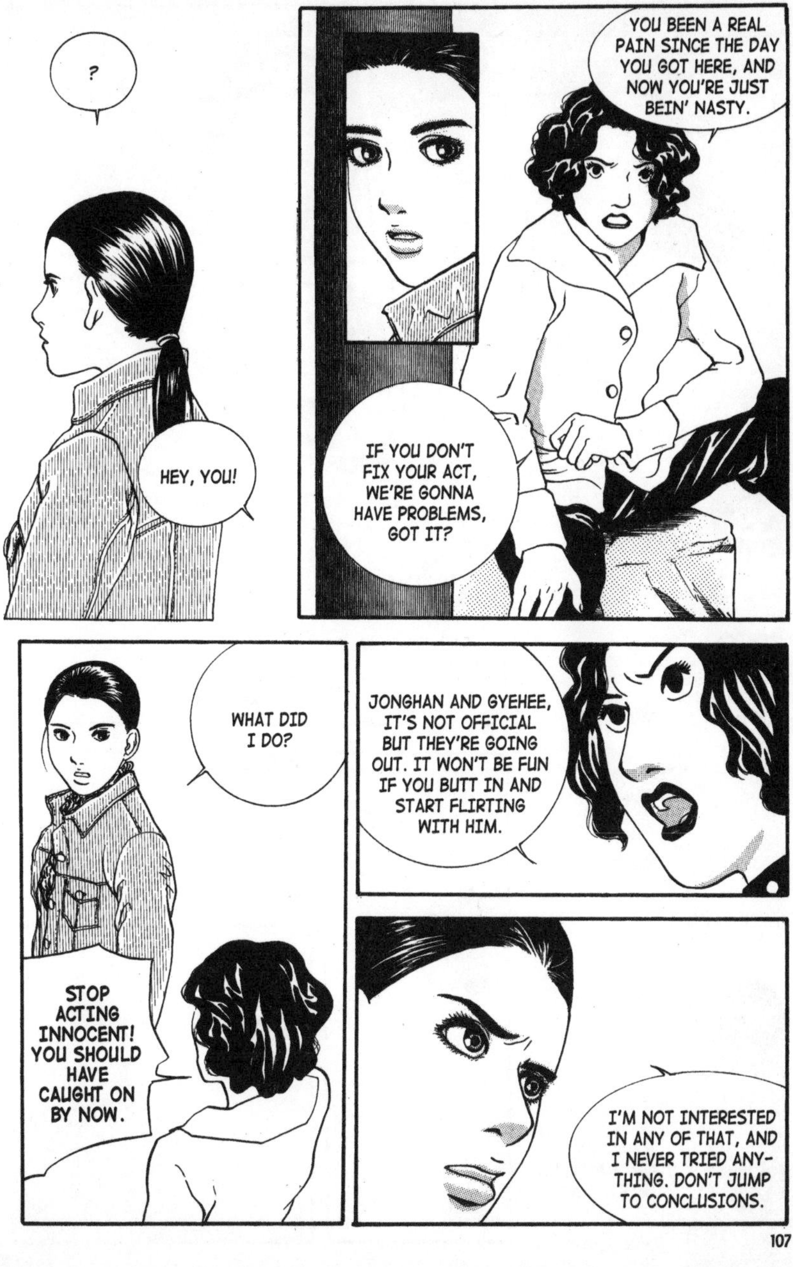
?
HEY, YOU!
YOU BEEN A REAL PAIN SINCE THE DAY YOU GOT HERE, AND NOW YOU'RE JUST BEIN' NASTY.
IF YOU DON'T FIX YOUR ACT, WE'RE GONNA HAVE PROBLEMS, GOT IT?
WHAT DID I DO?
STOP ACTING INNOCENT! YOU SHOULD HAVE CAUGHT ON BY NOW.
JONGHAN AND GYEHEE, IT'S NOT OFFICIAL BUT THEY'RE GOING OUT. IT WON'T BE FUN IF YOU BUTT IN AND START FLIRTING WITH HIM.
I'M NOT INTERESTED IN ANY OF THAT, AND I NEVER TRIED ANY-THING. DON'T JUMP TO CONCLUSIONS.

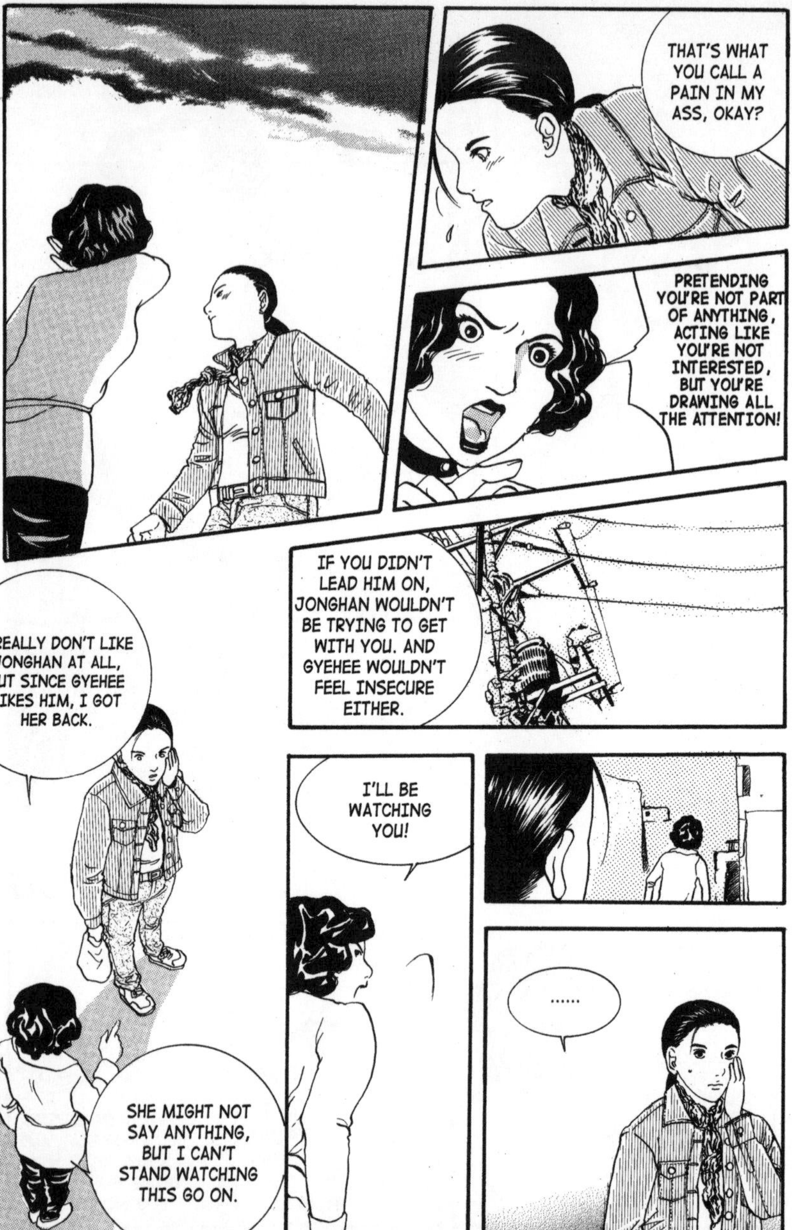
THAT'S WHAT YOU CALL A PAIN IN MY ASS, OKAY?
PRETENDING YOU'RE NOT PART OF ANYTHING, ACTING LIKE YOU'RE NOT INTERESTED, BUT YOU'RE DRAWING ALL THE ATTENTION!
IF YOU DIDN'T LEAD HIM ON, JONGHAN WOULDN'T BE TRYING TO GET WITH YOU. AND GYEHEE WOULDN'T FEEL INSECURE EITHER.
I REALLY DON'T LIKE JONGHAN AT ALL, BUT SINCE GYEHEE LIKES HIM, I GOT HER BACK.
SHE MIGHT NOT SAY ANYTHING, BUT I CAN'T STAND WATCHING THIS GO ON.
I'LL BE WATCHING YOU!
......

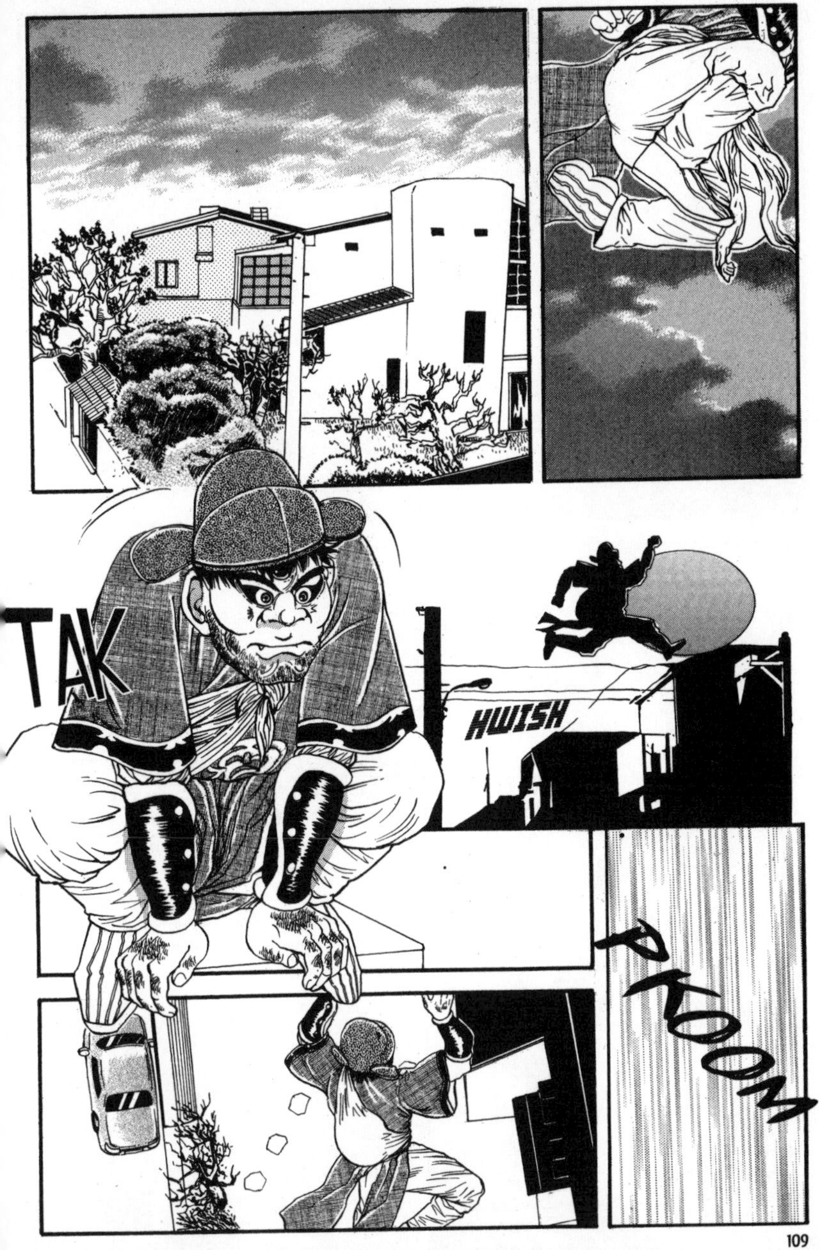
TAK
HWISH
PKOOM

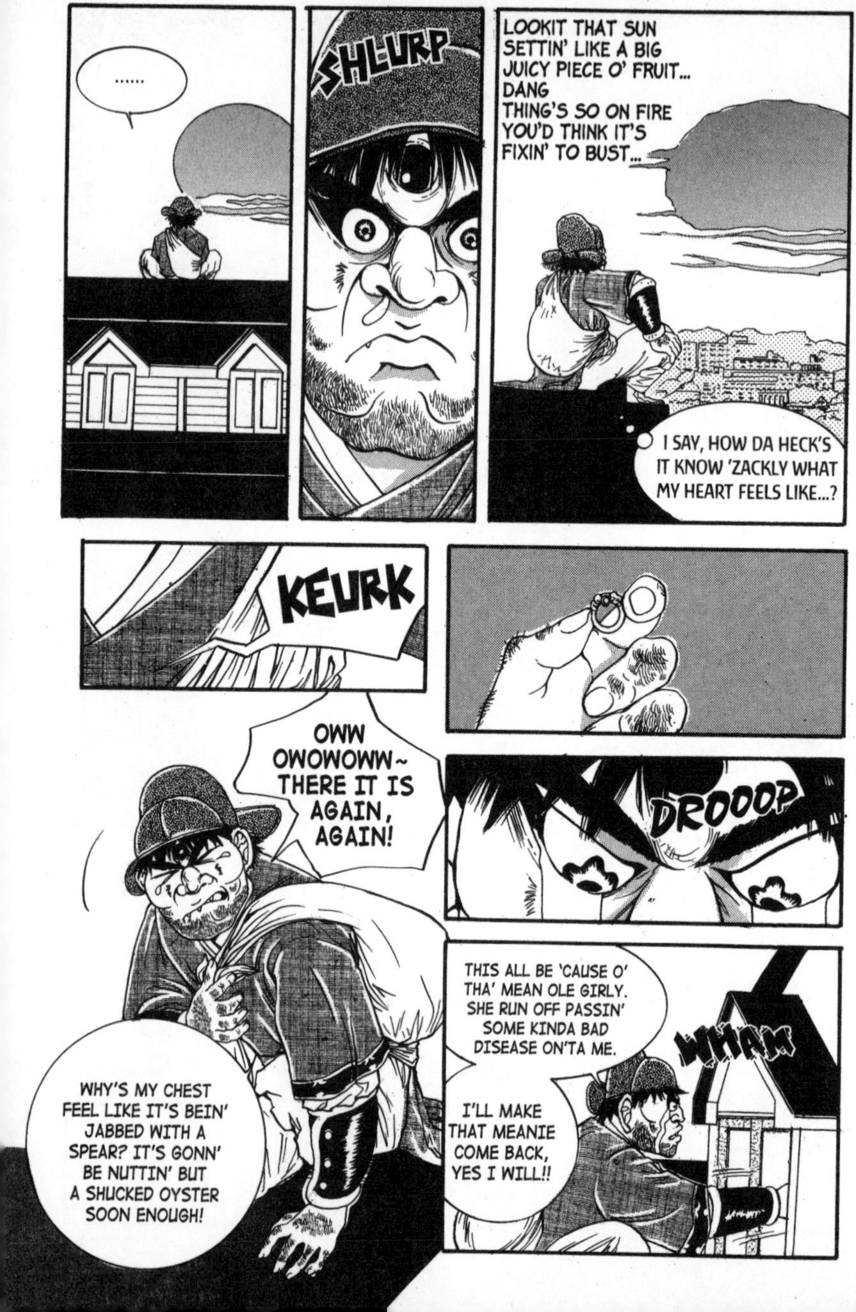
......
SHLURP
LOOKIT THAT SUN SETTIN' LIKE A BIG JUICY PIECE O' FRUIT... DANG THING'S SO ON FIRE YOU'D THINK IT'S FIXIN' TO BUST...
I SAY, HOW DA HECK'S IT KNOW 'ZACKLY WHAT MY HEART FEELS LIKE...?
KEURK
OWW OWOWOWW~ THERE IT IS AGAIN, AGAIN!
WHY'S MY CHEST FEEL LIKE IT'S BEIN' JABBED WITH A SPEAR? IT'S GONN' BE NUTTIN' BUT A SHUCKED OYSTER SOON ENOUGH!
DROOOP
THIS ALL BE 'CAUSE O' THA' MEAN OLE GIRLY. SHE RUN OFF PASSIN' SOME KINDA BAD DISEASE ON'TA ME.
WHAM
I'LL MAKE THAT MEANIE COME BACK, YES I WILL!!

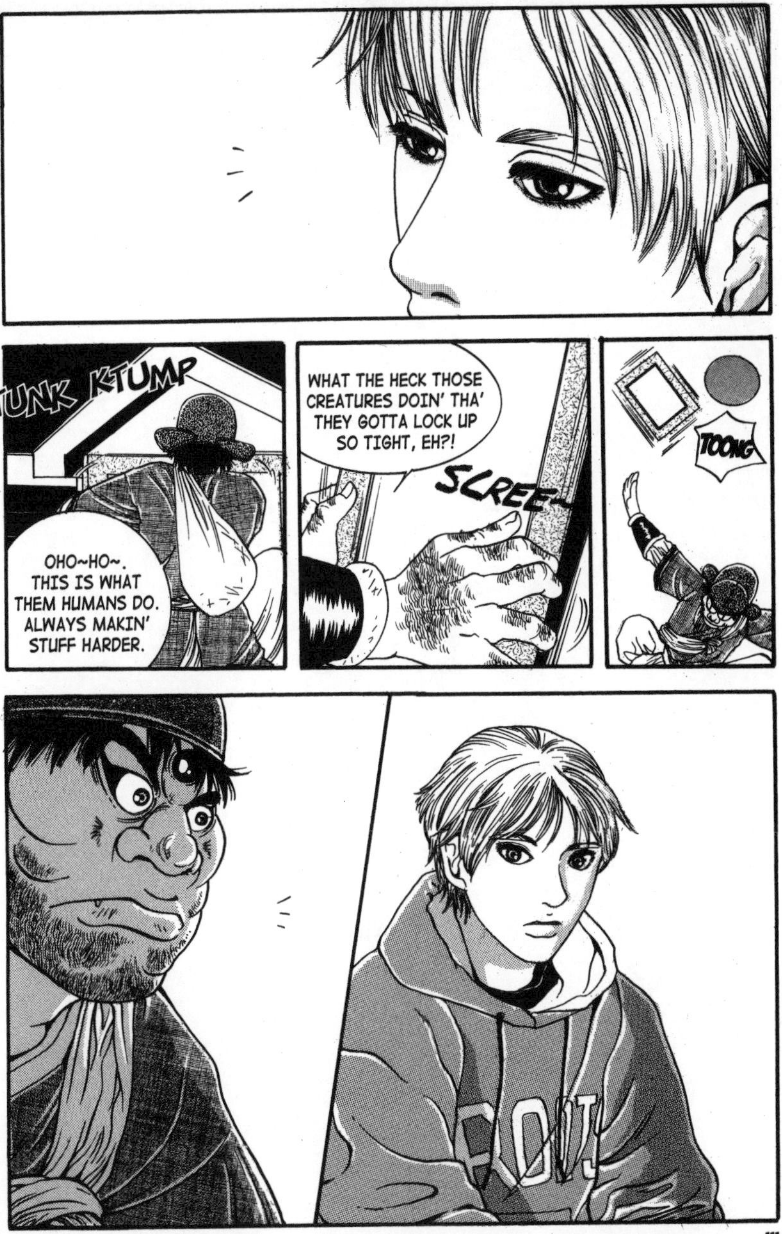
TUNK KTUMP
OHO~HO~. THIS IS WHAT THEM HUMANS DO. ALWAYS MAKIN' STUFF HARDER.
WHAT THE HECK THOSE CREATURES DOIN' THA' THEY GOTTA LOCK UP SO TIGHT, EH?!
SCREE-
TOONG

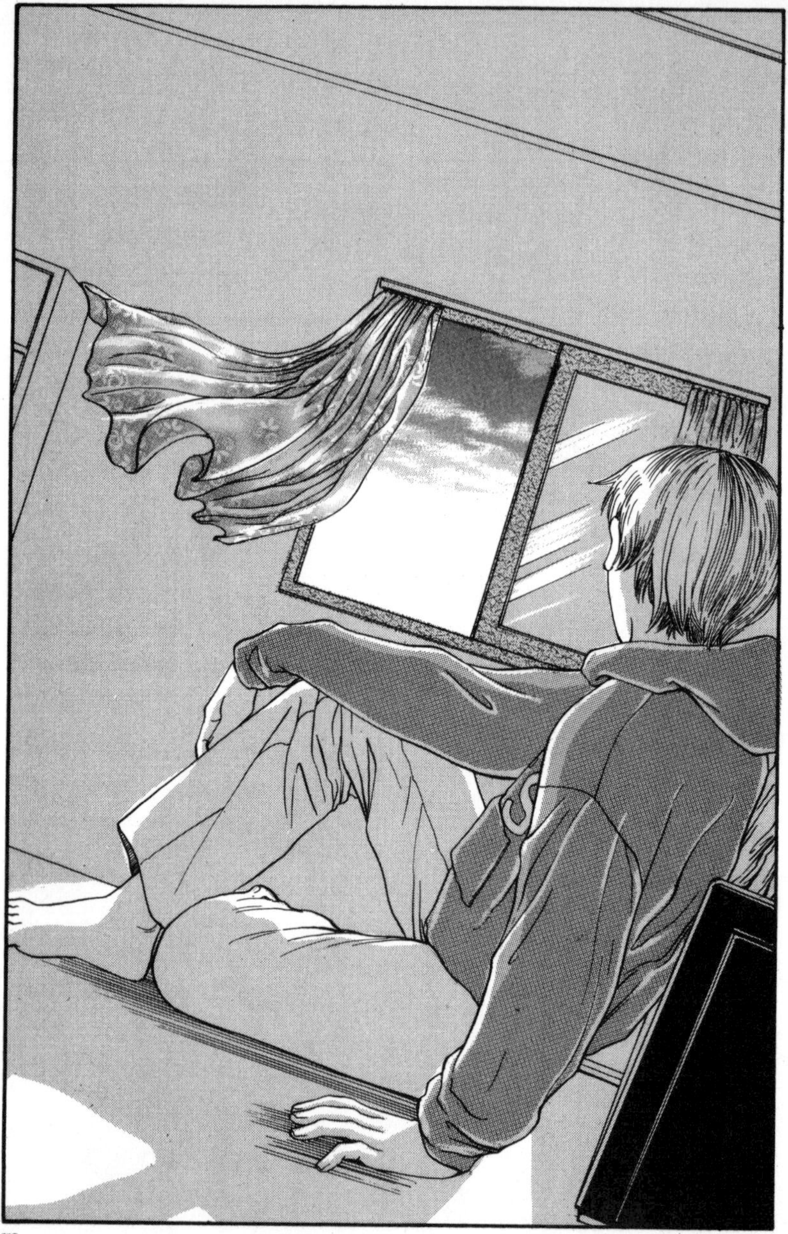

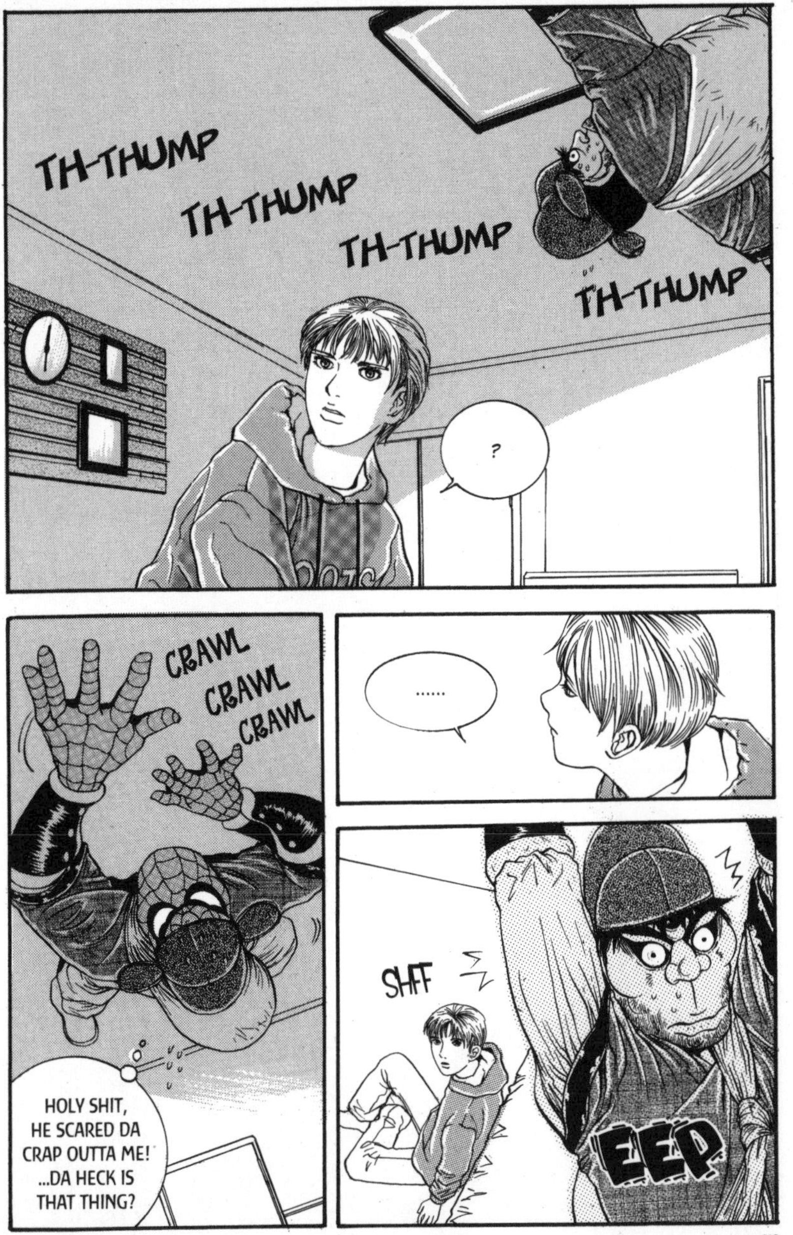
TH-THUMP
TH-THUMP
TH-THUMP
TH-THUMP
?
CRAWL
CRAWL
CRAWL
HOLY SHIT, HE SCARED DA CRAP OUTTA ME! ...DA HECK IS THAT THING?
......
SHFF
EEP

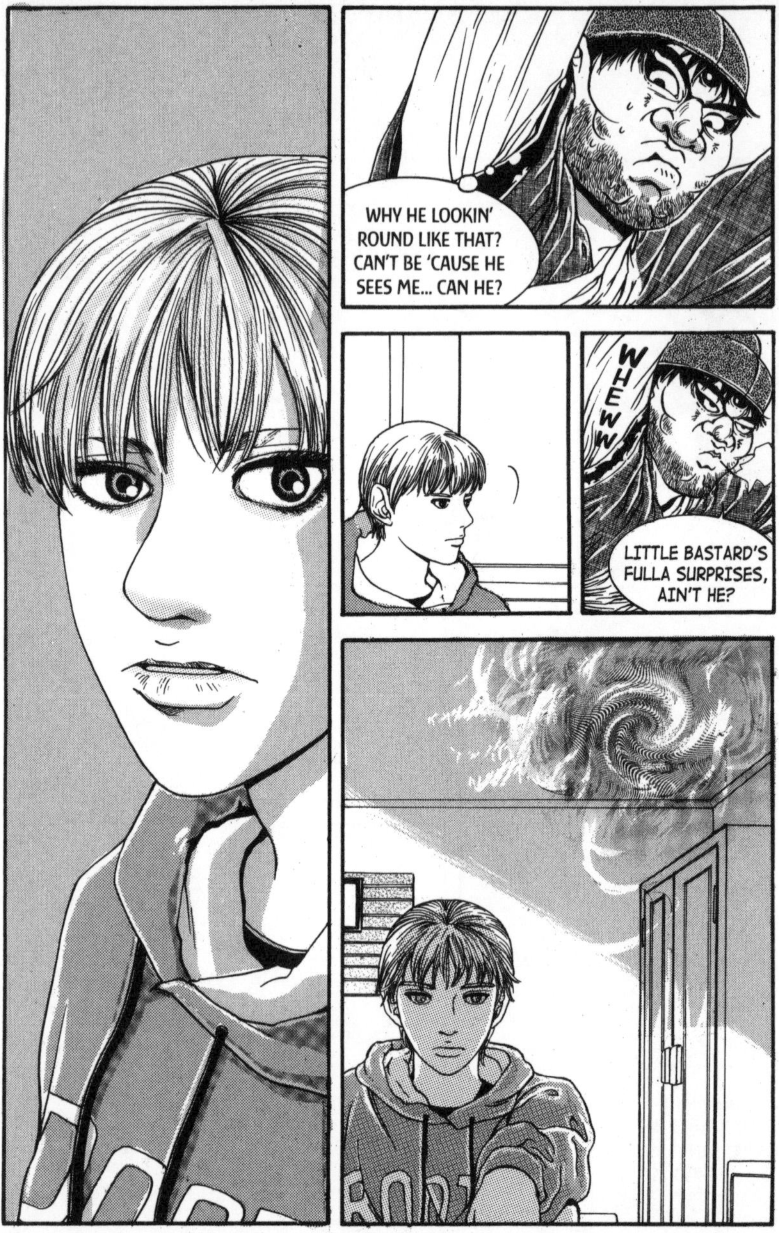
WHY HE LOOKIN' ROUND LIKE THAT? CAN'T BE 'CAUSE HE SEES ME... CAN HE?
WHEWW
LITTLE BASTARD'S FULLA SURPRISES, AIN'T HE?

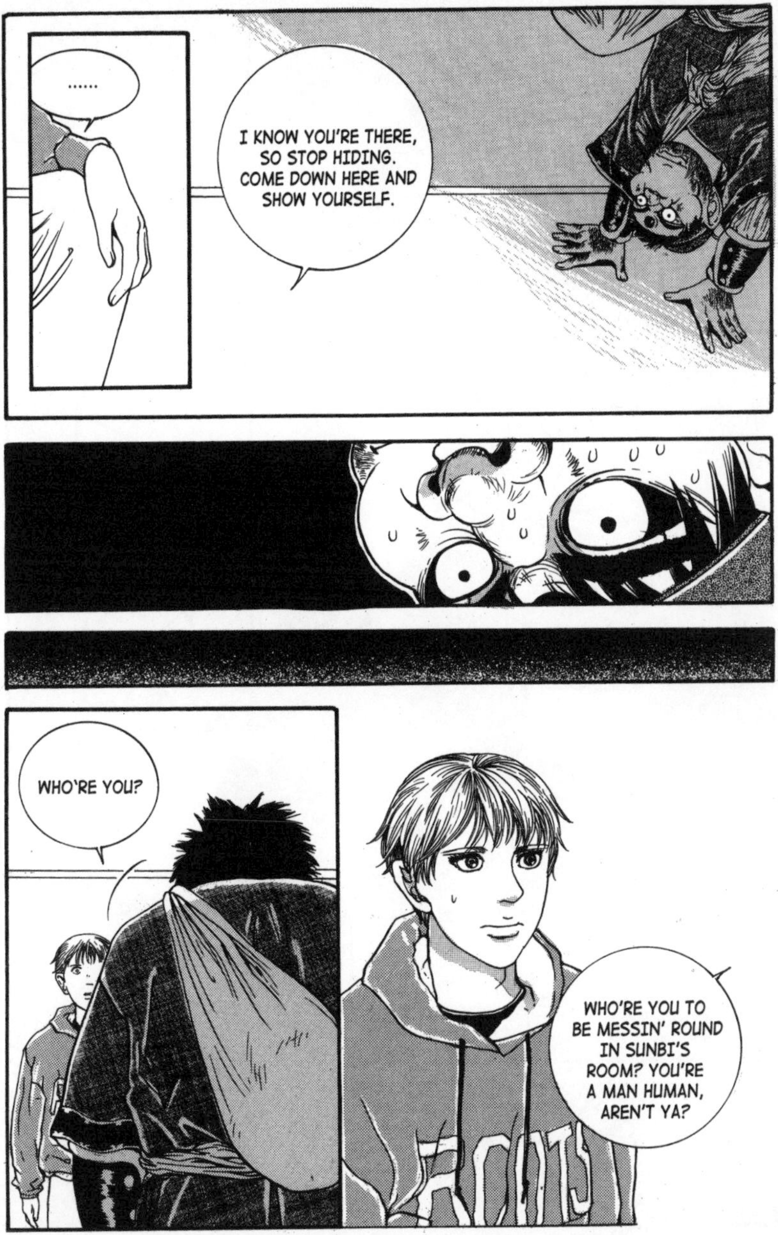
......
I KNOW YOU'RE THERE, SO STOP HIDING. COME DOWN HERE AND SHOW YOURSELF.
WHO'RE YOU?
WHO'RE YOU TO BE MESSIN' ROUND IN SUNBI'S ROOM? YOU'RE A MAN HUMAN, AREN'T YA?

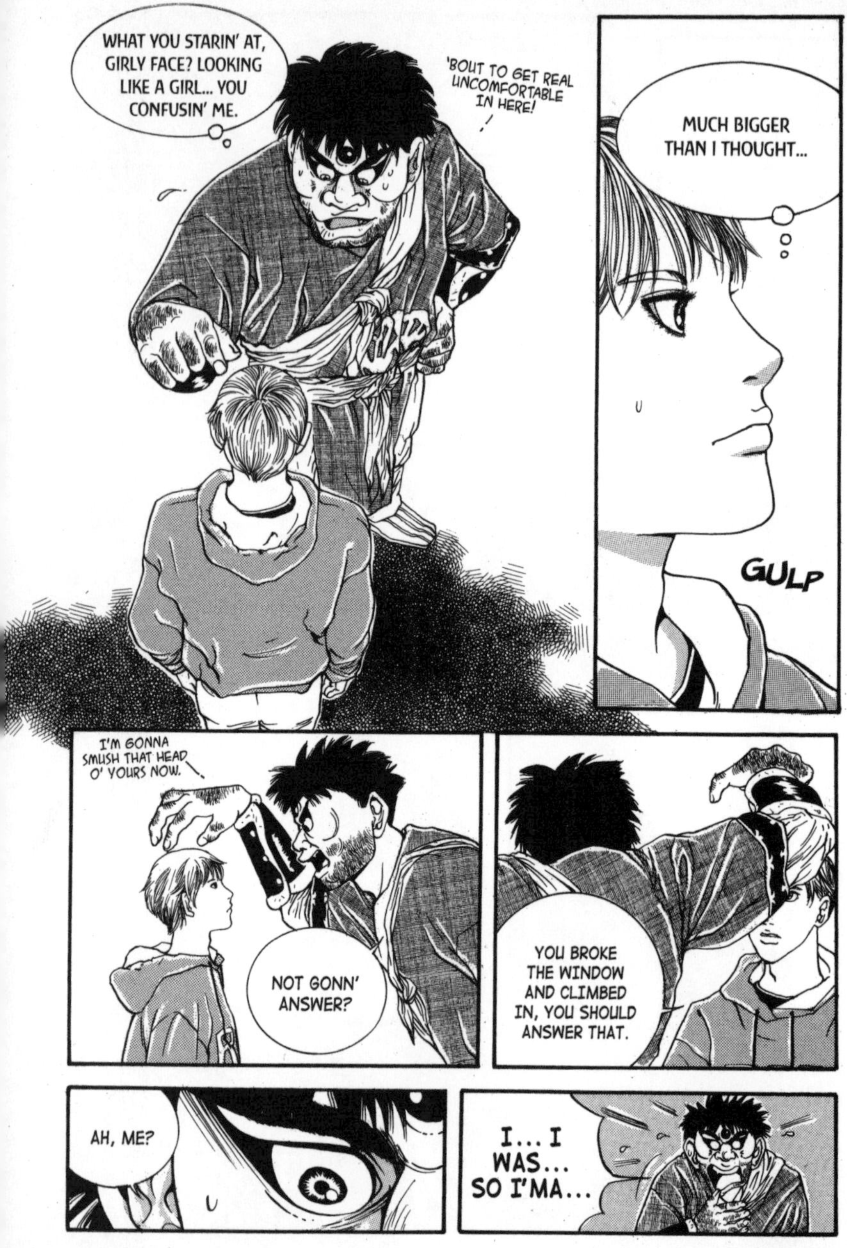
WHAT YOU STARIN' AT, GIRLY FACE? LOOKING LIKE A GIRL... YOU CONFUSIN' ME.
'BOUT TO GET REAL UNCOMFORTABLE IN HERE!
MUCH BIGGER THAN I THOUGHT...
GULP
I'M GONNA SMUSH THAT HEAD O' YOURS NOW.
NOT GONN' ANSWER?
YOU BROKE THE WINDOW AND CLIMBED IN, YOU SHOULD ANSWER THAT.
AH, ME?
I... I WAS... SO I'MA...

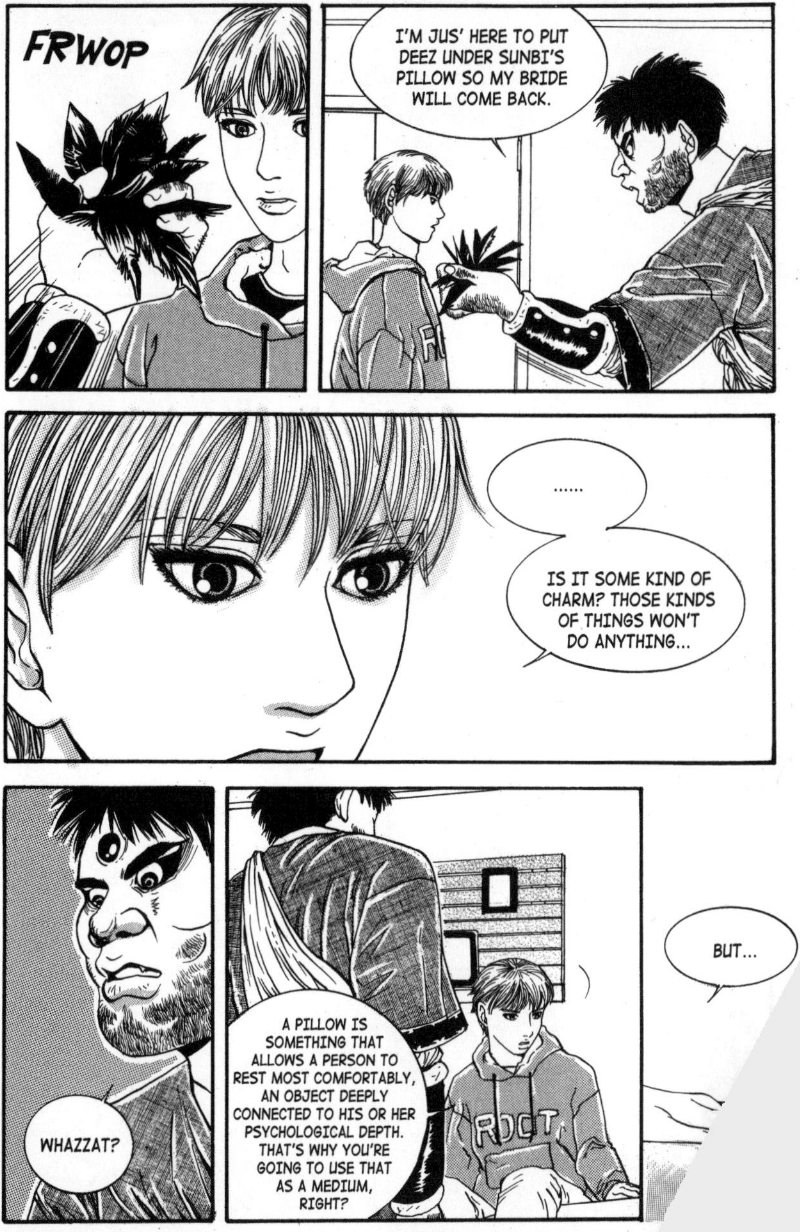
FRWOP
I'M JUS' HERE TO PUT DEEZ UNDER SUNBI'S PILLOW SO MY BRIDE WILL COME BACK.
......
IS IT SOME KIND OF CHARM? THOSE KINDS OF THINGS WON'T DO ANYTHING...
WHAZZAT?
A PILLOW IS SOMETHING THAT ALLOWS A PERSON TO REST MOST COMFORTABLY, AN OBJECT DEEPLY CONNECTED TO HIS OR HER PSYCHOLOGICAL DEPTH. THAT'S WHY YOU'RE GOING TO USE THAT AS A MEDIUM, RIGHT?
BUT...

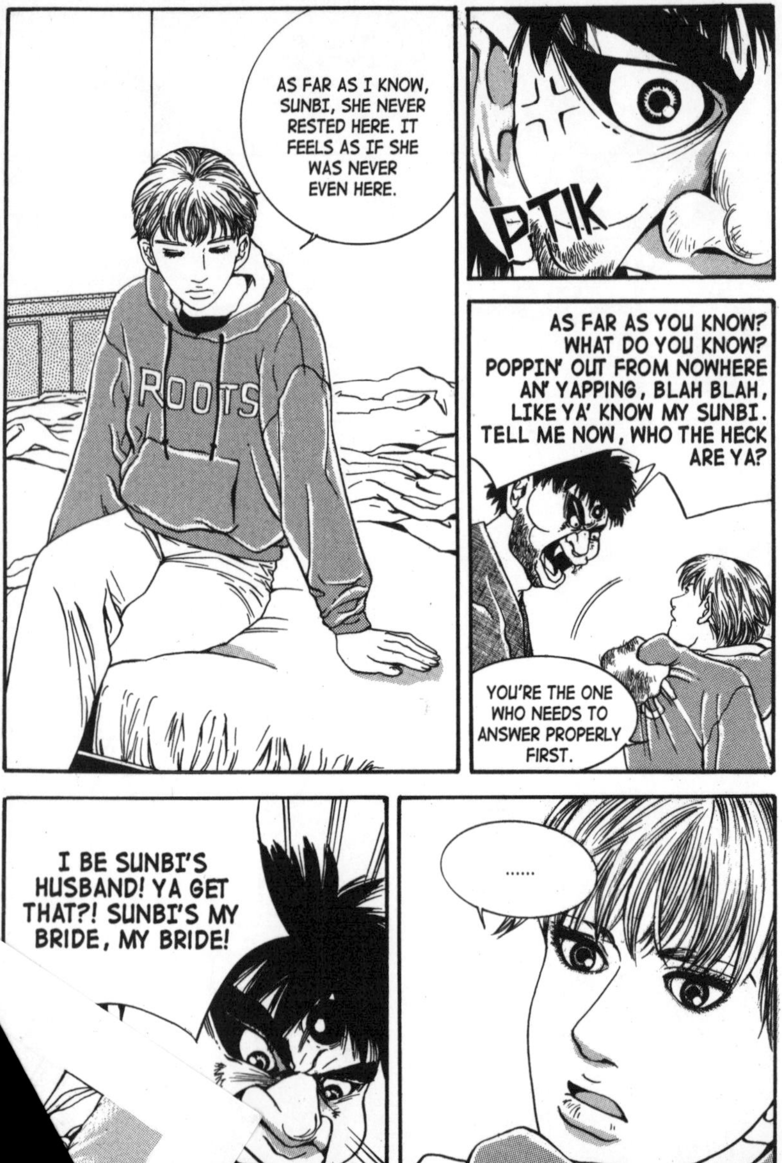
AS FAR AS I KNOW, SUNBI, SHE NEVER RESTED HERE. IT FEELS AS IF SHE WAS NEVER EVEN HERE.
PTIK
AS FAR AS YOU KNOW? WHAT DO YOU KNOW? POPPIN' OUT FROM NOWHERE AN' YAPPING, BLAH BLAH, LIKE YA' KNOW MY SUNBI. TELL ME NOW, WHO THE HECK ARE YA?
YOU'RE THE ONE WHO NEEDS TO ANSWER PROPERLY FIRST.
I BE SUNBI'S HUSBAND! YA GET THAT?! SUNBI'S MY BRIDE, MY BRIDE!
......

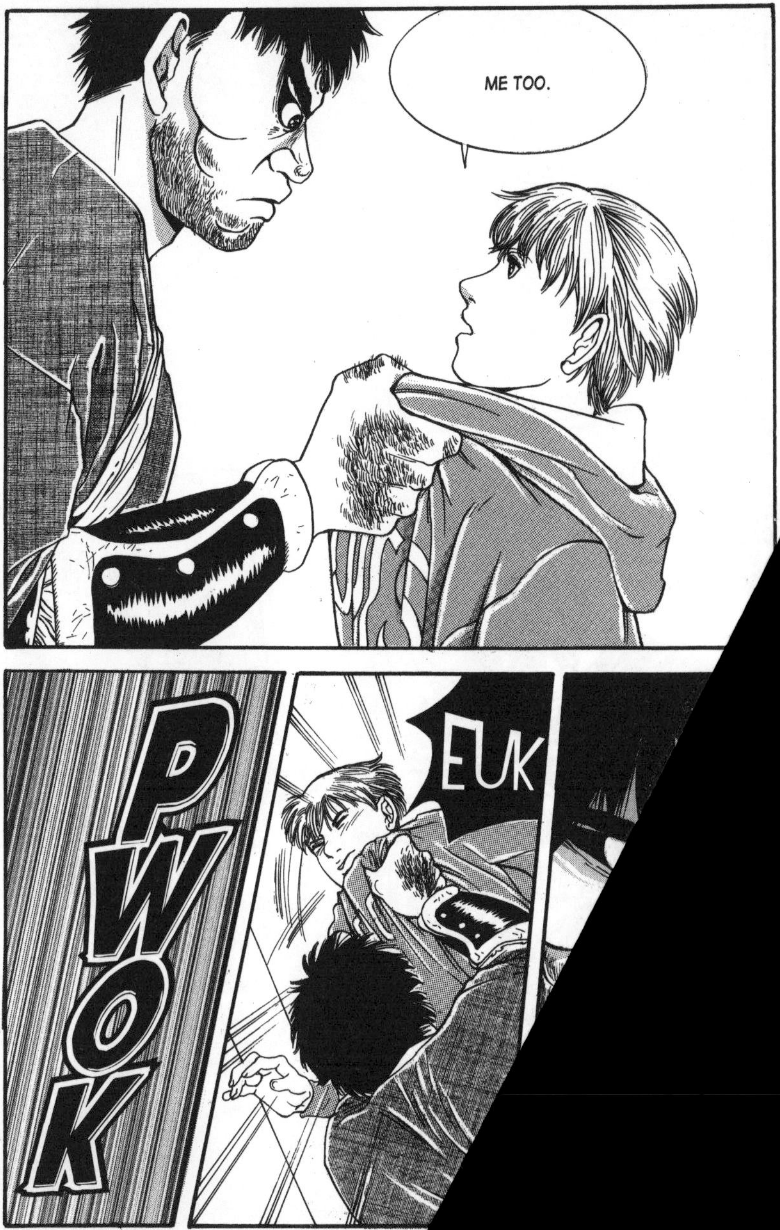
ME TOO.
PWOK
EUK

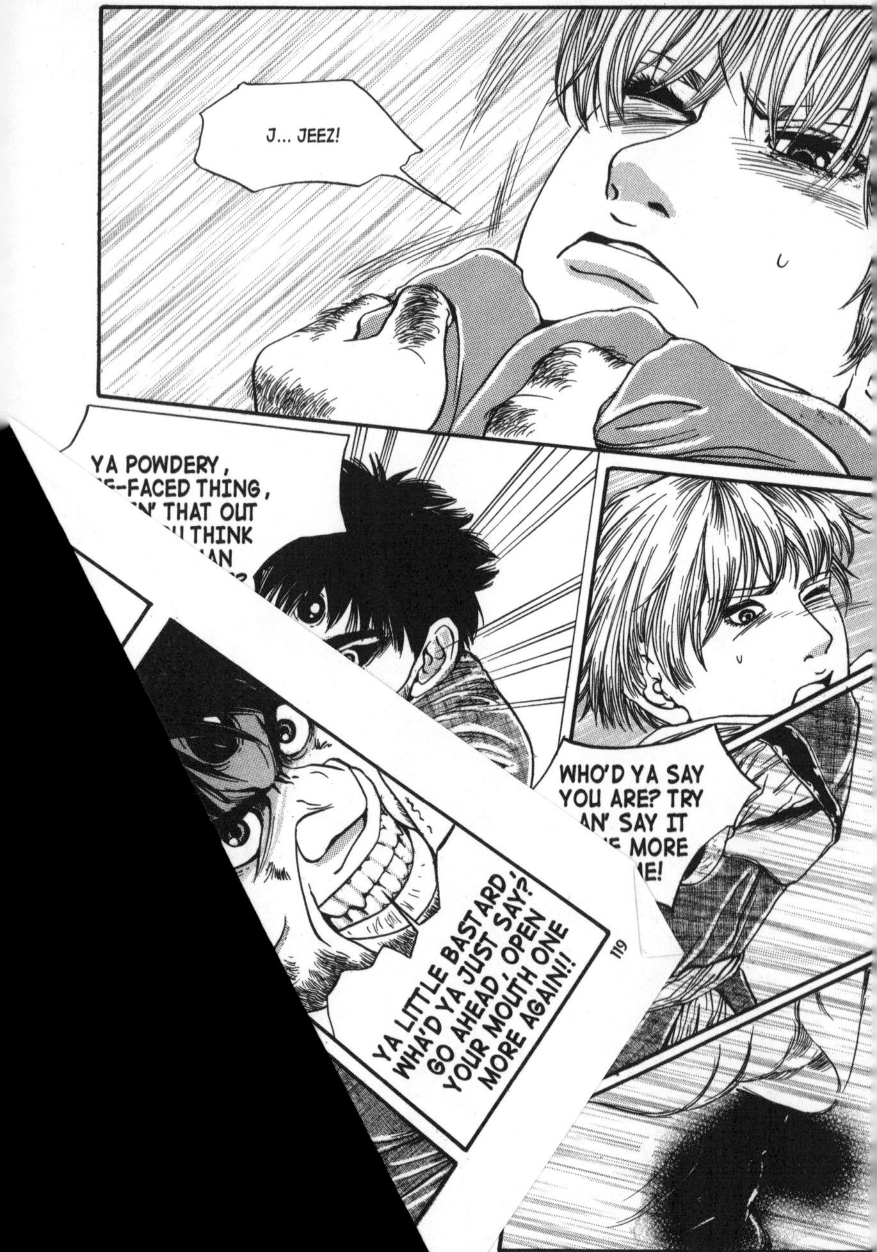
J... JEEZ!
YA POWDERY,
-FACED THING,
N' THAT OUT
U THINK
WHO'D YA SAY YOU ARE? TRY AN' SAY IT
E MORE
ME!
YA LITTLE BASTARD, WHA'D YA JUST SAY? GO AHEAD, OPEN YOUR MOUTH ONE MORE AGAIN!!

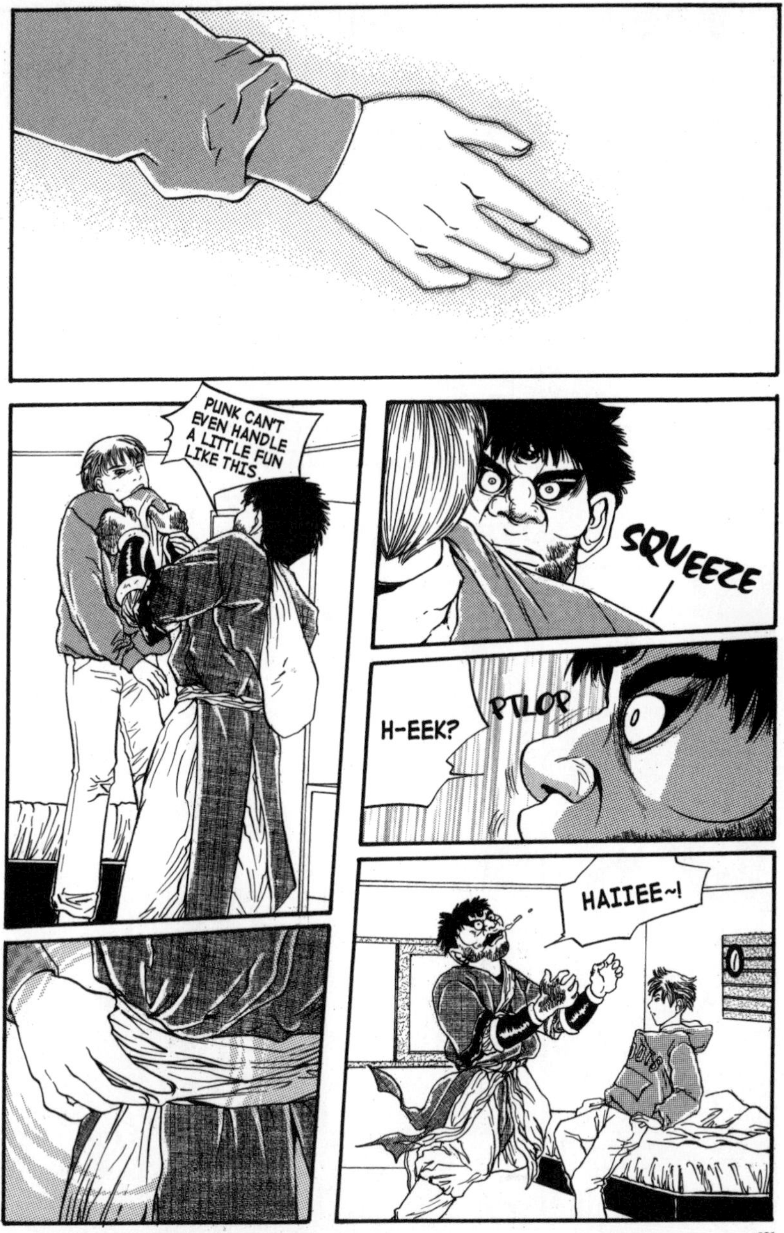
PUNK CAN'T EVEN HANDLE A LITTLE FUN LIKE THIS.
SQUEEZE
PTLOP
H-EEK?
HAIIEE~!

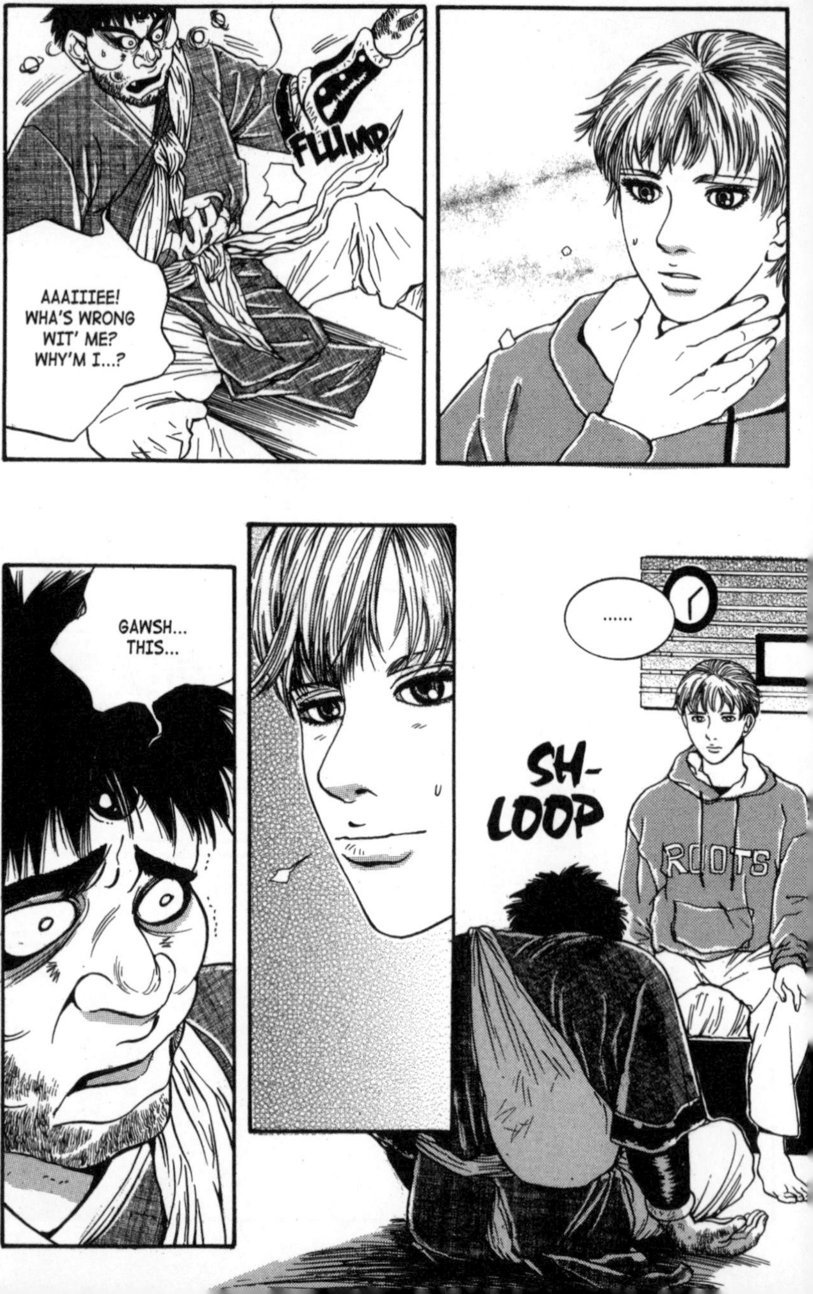
FLUMP
AAAIIIEE! WHA'S WRONG WIT' ME? WHY'M I...?
GAWSH... THIS...
......
SH-LOOP
ROOTS

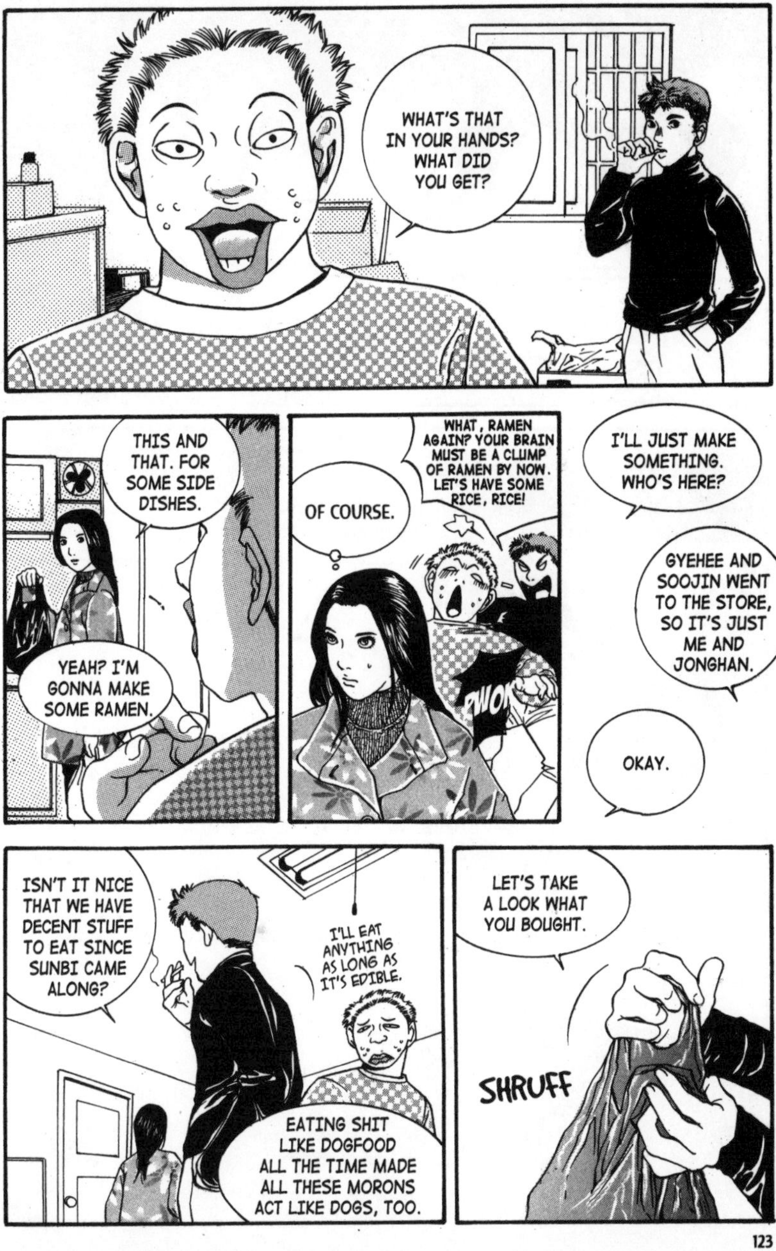
WHAT'S THAT IN YOUR HANDS? WHAT DID YOU GET?
THIS AND THAT. FOR SOME SIDE DISHES.
YEAH? I'M GONNA MAKE SOME RAMEN.
OF COURSE.
WHAT, RAMEN AGAIN? YOUR BRAIN MUST BE A CLUMP OF RAMEN BY NOW. LET'S HAVE SOME RICE, RICE!
PWOK
I'LL JUST MAKE SOMETHING. WHO'S HERE?
GYEHEE AND SOOJIN WENT TO THE STORE, SO IT'S JUST ME AND JONGHAN.
OKAY.
ISN'T IT NICE THAT WE HAVE DECENT STUFF TO EAT SINCE SUNBI CAME ALONG?
I'LL EAT ANYTHING AS LONG AS IT'S EDIBLE.
EATING SHIT LIKE DOGFOOD ALL THE TIME MADE ALL THESE MORONS ACT LIKE DOGS, TOO.
LET'S TAKE A LOOK WHAT YOU BOUGHT.
SHRUFF

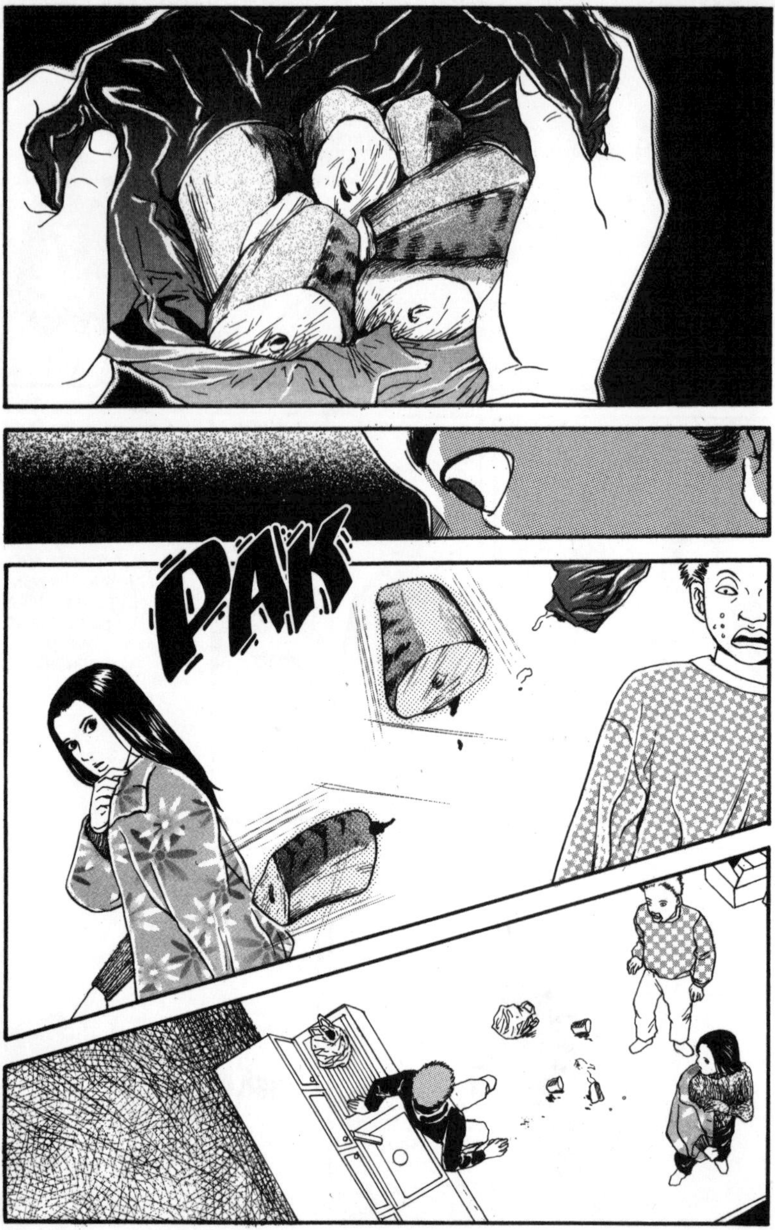
PAK

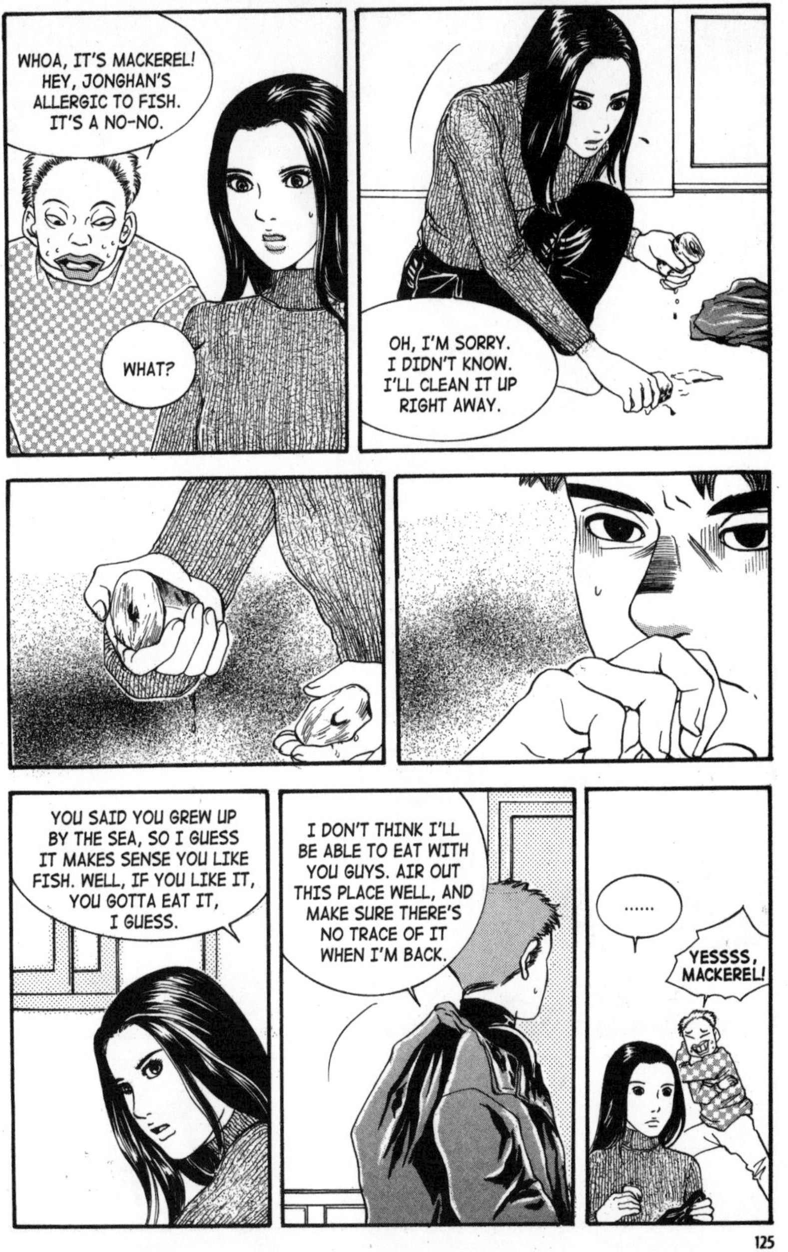
WHOA, IT'S MACKEREL! HEY, JONGHAN'S ALLERGIC TO FISH. IT'S A NO-NO.
WHAT?
OH, I'M SORRY. I DIDN'T KNOW. I'LL CLEAN IT UP RIGHT AWAY.
YOU SAID YOU GREW UP BY THE SEA, SO I GUESS IT MAKES SENSE YOU LIKE FISH. WELL, IF YOU LIKE IT, YOU GOTTA EAT IT, I GUESS.
I DON'T THINK I'LL BE ABLE TO EAT WITH YOU GUYS. AIR OUT THIS PLACE WELL, AND MAKE SURE THERE'S NO TRACE OF IT WHEN I'M BACK.
......
YESSSS, MACKEREL!

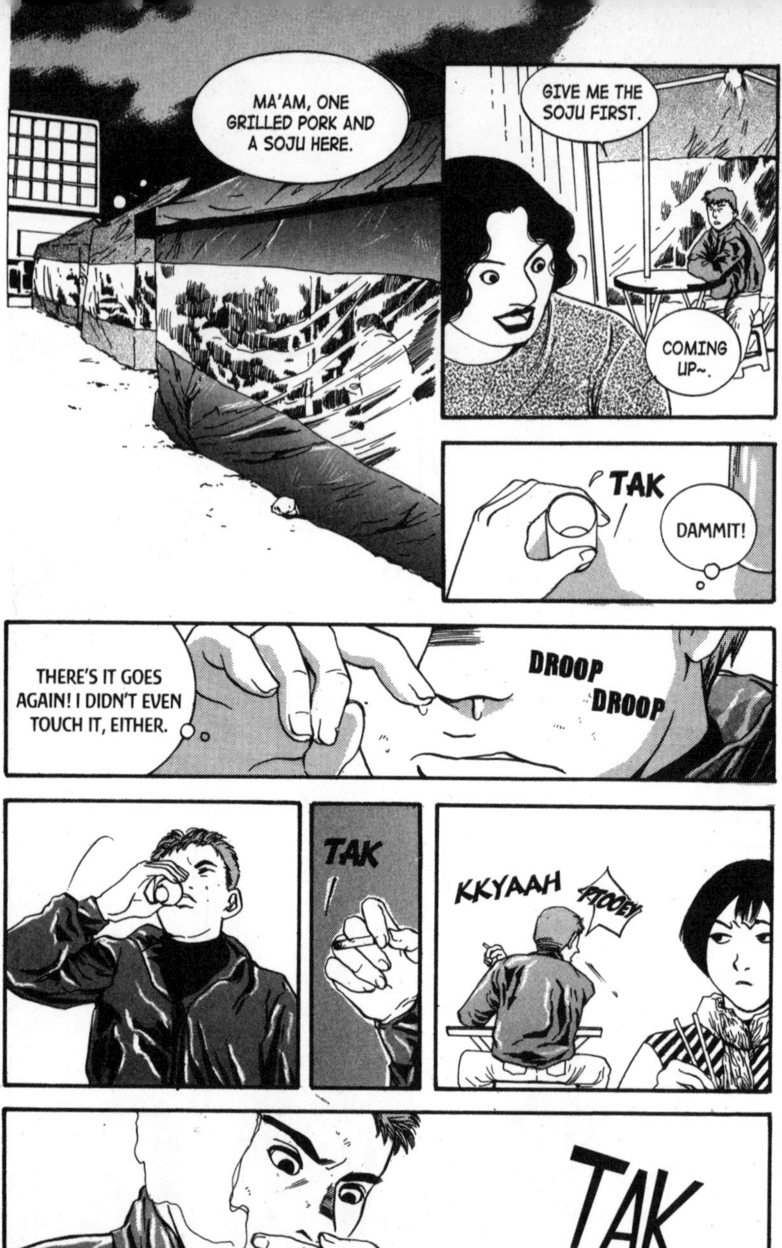
MA'AM, ONE GRILLED PORK AND A SOJU HERE.
GIVE ME THE SOJU FIRST.
COMING UP~.
TAK
DAMMIT!
THERE'S IT GOES AGAIN! I DIDN'T EVEN TOUCH IT, EITHER.
DROOP DROOP
TAK
KKYAAH
PTOOEY
TAK

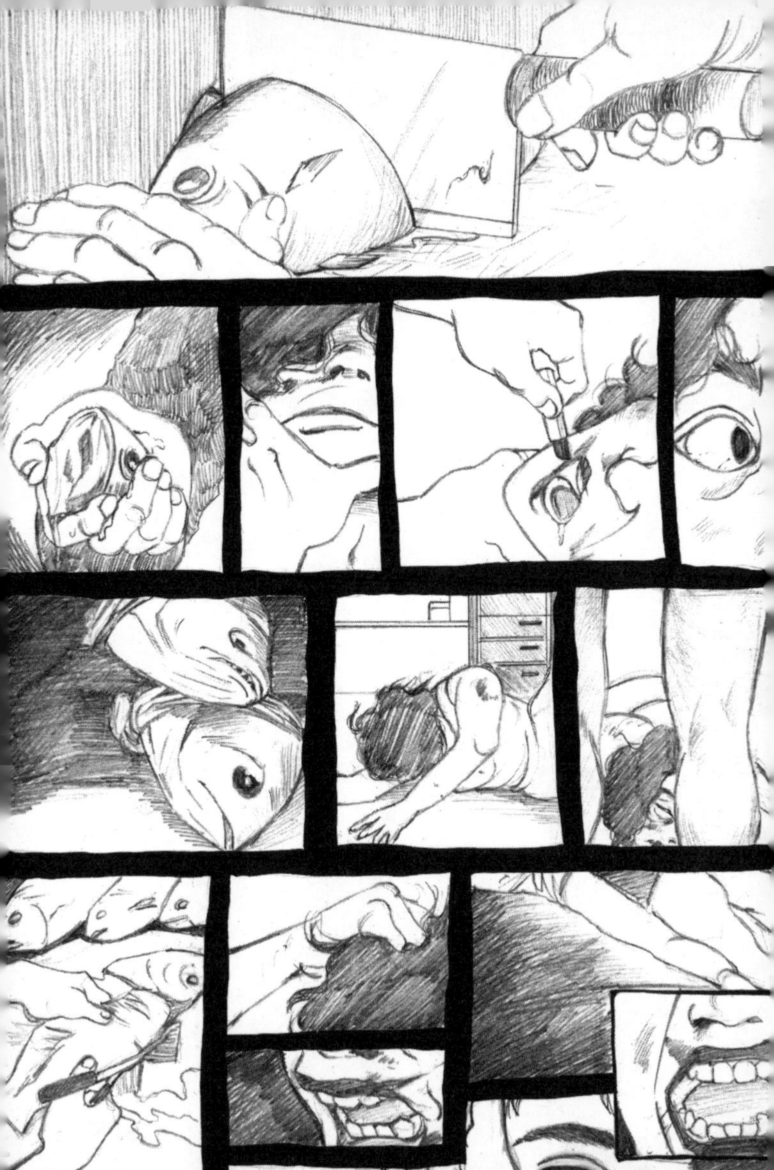

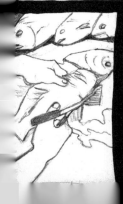

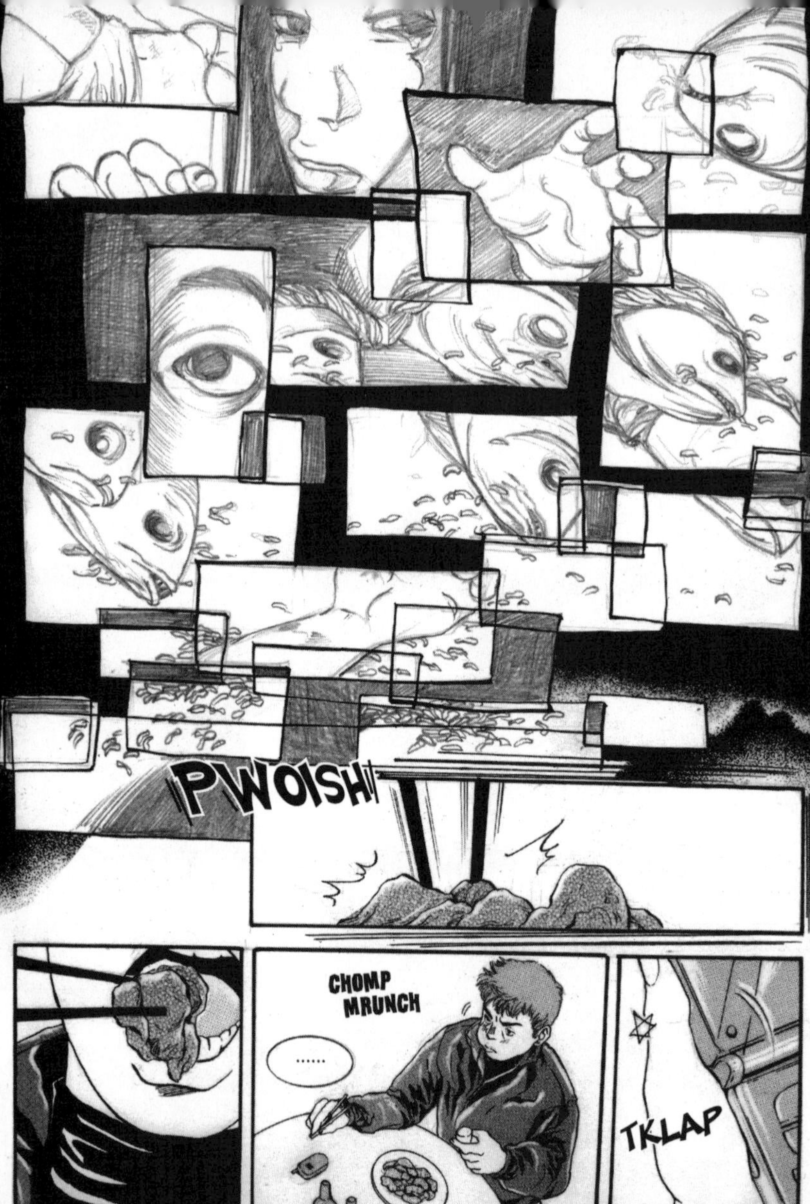
PWOISH
CHOMP
MRUNCH
......
TKLAP

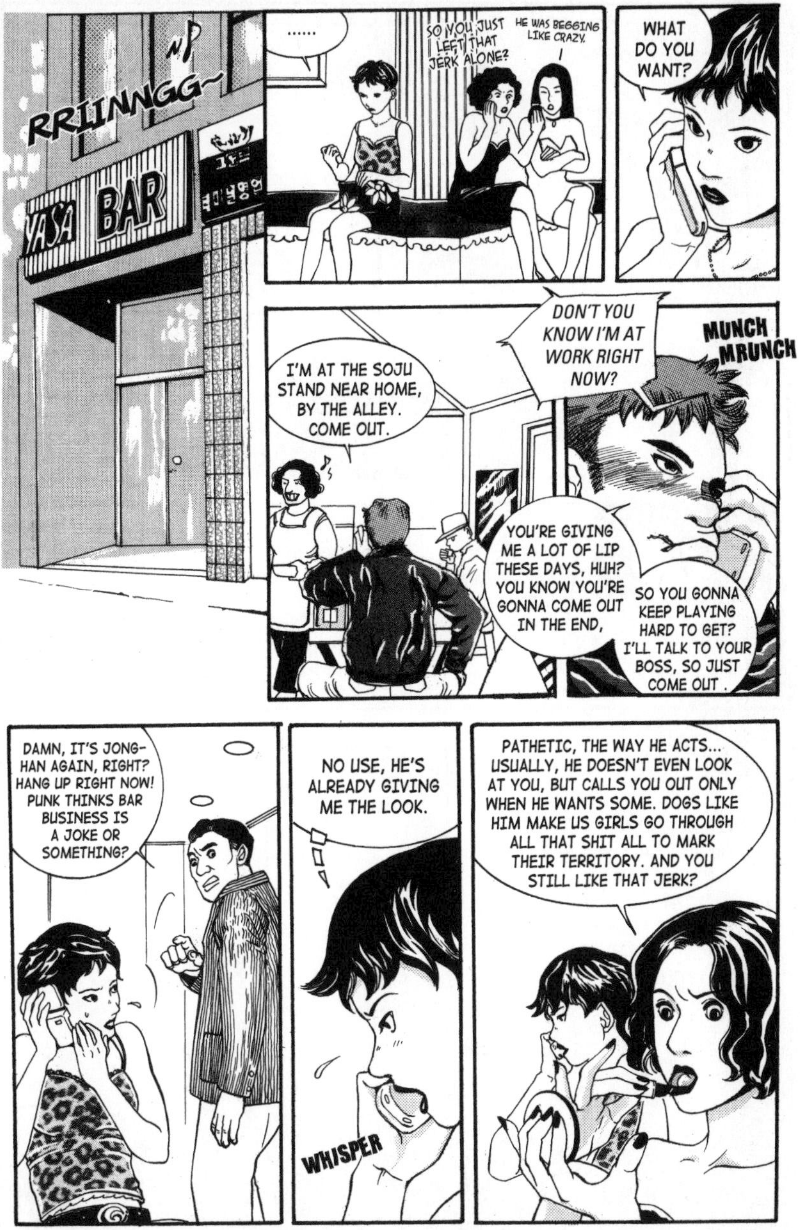
RRIINNGG~
YASA BAR
......
SO YOU JUST LEFT THAT JERK ALONE?
HE WAS BEGGING LIKE CRAZY.
WHAT DO YOU WANT?
I'M AT THE SOJU STAND NEAR HOME, BY THE ALLEY. COME OUT.
DON'T YOU KNOW I'M AT WORK RIGHT NOW?
MUNCH MRUNCH
YOU'RE GIVING ME A LOT OF LIP THESE DAYS, HUH? YOU KNOW YOU'RE GONNA COME OUT IN THE END,
SO YOU GONNA KEEP PLAYING HARD TO GET? I'LL TALK TO YOUR BOSS, SO JUST COME OUT .
DAMN, IT'S JONG-HAN AGAIN, RIGHT? HANG UP RIGHT NOW! PUNK THINKS BAR BUSINESS IS A JOKE OR SOMETHING?
NO USE, HE'S ALREADY GIVING ME THE LOOK.
WHISPER
PATHETIC, THE WAY HE ACTS... USUALLY, HE DOESN'T EVEN LOOK AT YOU, BUT CALLS YOU OUT ONLY WHEN HE WANTS SOME. DOGS LIKE HIM MAKE US GIRLS GO THROUGH ALL THAT SHIT ALL TO MARK THEIR TERRITORY. AND YOU STILL LIKE THAT JERK?

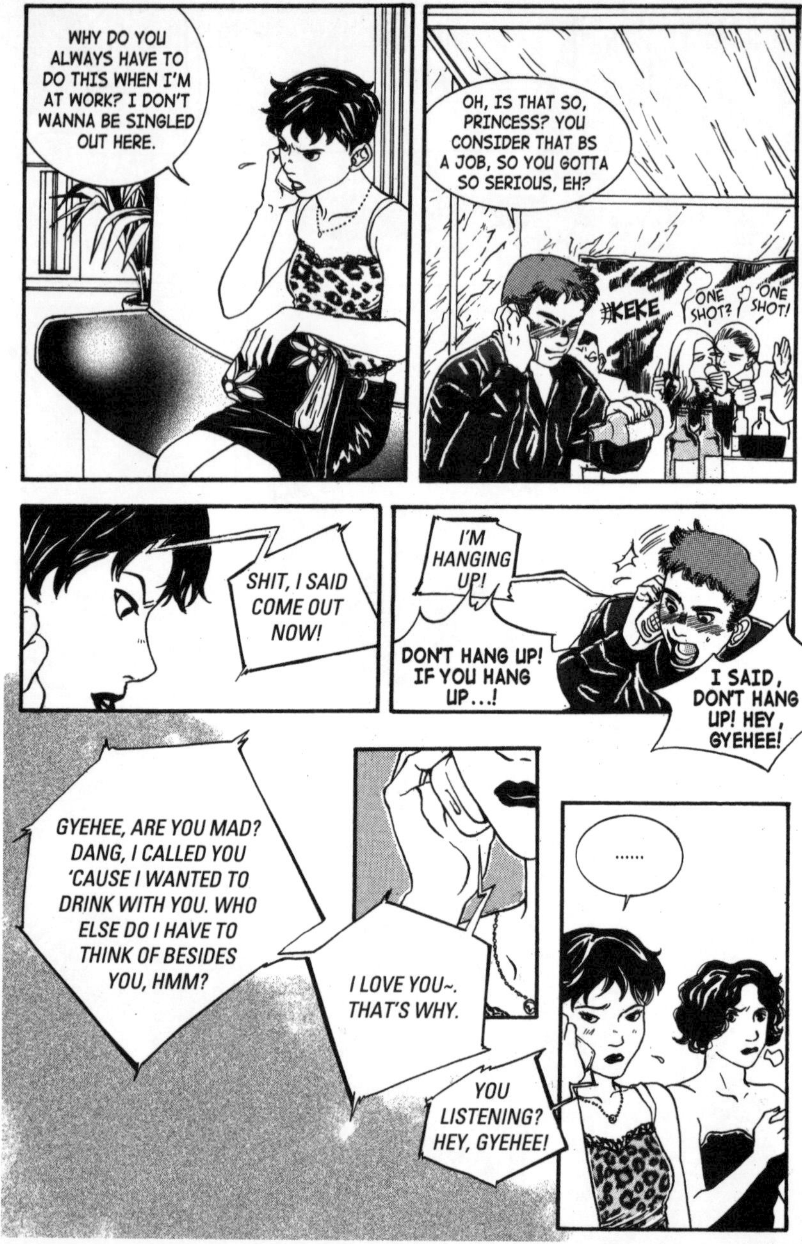
WHY DO YOU ALWAYS HAVE TO DO THIS WHEN I'M AT WORK? I DON'T WANNA BE SINGLED OUT HERE.
OH, IS THAT SO, PRINCESS? YOU CONSIDER THAT BS A JOB, SO YOU GOTTA SO SERIOUS, EH?
KEKE
ONE SHOT?
ONE SHOT!
SHIT, I SAID COME OUT NOW!
I'M HANGING UP!
DON'T HANG UP! IF YOU HANG UP...!
I SAID, DON'T HANG UP! HEY, GYEHEE!
GYEHEE, ARE YOU MAD? DANG, I CALLED YOU 'CAUSE I WANTED TO DRINK WITH YOU. WHO ELSE DO I HAVE TO THINK OF BESIDES YOU, HMM?
I LOVE YOU~. THAT'S WHY.
......
YOU LISTENING? HEY, GYEHEE!

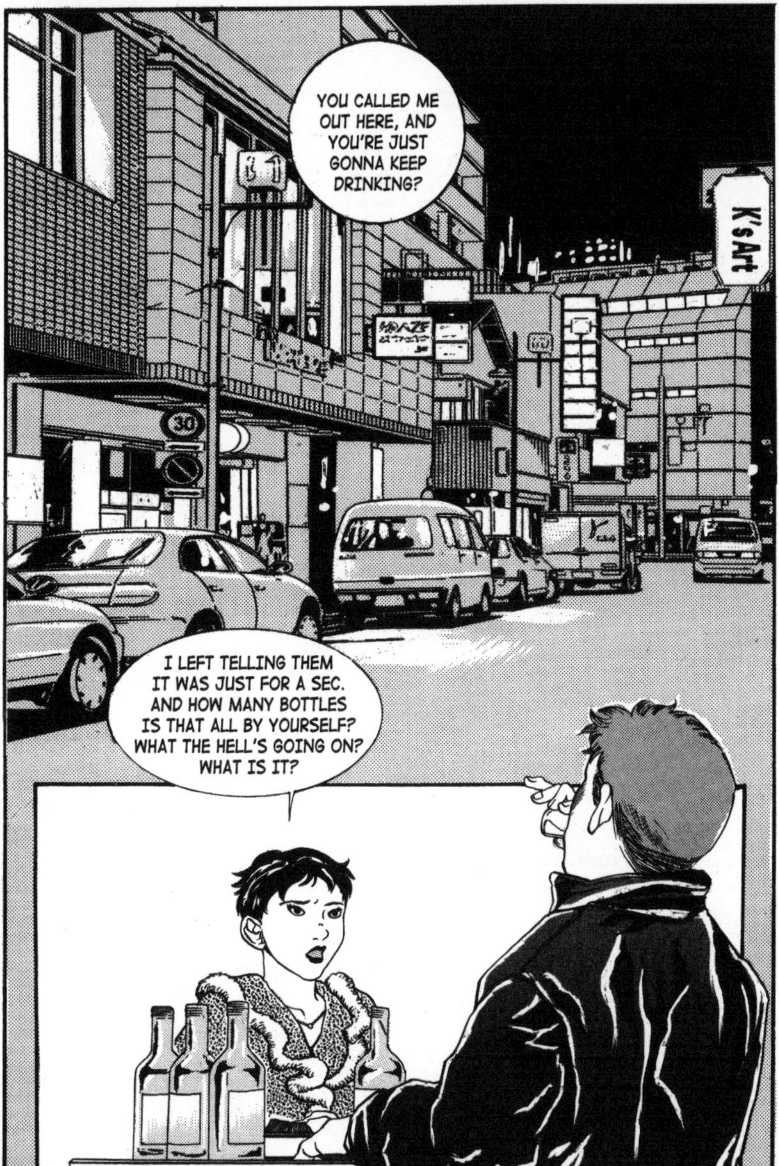
YOU CALLED ME OUT HERE, AND YOU'RE JUST GONNA KEEP DRINKING?
K'sArt
30
I LEFT TELLING THEM IT WAS JUST FOR A SEC. AND HOW MANY BOTTLES IS THAT ALL BY YOURSELF? WHAT THE HELL'S GOING ON? WHAT IS IT?

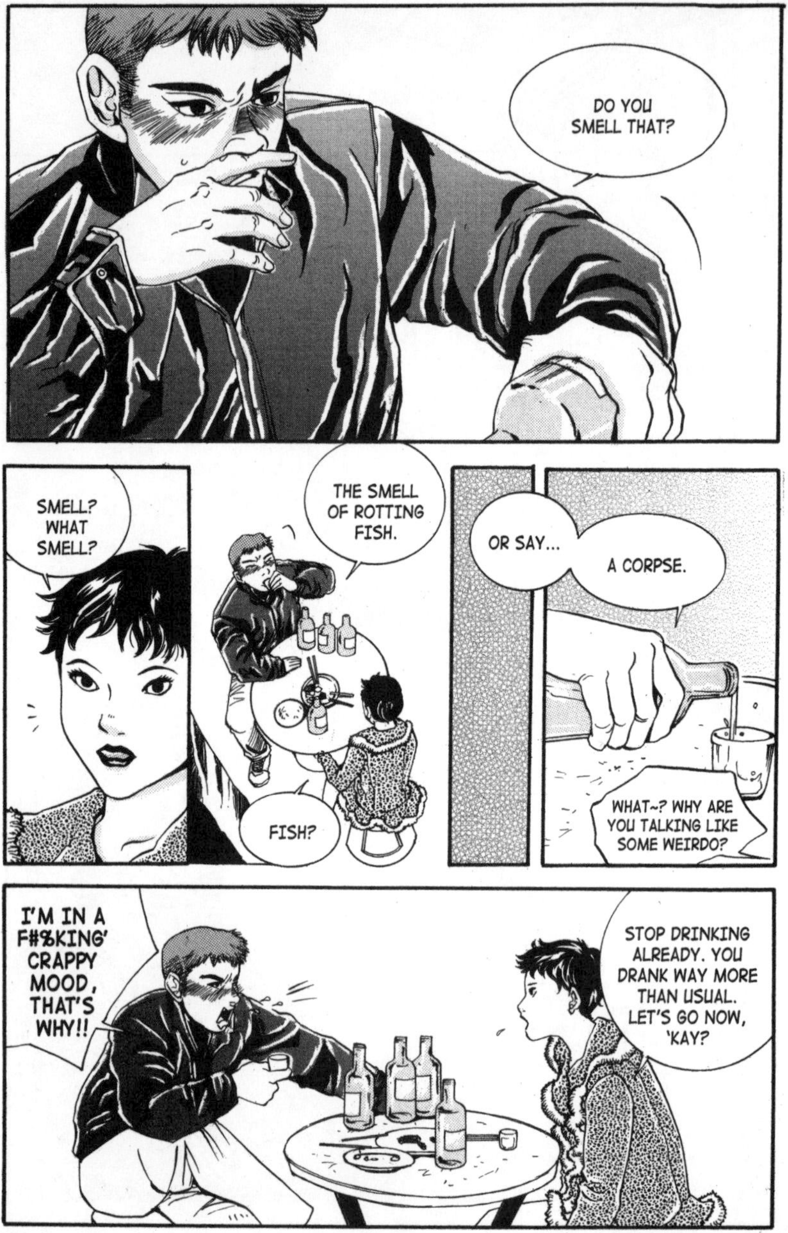
DO YOU SMELL THAT?
SMELL? WHAT SMELL?
THE SMELL OF ROTTING FISH.
FISH?
OR SAY...
A CORPSE.
WHAT~? WHY ARE YOU TALKING LIKE SOME WEIRDO?
I'M IN A F#%KING' CRAPPY MOOD, THAT'S WHY!!
STOP DRINKING ALREADY. YOU DRANK WAY MORE THAN USUAL. LET'S GO NOW, 'KAY?

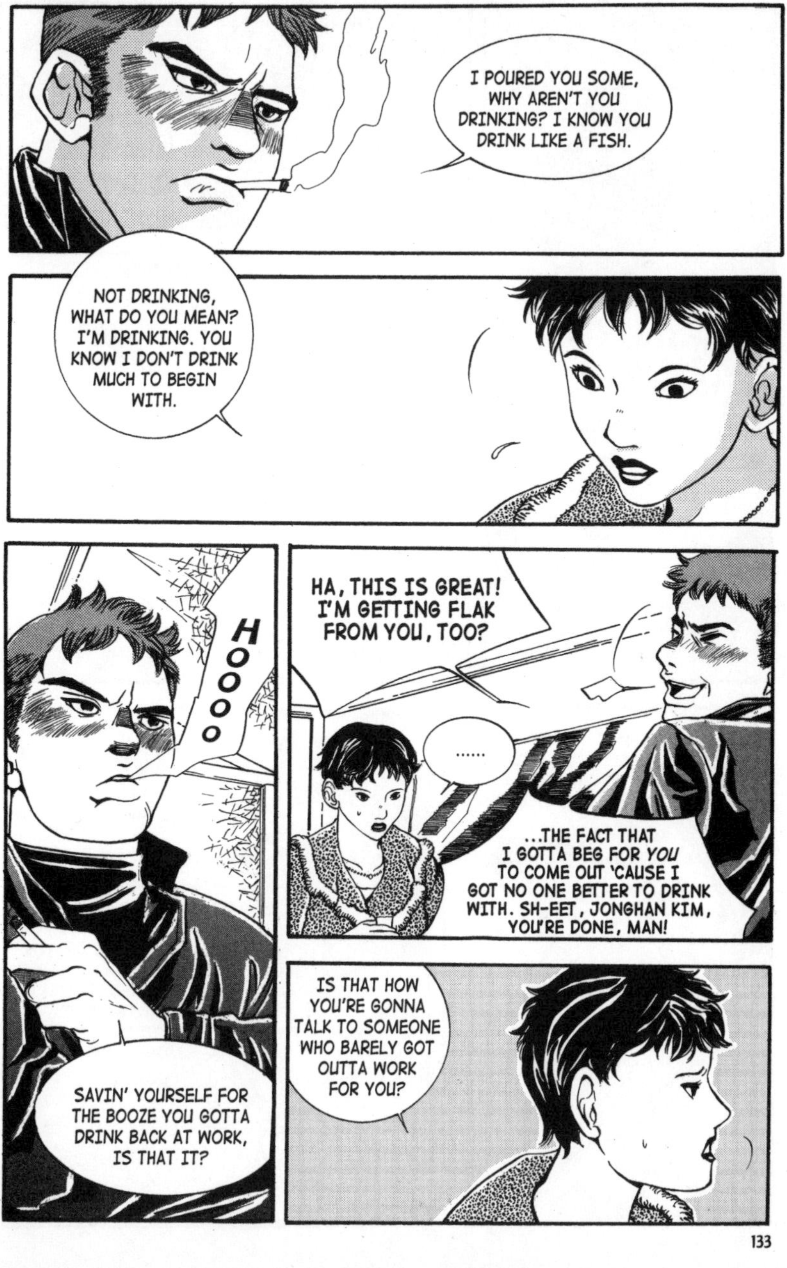
I POURED YOU SOME, WHY AREN'T YOU DRINKING? I KNOW YOU DRINK LIKE A FISH.
NOT DRINKING, WHAT DO YOU MEAN? I'M DRINKING. YOU KNOW I DON'T DRINK MUCH TO BEGIN WITH.
HOOOOO
SAVIN' YOURSELF FOR THE BOOZE YOU GOTTA DRINK BACK AT WORK, IS THAT IT?
HA, THIS IS GREAT! I'M GETTING FLAK FROM YOU, TOO?
......
...THE FACT THAT I GOTTA BEG FOR *YOU* TO COME OUT 'CAUSE I GOT NO ONE BETTER TO DRINK WITH. SH-EET, JONGHAN KIM, YOU'RE DONE, MAN!
IS THAT HOW YOU'RE GONNA TALK TO SOMEONE WHO BARELY GOT OUTTA WORK FOR YOU?

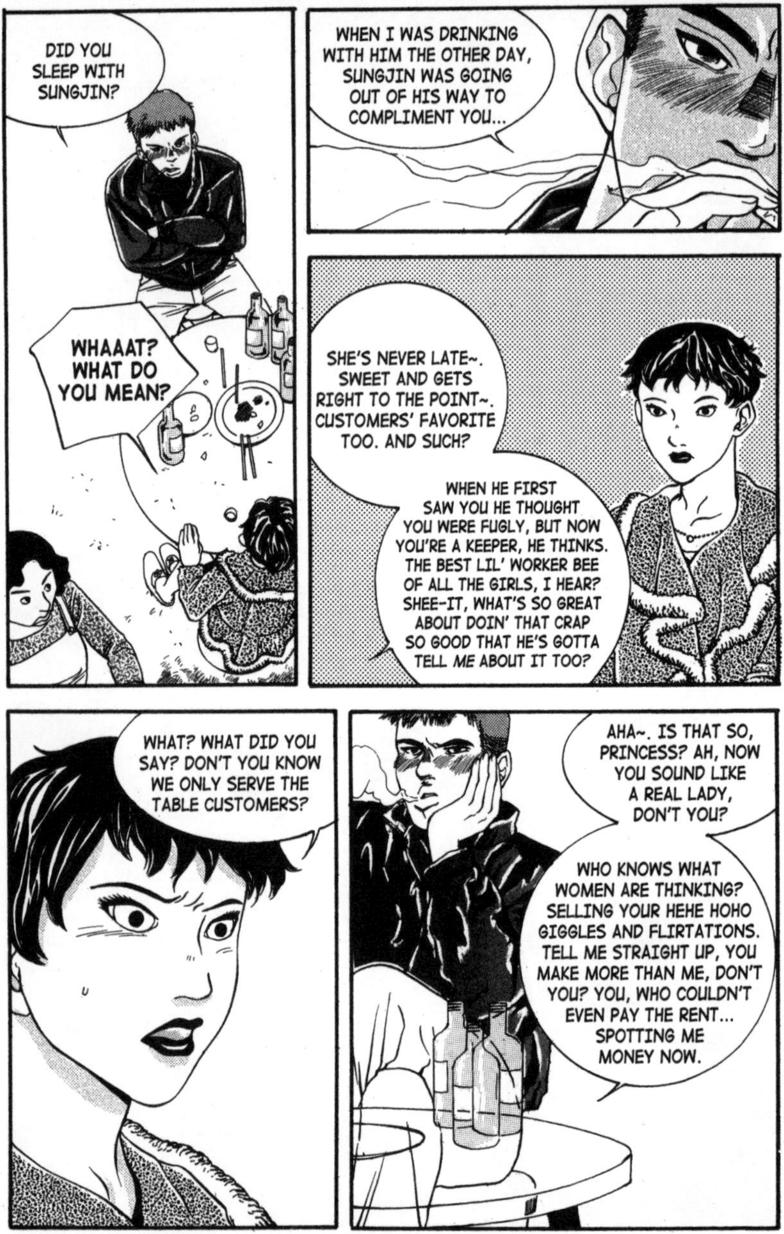
DID YOU SLEEP WITH SUNGJIN?
WHAAAT? WHAT DO YOU MEAN?
WHEN I WAS DRINKING WITH HIM THE OTHER DAY, SUNGJIN WAS GOING OUT OF HIS WAY TO COMPLIMENT YOU...
SHE'S NEVER LATE~. SWEET AND GETS RIGHT TO THE POINT~. CUSTOMERS' FAVORITE TOO. AND SUCH?
WHEN HE FIRST SAW YOU HE THOUGHT YOU WERE FUGLY, BUT NOW YOU'RE A KEEPER, HE THINKS. THE BEST LIL' WORKER BEE OF ALL THE GIRLS, I HEAR? SHEE-IT, WHAT'S SO GREAT ABOUT DOIN' THAT CRAP SO GOOD THAT HE'S GOTTA TELL *ME* ABOUT IT TOO?
WHAT? WHAT DID YOU SAY? DON'T YOU KNOW WE ONLY SERVE THE TABLE CUSTOMERS?
AHA~. IS THAT SO, PRINCESS? AH, NOW YOU SOUND LIKE A REAL LADY, DON'T YOU?
WHO KNOWS WHAT WOMEN ARE THINKING? SELLING YOUR HEHE HOHO GIGGLES AND FLIRTATIONS. TELL ME STRAIGHT UP, YOU MAKE MORE THAN ME, DON'T YOU? YOU, WHO COULDN'T EVEN PAY THE RENT... SPOTTING ME MONEY NOW.

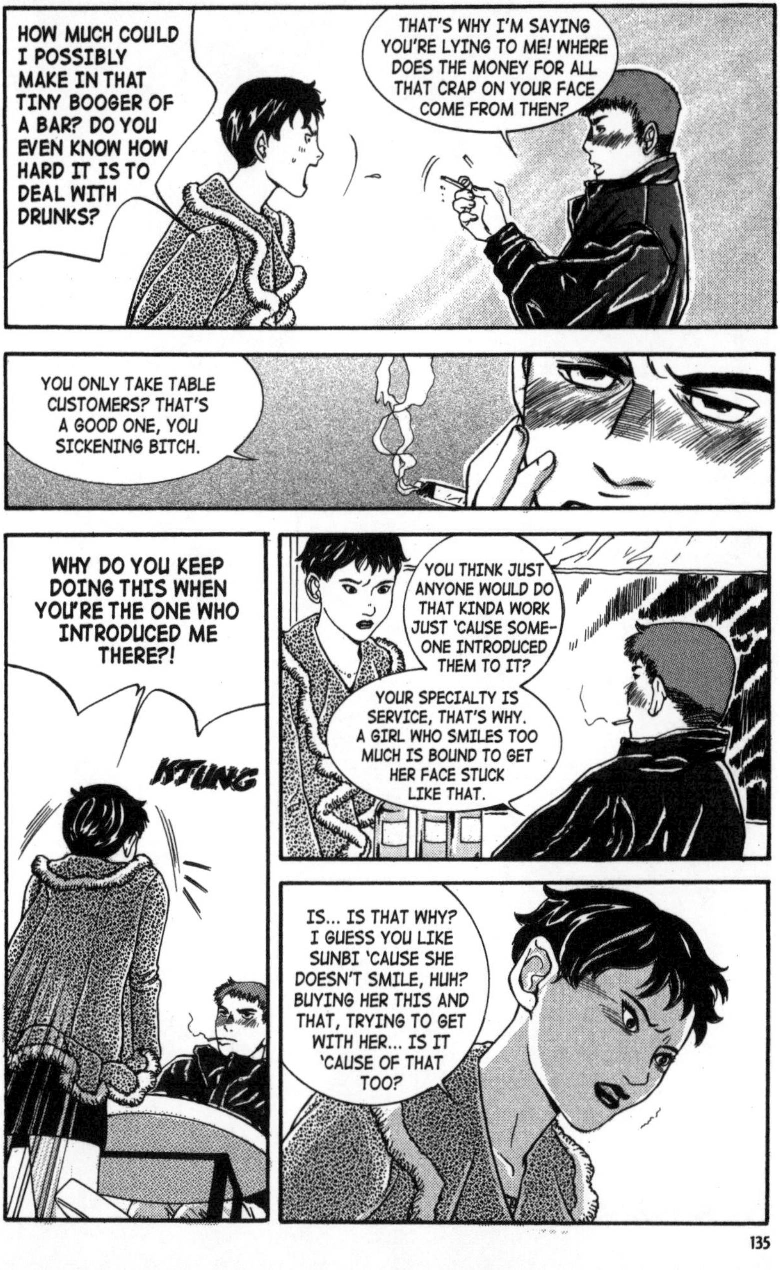
HOW MUCH COULD I POSSIBLY MAKE IN THAT TINY BOOGER OF A BAR? DO YOU EVEN KNOW HOW HARD IT IS TO DEAL WITH DRUNKS?
THAT'S WHY I'M SAYING YOU'RE LYING TO ME! WHERE DOES THE MONEY FOR ALL THAT CRAP ON YOUR FACE COME FROM THEN?
YOU ONLY TAKE TABLE CUSTOMERS? THAT'S A GOOD ONE, YOU SICKENING BITCH.
WHY DO YOU KEEP DOING THIS WHEN YOU'RE THE ONE WHO INTRODUCED ME THERE?!
KTUNG
YOU THINK JUST ANYONE WOULD DO THAT KINDA WORK JUST 'CAUSE SOME-ONE INTRODUCED THEM TO IT?
YOUR SPECIALTY IS SERVICE, THAT'S WHY. A GIRL WHO SMILES TOO MUCH IS BOUND TO GET HER FACE STUCK LIKE THAT.
IS... IS THAT WHY? I GUESS YOU LIKE SUNBI 'CAUSE SHE DOESN'T SMILE, HUH? BUYING HER THIS AND THAT, TRYING TO GET WITH HER... IS IT 'CAUSE OF THAT TOO?

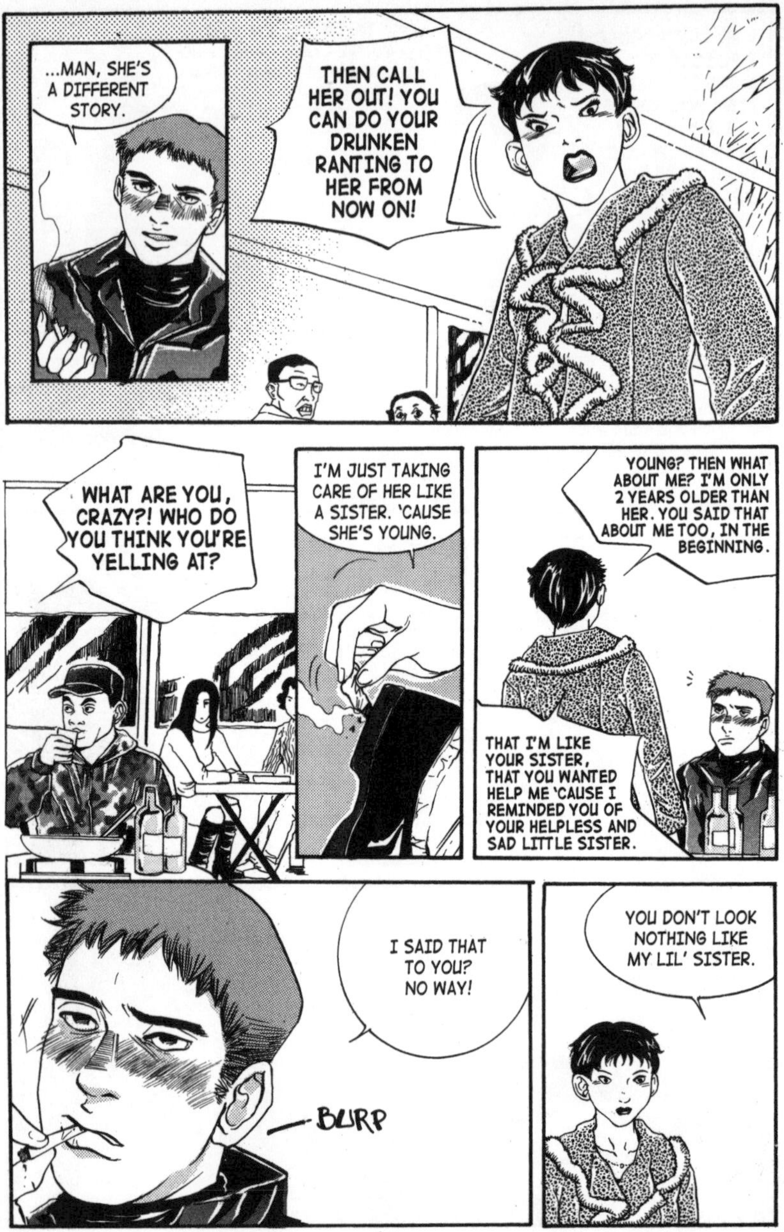

...MAN, SHE'S A DIFFERENT STORY.
THEN CALL HER OUT! YOU CAN DO YOUR DRUNKEN RANTING TO HER FROM NOW ON!
WHAT ARE YOU, CRAZY?! WHO DO YOU THINK YOU'RE YELLING AT?
I'M JUST TAKING CARE OF HER LIKE A SISTER. 'CAUSE SHE'S YOUNG.
YOUNG? THEN WHAT ABOUT ME? I'M ONLY 2 YEARS OLDER THAN HER. YOU SAID THAT ABOUT ME TOO, IN THE BEGINNING.
THAT I'M LIKE YOUR SISTER, THAT YOU WANTED HELP ME 'CAUSE I REMINDED YOU OF YOUR HELPLESS AND SAD LITTLE SISTER.
I SAID THAT TO YOU? NO WAY!
BURP
YOU DON'T LOOK NOTHING LIKE MY LIL' SISTER.

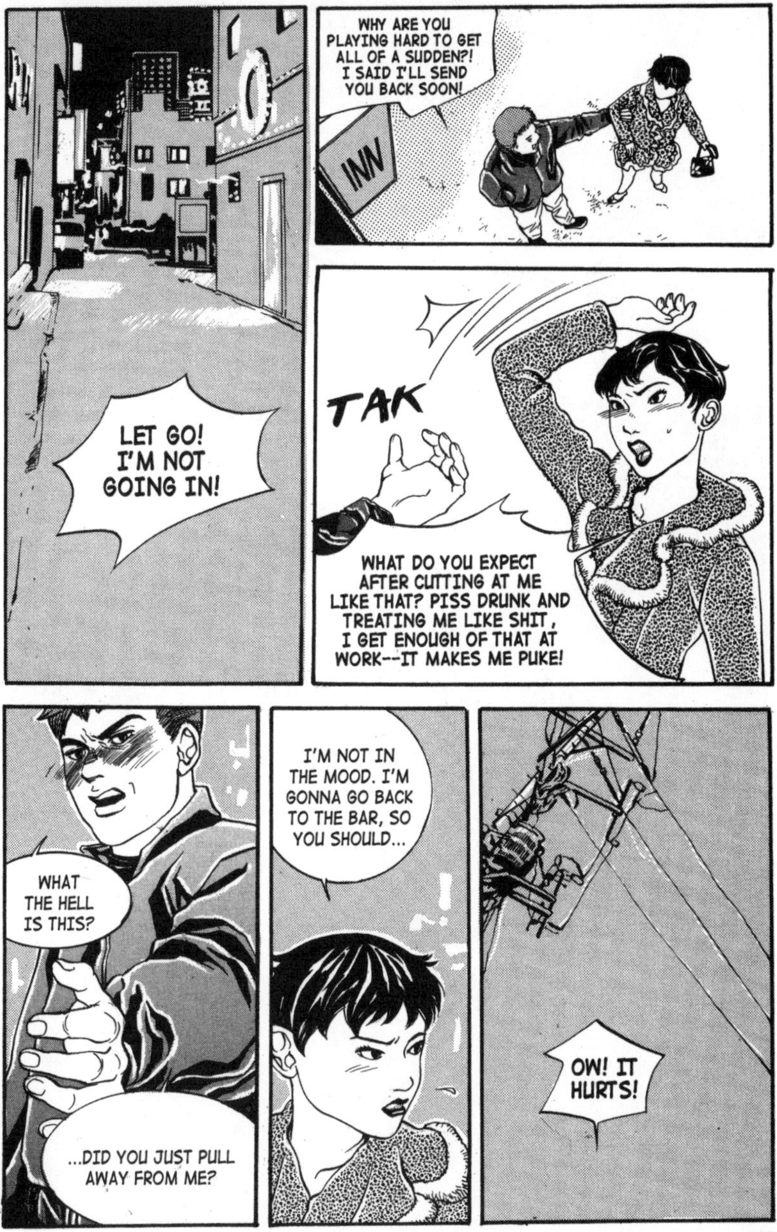
LET GO! I'M NOT GOING IN!
WHY ARE YOU PLAYING HARD TO GET ALL OF A SUDDEN?! I SAID I'LL SEND YOU BACK SOON!
INN
TAK
WHAT DO YOU EXPECT AFTER CUTTING AT ME LIKE THAT? PISS DRUNK AND TREATING ME LIKE SHIT, I GET ENOUGH OF THAT AT WORK--IT MAKES ME PUKE!
WHAT THE HELL IS THIS?
...DID YOU JUST PULL AWAY FROM ME?
I'M NOT IN THE MOOD. I'M GONNA GO BACK TO THE BAR, SO YOU SHOULD...
OW! IT HURTS!

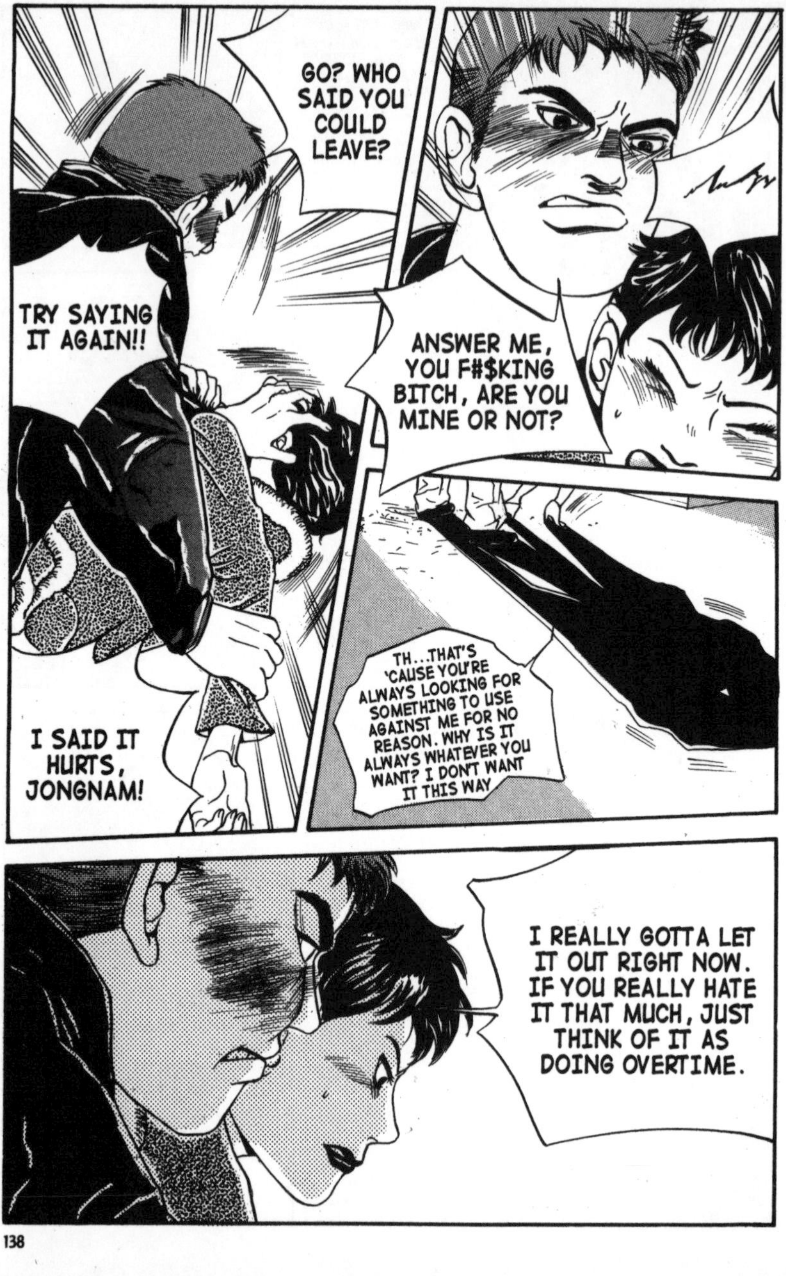
GO? WHO SAID YOU COULD LEAVE?
TRY SAYING IT AGAIN!!
I SAID IT HURTS, JONGNAM!
ANSWER ME, YOU F#$KING BITCH, ARE YOU MINE OR NOT?
TH...THAT'S 'CAUSE YOU'RE ALWAYS LOOKING FOR SOMETHING TO USE AGAINST ME FOR NO REASON. WHY IS IT ALWAYS WHATEVER YOU WANT? I DON'T WANT IT THIS WAY
I REALLY GOTTA LET IT OUT RIGHT NOW. IF YOU REALLY HATE IT THAT MUCH, JUST THINK OF IT AS DOING OVERTIME.

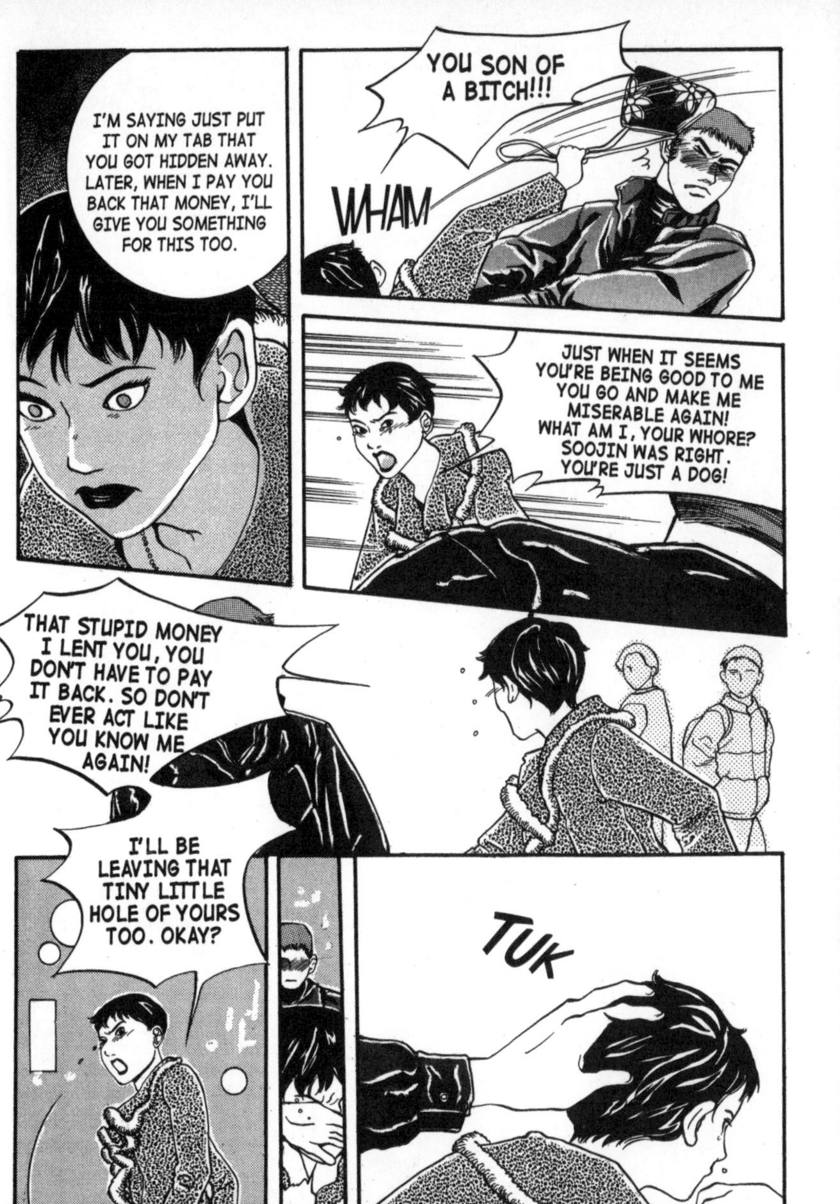
I'M SAYING JUST PUT IT ON MY TAB THAT YOU GOT HIDDEN AWAY. LATER, WHEN I PAY YOU BACK THAT MONEY, I'LL GIVE YOU SOMETHING FOR THIS TOO.
YOU SON OF A BITCH!!!
WHAM
JUST WHEN IT SEEMS YOU'RE BEING GOOD TO ME YOU GO AND MAKE ME MISERABLE AGAIN! WHAT AM I, YOUR WHORE? SOOJIN WAS RIGHT. YOU'RE JUST A DOG!
THAT STUPID MONEY I LENT YOU, YOU DON'T HAVE TO PAY IT BACK. SO DON'T EVER ACT LIKE YOU KNOW ME AGAIN!
I'LL BE LEAVING THAT TINY LITTLE HOLE OF YOURS TOO. OKAY?
TUK

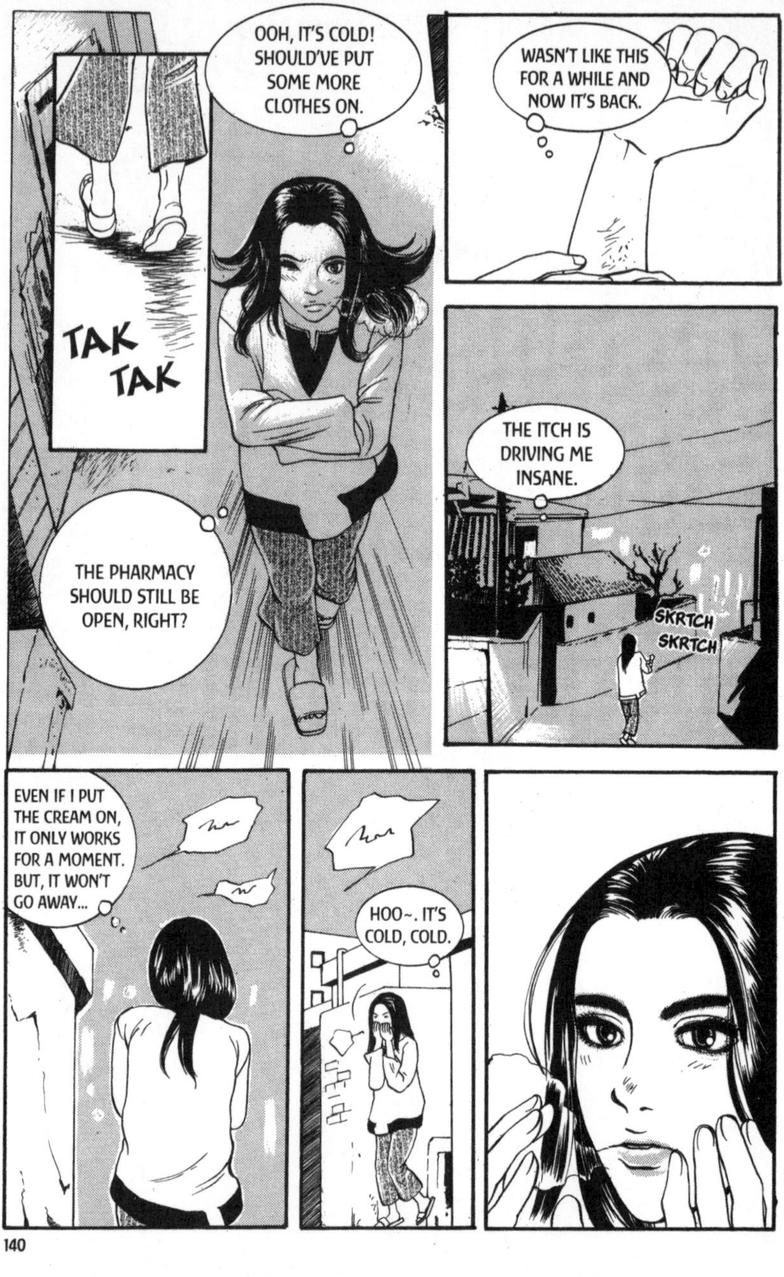
OOH, IT'S COLD! SHOULD'VE PUT SOME MORE CLOTHES ON.
TAK TAK
THE PHARMACY SHOULD STILL BE OPEN, RIGHT?
WASN'T LIKE THIS FOR A WHILE AND NOW IT'S BACK.
THE ITCH IS DRIVING ME INSANE.
SKRTCH SKRTCH
EVEN IF I PUT THE CREAM ON, IT ONLY WORKS FOR A MOMENT. BUT, IT WON'T GO AWAY...
HOO~. IT'S COLD, COLD.

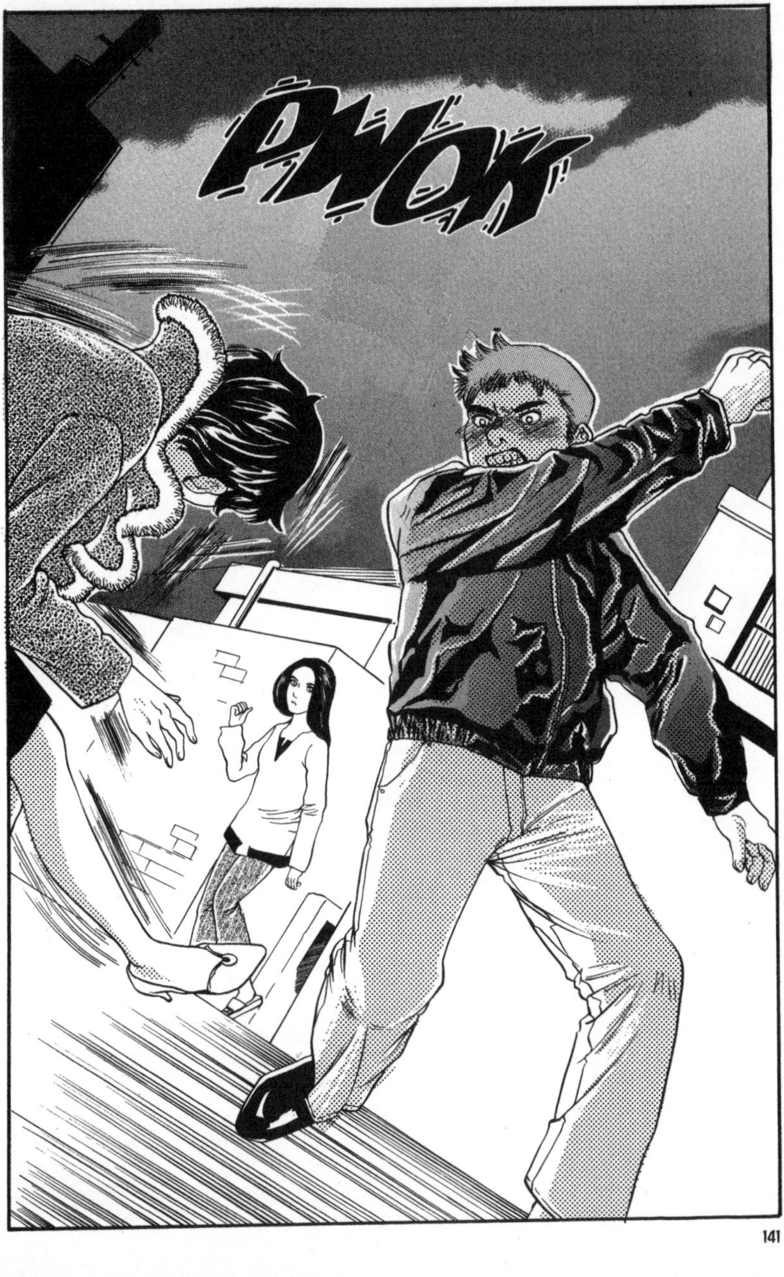
PWOK

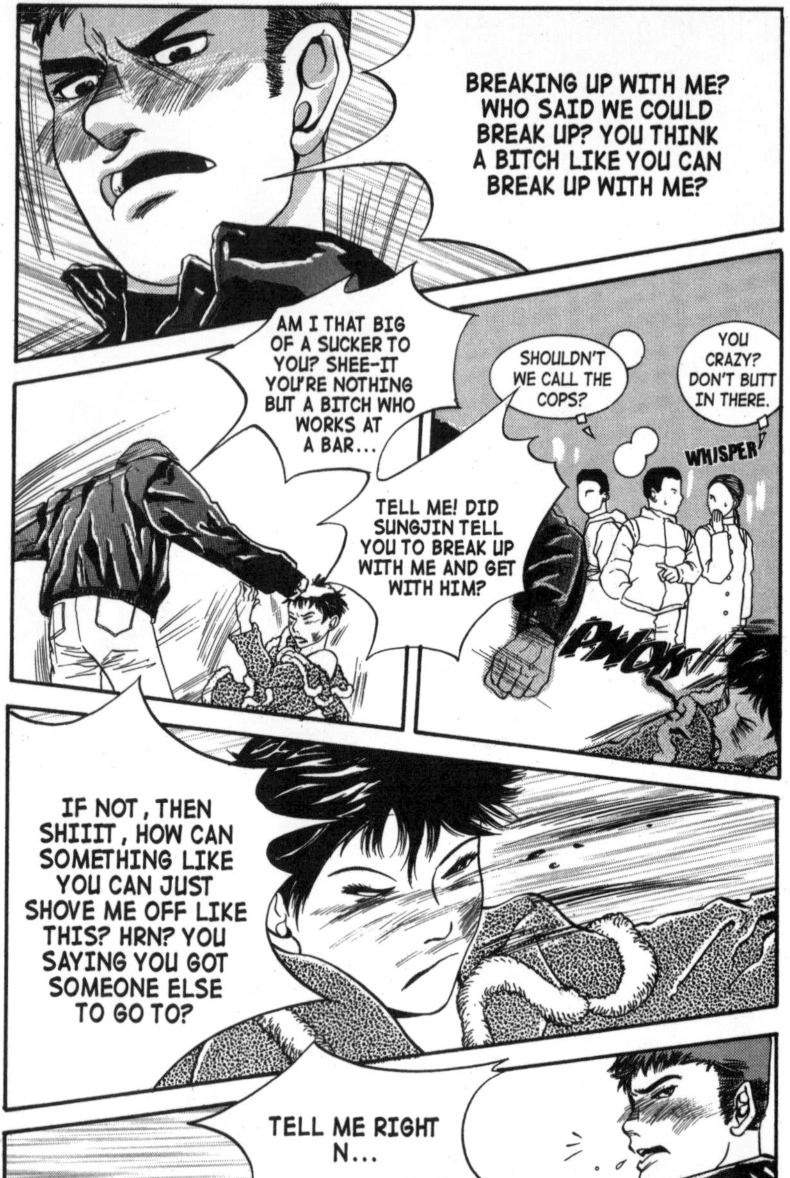
BREAKING UP WITH ME? WHO SAID WE COULD BREAK UP? YOU THINK A BITCH LIKE YOU CAN BREAK UP WITH ME?
AM I THAT BIG OF A SUCKER TO YOU? SHEE-IT YOU'RE NOTHING BUT A BITCH WHO WORKS AT A BAR...
TELL ME! DID SUNGJIN TELL YOU TO BREAK UP WITH ME AND GET WITH HIM?
SHOULDN'T WE CALL THE COPS?
YOU CRAZY? DON'T BUTT IN THERE.
WHISPER
PWOK
IF NOT, THEN SHIIIT, HOW CAN SOMETHING LIKE YOU CAN JUST SHOVE ME OFF LIKE THIS? HRN? YOU SAYING YOU GOT SOMEONE ELSE TO GO TO?
TELL ME RIGHT N...

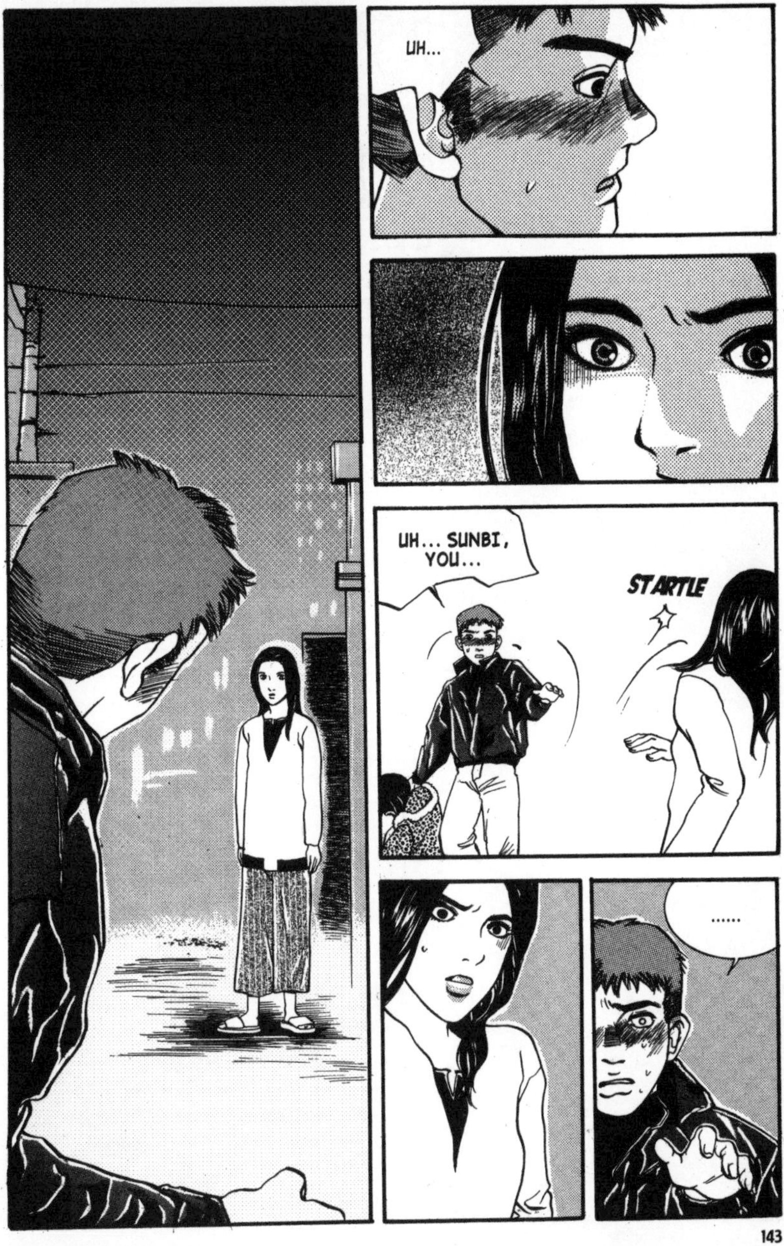
UH...
UH... SUNBI, YOU...
STARTLE
......

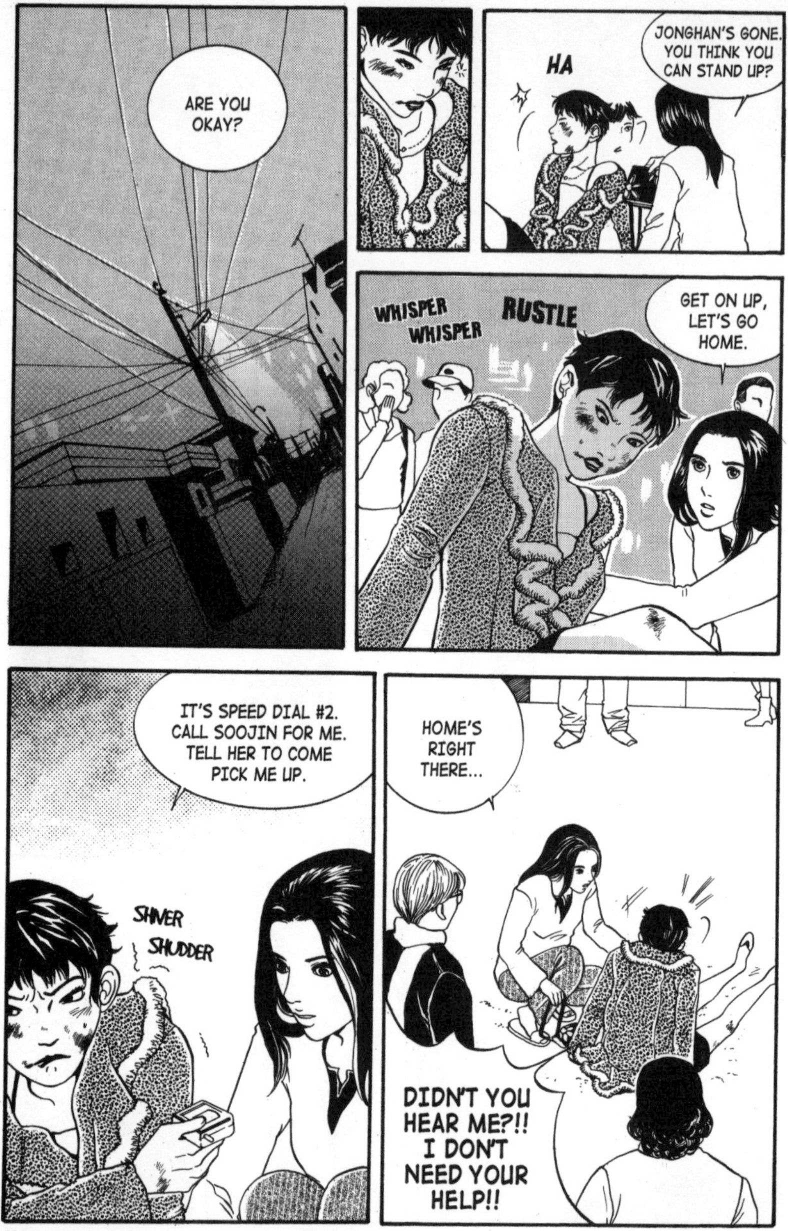

ARE YOU OKAY?
HA
JONGHAN'S GONE. YOU THINK YOU CAN STAND UP?
WHISPER WHISPER
RUSTLE
GET ON UP, LET'S GO HOME.
IT'S SPEED DIAL #2. CALL SOOJIN FOR ME. TELL HER TO COME PICK ME UP.
SHIVER
SHUDDER
HOME'S RIGHT THERE...
DIDN'T YOU HEAR ME?!! I DON'T NEED YOUR HELP!!

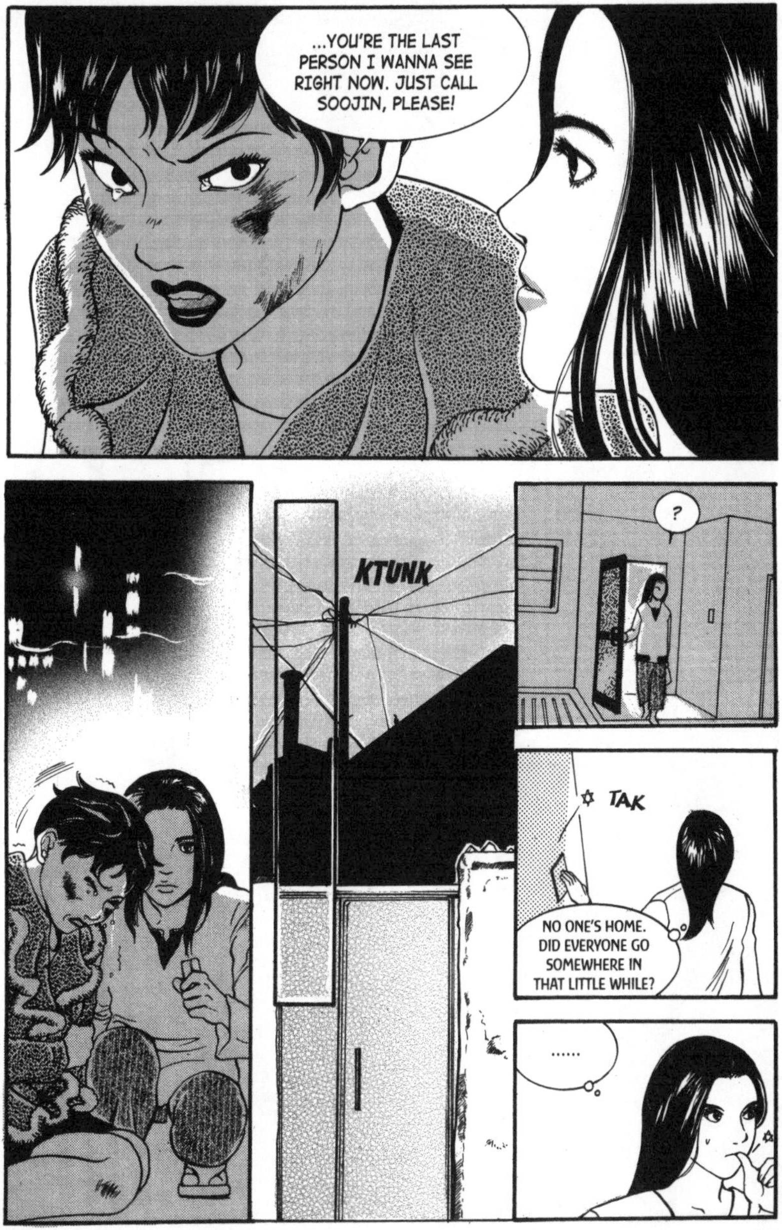
...YOU'RE THE LAST PERSON I WANNA SEE RIGHT NOW. JUST CALL SOOJIN, PLEASE!
KTUNK
?
TAK
NO ONE'S HOME. DID EVERYONE GO SOMEWHERE IN THAT LITTLE WHILE?
......

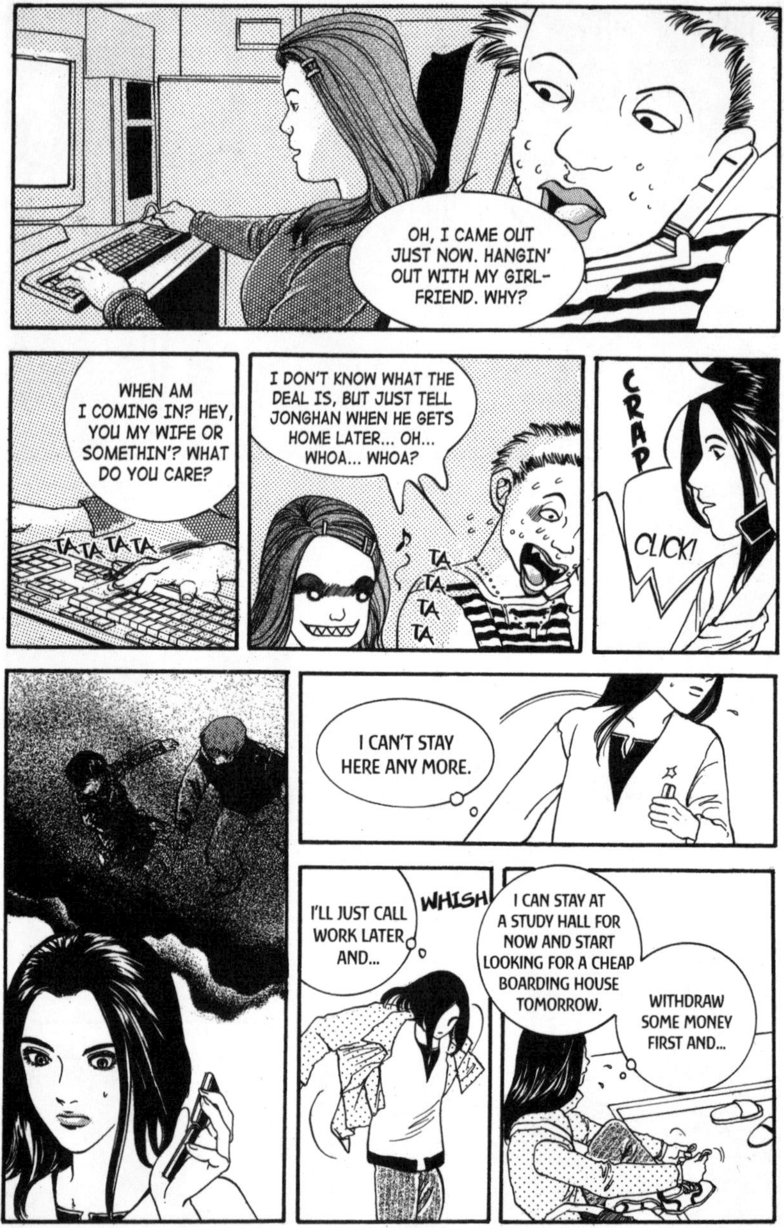
OH, I CAME OUT JUST NOW. HANGIN' OUT WITH MY GIRL-FRIEND. WHY?
WHEN AM I COMING IN? HEY, YOU MY WIFE OR SOMETHIN'? WHAT DO YOU CARE?
TA TA TA TA
I DON'T KNOW WHAT THE DEAL IS, BUT JUST TELL JONGHAN WHEN HE GETS HOME LATER... OH... WHOA... WHOA?
TA TA TA TA
CRAP
CLICK!
I CAN'T STAY HERE ANY MORE.
I'LL JUST CALL WORK LATER AND...
WHISH
I CAN STAY AT A STUDY HALL FOR NOW AND START LOOKING FOR A CHEAP BOARDING HOUSE TOMORROW.
WITHDRAW SOME MONEY FIRST AND...

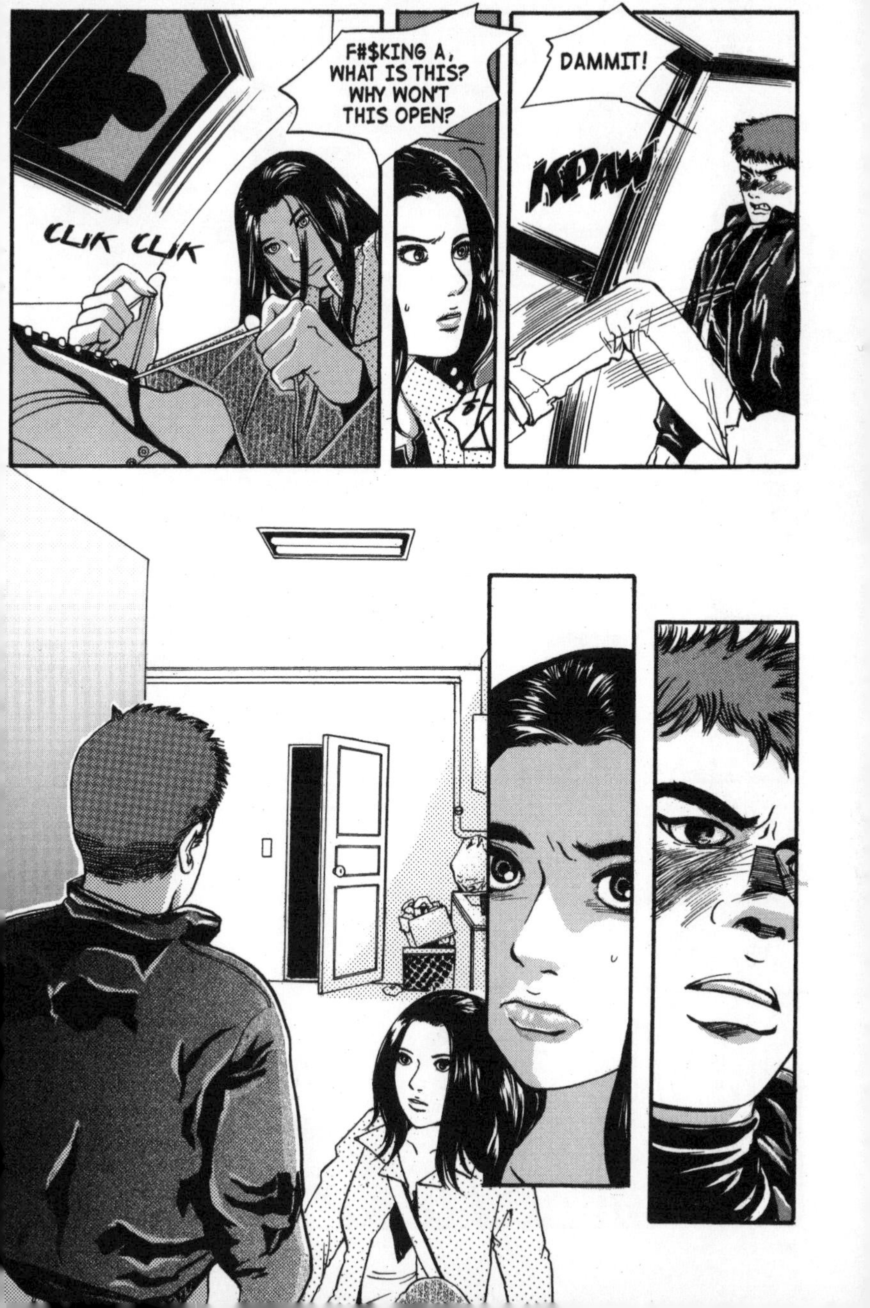
CLIK CLIK
F#$KING A, WHAT IS THIS? WHY WON'T THIS OPEN?
DAMMIT!
KPAW

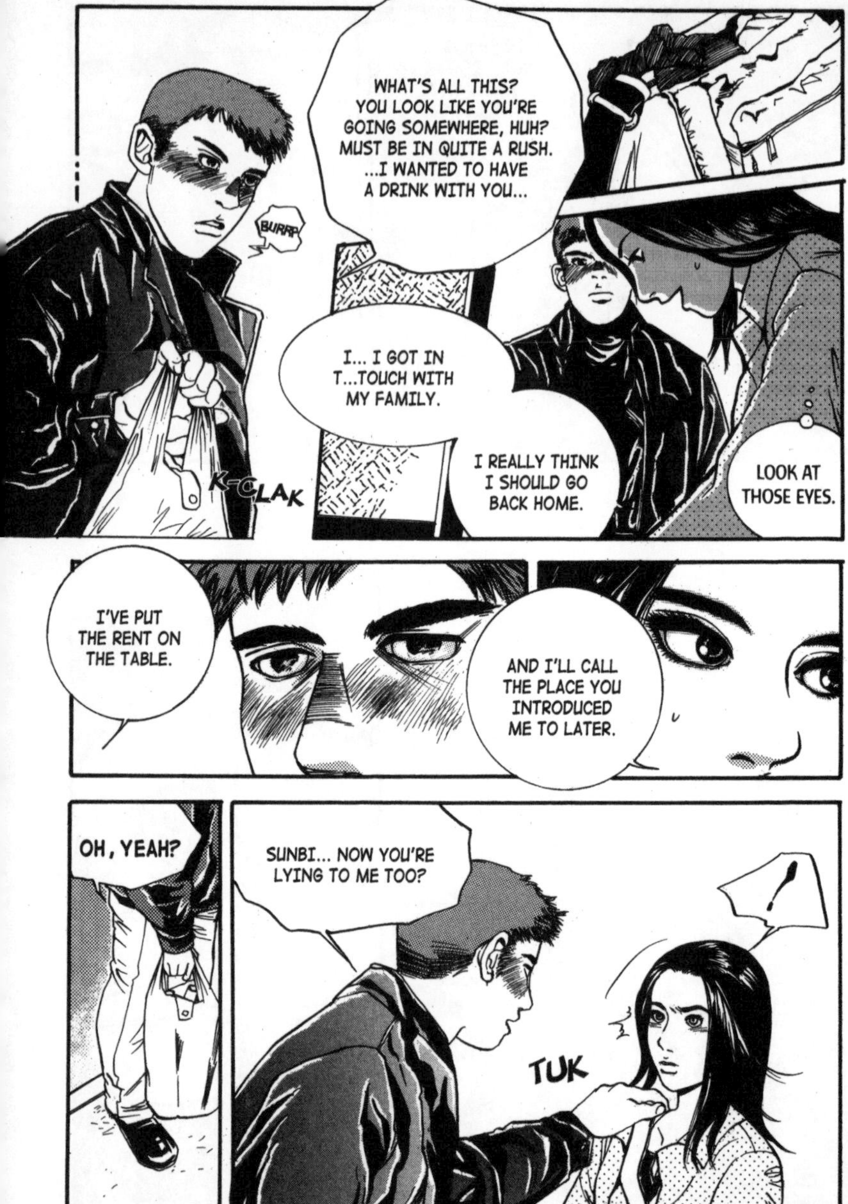

BURRP
K-CLAK
WHAT'S ALL THIS? YOU LOOK LIKE YOU'RE GOING SOMEWHERE, HUH? MUST BE IN QUITE A RUSH. ...I WANTED TO HAVE A DRINK WITH YOU...
I... I GOT IN T...TOUCH WITH MY FAMILY.
I REALLY THINK I SHOULD GO BACK HOME.
LOOK AT THOSE EYES.
I'VE PUT THE RENT ON THE TABLE.
AND I'LL CALL THE PLACE YOU INTRODUCED ME TO LATER.
OH, YEAH?
SUNBI... NOW YOU'RE LYING TO ME TOO?
!
TUK

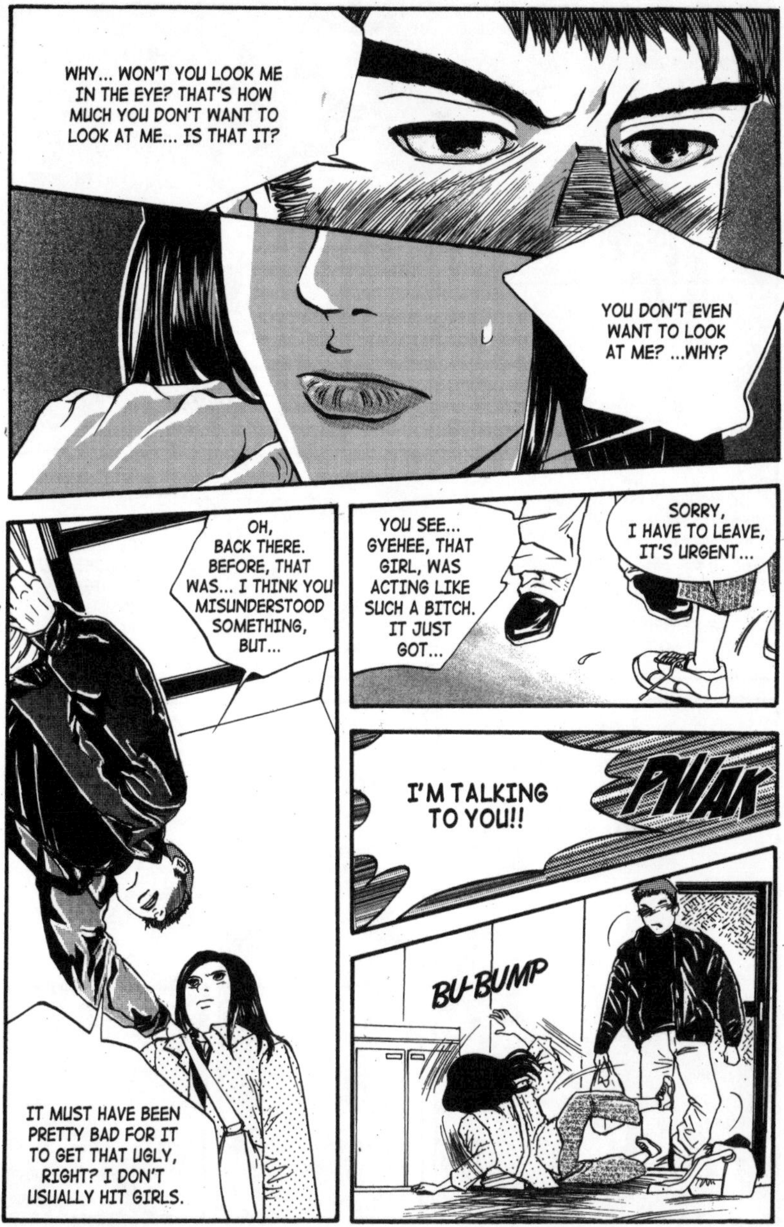
WHY... WON'T YOU LOOK ME IN THE EYE? THAT'S HOW MUCH YOU DON'T WANT TO LOOK AT ME... IS THAT IT?
YOU DON'T EVEN WANT TO LOOK AT ME? ...WHY?
OH, BACK THERE. BEFORE, THAT WAS... I THINK YOU MISUNDERSTOOD SOMETHING, BUT...
IT MUST HAVE BEEN PRETTY BAD FOR IT TO GET THAT UGLY, RIGHT? I DON'T USUALLY HIT GIRLS.
YOU SEE... GYEHEE, THAT GIRL, WAS ACTING LIKE SUCH A BITCH. IT JUST GOT...
SORRY, I HAVE TO LEAVE, IT'S URGENT...
I'M TALKING TO YOU!!
PWAK
BU-BUMP

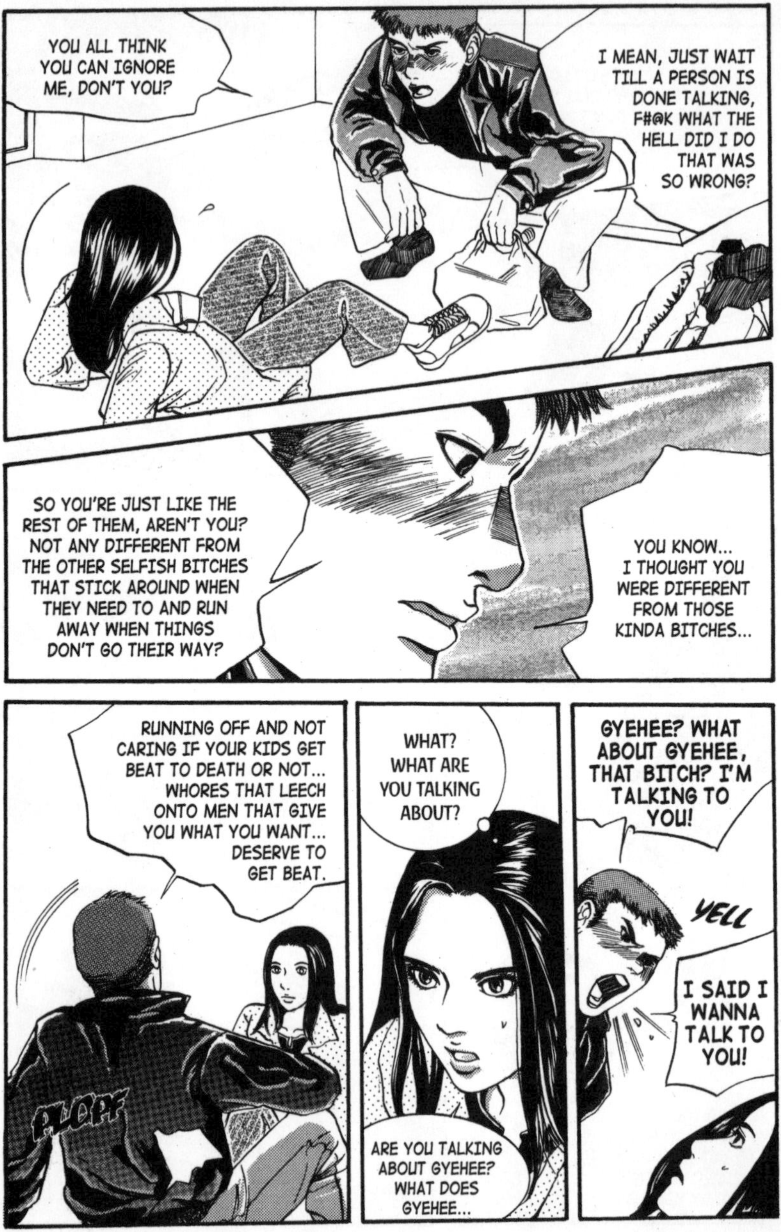
YOU ALL THINK YOU CAN IGNORE ME, DON'T YOU?
I MEAN, JUST WAIT TILL A PERSON IS DONE TALKING, F#@K WHAT THE HELL DID I DO THAT WAS SO WRONG?
SO YOU'RE JUST LIKE THE REST OF THEM, AREN'T YOU? NOT ANY DIFFERENT FROM THE OTHER SELFISH BITCHES THAT STICK AROUND WHEN THEY NEED TO AND RUN AWAY WHEN THINGS DON'T GO THEIR WAY?
YOU KNOW... I THOUGHT YOU WERE DIFFERENT FROM THOSE KINDA BITCHES...
RUNNING OFF AND NOT CARING IF YOUR KIDS GET BEAT TO DEATH OR NOT... WHORES THAT LEECH ONTO MEN THAT GIVE YOU WHAT YOU WANT... DESERVE TO GET BEAT.
PLOPF
WHAT? WHAT ARE YOU TALKING ABOUT?
ARE YOU TALKING ABOUT GYEHEE? WHAT DOES GYEHEE...
GYEHEE? WHAT ABOUT GYEHEE, THAT BITCH? I'M TALKING TO YOU!
YELL
I SAID I WANNA TALK TO YOU!

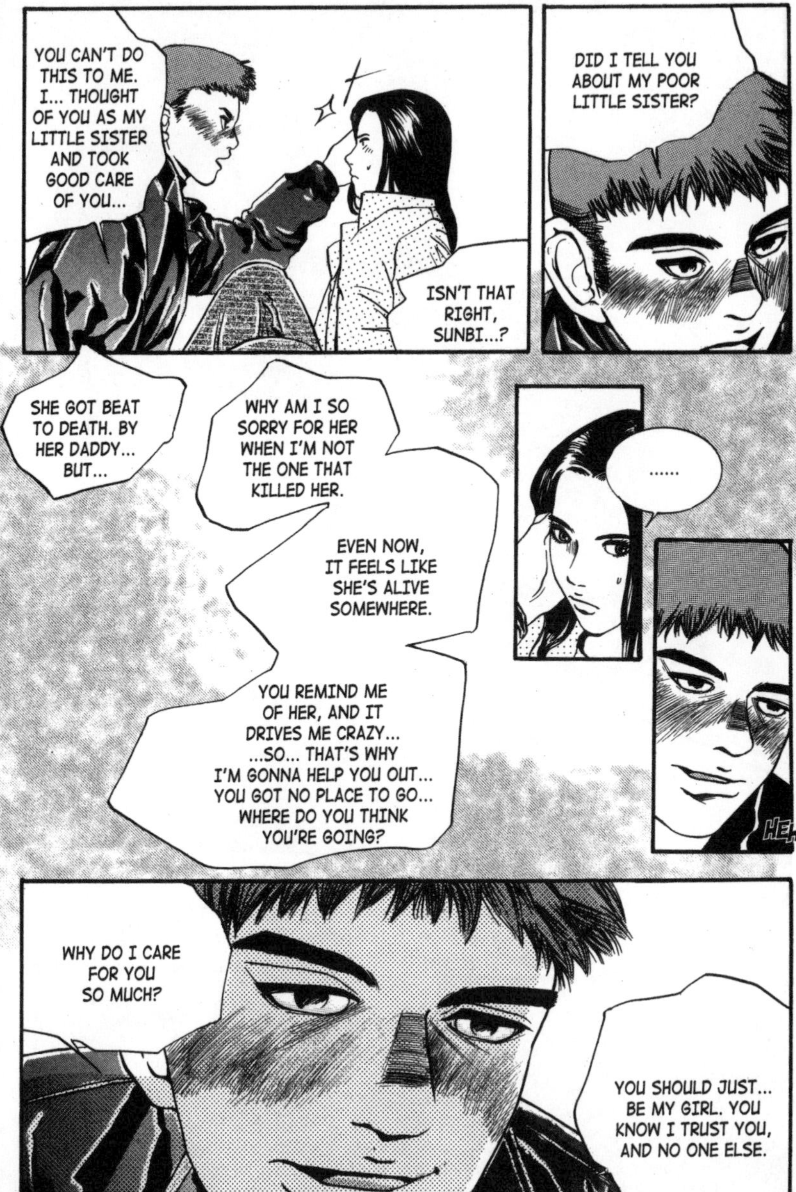
YOU CAN'T DO THIS TO ME. I... THOUGHT OF YOU AS MY LITTLE SISTER AND TOOK GOOD CARE OF YOU...
ISN'T THAT RIGHT, SUNBI...?
DID I TELL YOU ABOUT MY POOR LITTLE SISTER?
SHE GOT BEAT TO DEATH. BY HER DADDY... BUT...
WHY AM I SO SORRY FOR HER WHEN I'M NOT THE ONE THAT KILLED HER.
EVEN NOW, IT FEELS LIKE SHE'S ALIVE SOMEWHERE.
YOU REMIND ME OF HER, AND IT DRIVES ME CRAZY... ...SO... THAT'S WHY I'M GONNA HELP YOU OUT... YOU GOT NO PLACE TO GO... WHERE DO YOU THINK YOU'RE GOING?
......
HEH
WHY DO I CARE FOR YOU SO MUCH?
YOU SHOULD JUST... BE MY GIRL. YOU KNOW I TRUST YOU, AND NO ONE ELSE.

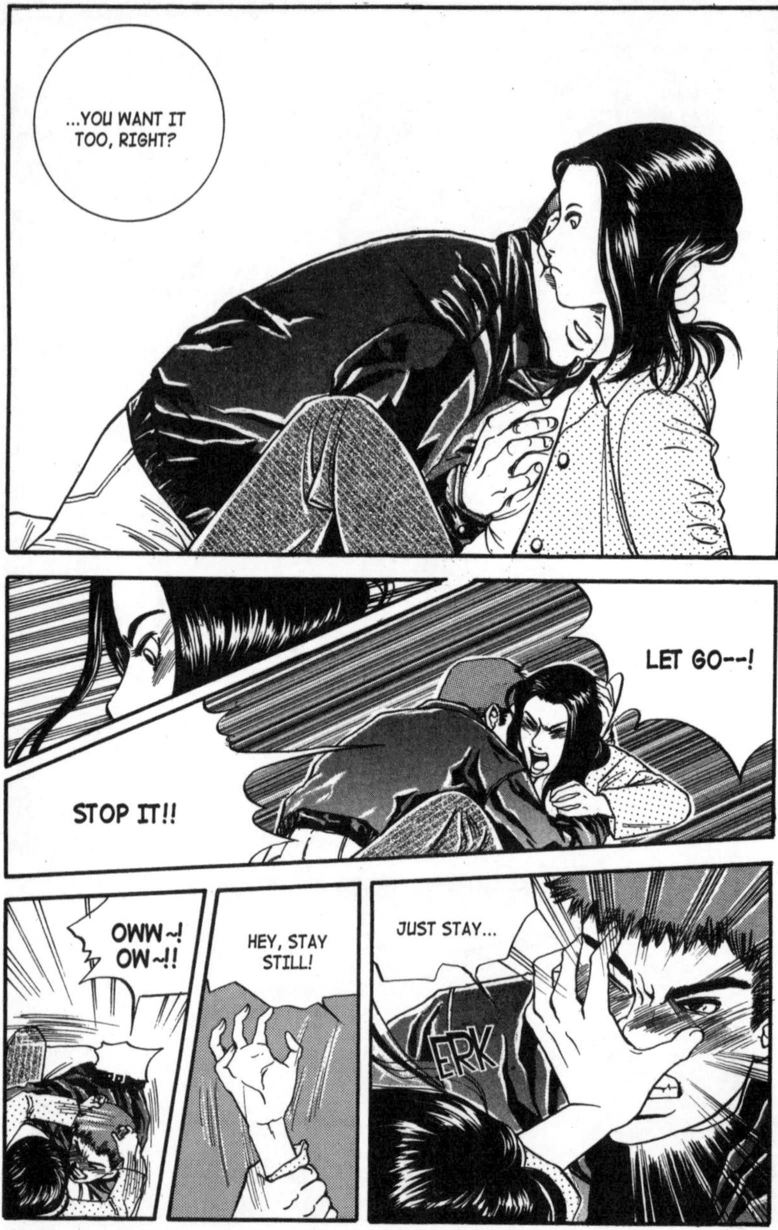
...YOU WANT IT TOO, RIGHT?
STOP IT!!
LET GO--!
OWW~! OW~!!
HEY, STAY STILL!
JUST STAY...
ERK

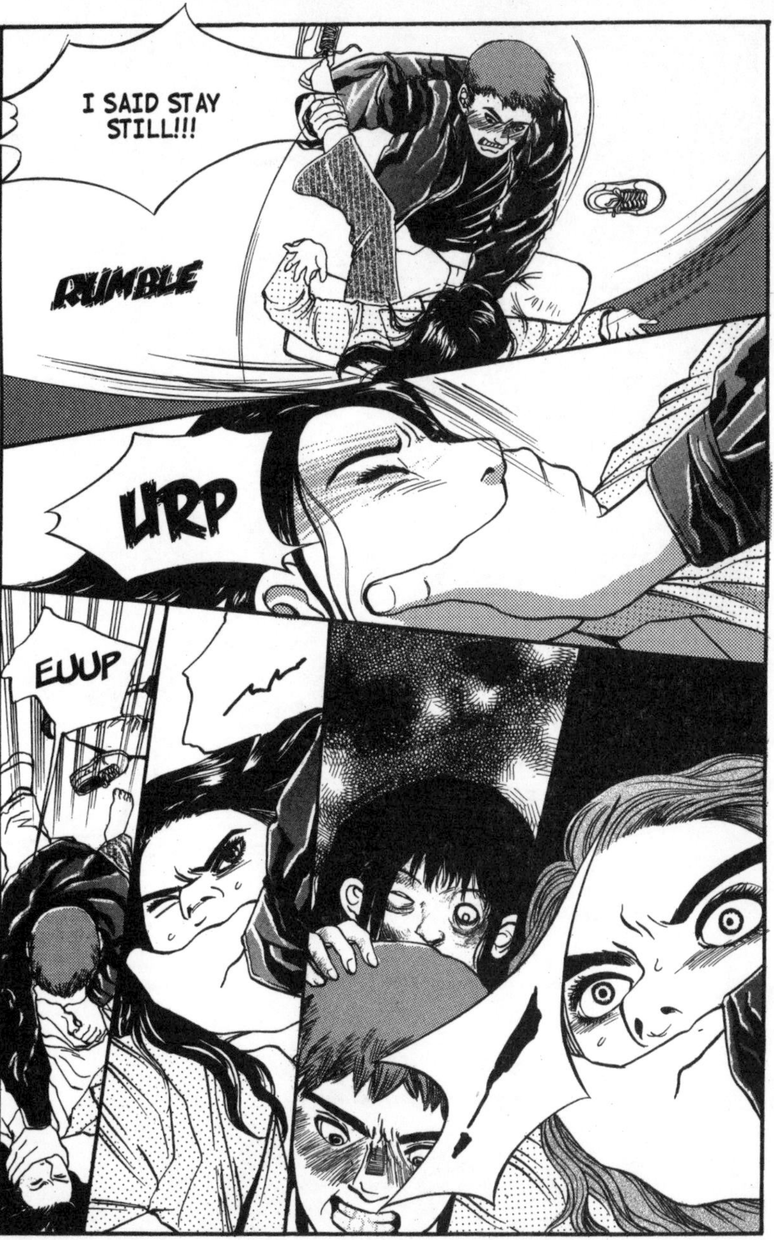
I SAID STAY STILL!!!
RUMBLE
URP
EUUP
!

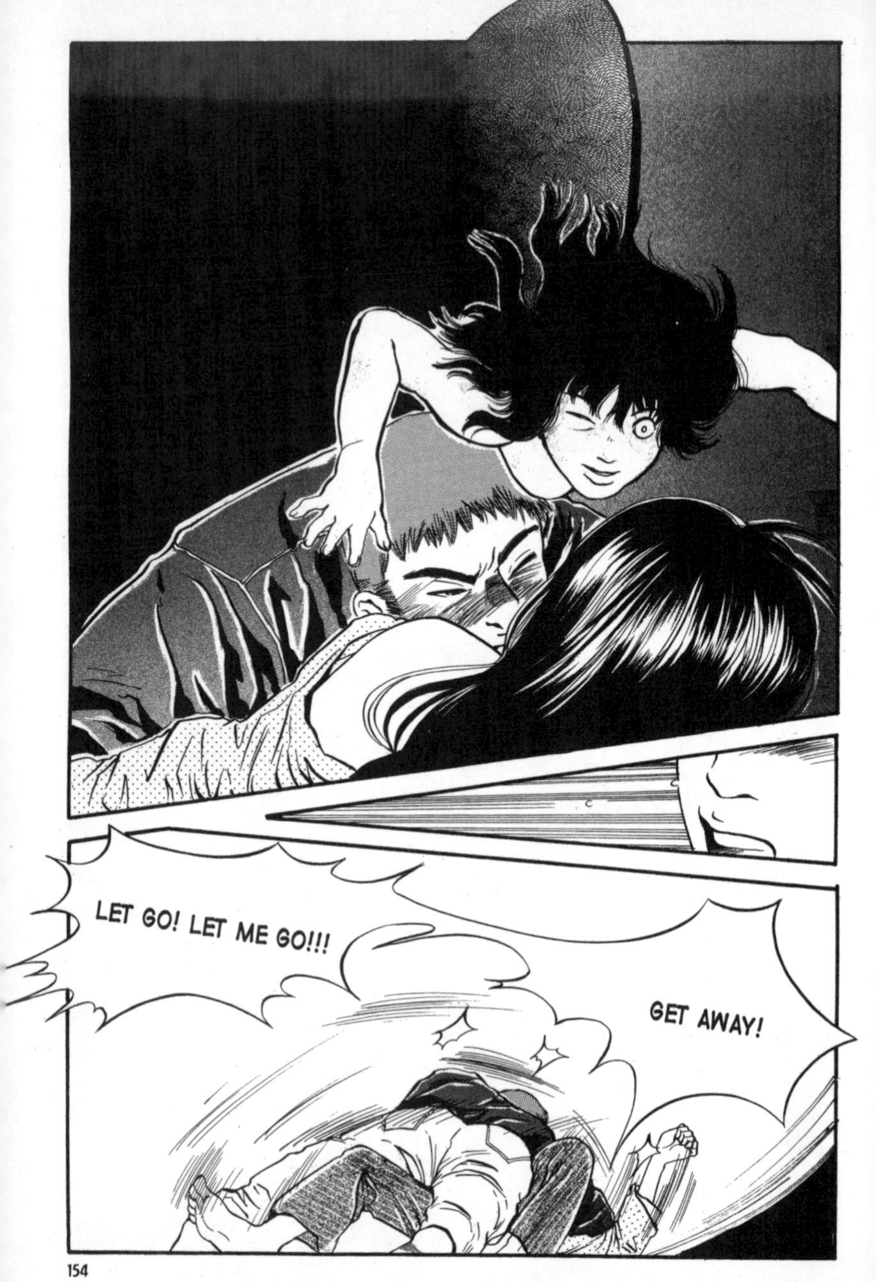
LET GO! LET ME GO!!!
GET AWAY!

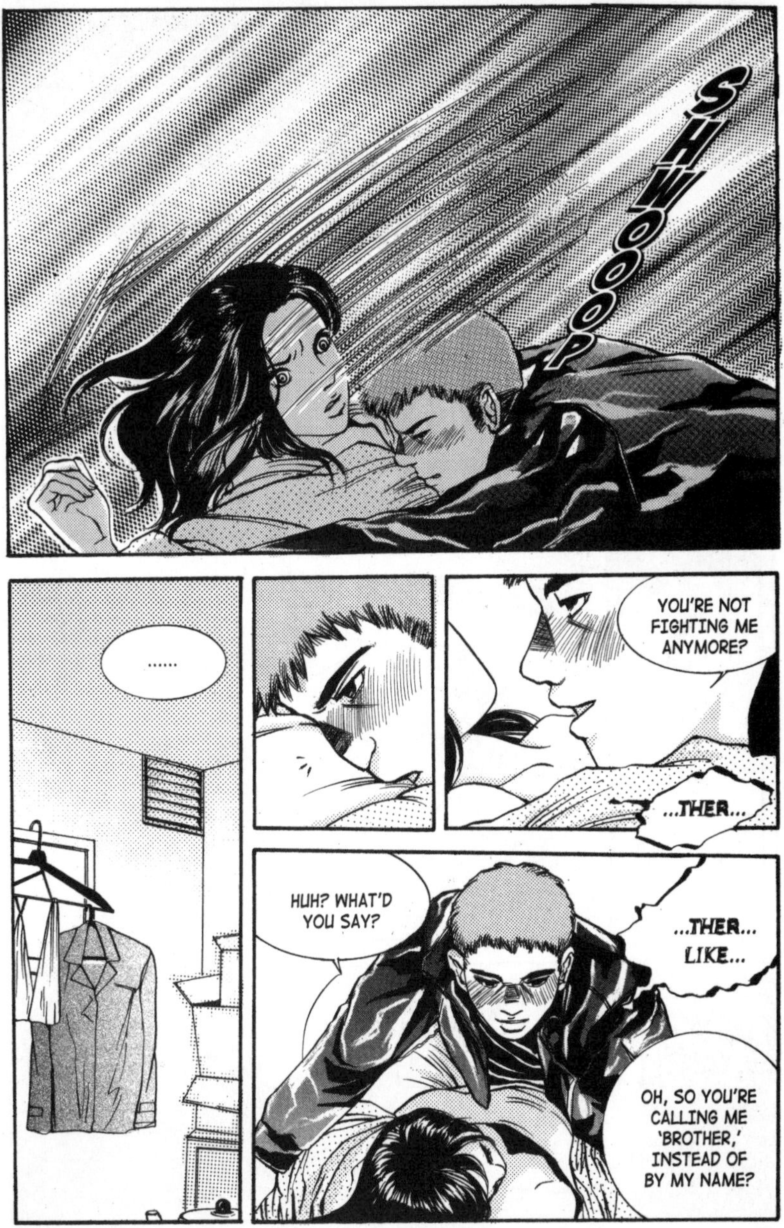
SHWOOOP
......
YOU'RE NOT FIGHTING ME ANYMORE?
...THER...
HUH? WHAT'D YOU SAY?
...THER... LIKE...
OH, SO YOU'RE CALLING ME 'BROTHER,' INSTEAD OF BY MY NAME?

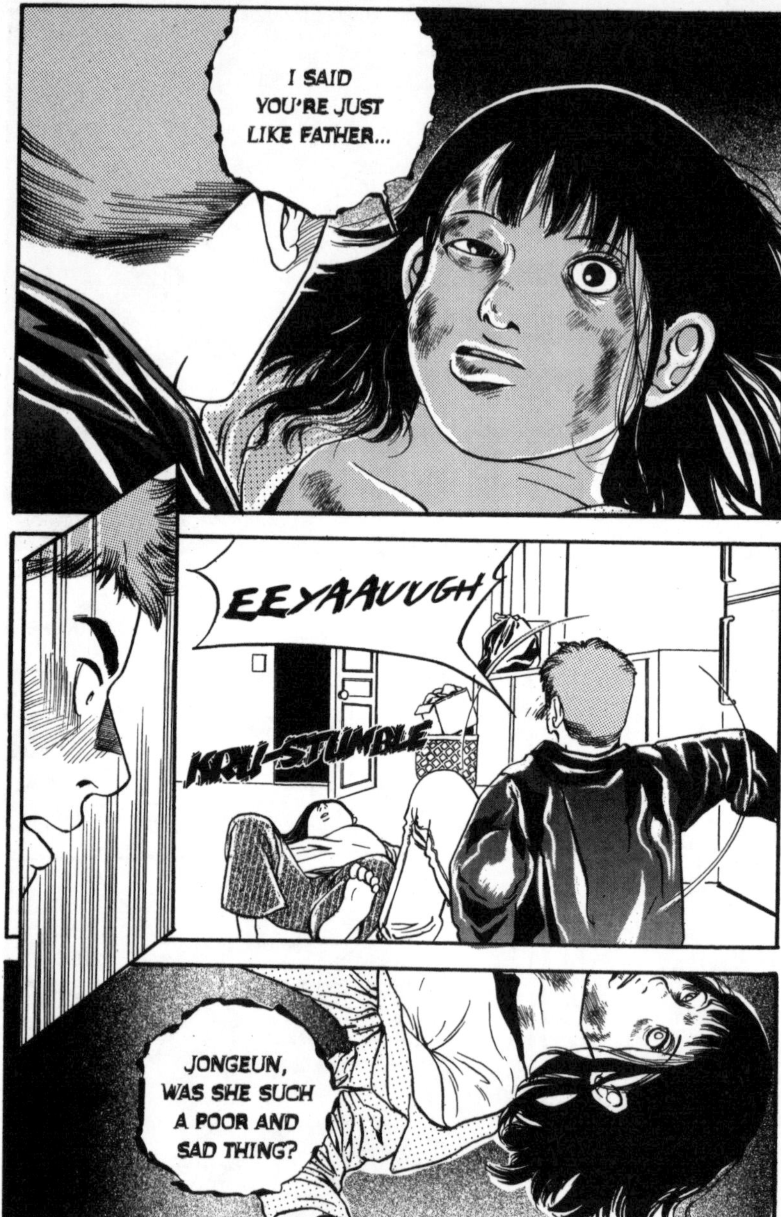
I SAID YOU'RE JUST LIKE FATHER...
EEYAAUUGH
KRU-STUMBLE
JONGEUN, WAS SHE SUCH A POOR AND SAD THING?

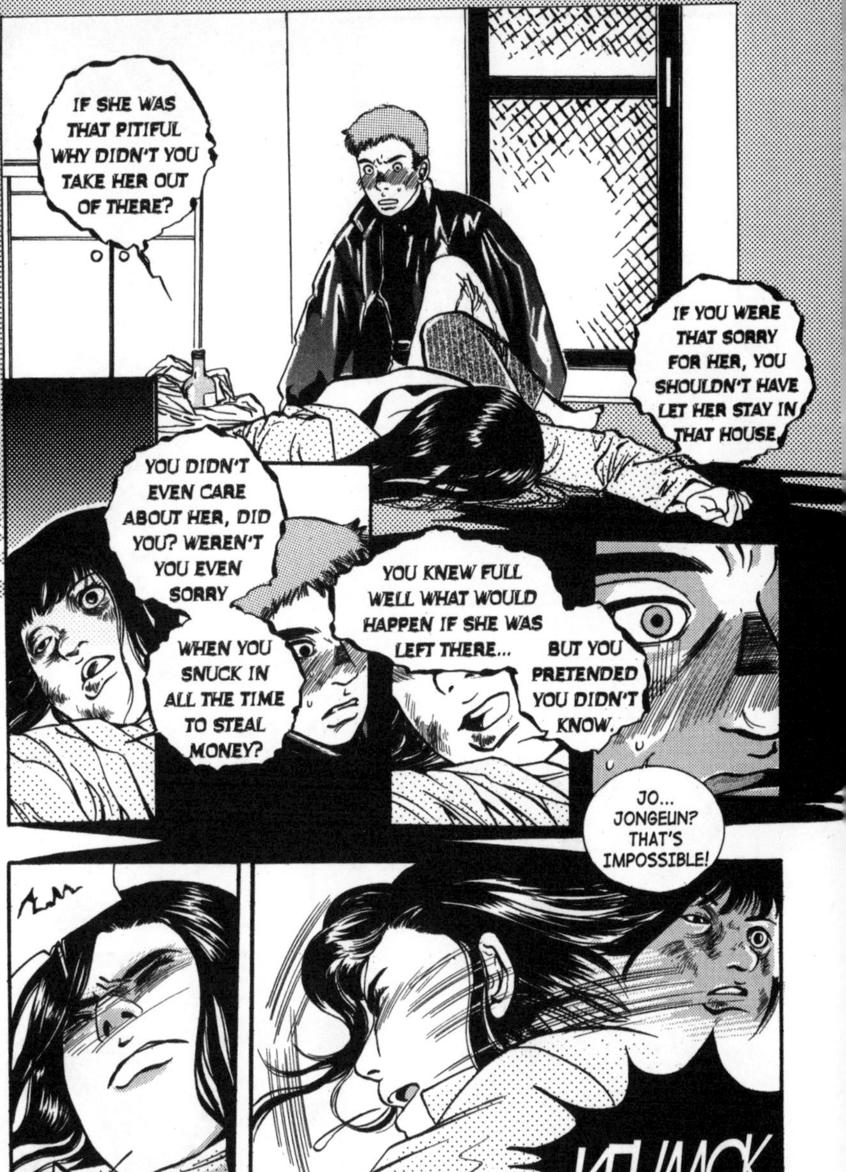

IF SHE WAS THAT PITIFUL WHY DIDN'T YOU TAKE HER OUT OF THERE?
IF YOU WERE THAT SORRY FOR HER, YOU SHOULDN'T HAVE LET HER STAY IN THAT HOUSE.
YOU DIDN'T EVEN CARE ABOUT HER, DID YOU? WEREN'T YOU EVEN SORRY
WHEN YOU SNUCK IN ALL THE TIME TO STEAL MONEY?
YOU KNEW FULL WELL WHAT WOULD HAPPEN IF SHE WAS LEFT THERE...
BUT YOU PRETENDED YOU DIDN'T KNOW.
JO... JONGEUN? THAT'S IMPOSSIBLE!
EURP
KEHAACK

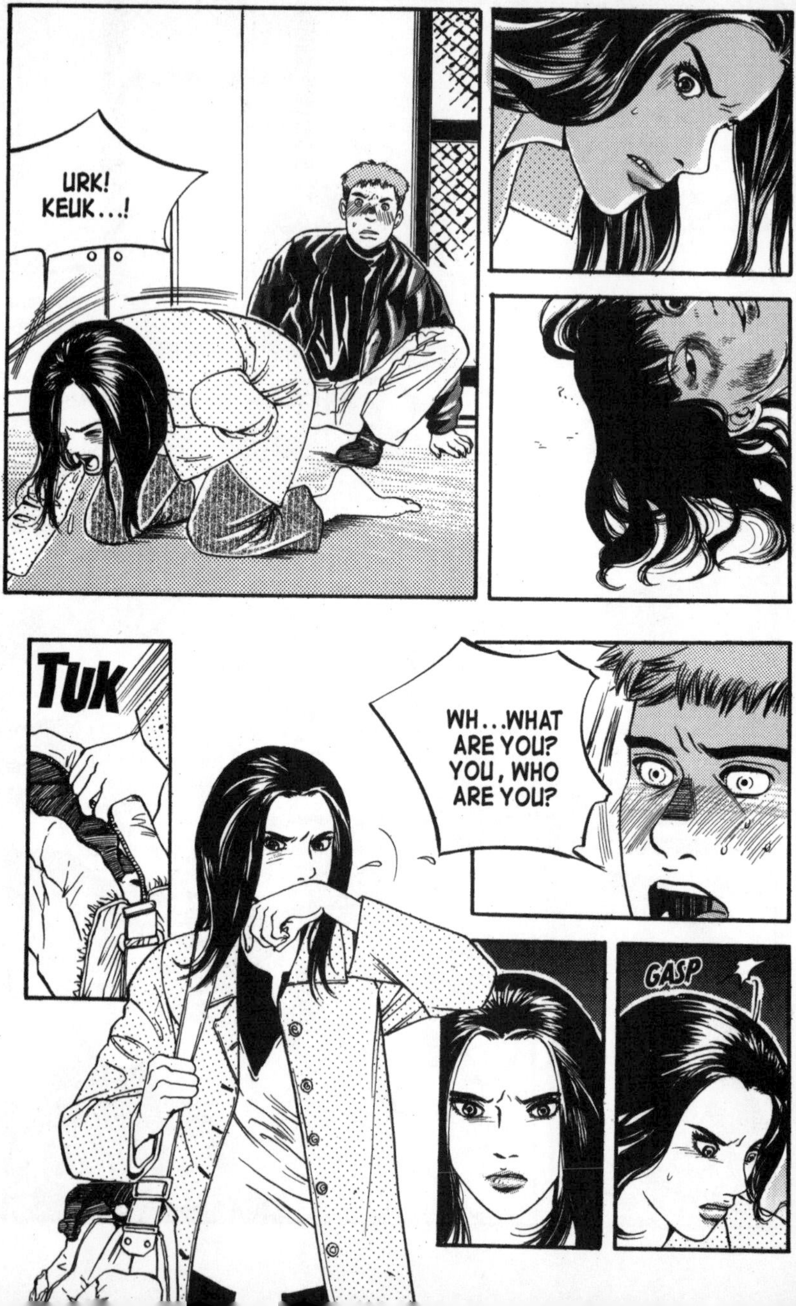
URK! KEUK...!
TUK
WH...WHAT ARE YOU? YOU, WHO ARE YOU?
GASP

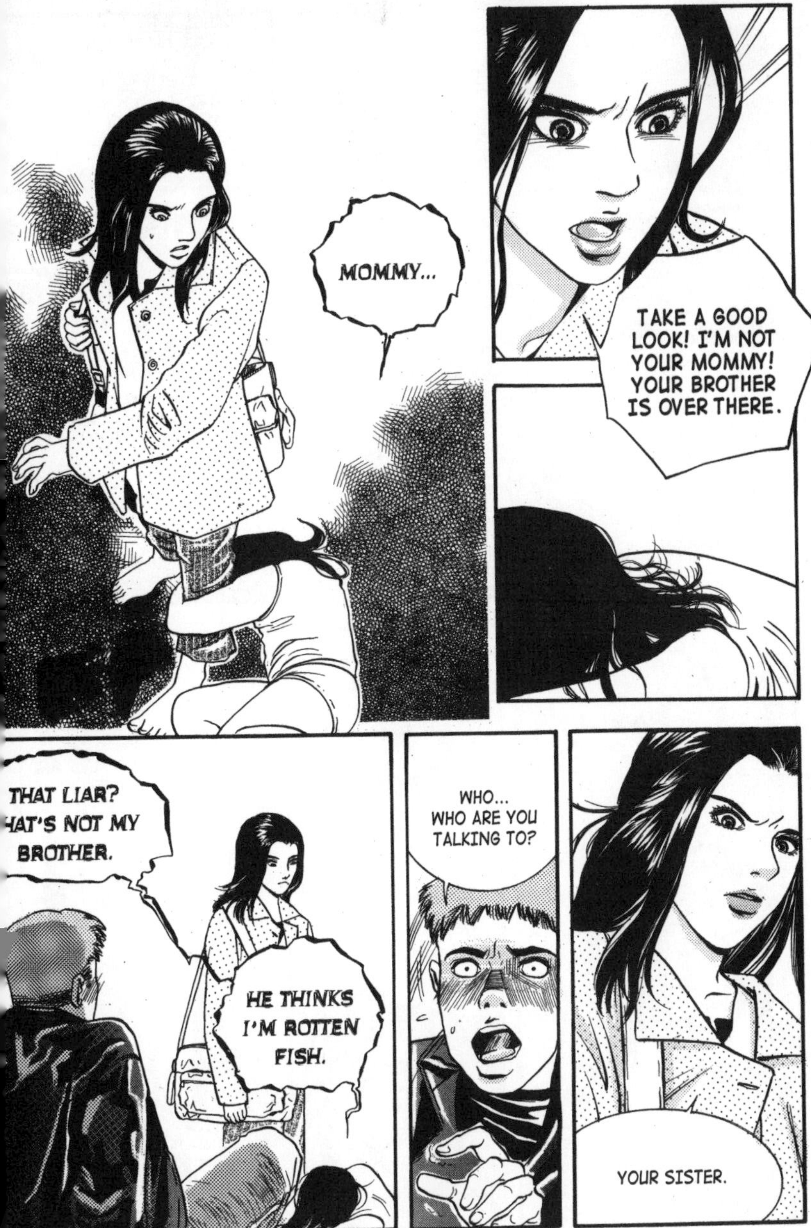
MOMMY...
TAKE A GOOD LOOK! I'M NOT YOUR MOMMY! YOUR BROTHER IS OVER THERE.
THAT LIAR? HAT'S NOT MY BROTHER.
HE THINKS I'M ROTTEN FISH.
WHO... WHO ARE YOU TALKING TO?
YOUR SISTER.

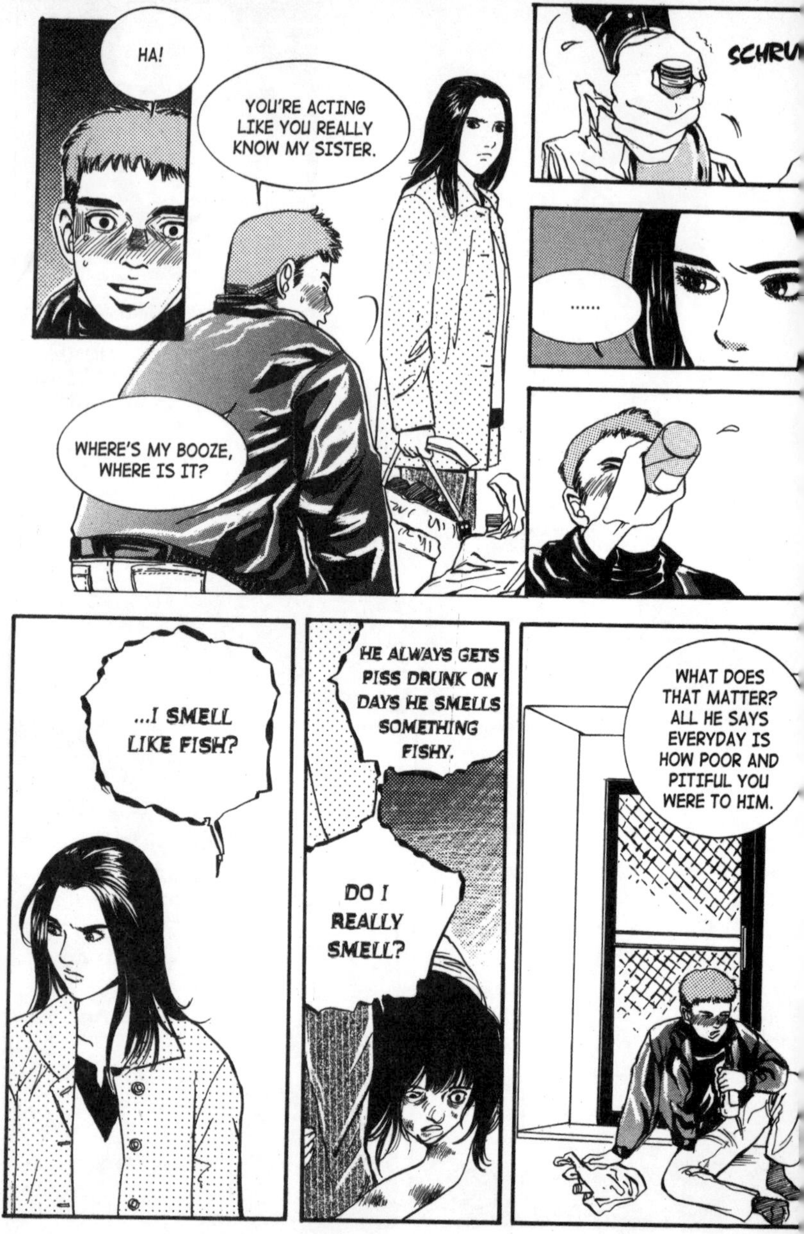
HA!
YOU'RE ACTING LIKE YOU REALLY KNOW MY SISTER.
WHERE'S MY BOOZE, WHERE IS IT?
SCHRU
......
...I SMELL LIKE FISH?
HE ALWAYS GETS PISS DRUNK ON DAYS HE SMELLS SOMETHING FISHY.
DO I REALLY SMELL?
WHAT DOES THAT MATTER? ALL HE SAYS EVERYDAY IS HOW POOR AND PITIFUL YOU WERE TO HIM.

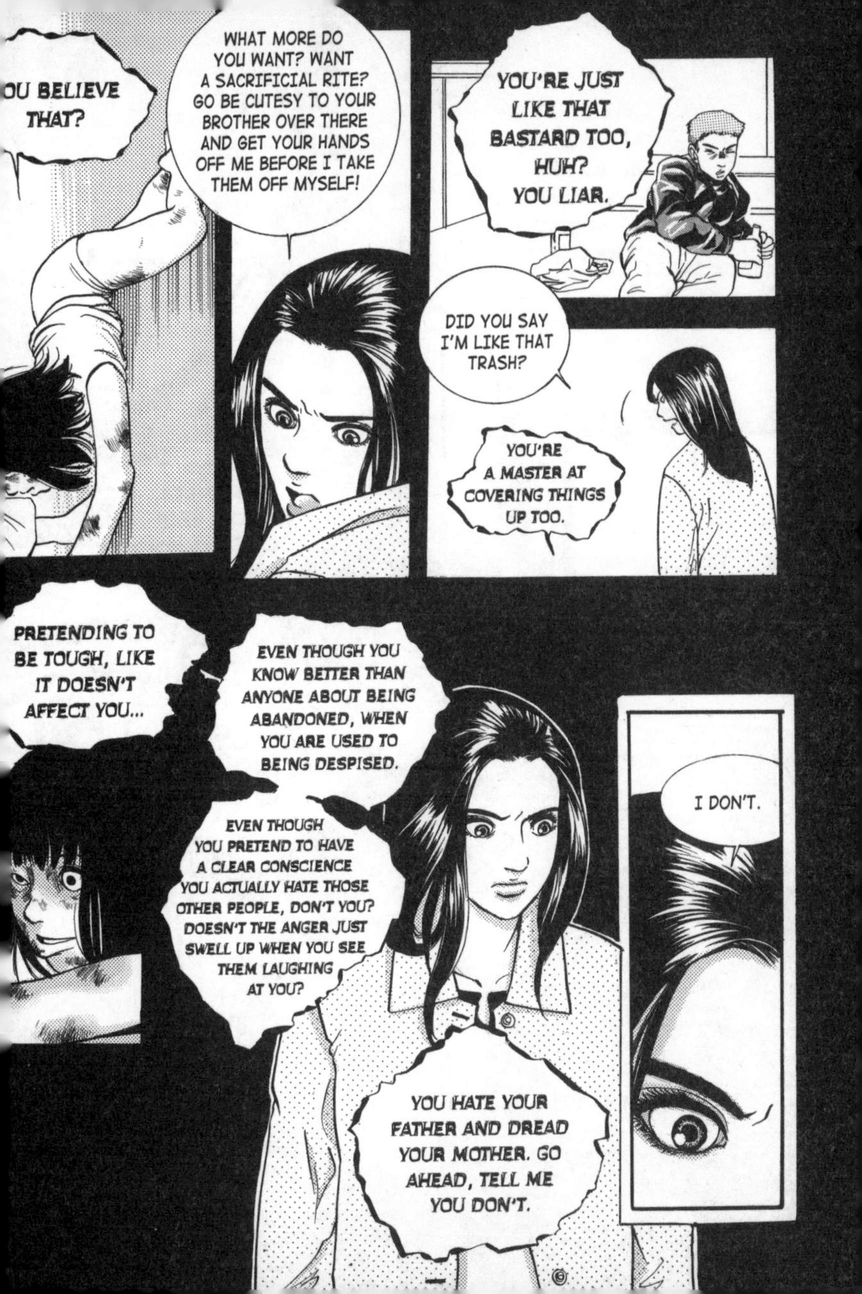
OU BELIEVE THAT?
WHAT MORE DO YOU WANT? WANT A SACRIFICIAL RITE? GO BE CUTESY TO YOUR BROTHER OVER THERE AND GET YOUR HANDS OFF ME BEFORE I TAKE THEM OFF MYSELF!
YOU'RE JUST LIKE THAT BASTARD TOO, HUH? YOU LIAR.
DID YOU SAY I'M LIKE THAT TRASH?
YOU'RE A MASTER AT COVERING THINGS UP TOO.
PRETENDING TO BE TOUGH, LIKE IT DOESN'T AFFECT YOU...
EVEN THOUGH YOU KNOW BETTER THAN ANYONE ABOUT BEING ABANDONED, WHEN YOU ARE USED TO BEING DESPISED.
EVEN THOUGH YOU PRETEND TO HAVE A CLEAR CONSCIENCE YOU ACTUALLY HATE THOSE OTHER PEOPLE, DON'T YOU? DOESN'T THE ANGER JUST SWELL UP WHEN YOU SEE THEM LAUGHING AT YOU?
YOU HATE YOUR FATHER AND DREAD YOUR MOTHER. GO AHEAD, TELL ME YOU DON'T.
I DON'T.

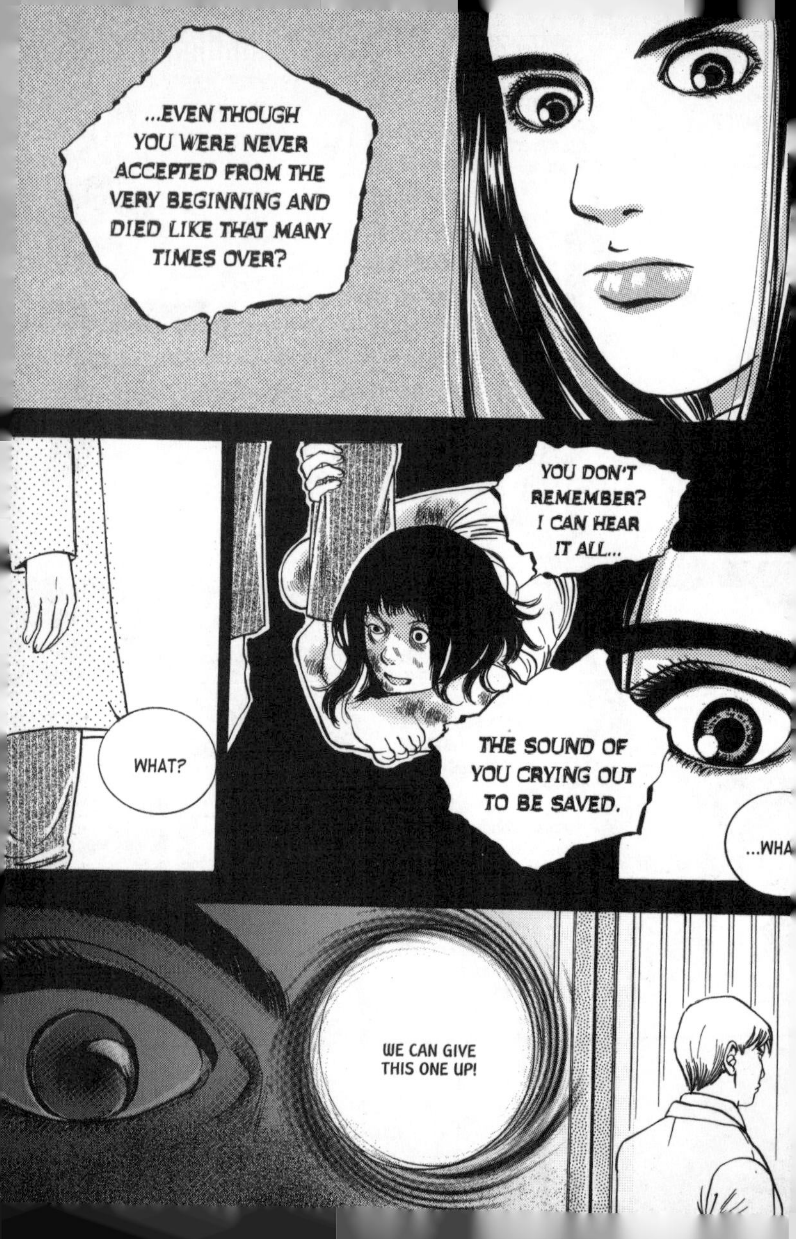
...EVEN THOUGH YOU WERE NEVER ACCEPTED FROM THE VERY BEGINNING AND DIED LIKE THAT MANY TIMES OVER?
WHAT?
YOU DON'T REMEMBER? I CAN HEAR IT ALL...
THE SOUND OF YOU CRYING OUT TO BE SAVED.
...WHA
WE CAN GIVE THIS ONE UP!

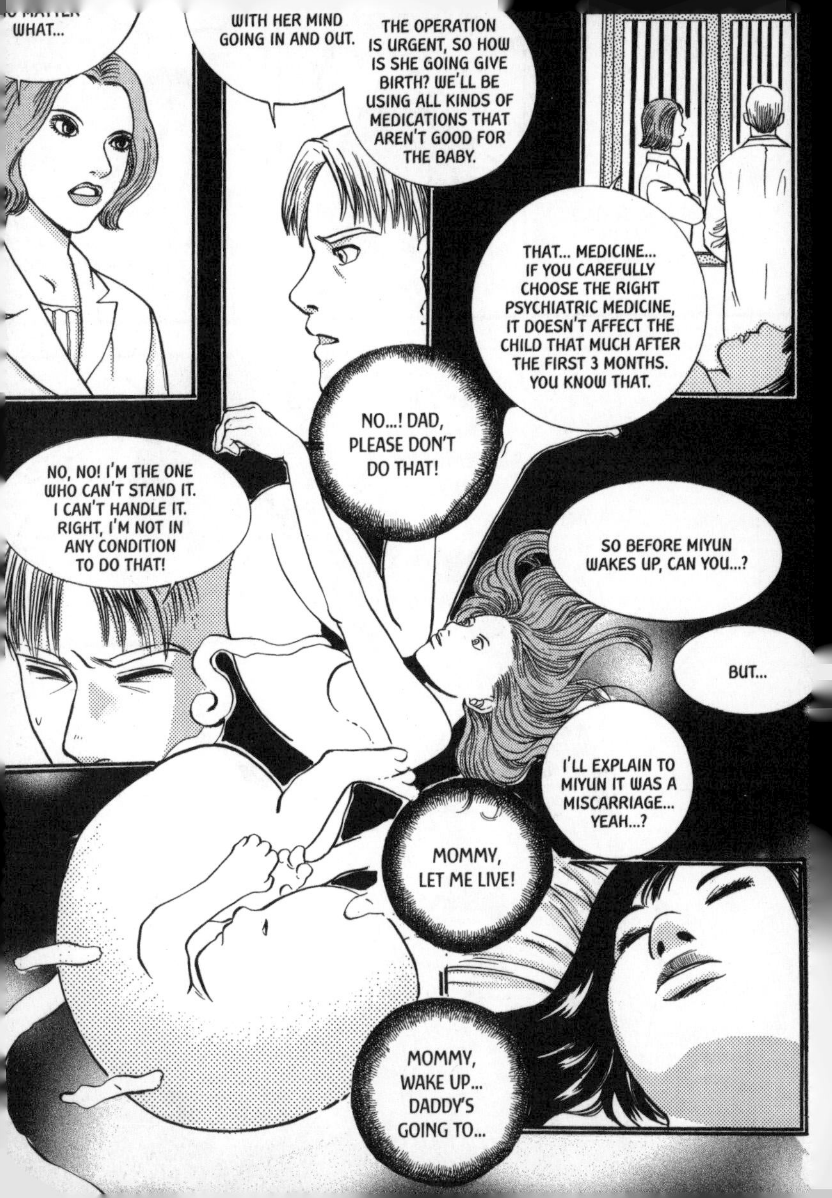
WHAT...
WITH HER MIND GOING IN AND OUT.
THE OPERATION IS URGENT, SO HOW IS SHE GOING GIVE BIRTH? WE'LL BE USING ALL KINDS OF MEDICATIONS THAT AREN'T GOOD FOR THE BABY.
THAT... MEDICINE... IF YOU CAREFULLY CHOOSE THE RIGHT PSYCHIATRIC MEDICINE, IT DOESN'T AFFECT THE CHILD THAT MUCH AFTER THE FIRST 3 MONTHS. YOU KNOW THAT.
NO, NO! I'M THE ONE WHO CAN'T STAND IT. I CAN'T HANDLE IT. RIGHT, I'M NOT IN ANY CONDITION TO DO THAT!
NO...! DAD, PLEASE DON'T DO THAT!
SO BEFORE MIYUN WAKES UP, CAN YOU...?
BUT...
I'LL EXPLAIN TO MIYUN IT WAS A MISCARRIAGE... YEAH...?
MOMMY, LET ME LIVE!
MOMMY, WAKE UP... DADDY'S GOING TO...

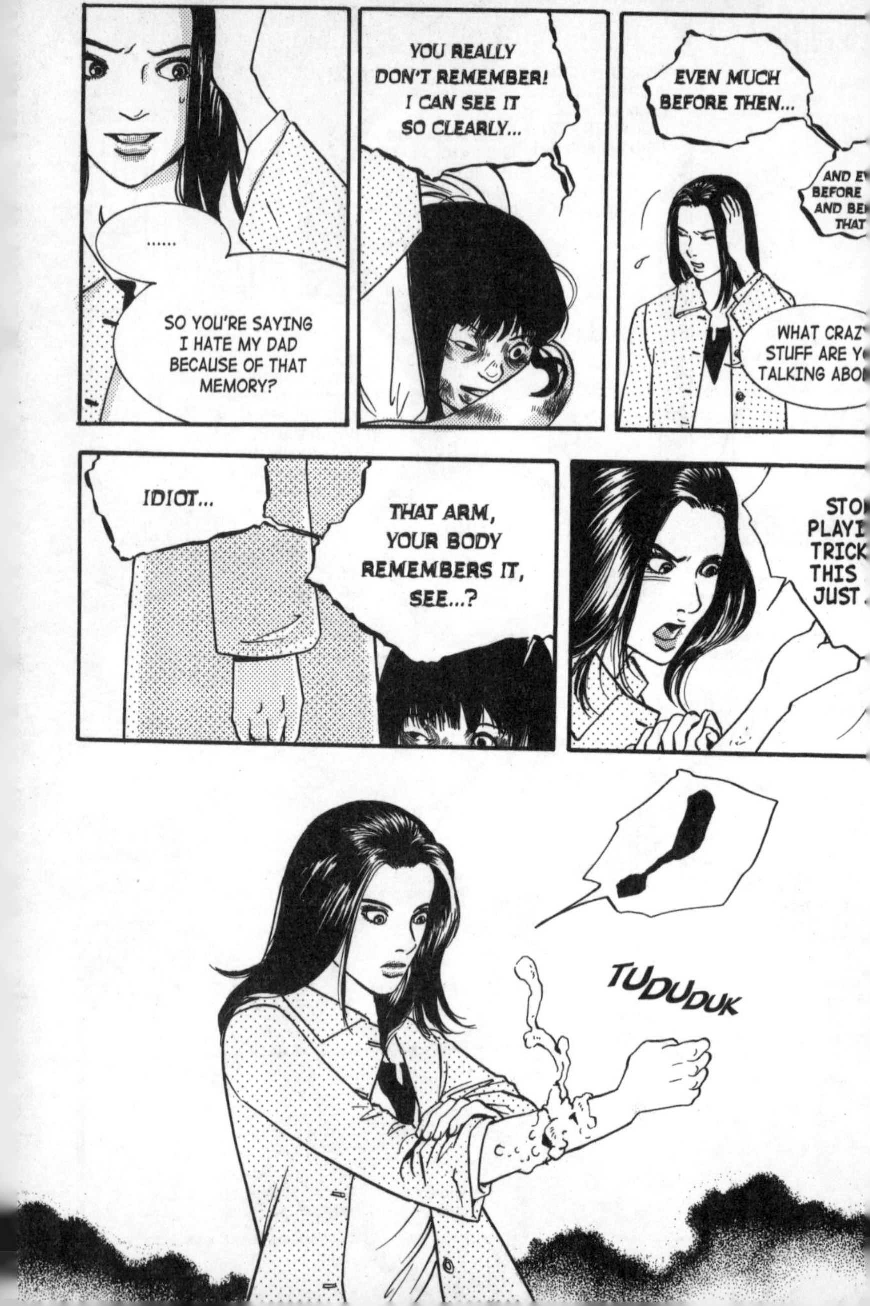
......
SO YOU'RE SAYING I HATE MY DAD BECAUSE OF THAT MEMORY?
YOU REALLY DON'T REMEMBER! I CAN SEE IT SO CLEARLY...
EVEN MUCH BEFORE THEN...
AND E BEFORE AND BE THAT
WHAT CRAZ STUFF ARE Y TALKING ABO
IDIOT...
THAT ARM, YOUR BODY REMEMBERS IT, SEE...?
STO PLAYI TRICK THIS JUST
TUDUDUK

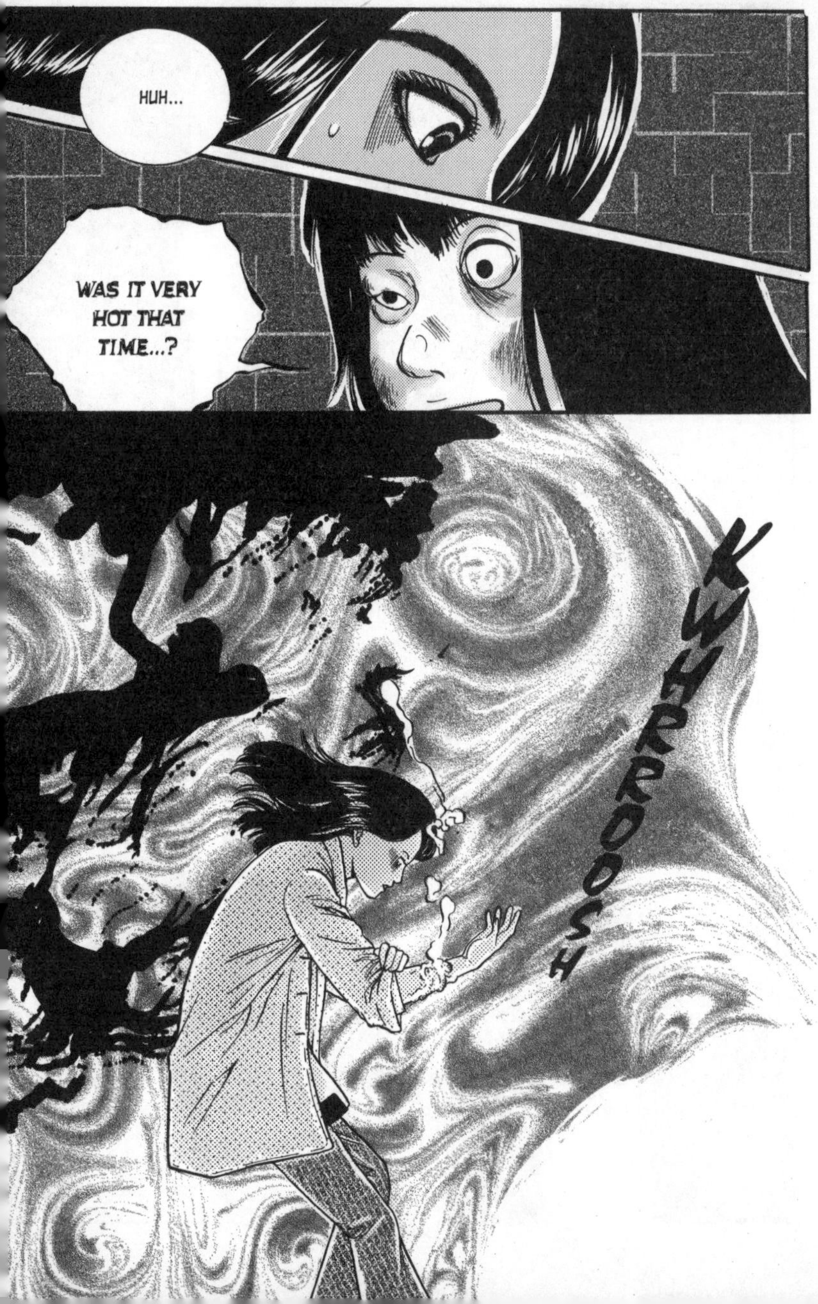
HUH...
WAS IT VERY HOT THAT TIME...?
KWHRROOSH

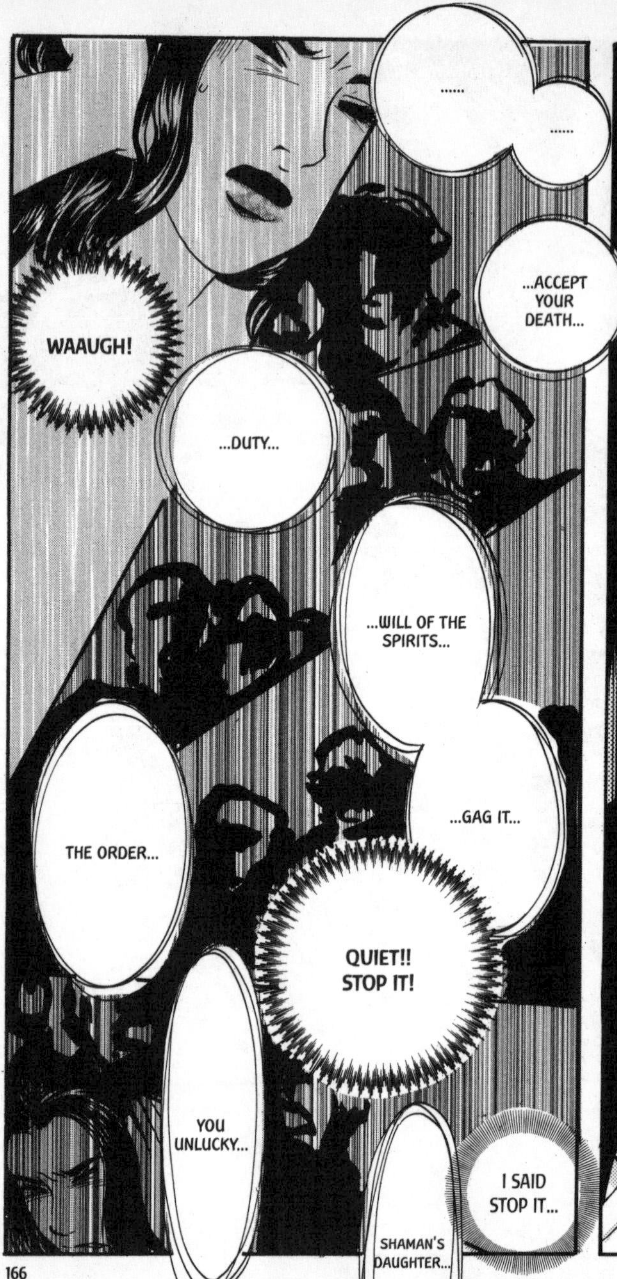
......
......
WAAUGH!
...ACCEPT YOUR DEATH...
...DUTY...
...WILL OF THE SPIRITS...
THE ORDER...
...GAG IT...
QUIET!! STOP IT!
YOU UNLUCKY...
SHAMAN'S DAUGHTER...
I SAID STOP IT...
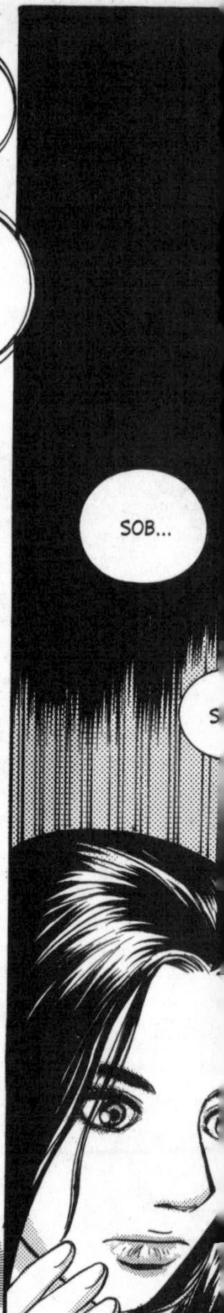
SOB...

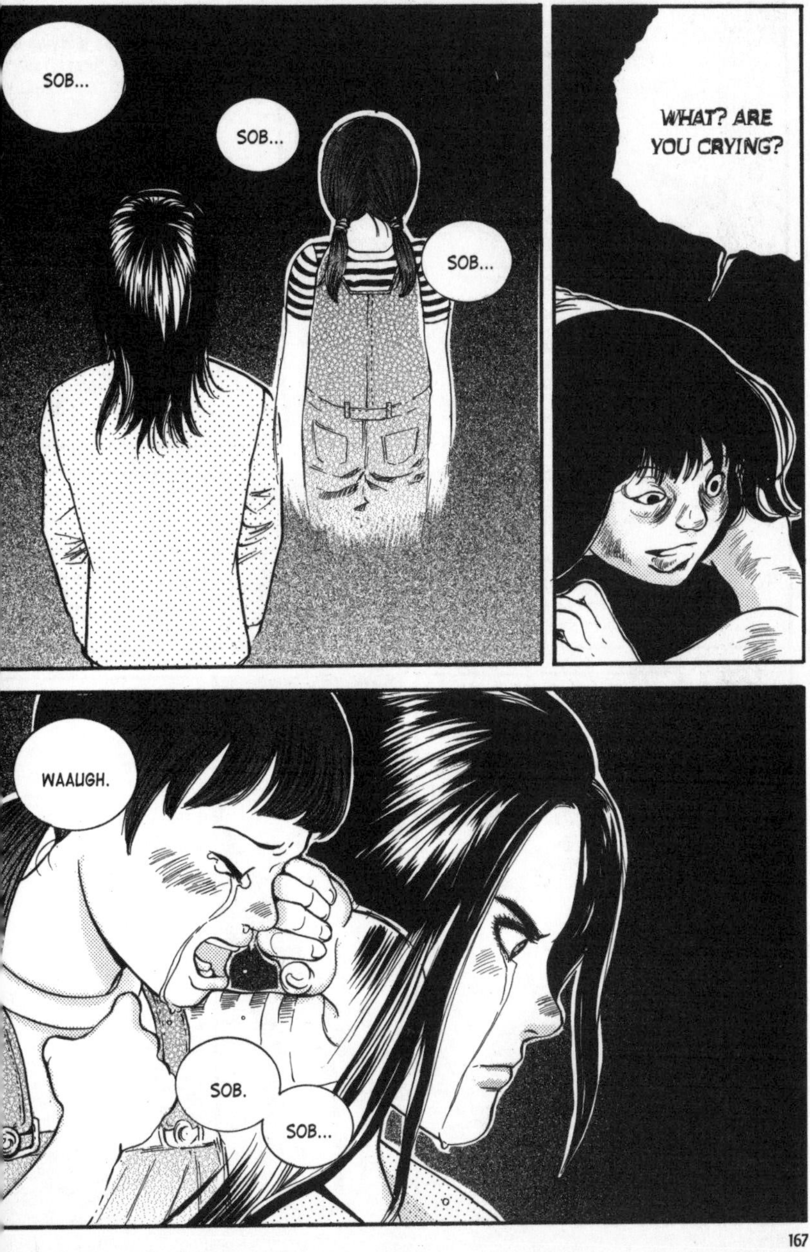
SOB...
SOB...
SOB...
WHAT? ARE YOU CRYING?
WAAUGH.
SOB.
SOB...

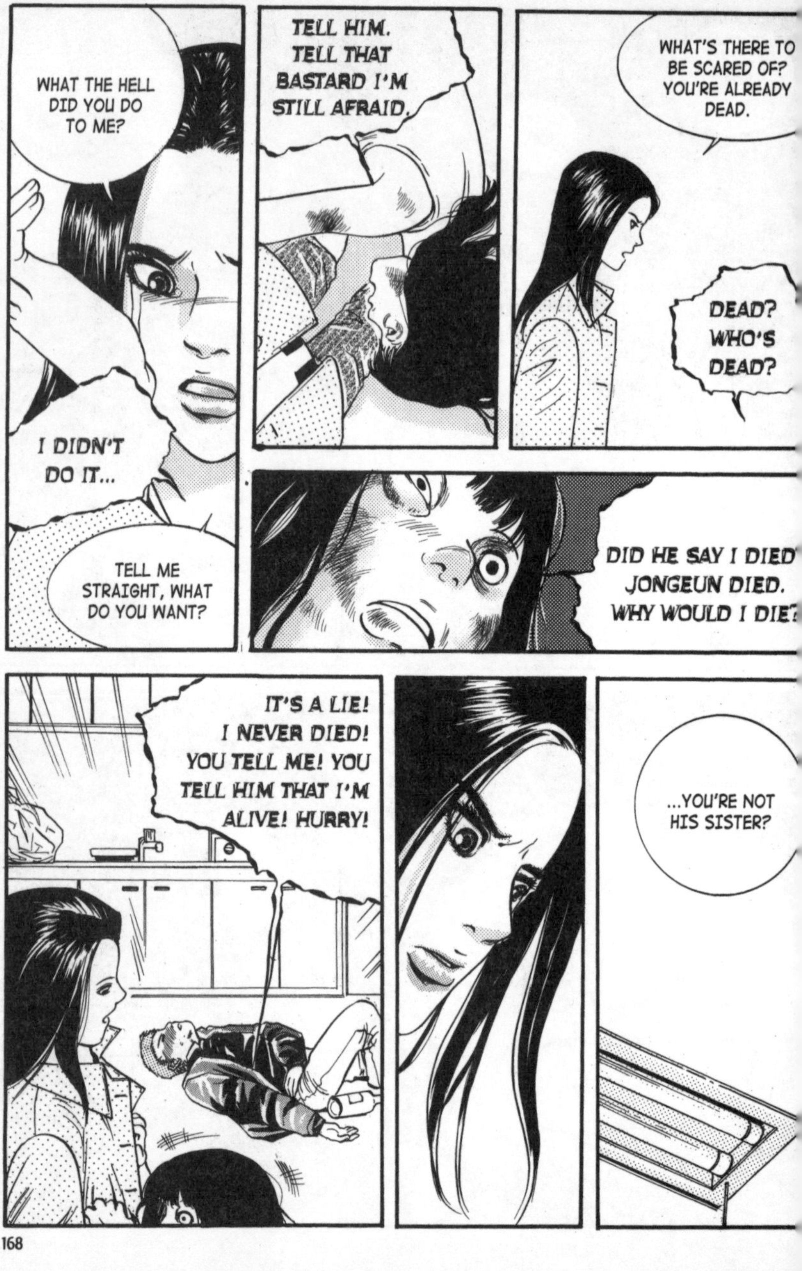

WHAT THE HELL DID YOU DO TO ME?
I DIDN'T DO IT...
TELL ME STRAIGHT, WHAT DO YOU WANT?
TELL HIM. TELL THAT BASTARD I'M STILL AFRAID.
WHAT'S THERE TO BE SCARED OF? YOU'RE ALREADY DEAD.
DEAD? WHO'S DEAD?
DID HE SAY I DIED JONGEUN DIED. WHY WOULD I DIE
IT'S A LIE! I NEVER DIED! YOU TELL ME! YOU TELL HIM THAT I'M ALIVE! HURRY!
...YOU'RE NOT HIS SISTER?

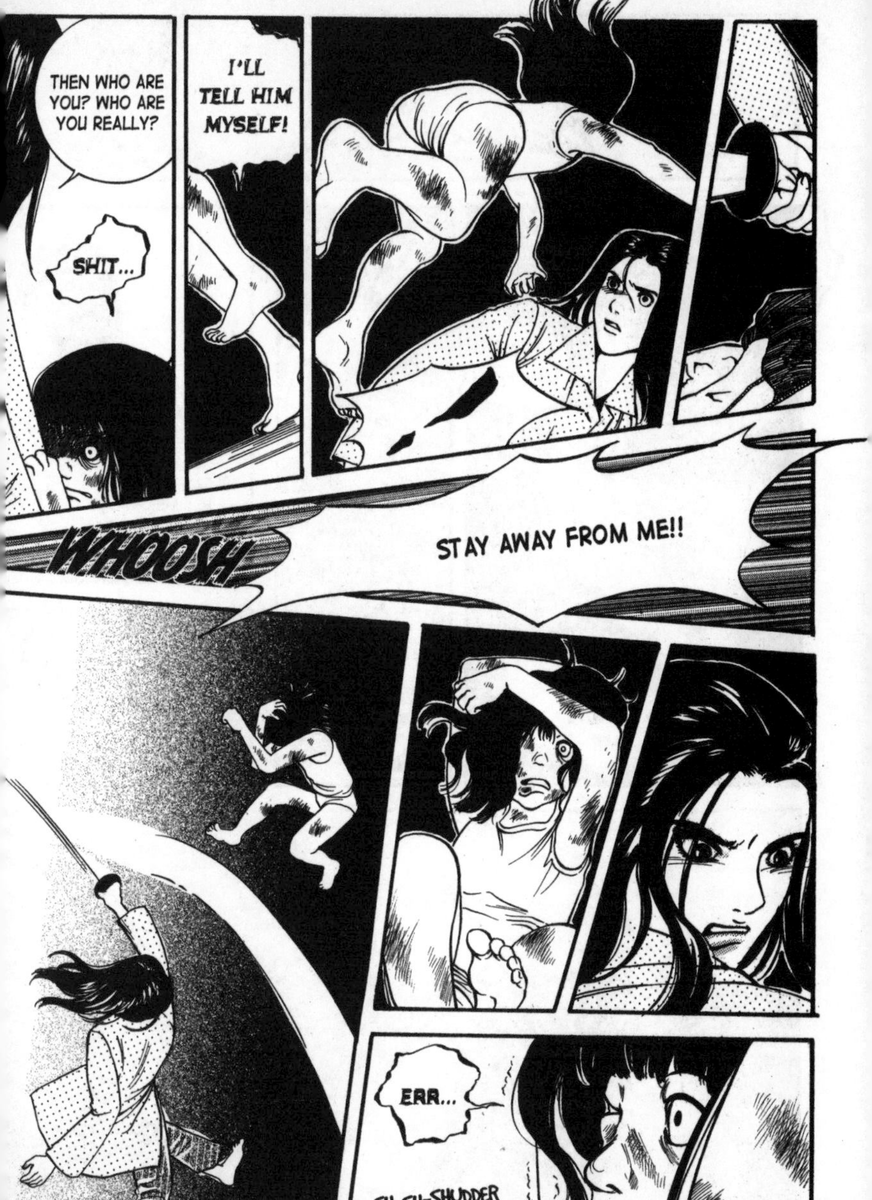
THEN WHO ARE YOU? WHO ARE YOU REALLY?
SHIT...
I'LL TELL HIM MYSELF!
WHOOSH
STAY AWAY FROM ME!!
ERR...
SH-SH-SHUDDER

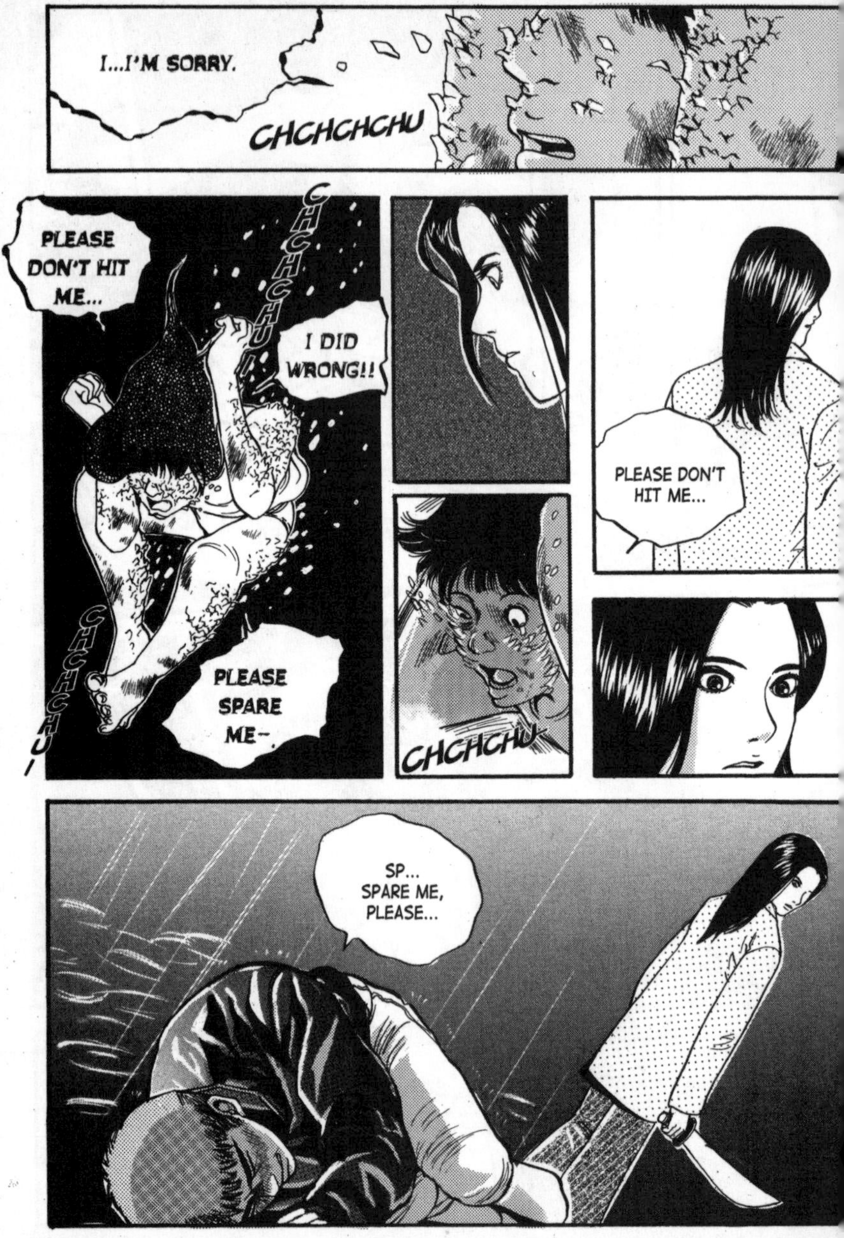
I...I'M SORRY.
CHCHCHCHU
PLEASE DON'T HIT ME...
CHCHCHCHU!
I DID WRONG!!
CHCHCHCHU!
PLEASE SPARE ME~
CHCHCHU
PLEASE DON'T HIT ME...
SP... SPARE ME, PLEASE...

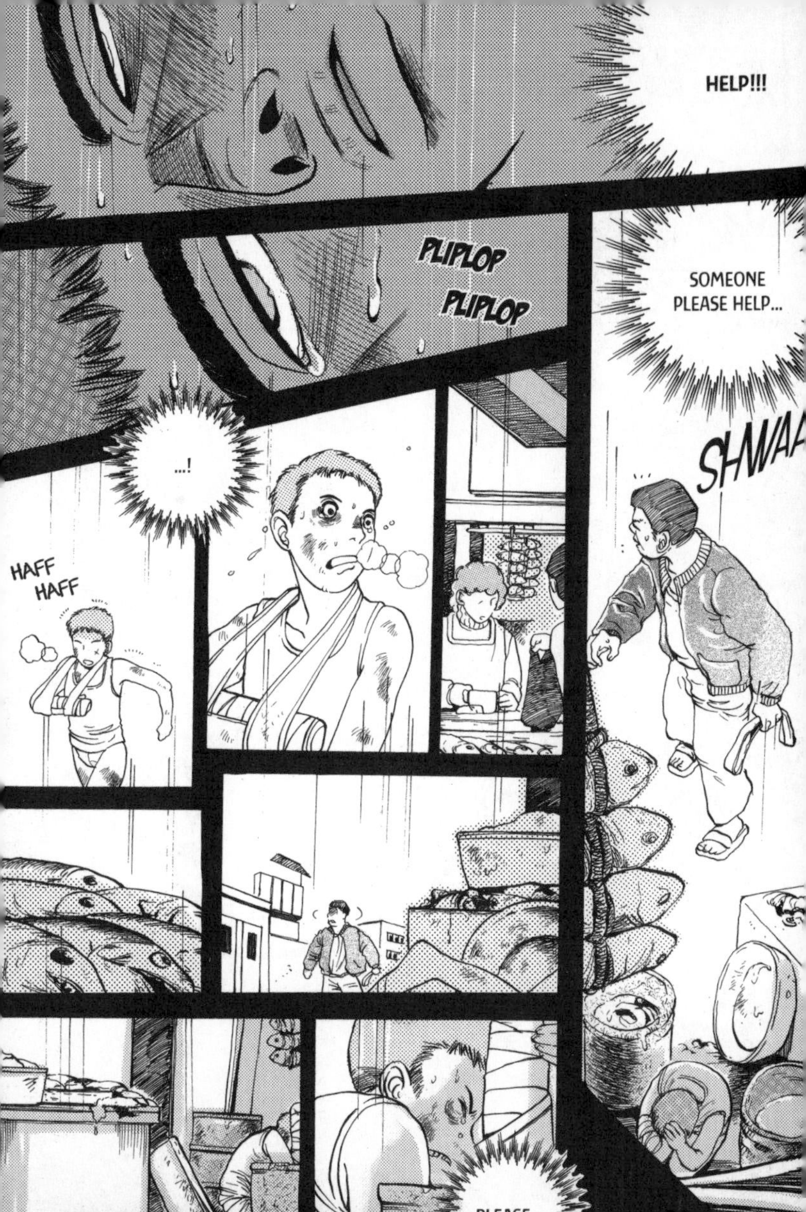

HELP!!!
PLIPLOP
PLIPLOP
SOMEONE PLEASE HELP...
...!
HAFF HAFF

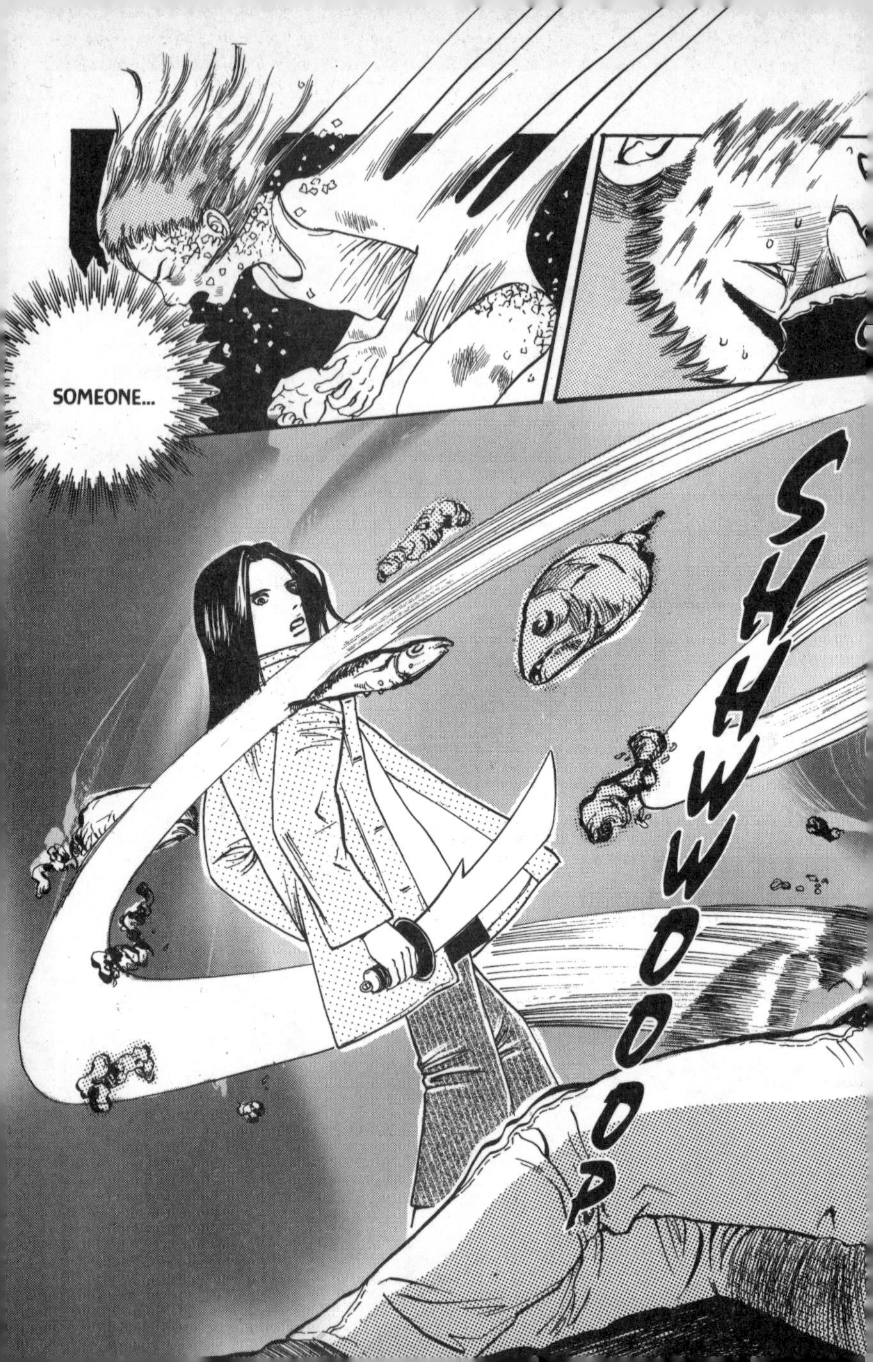
SOMEONE...
SHHWWOOOOP

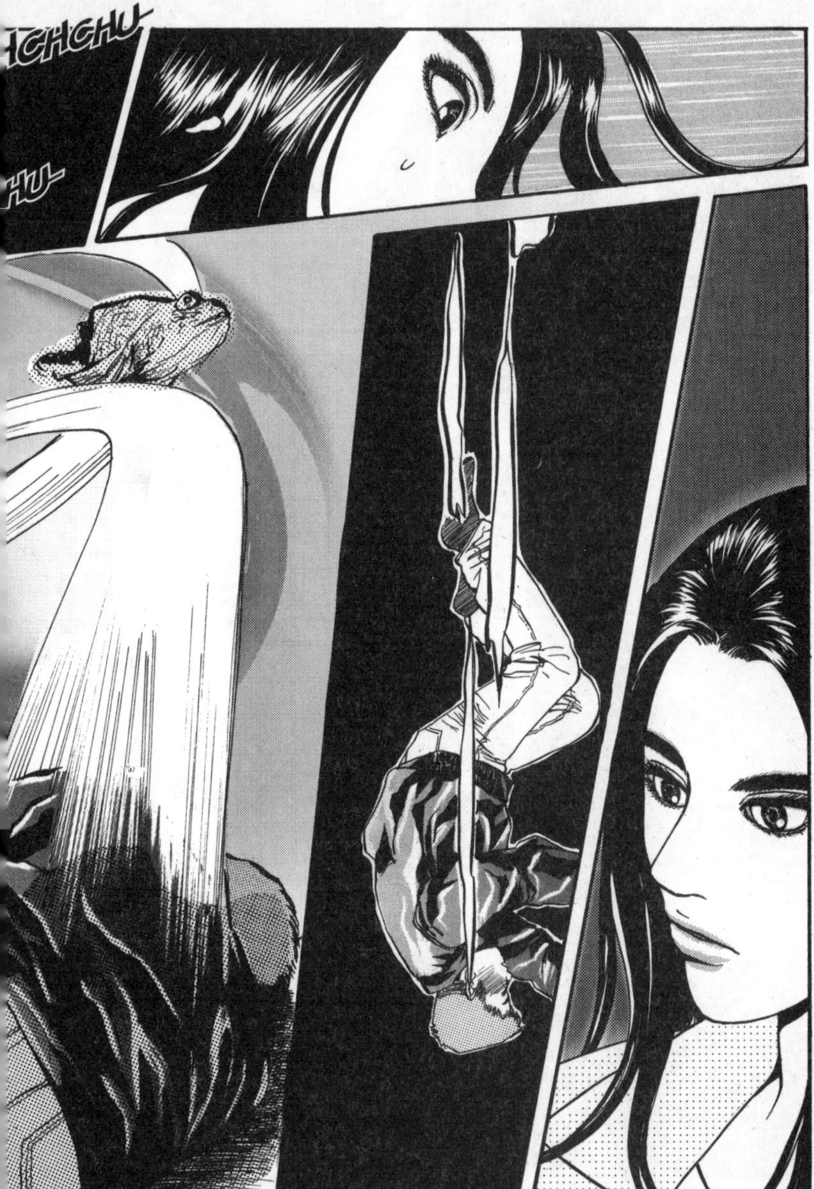
CHCHU
HU-

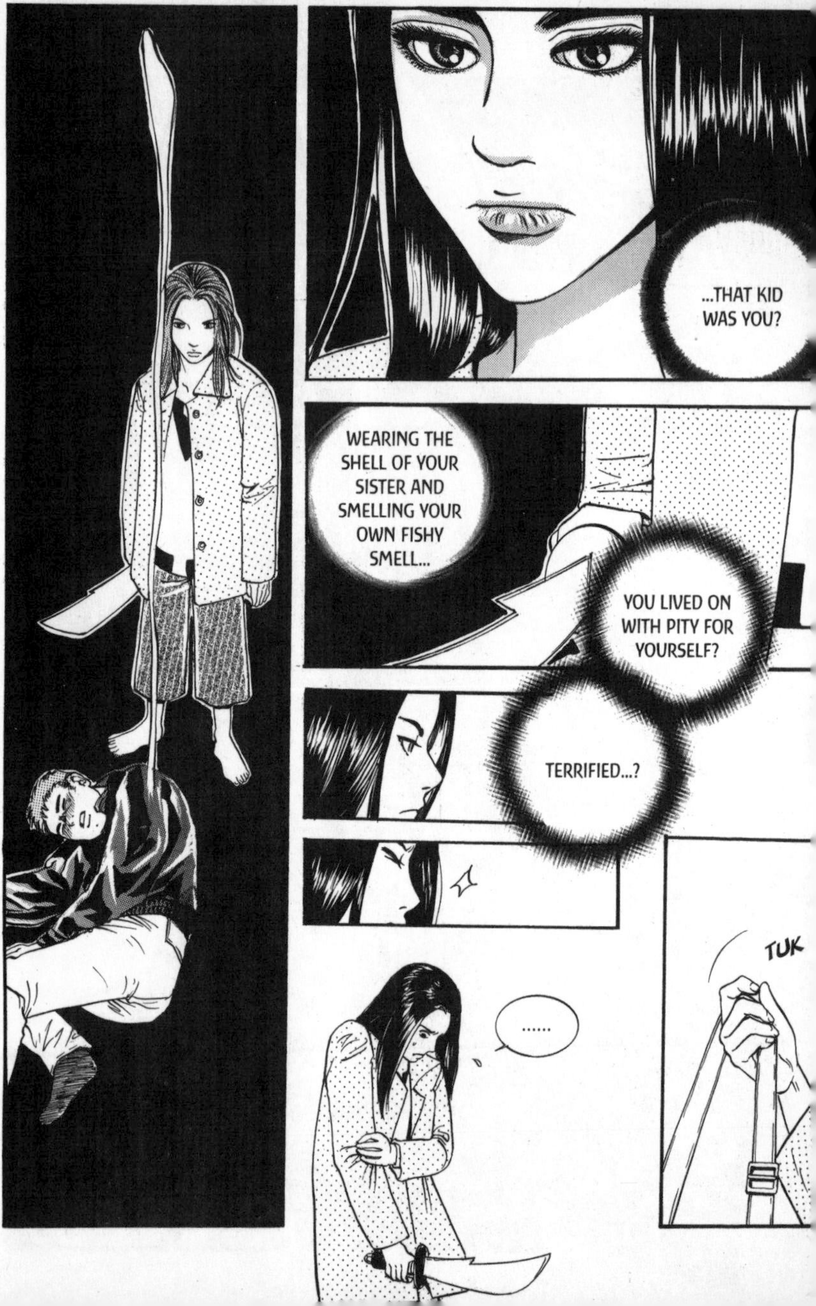
...THAT KID WAS YOU?
WEARING THE SHELL OF YOUR SISTER AND SMELLING YOUR OWN FISHY SMELL...
YOU LIVED ON WITH PITY FOR YOURSELF?
TERRIFIED...?
......
TUK

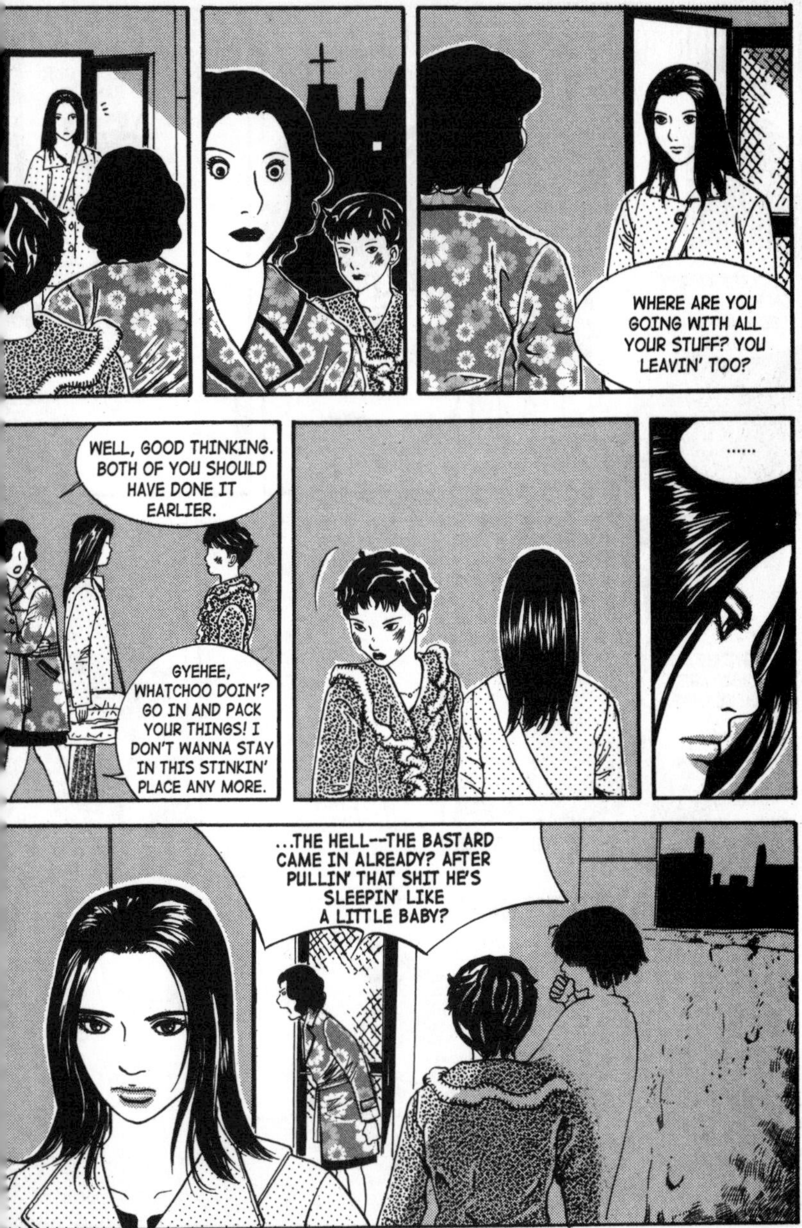
WHERE ARE YOU GOING WITH ALL YOUR STUFF? YOU LEAVIN' TOO?
WELL, GOOD THINKING. BOTH OF YOU SHOULD HAVE DONE IT EARLIER.
GYEHEE, WHATCHOO DOIN'? GO IN AND PACK YOUR THINGS! I DON'T WANNA STAY IN THIS STINKIN' PLACE ANY MORE.
......
...THE HELL--THE BASTARD CAME IN ALREADY? AFTER PULLIN' THAT SHIT HE'S SLEEPIN' LIKE A LITTLE BABY?

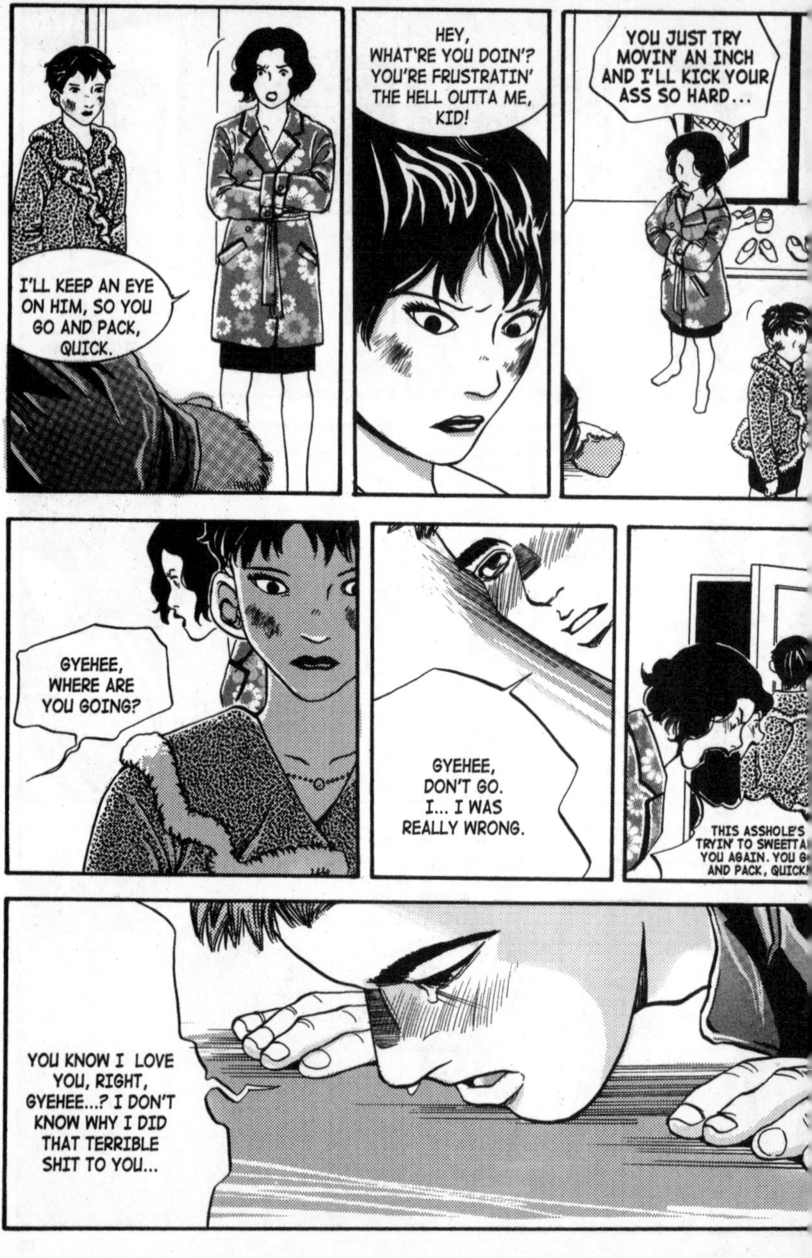
I'LL KEEP AN EYE ON HIM, SO YOU GO AND PACK, QUICK.
HEY, WHAT'RE YOU DOIN'? YOU'RE FRUSTRATIN' THE HELL OUTTA ME, KID!
YOU JUST TRY MOVIN' AN INCH AND I'LL KICK YOUR ASS SO HARD...
GYEHEE, WHERE ARE YOU GOING?
GYEHEE, DON'T GO. I... I WAS REALLY WRONG.
THIS ASSHOLE'S TRYIN' TO SWEETTA
YOU AGAIN. YOU G
AND PACK, QUICK
YOU KNOW I LOVE YOU, RIGHT, GYEHEE...? I DON'T KNOW WHY I DID THAT TERRIBLE SHIT TO YOU...

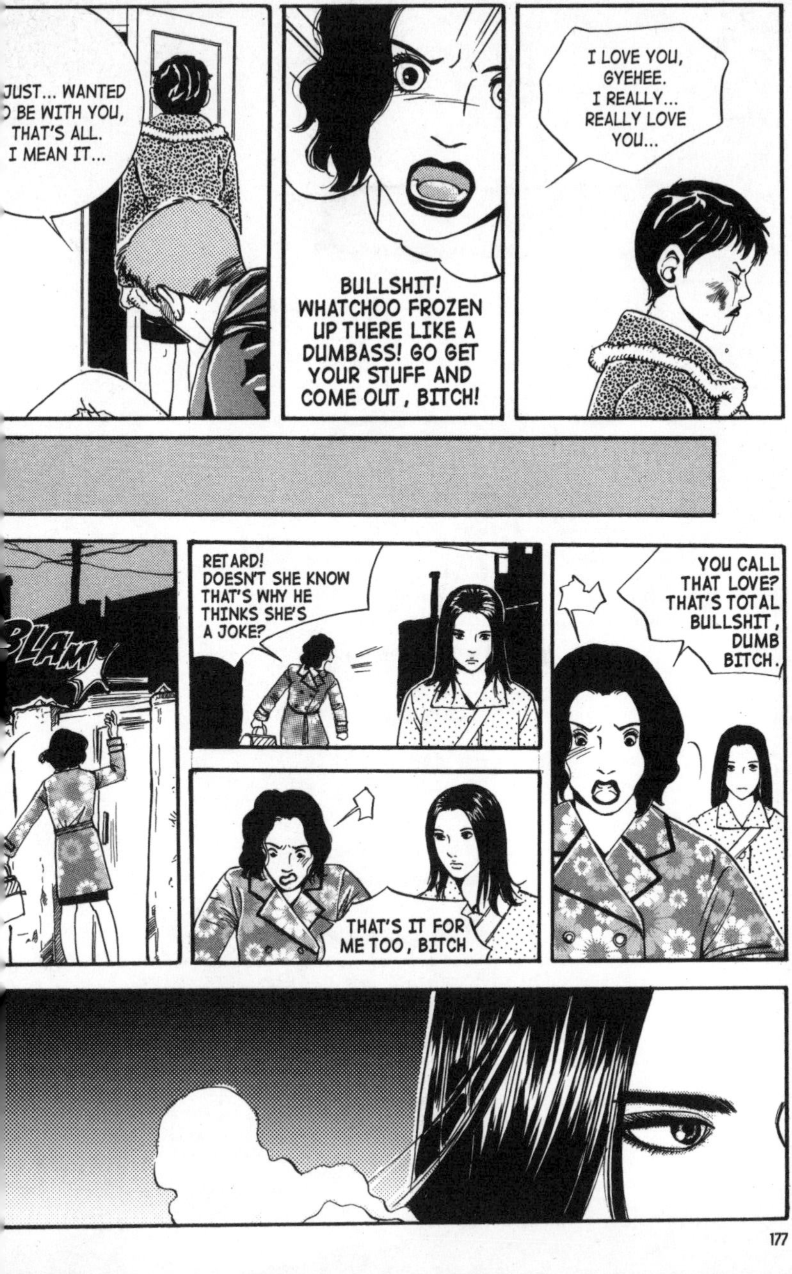
JUST... WANTED BE WITH YOU, THAT'S ALL. I MEAN IT...
BULLSHIT! WHATCHOO FROZEN UP THERE LIKE A DUMBASS! GO GET YOUR STUFF AND COME OUT, BITCH!
I LOVE YOU, GYEHEE. I REALLY... REALLY LOVE YOU...
BLAM
RETARD! DOESN'T SHE KNOW THAT'S WHY HE THINKS SHE'S A JOKE?
THAT'S IT FOR ME TOO, BITCH.
YOU CALL THAT LOVE? THAT'S TOTAL BULLSHIT, DUMB BITCH.

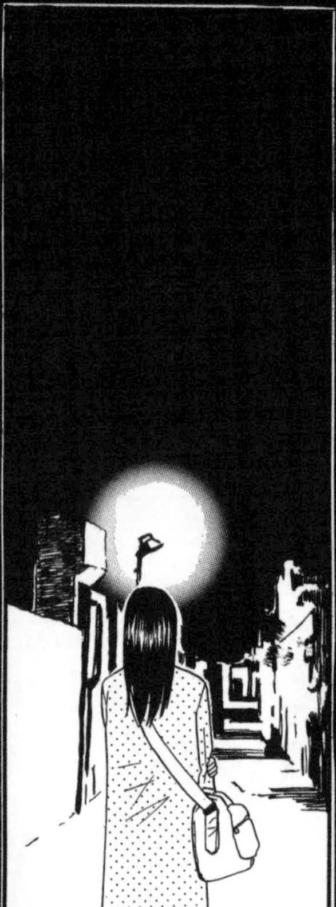

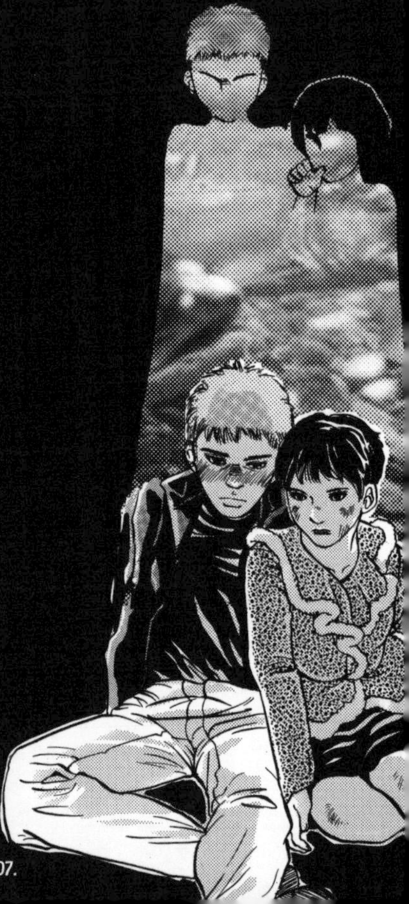

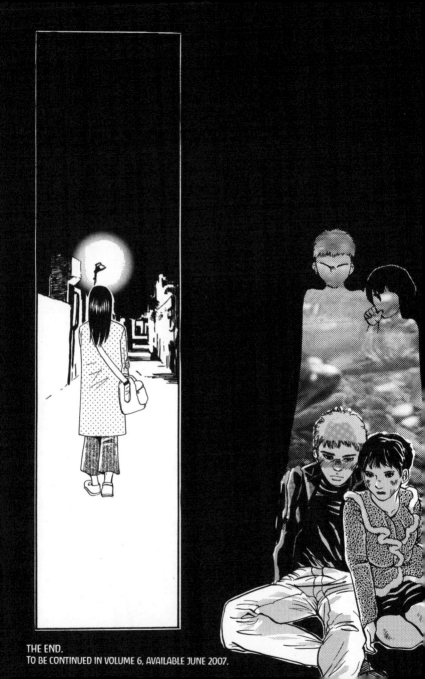

THE END.
TO BE CONTINUED IN VOLUME 6, AVAILABLE JUNE 2007.

10, 20, and 30

vol. 1

Morim Kang

10 20 and 30

*Cover not final

by Morim Kang

Three extraordinary women in three age groups with three unforgettable lives intersect in Morim Kang's fascinating *10, 20, and 30*. Yuhrin is a clumsy, scatterbrained widow in her 30's whose teenage daughter, Kangae, is forced to take care of her. Meanwhile, Kangae's jaded, twenty-something cousin Ami suffers a messy breakup with her boyfriend. Finally, Kangae, who dreads the thought of growing up and its attendant responsibilities, hates men and is sure to complicate matters. Get ready for one wild ride with *10, 20, and 30*.

Read it ahead at www.NETCOMICS.com!

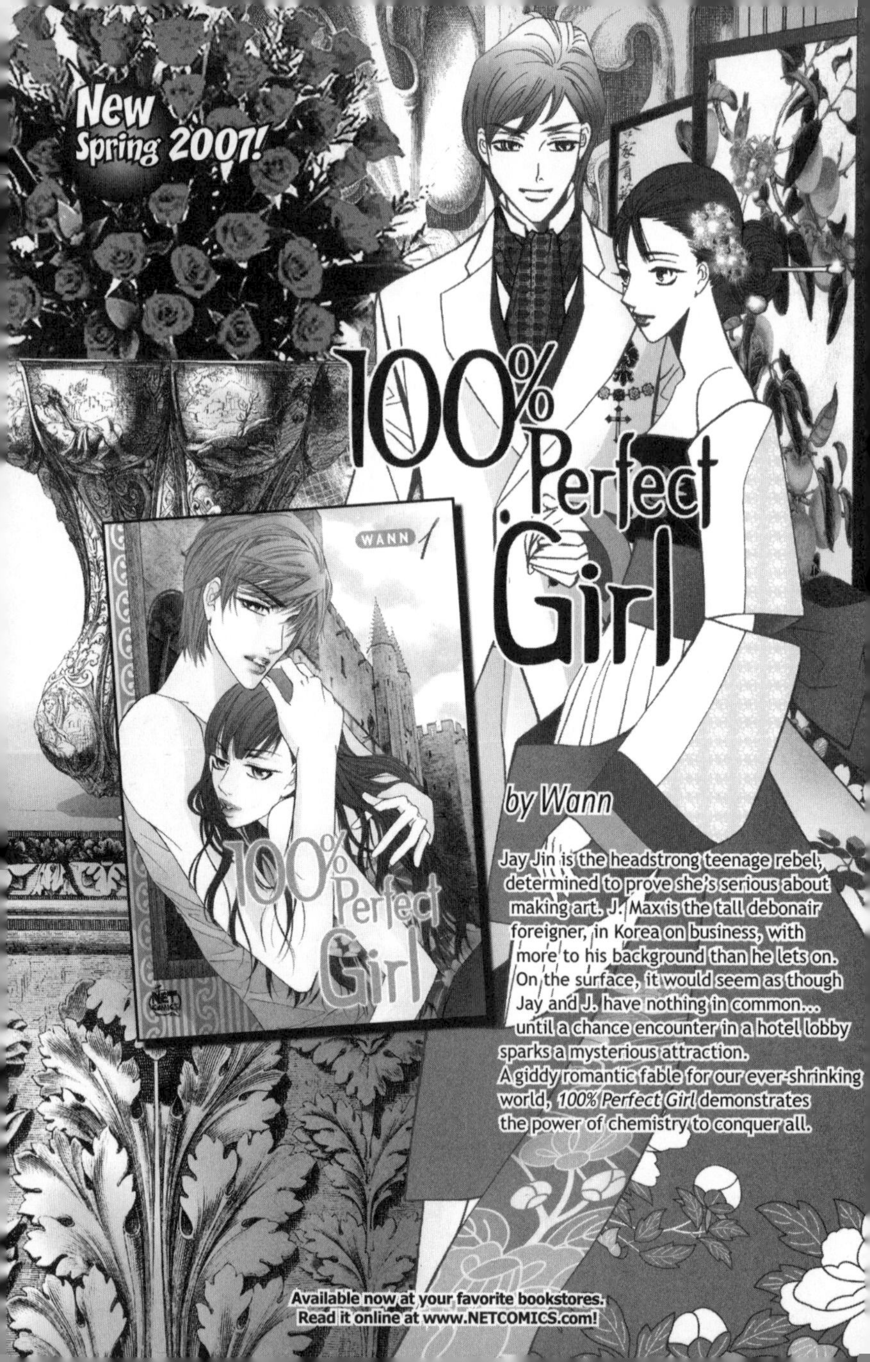
New Spring 2007!
100% Perfect Girl
WANN 1
100% Perfect Girl
NETCOMICS
by Wann
Jay Jin is the headstrong teenage rebel, determined to prove she's serious about making art. J. Max is the tall debonair foreigner, in Korea on business, with more to his background than he lets on. On the surface, it would seem as though Jay and J. have nothing in common... until a chance encounter in a hotel lobby sparks a mysterious attraction.
A giddy romantic fable for our ever-shrinking world, *100% Perfect Girl* demonstrates the power of chemistry to conquer all.
Available now at your favorite bookstores.
Read it online at www.NETCOMICS.com!

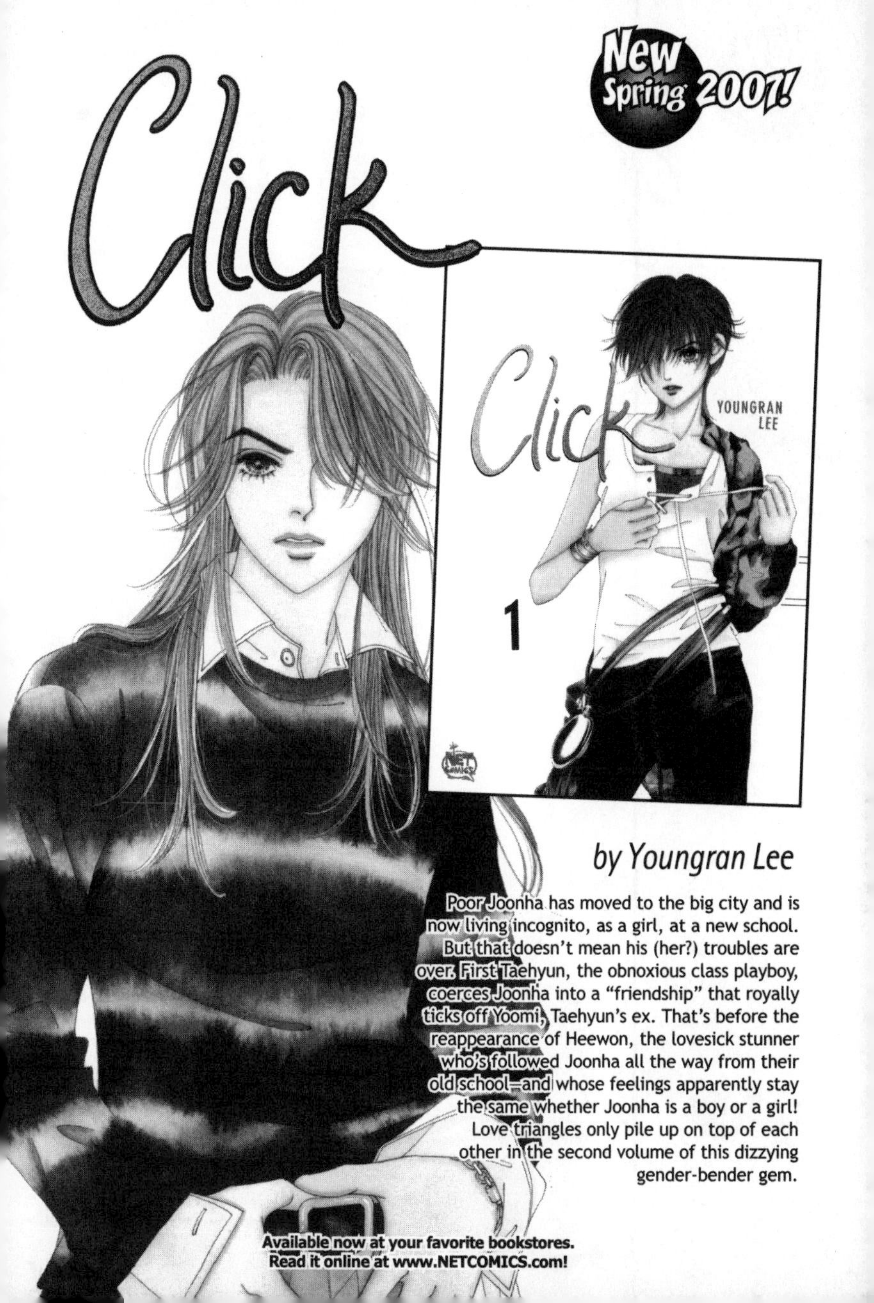
New Spring 2007!
Click
Click
YOUNGRAN LEE
1
by Youngran Lee
Poor Joonha has moved to the big city and is now living incognito, as a girl, at a new school. But that doesn't mean his (her?) troubles are over. First Taehyun, the obnoxious class playboy, coerces Joonha into a "friendship" that royally ticks off Yoomi, Taehyun's ex. That's before the reappearance of Heewon, the lovesick stunner who's followed Joonha all the way from their old school—and whose feelings apparently stay the same whether Joonha is a boy or a girl! Love triangles only pile up on top of each other in the second volume of this dizzying gender-bender gem.
Available now at your favorite bookstores.
Read it online at www.NETCOMICS.com!

In the Starlight VOL. 1

by Kyungok Kang

Ever since Shinhye was young, when she used to sit on a hill watching the night sky with her father, she has always admired the stars and dreamed of what is out there in the universe. But she never expected that her dreams—and nightmares— would come true. As a beautiful and intelligent 17-year-old, she attracts the attention of Donghoon, whose uncle works with the Department of Science. As it happens, Donghoon's uncle is in charge of finding a home for a visiting foreigner... who has ESP! Guess who the foreigner shacks up with?

A brand-new title from Kyungok Kang, author of *In the Starlight* & *Narration of Love at 17*

Two Will Come

Ordinary high school girl Jina discovers that she is heir to a terrible legacy handed down from her family's sinister history. Long ago, her ancestors killed a magical serpent known as an Imugi, believing that it would bring them good luck. Unfortunately, the creature cursed them as it died, decreeing that one family member of each generation from that day forth will be killed by two people closely acquainted with that person. In this day and age, no one wants to believe in such outmoded superstitions, but one of Jina's relatives has been murdered without fail in every generation. Now, Jina has been informed that she will be next to die…